JACKSONVILLE FOOD TRUCKS

STORIES & RECIPES FROM THE ROAD

NANCY WHITE

AMERICAN PALATE

Published by American Palate
A Division of The History Press
Charleston, SC 29403
www.historypress.net

All images are courtesy of the author unless otherwise noted.

First published 2015

Manufactured in the United States

ISBN 978.1.62619.765.7

Library of Congress Control Number: 2015931109

Notice: The information in this book is true and complete to the best of our knowledge. It is offered without guarantee on the part of the author or The History Press. The author and The History Press disclaim all liability in connection with the use of this book.

For the truckies…

CONTENTS

ACKNOWLEDGEMENTS

I owe a debt of gratitude to Amy O'Grady of Jax Truckies and Driftwood BBQ and Chef Chriss Brown of 927 Events and the Beaver Street Commissary for their support and encouragement throughout this project. To everyone who volunteers their time for the good of the group, thank you for supporting local food businesses and having one another's backs out there.

We, all of us who love food trucks in Jacksonville, have Jax Truckies founders Mike Field, Caron Streibich, Ennis Davis and Stacey Steiner to thank for being the spark that lit the food truck flame. Mike and Caron are so humble when they look back at everything they accomplished in a few short years—bringing trucks together as one voice and bringing an audience of curious and hungry diners to the trucks through their award-winning Facebook page, events and promotions. Your dogged advocacy helped build bridges and smooth roads between city hall and the people of the First Coast who embraced the trucks from day one. Thank you for providing a roadmap for this cultural convoy that just keeps on rolling!

There are so many people to thank for making this book possible.

To The History Press and my commissioning editor, Alyssa Kate Pierce, thank you for providing an outlet to tell the stories of some of Jacksonville's most iconic eateries. To my project editor, Julia Turner, and the whole crew of talented designers and editors whose work you see here, thanks for your guidance and support through the daunting process of birthing my first book. I have the deepest respect for all of you.

Where would I be without my family and friends?

To my mom, Virginia, who didn't bat an eye when I told her I was entering into a project that would consume much of my time for half the year, thanks for understanding and supporting me as only you can. To my sister Maureen and niece Kelly, thanks for being good sports and coming along on so many edible adventures and for alerting me whenever you spotted a new truck alongside the road!

Thanks to all my friends who have accompanied me to lunches, brunches, happy hours, dinners and a few fabulous road trips.

My Ex-Pat sisters and the fabulous V-Jewels, you have kept me sane and pleasantly entertained during our monthly brunch dates and regular super-secret Facebook cheering squad sessions. Thanks for always being there when I need a virtual hug, a prayer or a culinary partner in crime.

My editors and friends at the *Florida Times-Union* have been extremely supportive throughout this process. Thanks to Carole Fader for your patience when my Dining Notes column has been an hour or two later than usual due to my dashing across town to grab lunch at yet another food truck. Thanks to Tom Szaroleta for being an all-around mensch and to *T-U*'s digital director Gary T. Mills for all your help and advice and for building Dining Notes into a respected source for information on the First Coast's food and dining scene. You set the bar pretty high, my friend.

Cinda, thanks for opening the pages of *Arbus* magazine to me and introducing me to some of the area's most interesting chefs—and some mighty fine wine in the bargain. Florence, thanks for reminding me of the restorative power of food and prayer.

Similarly, to my food-loving friends—the chefs, restaurant owners, industry workers, farmers, craft brewers, purveyors of handmade food products and their chroniclers, my fellow food writers and photographers—thanks for all you do to elevate the area's food scene. You make living on Florida's First Coast a delicious proposition.

Lastly, to the truckies—especially those of you who have honored me with your time and generously sharing your stories and your delightful food—I am beyond impressed by your talent, your passion, your generosity and your seemingly boundless energy. Thank you for your enthusiasm and encouragement for this book. I hope I have done your stories justice.

INTRODUCTION

My blog, "Nourish the Beast," began as a way to flex my creative writing muscles after decades of writing in the voice of the various corporations and organizations I represented as a public relations practitioner. I had no idea back in 2005 that ten years later I would still be writing about food and be more passionate than ever about doing so.

When I was approached to write this book, I knew I would be in for a wild ride. The food truck scene in Jacksonville is growing exponentially right now, and while city officials were unsympathetic at first, one by one they are realizing that food truck operators are legitimate business owners and tax-paying residents who deserve their full support as much as the owners of brick-and-mortar businesses.

Jax Truckies has been a major catalyst to the food truck scene here in Jacksonville, and I was fortunate to serve as a media advisor to its leader, Amy O'Grady, in her first months at the helm. During that time, I got to meet many of the truck owners, chefs and crew members whose names fill these pages. I take great pleasure in shining what little spotlight I have at my disposal squarely on them here.

Corner Taco chef and owner Chris Dickerson issued this challenge to Jacksonville diners: "Attention all foodies: Bored of average fare? If you agree that Jacksonville is becoming a serious food city, here's how you can help. Demand higher quality, not bigger portions or lower prices. Vote with your dollars and support local restaurants trying to raise the bar."

I agree 100 percent.

To the hungry fans who seek out and support Jacksonville's food trucks, please know how important you are to the success of these small businesses. Together, you play a key role in our city's cultural expansion. When you choose to spend your time and money in support of local food businesses, you are building a better

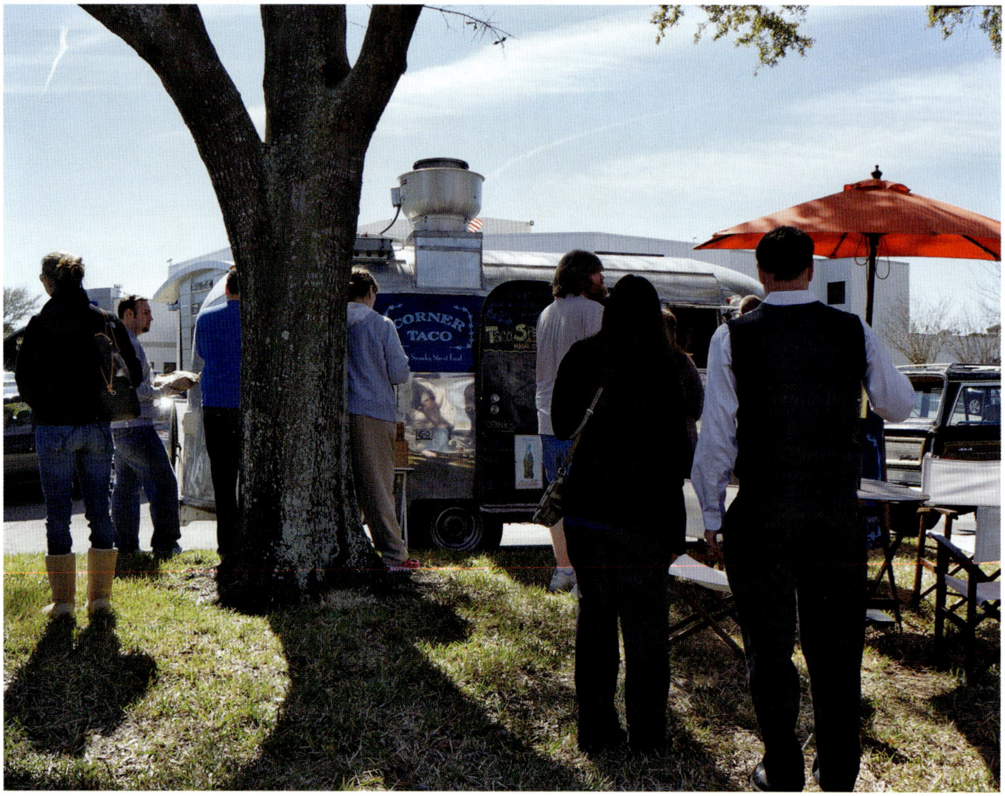

Corner Taco serving the lunch crowd at Key Buick.

place to live, work, grow and eat. To the last, each food truck operator I interviewed for this book told me he or she was amazed and humbled by your outpouring of solidarity and support. Thanks for continuing to spread your love for the food trucks of Florida's First Coast.

In this book, you will find the stories of hardworking business owners, passionate chefs and community volunteers. You'll learn how some of your favorite food truck chefs came to choose that road and where it is leading them next. Some have shared recipes for dishes they serve on the trucks, scaled down somewhat for home cooking. Many have given us a glimpse into the daily life of a food truck owner, which (no shock here) is far different from the way it is portrayed in films and on television.

I wish that we had more time and space to cover all the great rolling kitchens out there, but I have tried to select a representative sample of all that our food trucks have to offer. If your favorite is not featured here, it simply means I wasn't able to get to it or its owner(s) was (were) not able to spend time with me for this

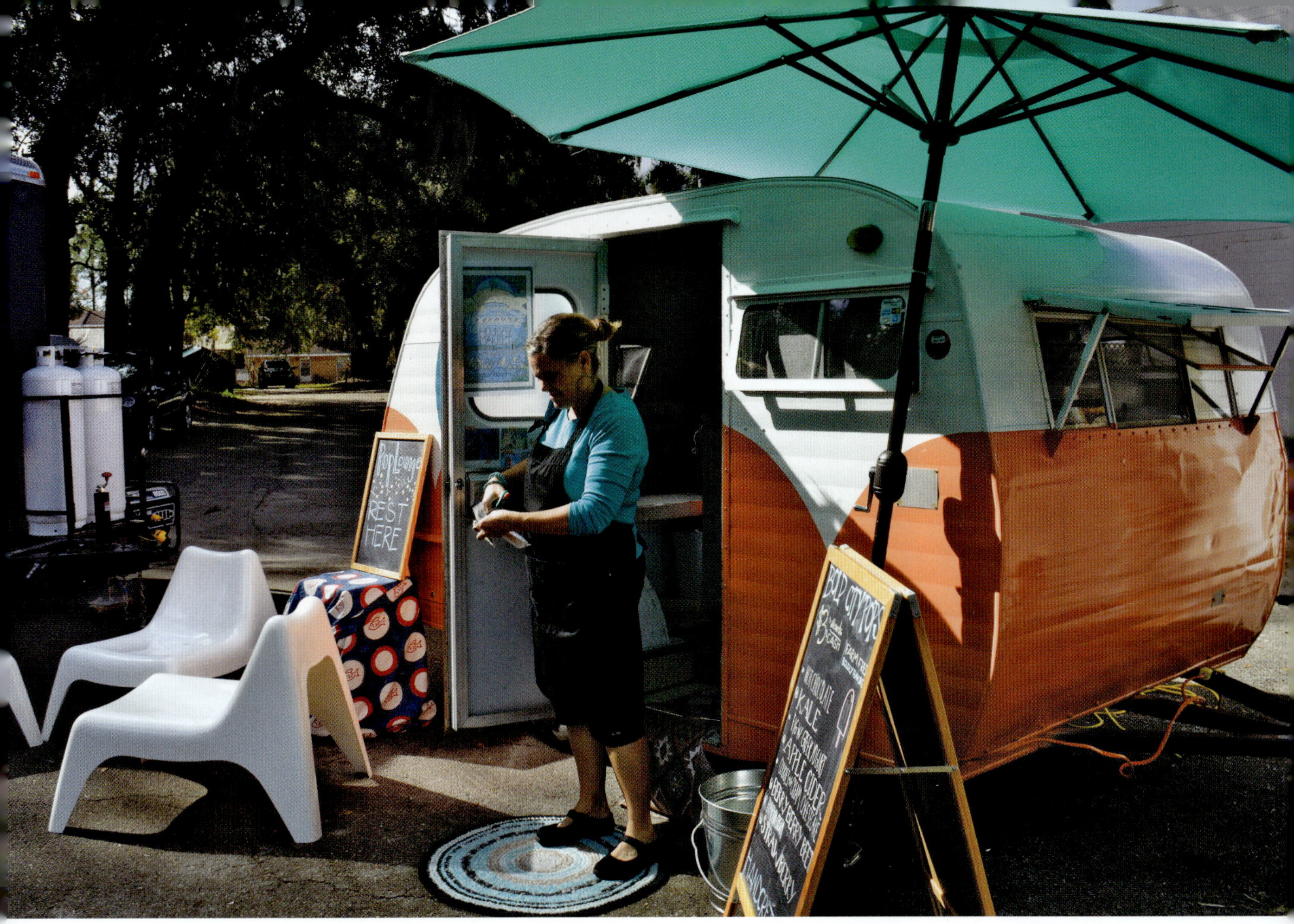

Bold City Pops at Jax Food Truck Food Court.

project. With any luck, there will be a sequel!

A bit of housekeeping, if I may. When I say "truckies" or "trucks" in this book, I am referring to businesses that are run from an actual truck, a trailer or, as with two businesses profiled here, something a bit, well, smaller. I have attempted to differentiate this in my writing, but in practical terms they are all "truckies" to local fans.

Let's get trucking!

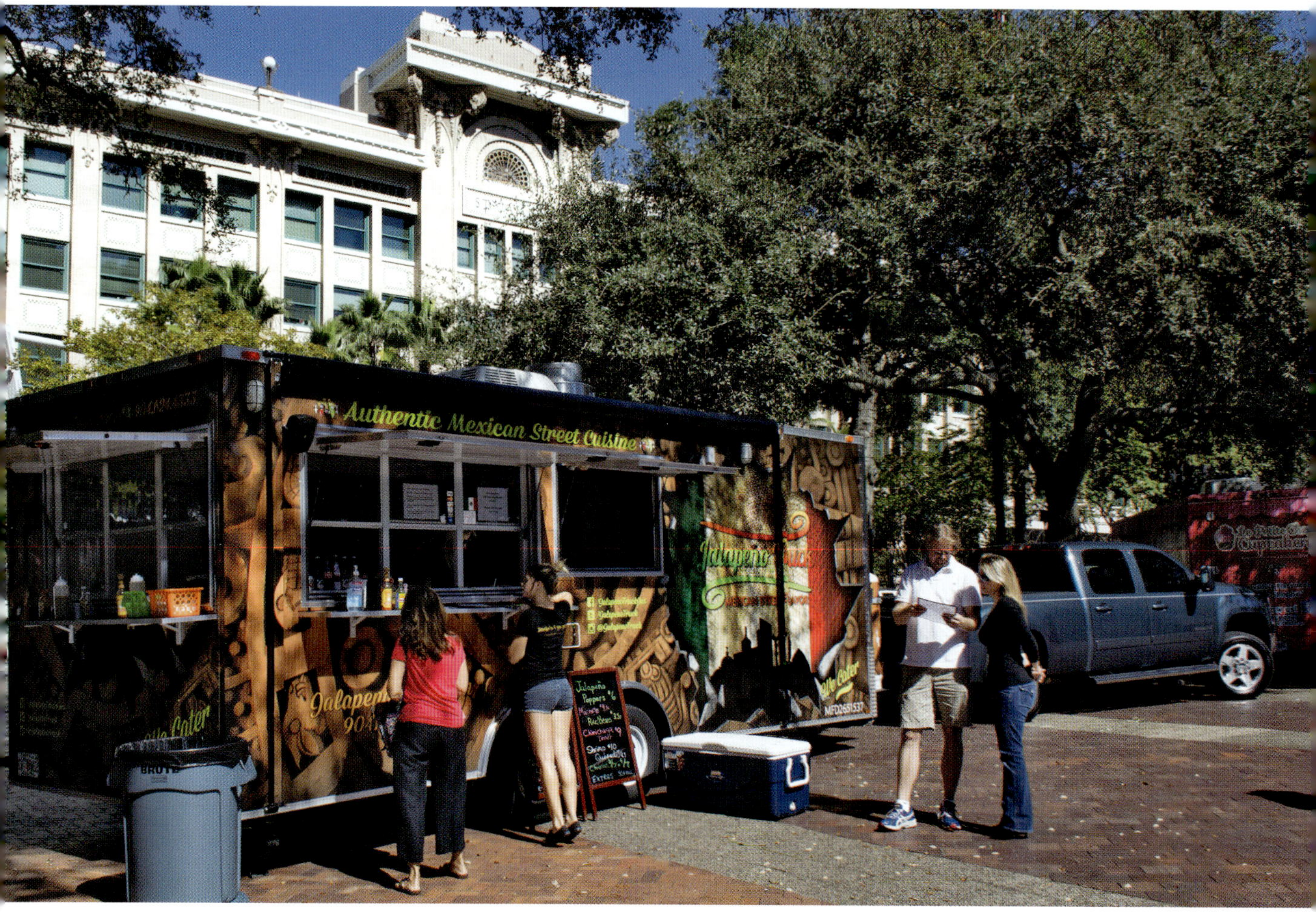

Food trucks at Hemming Park, located steps from city hall.

THE SCENE

THE LOCAL FOOD TRUCK CULTURE

There is a strong and growing food culture in Jacksonville and throughout Florida's First Coast. We're a bighearted bunch, and we value small business and the entrepreneurial spirit. A growing number of us also want to be closer to the source of our food, whether that means frequenting one of the many farmers' markets popping up around town, buying gluten-free cupcakes from a small-batch craft bakery or rushing to try the newly opened "mom and pop" restaurant across town. Food trucks fit perfectly into our diverse, evolving social structure.

Far from its disruptive, subculture roots, the food truck movement in Jacksonville is on the road to becoming mainstream. Where trucks once were blocked from doing business, they now regularly take part in many of our city's signature events and are invited to set up shop and serve their fare in some of our most iconic public spaces. Food trucks were voted the area's top trend by the readers of *Void Magazine* and *Folio Weekly*—not just top food trend, but top trend, period.

Jax Truckies, a local group of food truck operators and fans offering advocacy and support to the area's mobile food vendors, took top honors in social media in a *Jacksonville Business Journal* readers' poll in 2014,and "Best Facebook Page" in *Folio Weekly*'s Best of Jax readers' polls three years running from 2012 to 2014. Their popularity is due in no small part to the group's 27,450-plus followers on Facebook, many of whom return frequently to find out where their favorite trucks will be serving.

From their upstart beginnings to eventual mainstream popularity and acceptance, the real story of food trucks on the First Coast is about the people at the heart of those businesses,

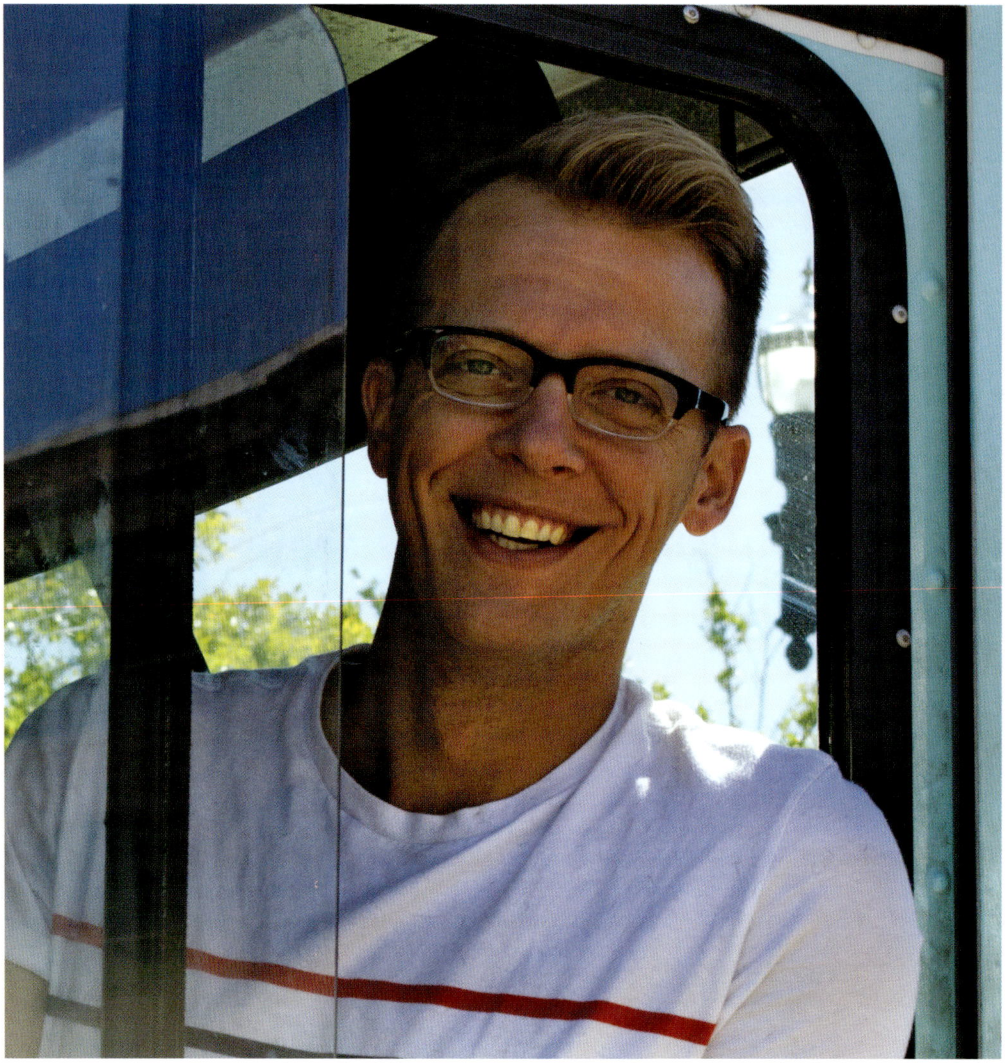

Mild-mannered Dale Stoudt of Super Food.

and of course, the food they serve. I can think of no better place to start than at the beginning of what was, for a time, a very rocky road to success.

FOOD TRUCKS COME TO JACKSONVILLE

Jax Truckies

Even as a board member for nonpartisan urban advocacy organization Transform Jax, Mike Field never thought he would be spending so much time in city hall meetings.

Jax Truckies began in 2012 as a passion-driven hobby for Mike and his girlfriend, Caron Streibich. Under their leadership, the group's following reached over twenty-two thousand people in less than two years.

In 2014, the day-to-day operation of Jax Truckies was passed on to Amy O'Grady, who, with husband Patrick, owns one of Jacksonville's longest-running mobile food businesses, Driftwood BBQ. The organization's Facebook following was just over 26,800 when I was writing this. The organization is growing, and Amy is honored to be responsible for the continued success of Jax Truckies. It is her mission to nurture and grow a collaboration with local food truck vendors, patrons, bloggers and other entrepreneurs.

In 2012, it was rough going for the trucks, which were routinely asked to leave their lunch spots, despite sometimes even being on private property with the owner's approval. Drew and Curt Cavins had a scrapbook of all the tickets they received while trying to bring their food bus, called Bus'In Your Chops, to town. Mike, in his work with Transform Jax, could see the need for a sea change in policy and the city's approach to business development when it came to mobile food vendors. His advice to city hall, then and now, is be a moderator, not a gatekeeper.

I sat down with Mike and now fiancée Caron at the Blind Rabbit in Riverside to get the story behind Jax Truckies. They were looking for ways to convince the city to embrace the growing food truck culture, and they thought—how cool would it be to have food trucks at Hemming all the time? If you know Jax, you know that Hemming Park is Jacksonville's unofficial "town square," in the heart of downtown, smack dab in front of city hall.

Thinking it would be an easy sell, that the city would embrace the opportunity, they reached out to the office of special events, which basically said thanks, but no thanks. At least one city official offered to help them navigate the process, but the map for success at that point consisted more of roadblocks than road.

Undaunted, they formed a group in January 2012 and began planning the first of several successful food truck events, this time looking just beyond

JAX TRUCKIES

facebook.com/jaxtruckies
twitter.com/jaxtruckies

Jax Truckies. *Logo designed by Caron Streibich.*

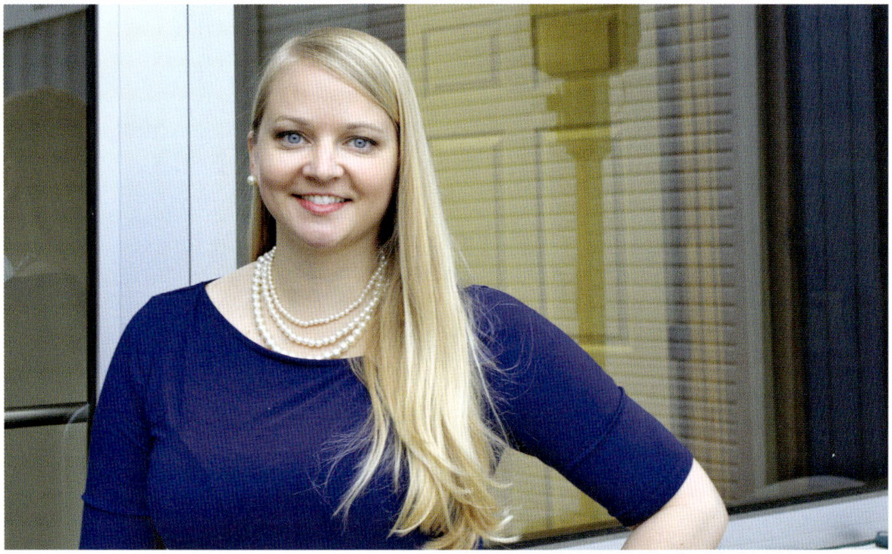

Amy O'Grady, president of Jax Truckies.

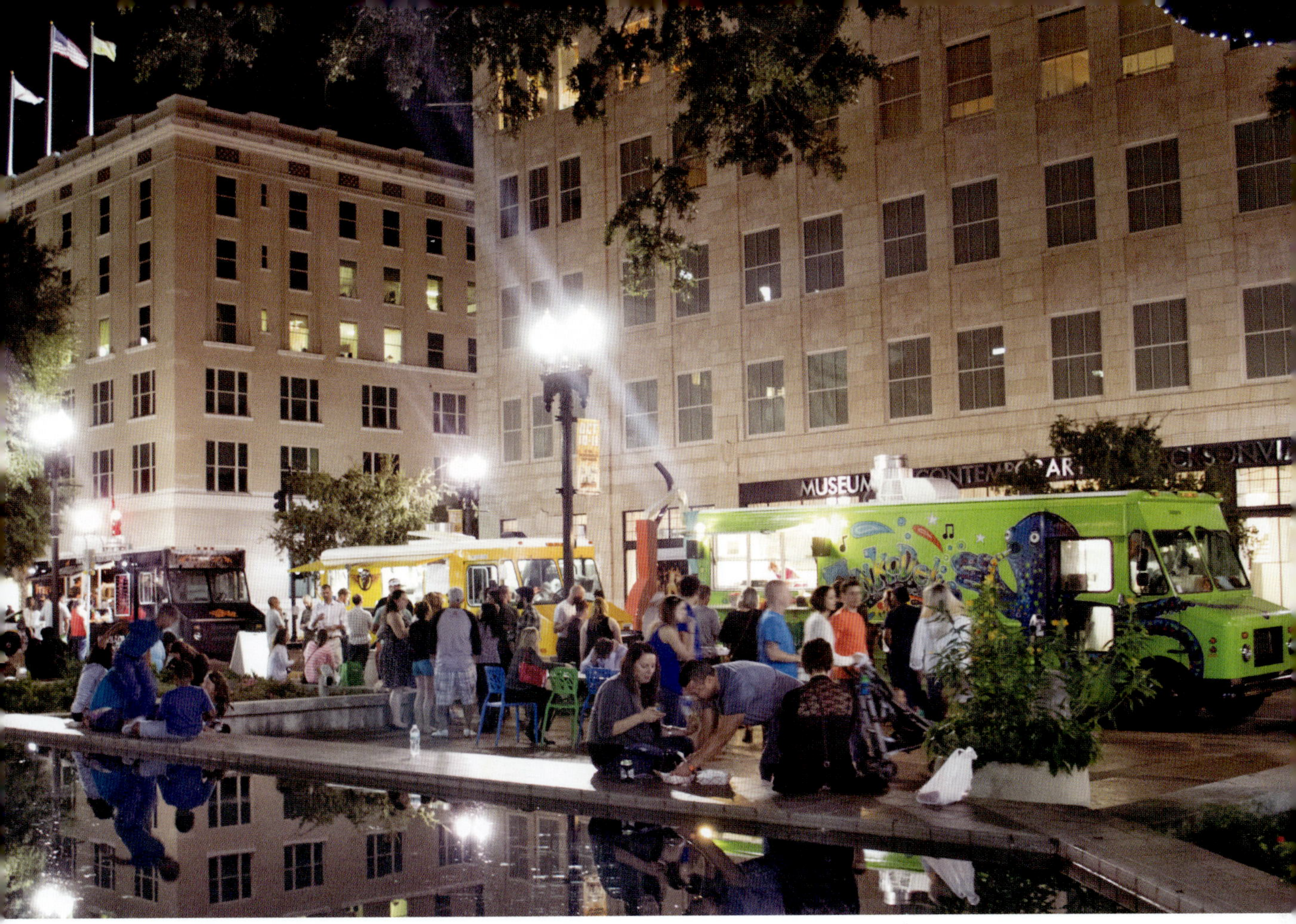

Food Trucks in Hemming Park, Jaxsons Night Market, 2014.

downtown to the Riverside area. Stanton Hudmon at Pine Street/RPS and Susan Miller at Bold City Brewery agreed to host them at the brewery on Rosselle Street. Ennis Davis at metrojacksonville.com created an online ticket outlet, and Stacey Steiner handled PR, getting them on the news to promote the event and starting the conversation on social media.

The name "Jax Truckies" came about almost by accident. Mike was thinking of names for the awards for the event and thought, "How cool would it be to say, 'I won a Truckie!'" Caron designed the logo (with Mike over her shoulder like *every* graphic designer's favorite client) and the event poster, and the branding launched on their Facebook page in February 2012. Soon the truck operators, along with thousands of enthusiastic food truck fans, were calling themselves truckies. A brand was born.

About a year before the legislation in Jacksonville Beach went through, Jax Truckies teamed up with Beaches Watch, an advocacy group, and held a public forum at the Jacksonville Public Library, Neptune Beach Branch.

Tony Sleiman, CEO of Sleiman Enterprises, also helped when it came to convincing Jacksonville Beach to permit trucks to operate there. He sat down with city council members and told them firsthand how his businesses benefited from having the trucks nearby and addressed the concerns of a small group of restaurant owners who were seeking to block the trucks from operating at the beach.

The Jacksonville Beach City Council had an election coming up, and certain council members made food trucks a campaign issue. Mike cites Christine Hoffman as advocating that the beaches should be welcoming small businesses, singling out food trucks as an example of the kind of development that was good for the community.

A Labor of Love

While firmly placing the focus on how a thriving food truck scene would impact Jacksonville businesses, for Jax Truckies founders Mike and Caron, it was never about the money. At the height of their involvement, they were each easily putting in thirty to forty volunteer hours per week. Mike chased down legislation and facilitated key alliances, and Caron worked with truck operators to create their social media profiles, advised them on marketing and what to serve at events and answered myriad questions. They planned and executed several major events—all of this while they both held demanding full-time jobs. Jacksonville's food truck scene would not have taken root so quickly or blossomed so fully had it not been for their tireless efforts. For them, it was truly a labor of love.

Back in Jacksonville, Jack Shad, officer in the city's Office of Public Parking, combed through the section of the municipal code referring to transit merchants. He proposed an

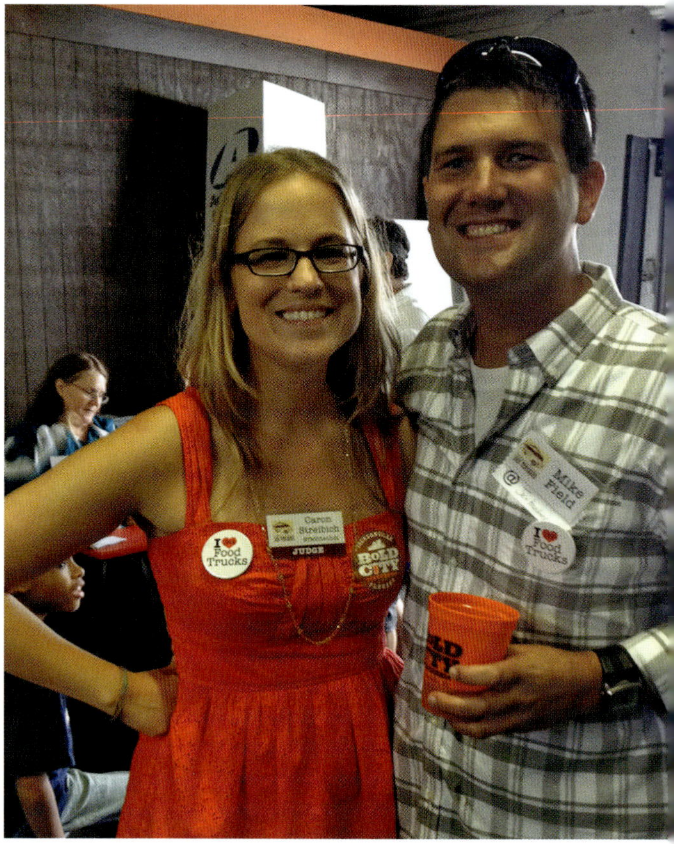

Jax Truckies founders, Caron Streibich and Mike Field, celebrate the inaugural Jax Truckies Food Truck Championship at Bold City Brewery. *Photograph by Ennis Davis of Metro Jacksonville.*

alternative interpretation of the ordinance that could give the city leverage to allow trucks to park downtown. Over 250 people showed up at a scheduled public hearing on a Wednesday afternoon to participate in the debate. The city was overwhelmed by the response.

Many business owners made it clear that they stood with the trucks. Brian Bush from Tom Bush Mazda circulated a petition, and within seventy-two hours, he got over ten thousand signatures. After everything that had already happened, Mike was shocked by such a swift and decisive response; it was clear Jaxsons wanted food trucks in their city.

One thing Mike is particularly proud of is that they developed successful pilot programs with both the PGA Tour and the Jacksonville Jaguars to introduce food trucks at PGA Tour events and tailgate areas outside NFL games. Those types of strategic partnerships were key to the success of the group, which literally had no operating budget.

Partnering with charities that in turn promoted the events to their followings turned out to be a great idea as well. The trucks benefitted from new, engaged followers, and the charities received typically 10 percent of the proceeds from the trucks. Every large event that Jax Truckies produced had a charitable component. Over the years that Mike and Caron operated the group, Jax Truckies raised over $27,000 for local charities.

As food truck fervor continues to grow in Jacksonville, Jax Truckies has become the largest source of information on the local food truck scene. Jax Truckies was doing a bang-up job of posting the trucks' whereabouts on their Facebook page, and they began holding events to raise awareness and garner public support. The more trucks that were licensed in town, the more the fan base grew.

JAX TRUCKIES FOOD TRUCK EVENTS

2012 Food Truck Championship

On March 31, 2012, the Jax Truckies Jacksonville Food Truck Championship was held at Bold City Brewery. Ticket sales were limited to 350 to ensure that people's first food truck experience wouldn't be standing in line for an hour. Proceeds benefitted Second Harvest Food Bank.

The event included a contest for Best Sandwich and Best Side Item. In addition, participants had the opportunity to select a people's choice award. Guest judges included Caron (in her capacity as hostess of *Folio Weekly*'s Bite Club), *Jacksonville Magazine*'s Kerry "The Specktator" Speckman (pre-mohawk) and Cole Pepper from the Jacksonville Backyard BBQ Championship.

2012 Food Truck Championship Winners

Best Sandwich: Mike B's—the Cleveland
Best Side Item: Monroe's BBQ—Collard Greens
Judges' Choice: On the Fly
People's Choice: On the Fly

Jax Truckies Food Truck Rally

The next major event was a Food Truck Rally on June 9, 2012, this time in downtown Jacksonville, using the parking lot adjacent to Burrito Gallery on Adams Street. Ten trucks participated. For some, this was one of their first outings. Super Food had been built just three months prior, and Gourmet Aviator was only a month old. The event was heavily promoted through social media thanks to Caron, Mike and Stacey Steiner, who garnered the group some much-welcomed positive media attention.

The maverick "truckies" didn't have a permit and basically were just daring the city to shut them down in front of thousands of local residents who had swarmed to the event. Mike recalls a heart-stopping moment when five uniformed firemen and police officers walked in, and he thought, "OK, here we go, they're going to shut us down right here." In actuality, they were on their lunch break and just looking for something to eat! A relieved Mike welcomed them in for their first taste of local food truck fare.

2013 Food Truck Championship

The 2013 Food Truck Championship was also at the Burrito Gallery lot on Adams on June 15, 2013. Intuition Ale Works and Digital Billboard came on board to help with advertising. The event was heavily promoted through TV, radio, print, outdoor and social media. They knew it was going to be big; they just didn't know how big.

The huge crowd waited in long lines, mostly with smiles intact, for a chance to support the trucks. Whether you ate at a truck or, like me, came downtown just to soak up the atmosphere (and a couple of Intuition Ale Works brews), it was obvious Jax Truckies could deliver on its promise to bring foot traffic to downtown. Businesses adjacent to the event reported having their best nights in a long time, including several restaurants that benefitted from hungry diners not wanting to wait in line.

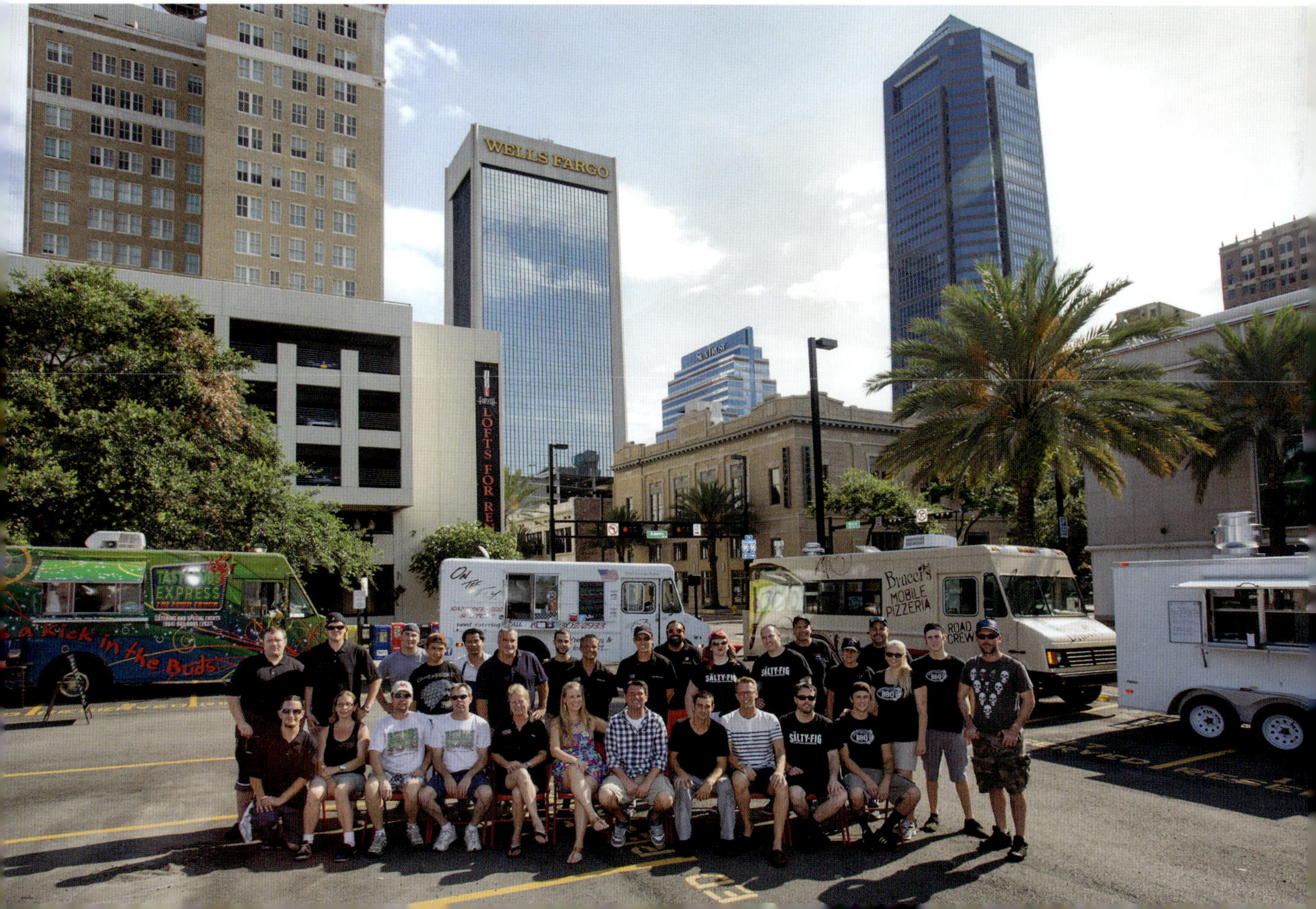

Jax Truckies second Food Truck Championship took place on June 15, 2013, at the Burrito Gallery lot in downtown Jacksonville. *Photograph by Laura Evans Photography.*

2013 Food Truck Championship Winners

Best BBQ: Driftwood BBQ—Brisket Stack atop blue cheese mashed potatoes
Best Taco: Monroe's BBQ—Spicy Pulled Pork with creamy slaw and Sriracha
Best Sandwich: Taste Buds Express—Chicken Shawarma Flauta
Most Innovative: The Happy Grilled Cheese—Crunch Melt with Mac 'n' Cheese and Tomato Soup
Sweet Tooth: On the Fly—Chocolate Peanut Butter Pretzel Bar
Judges' Choice: On the Fly
People's Choice: On the Fly

Tony Sleiman was there, and clearly he saw the potential. He offered the Jacksonville Landing, his prime waterfront retail development, as a venue for future events. He also lent his voice and considerable influence to the growing chorus of food truck supporters. For the truckies, it was the validation they needed. Here was the biggest landlord of restaurant businesses in town welcoming food trucks to his property.

In December 2013, Jax Truckies were "Truckin on the River" in partnership with the Jacksonville Landing and benefitting Children's Miracle Network. Eleven food trucks, cold beer, sodas, good music and an unbeatable view made for a great event for thousands. The Happy Grilled Cheese was voted by fans as the "Children's Champion."

2014 Food Truck Championship

Jax Truckies partnered with Big Brothers Big Sisters of Northeast Florida to co-host the Third Annual Jax Truckies Food Truck Championship. More than two dozen trucks competed for the 2014 People's Choice and Judges' Choice awards. The event, in its new home at the Jacksonville Landing, featured music, giveaways, a raffle and, of course, lots of great food.

2014 Food Truck Championship Winners

Best Global Cuisine: Blue Pacific Taco—Malaysian Chicken Satay
Best Taco: Taste Buds Express—Billy's Favorite Taco
Best Sandwich: Chunky Tomato—Mozzarella & Tomato Panini
Most Innovative: Fusion—Banana Curry
Sweet Tooth: The Loving Cup—Butter Beer
Judges' Choice: What's the Catch
People's Choice: The Happy Grilled Cheese

JACKSONVILLE FOOD TRUCKS (JFT)

Tom Wilbers of Up in Smoke BBQ and Alex Montanez of Gourmet Aviator are the founding members of Jacksonville Food Trucks (JFT). The group holds monthly meetings to share information and plan events. It also manages the JFT Warehouse off Powers Avenue next to Restaurant Depot, which offers sheltered parking, dry goods storage, water service and waste disposal to food trucks.

BEER HERE

If Jacksonville didn't have such great local breweries, it's not clear whether our food truck scene would have ever taken off the way it has.

Susan Miller of Bold City Brewery and Cari Sanchez-Potter from Intuition Ale Works invited some of the first trucks to serve in their breweries' private courtyards, and the very first Jax Truckies event was held at Bold City Brewery. At the beach, On the Fly found early refuge at Green Room Brewing while Engine 15 tried to host a truck, but the city put an end to both those arrangements before revisiting its stance on food trucks. More recently, Aardwolf and Veterans United have joined the fun and have proved popular spots for a rotation of trucks. A special sympathy exists between the trucks and the breweries, with both camps having to deal with pending legislation that could seriously impede their progress.

TO MARKET, TO MARKET

Cari Sanchez-Potter and friends started the King Street Farmers' Market, inviting trucks to operate there each Wednesday. For many of us, myself included, it was our first introduction to our food trucks. Gourmet Aviator, Salty Fig and Corner Taco were regulars, and the lines at times were so long it wasn't clear if you would get your order in time to devour it and head back to work. What was clear, though, was that people from all parts of Jacksonville were beginning to hear about, and travel to eat from the trucks.

Still more trucks began testing the waters as tent vendors at the Riverside Arts Market (RAM). Tom and Jen Wilbers sold BBQ under their Up in Smoke name before their big red trailer hit the streets, and Izzy Tahil of Blue Pacific Grill and Taco Bar got his start at RAM before purchasing his trailer from a fellow market vendor. Amy and Patrick O'Grady sold their Driftwood BBQ at RAM on weekends and ran their trailer during the week.

Jacksonville Farmers' Market and smaller markets around town have continued the trend of inviting trucks to serve at their events and in their spaces.

BEAVER STREET COMMISSARY AND THE LOT

Chef, caterer, commissary manager, food biz startup counselor and food truck wrangler Chriss Brown may well be the most hardworking person I know. As partner-manager at Jacksonville's 927 Events, Chriss sets the stage for special events, meetings, parties, receptions and more in a one-of-a-kind downtown venue.

As she searched for a commissary kitchen in Jacksonville, she wasn't finding any that met her needs. Sensing a business opportunity, she consulted her friend and business partner Paul, who owned a warehouse on Beaver Street that would make an ideal commissary space. The two decided to build a facility big enough for startups and small business entrepreneurs looking for a licensed facility for their operations to join. Thus was born the Beaver Street Commissary.

In 2012, Chriss got involved in promoting and assisting new food truck businesses in Jacksonville, and in 2013, she and Paul created a space solely for the use and convenience of food trucks. Located across from the commissary, "the Lot" features secure parking and surveillance for food trucks and vendor carts, with available individual electric, garbage, grease disposal and water setups. There are plans to expand offerings and plenty of space in which to grow.

As an advisor to Jax Truckies, Chriss has been a frequent visitor to city hall during the last rounds of legislation. She contributed to the passing of a compromise bill that would allow trucks and restaurants to peaceably coexist in Jacksonville.

With as much time as Chriss has spent around food trucks, it should come as no surprise that she would eventually own one. Say hello to Say Cheese! "Jacksonville's Grooviest Grilled Cheese." I got to sample some of the tasty, toasty grilled cheese sandwiches as they were developing the recipe, and I'm happy to report that Jacksonville's food truck scene just got significantly cheesier!

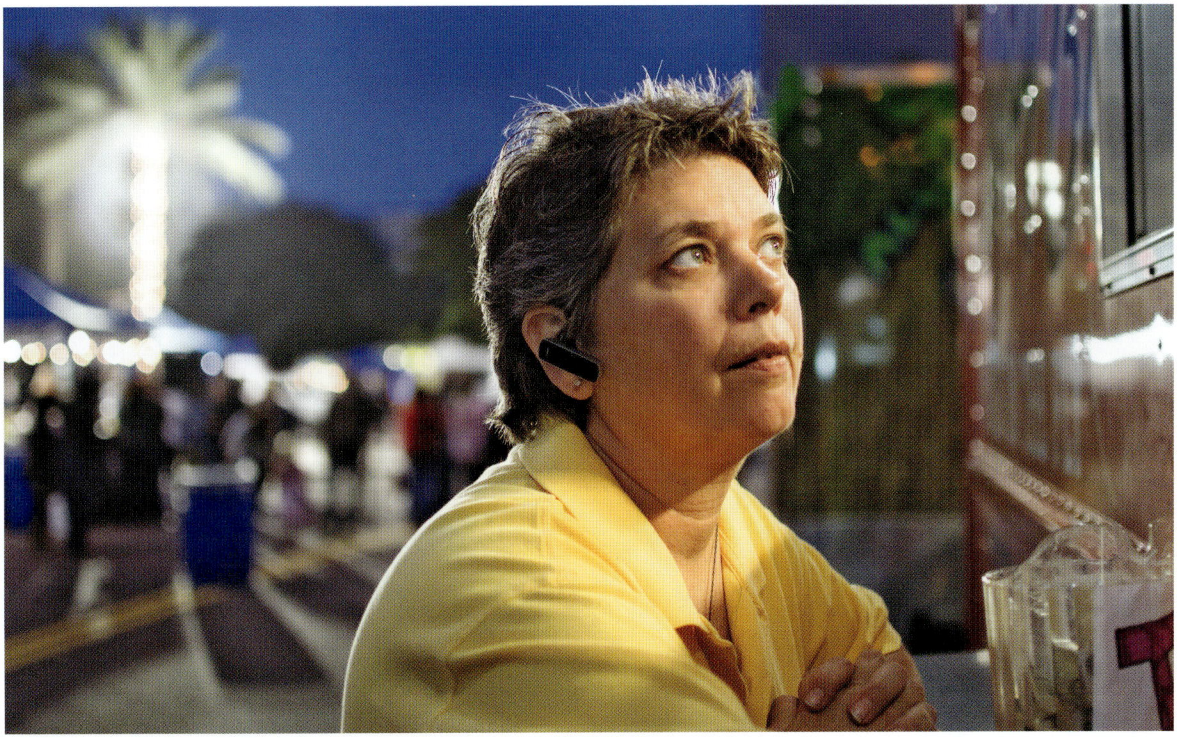

Chef Chriss Brown of 927 Events.

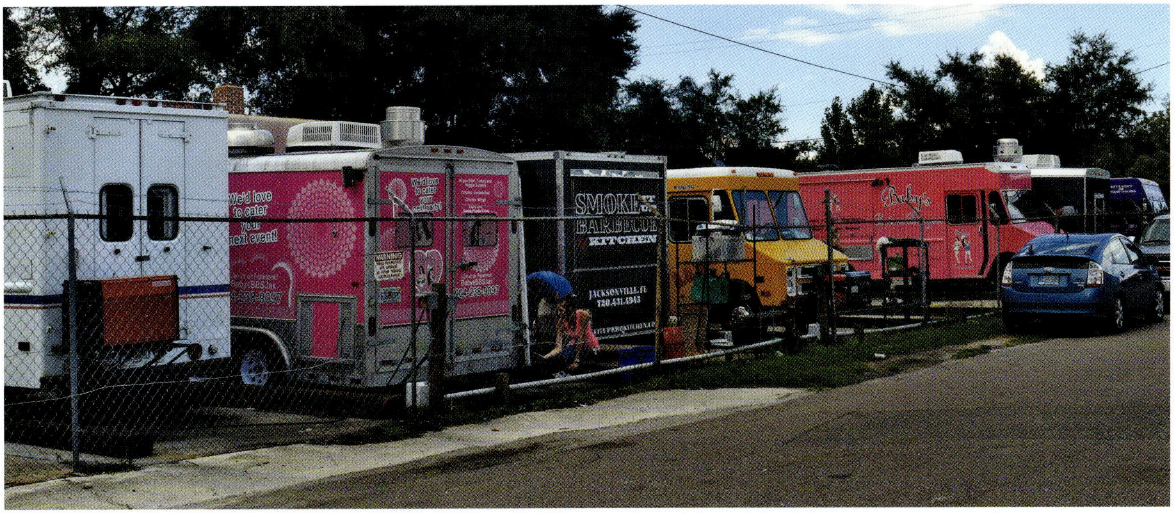

The Lot at Beaver Street Commissary.

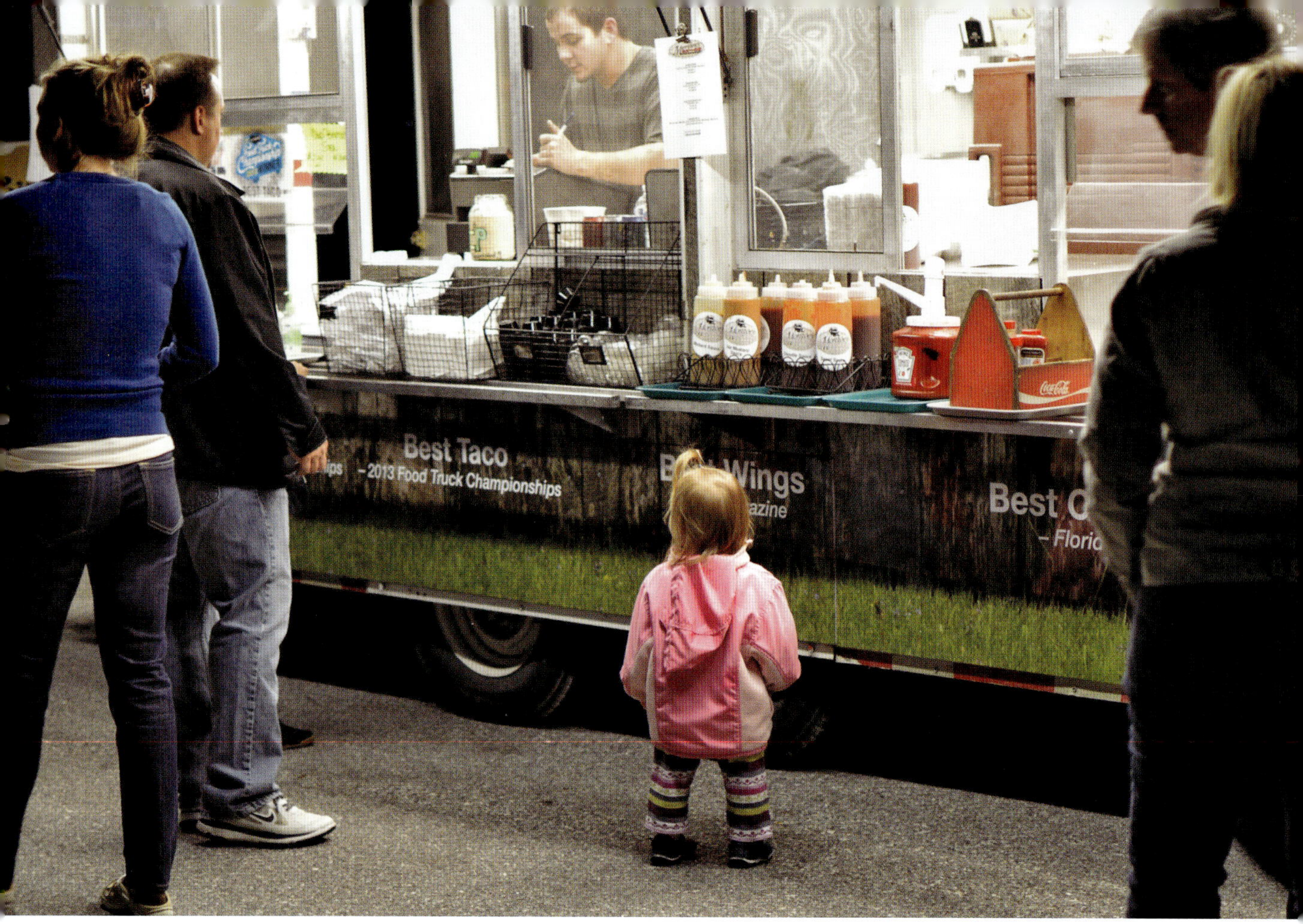

Fearless food truck fan at Nocatee.

THE NEXT GENERATION

The next generation of truckies is already being groomed. Jax Truckies, Corner Taco, Monroe's Smokehouse Bar-B-Q & Catering and the Happy Grilled Cheese all sit on an advisory board offering support to an innovative new workforce development program for Duval County Public Schools, in partnership with the JAX Chamber, where high school students will learn to run food truck businesses.

THE TRUCKS

THE BLIND RABBIT (FORMERLY THE SALTY FIG)

Jeff Stanford

One of the earliest mobile food vendors on the scene locally was the Salty Fig.

Jeff Stanford was born in Mississippi but moved to Florida in 1998, the same year I did. He attended Nease High School in Ponte Vedra, where I live. While there, he played soccer against a young Patrick O'Grady from Fletcher High, now owner-operator of Driftwood BBQ. When Jeff went to Florida State College–Jacksonville (FSCJ) to earn his culinary degree, he was in the same class as Blake Burnett from Chew Chew. Jacksonville is, on one hand, the largest city in the United States by landmass and, on the other hand, a small world after all.

After college, Jeff took the corporate route, working for Bonefish. He lived out of a suitcase for years while he opened about fifty stores for them. He served as regional R&D director and then national culinary director for Bonefish before spending some time at another seafood restaurant in town. Then he served as chef de cuisine at the Omni in Amelia Island. Through this progression, he learned the restaurant business inside and out. At the Omni, he developed the discipline to produce mass amounts of food, but he wanted to work somewhere with more of a southern soul. His stunning résumé got him a job in New Orleans, where he became chef de partie at Commander's Palace.

Jeff left a great-paying, prestigious job at one of the best restaurants in the country to come back to Jacksonville in January 2012 and create the Salty Fig Gastropub with his brother, John.

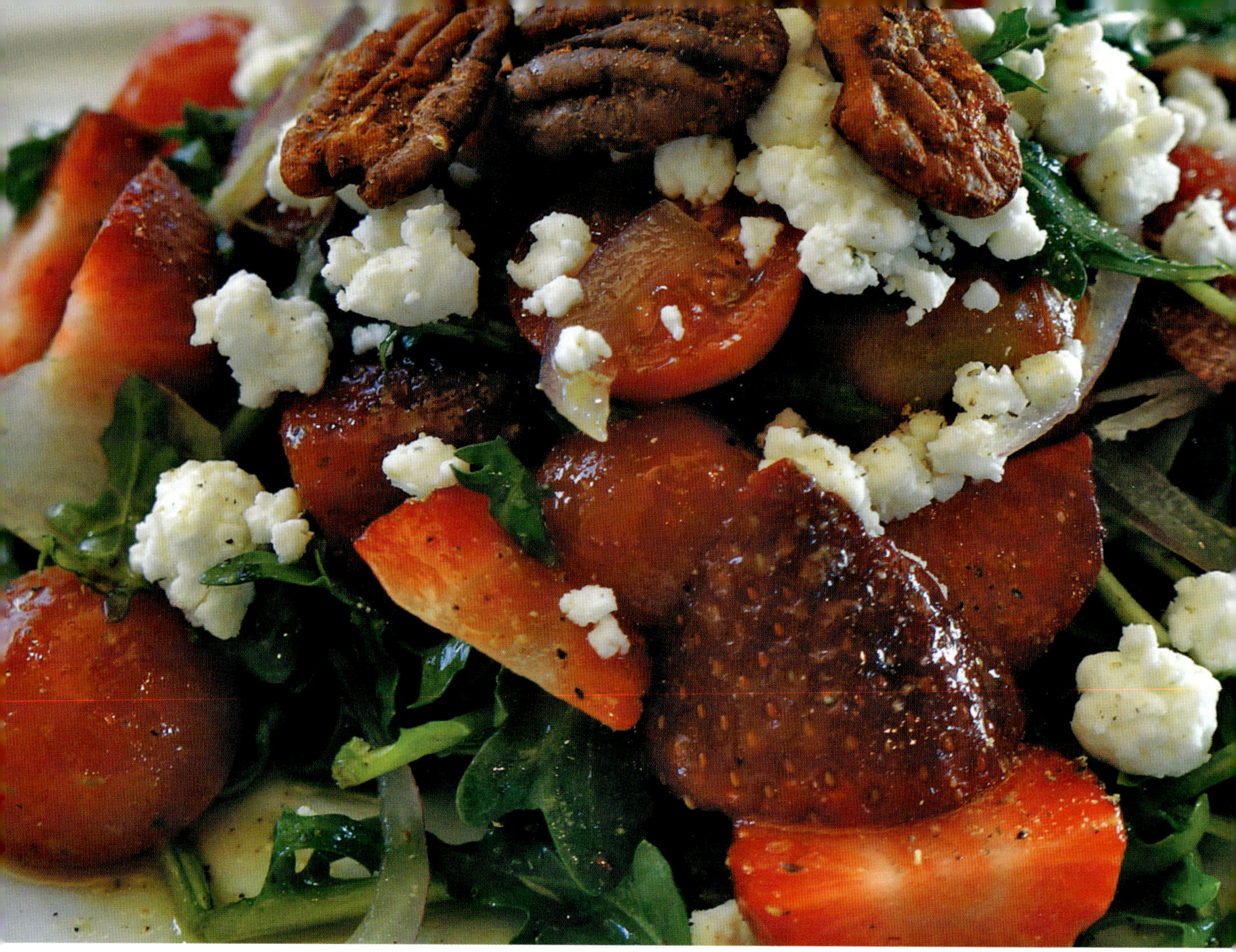

Summer Strawberry Salad from Salty Fig.

In March 2012, the brothers signed a lease on a building at the corner of College and King Streets in Riverside. With the deposit, lease and architectural fees, they had already invested $50,000 when, reacting against commercial growth in the largely residential area, Jacksonville City Council passed a moratorium—no more new bars or restaurants could open on the street, specifically from College to King. There was no getting out of the lease, so the fight was on. They fought city council, they fought the Riverside Area Preservation (RAP) group and they fought the perception that a gastropub was merely another bar. Not wanting to lay out more cash for construction until the moratorium was lifted, Jeff started looking at a food truck as a way to generate cash flow and started testing menu items.

He found a concession trailer on eBay, and in April 2012, he drove to Fayetteville, North Carolina; paid the seller $15,000 in cash; and towed it back home to Jacksonville. They added a generator, propane tanks and the requisite Ansul fire suppression system.

The atmosphere for food trucks at that time was not much better than for new restaurants, but Salty Fig was able to park a few days a week on a vacant lot at the corner of Stockton and Osceola Streets in Riverside, and the Stanfords frequented the King Street Farmers' Market on Wednesdays.

My favorite item from their truck was a salad that was mostly spring mix, arugula, seasonal fruit and candied nuts. I would order the salad and a side of creamy, stone-ground goat cheese grits and take them back to my desk for a cool feast in the heat of the summer. It was an at least weekly treat when I worked on that side of town. When they finally opened the brick-and-mortar version of Salty Fig, my salad and grits ritual was kicked up a few notches, as another New Orleans chef would say. It was the same great combo, just in more posh surroundings, with, you know, tables, chairs, air conditioning, etc. I can see why some food truck owners just can't wait to start their restaurants.

Once he and John got Salty Fig the restaurant up and running, Jeff struck out on his own to Jacksonville Beach and created the Blind Rabbit, A Burger and Whiskey Bar. The 5,500-square-foot restaurant seats 230, right in the heart of the central business district in Jacksonville Beach. When this more casual concept took off, he decided to rebrand Salty Fig as the Blind Rabbit. The next step would be to rewrap the Salty Fig trailer, which had been parked along College next to the restaurant. Alas, it was hit by someone texting and driving. The driver was not seriously injured, but the Salty Fig was beyond repair. Jeff is in the design phase for a second truck for their catering, events and festival participation. M&R Specialty Trailers is fabricating it, and with a little luck, it will be rolling down the streets of town by now. Find the Blind Rabbit online at theblindrabbitwhiskeybar.com.

THE BLU CLAW

Wayne and Tonie Davis

Wayne Davis grew up in Jamaica, where, he says, "you can find wonderful food on the side of the road, and cooking is in your blood." As a teenager, Wayne moved to Maryland, where he gained an appreciation of the blue crabs that were so plentiful in the Chesapeake Bay.

In 2009, Wayne and his wife, Tonie, moved to Florida, and in 2011, they opened the Blu Claw as a food vendor at the Pecan Park Flea Market. After a few years, they decided to join the food truck movement, and in May 2014, they purchased a trailer from Southern Dimensions Group. The couple designed the trailer's kitchen layout themselves, and Precision Cut did the colorful wrap.

In January 2015, Wayne and Tonie took the leap to close the Pecan Park location and become totally mobile. The plan is to take their style of cooking to the greater metropolitan Jacksonville area and beyond. They hope to participate in festivals and larger events

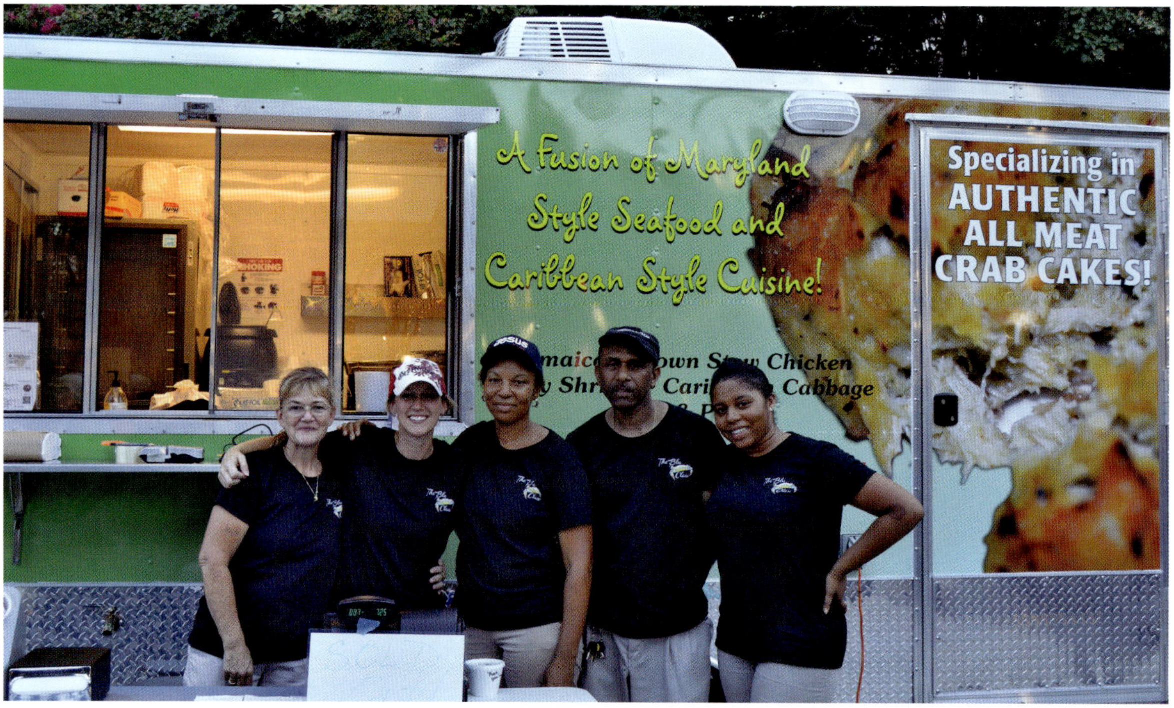

(Left to right) April, Kathy, Tonie, Wayne and daughter Endia all pitched in at the Blu Claw during the Jax Truckies Block Party at the Jacksonville Landing.

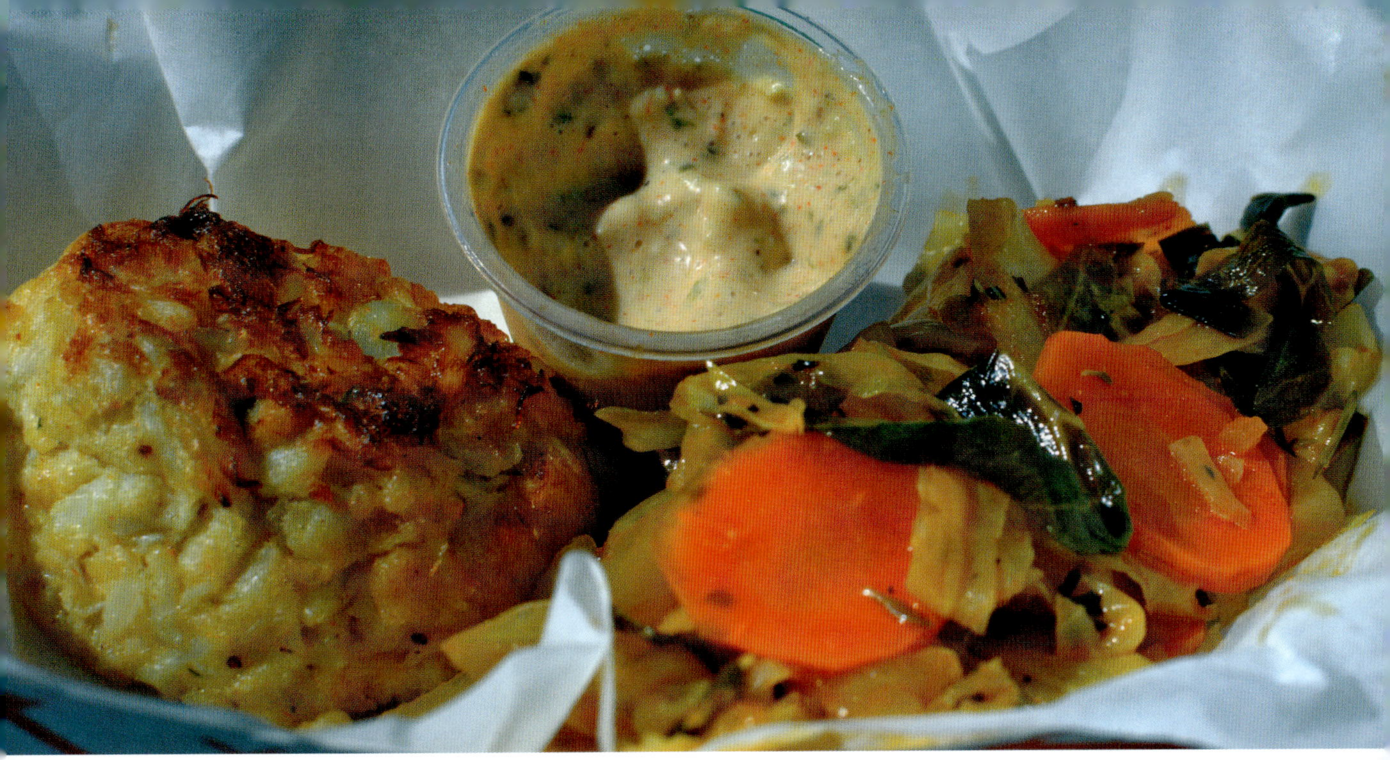

Above: The Blu Claw's mini crab cake sampler includes a dollop of tart and tangy remoulade, a perfect complement to the sweet crab.

Below: Curry Shrimp from the Blu Claw is a satisfying choice for lunch, served with gungo (pigeon peas) and rice and savory Jamaican cabbage.

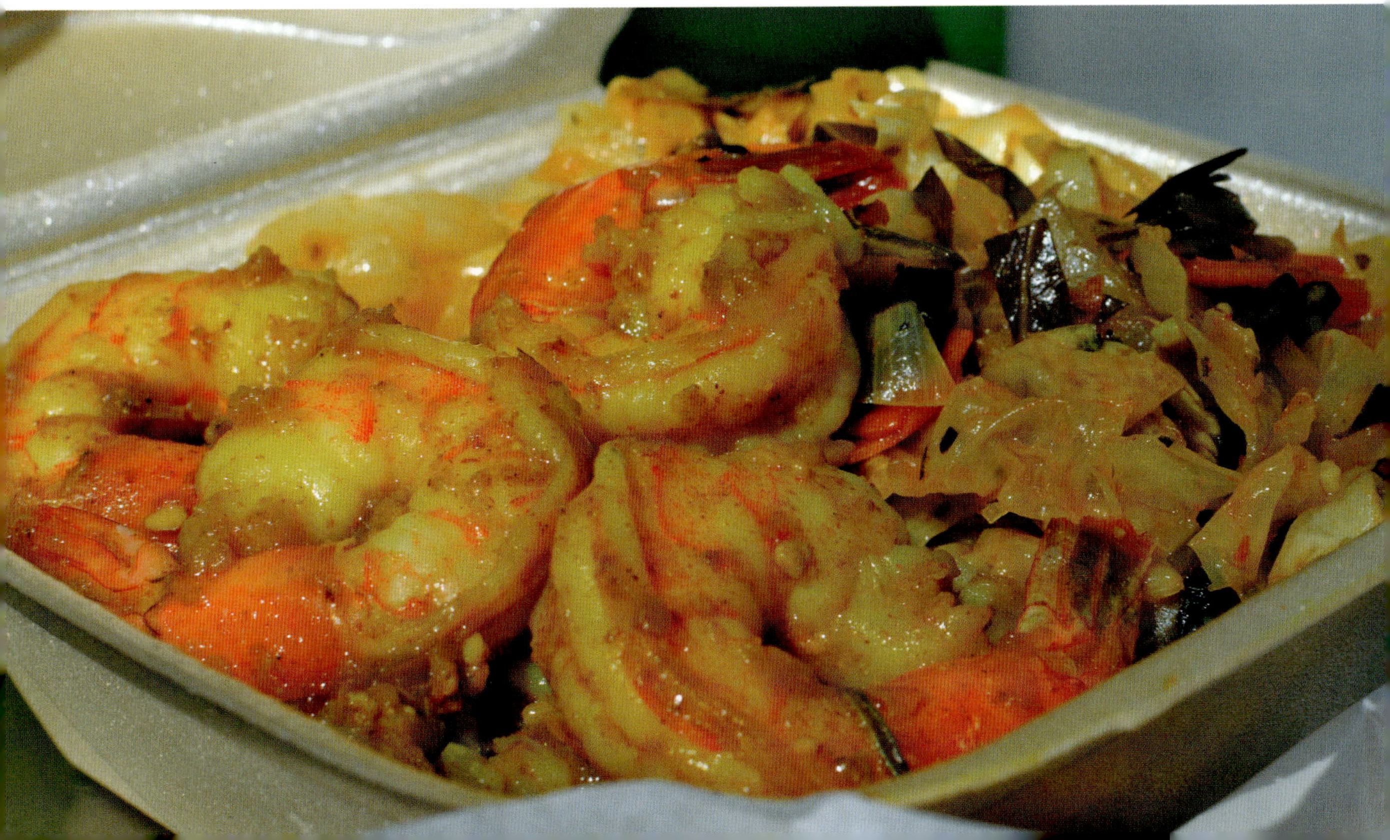

as well as find more regular lunch and dinner service locations.

With culinary inspiration from Wayne's Jamaican grandmother, Wayne and Tonie are turning out Jamaican-style street cooking, with Maryland influences. The combination is a winner in dishes like their Maryland-Style Crab Cakes, Caribbean Cabbage and golden Curry Shrimp.

Having no formal culinary training prior to running the Blu Claw, Tonie says it was a surprise to her at first how much time and effort it takes to make lunch and dinner service go smoothly. "Prep, prep and prep is all I can say," she cautions. "It's the difference between keeping up or drowning."

The couple suffered a setback in November 2014 when thieves broke into their storage lot and stole their brand-new generator and license plates. They persevered through the unexpected hardship, and their fans rallied around them.

The positive feedback and interaction with their customers is what keeps them going. Tonie credits God, and the couple is thankful for the support of family, customers who drove to Pecan Park from all over and the snowbirds. The Davises enjoyed meeting the people who made the Blu Claw a part of their itinerary as they traveled south, and they hope folks will continue to seek them out now that they've taken to the streets. Find the Blu Claw online at facebook.com/thebluclaw.

BLUE PACIFIC GRILL AND TACO BAR

Esmael "Izzy" Tahil

In Izzy Tahil's family, everyone either cooks very well or eats very well.

Born and raised in Singapore, Izzy has lived in Egypt, Thailand, New York and Hawaii and has traveled throughout the world. He was exposed to a lot of different cuisines growing up, mostly Asian. Any food he produces for his Blue Pacific Grill and Taco Bar today is reminiscent of a place he has traveled and something that he has tried and liked, often from street food vendors.

Izzy has worked in hotels and restaurants in New York and Hawaii. He found working in fine-dining restaurants to be a good learning experience, but he longed for a venue to express his individuality and creativity.

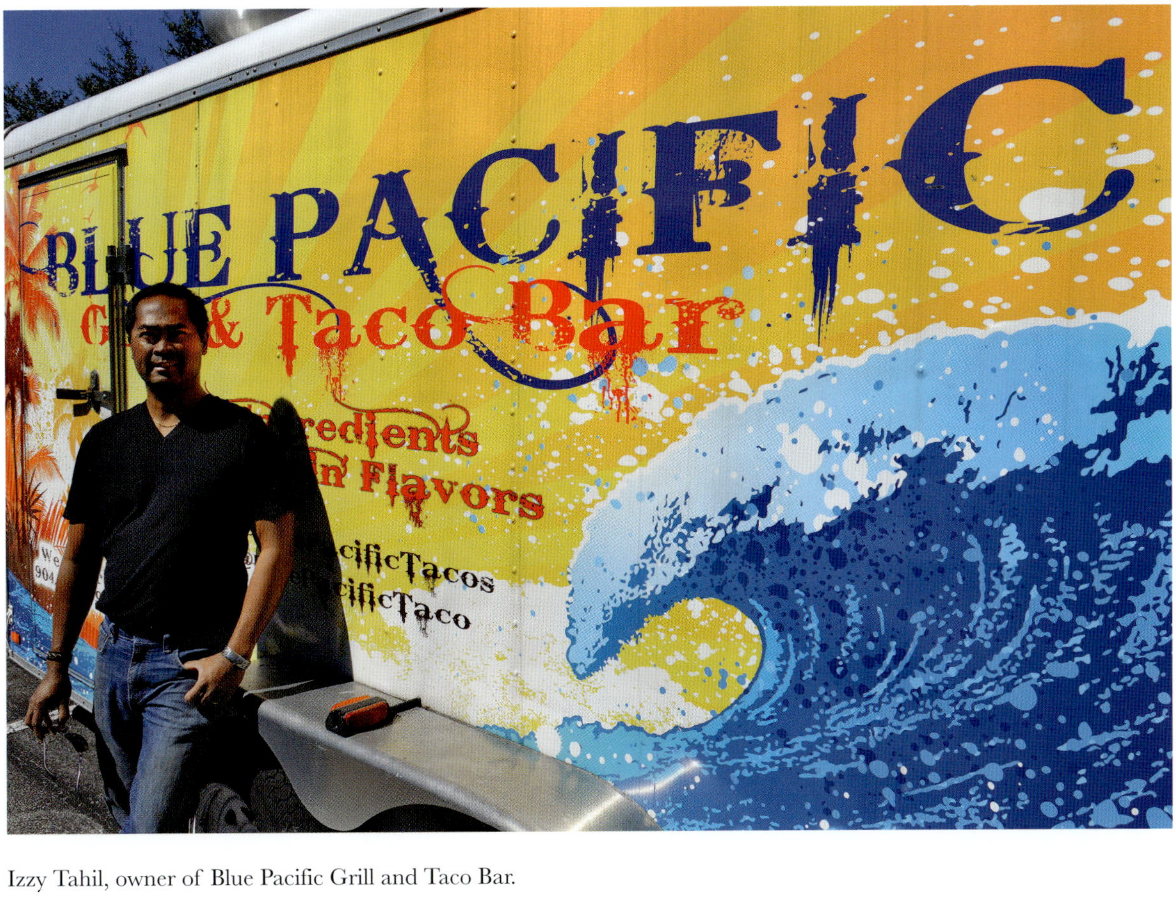

Izzy Tahil, owner of Blue Pacific Grill and Taco Bar.

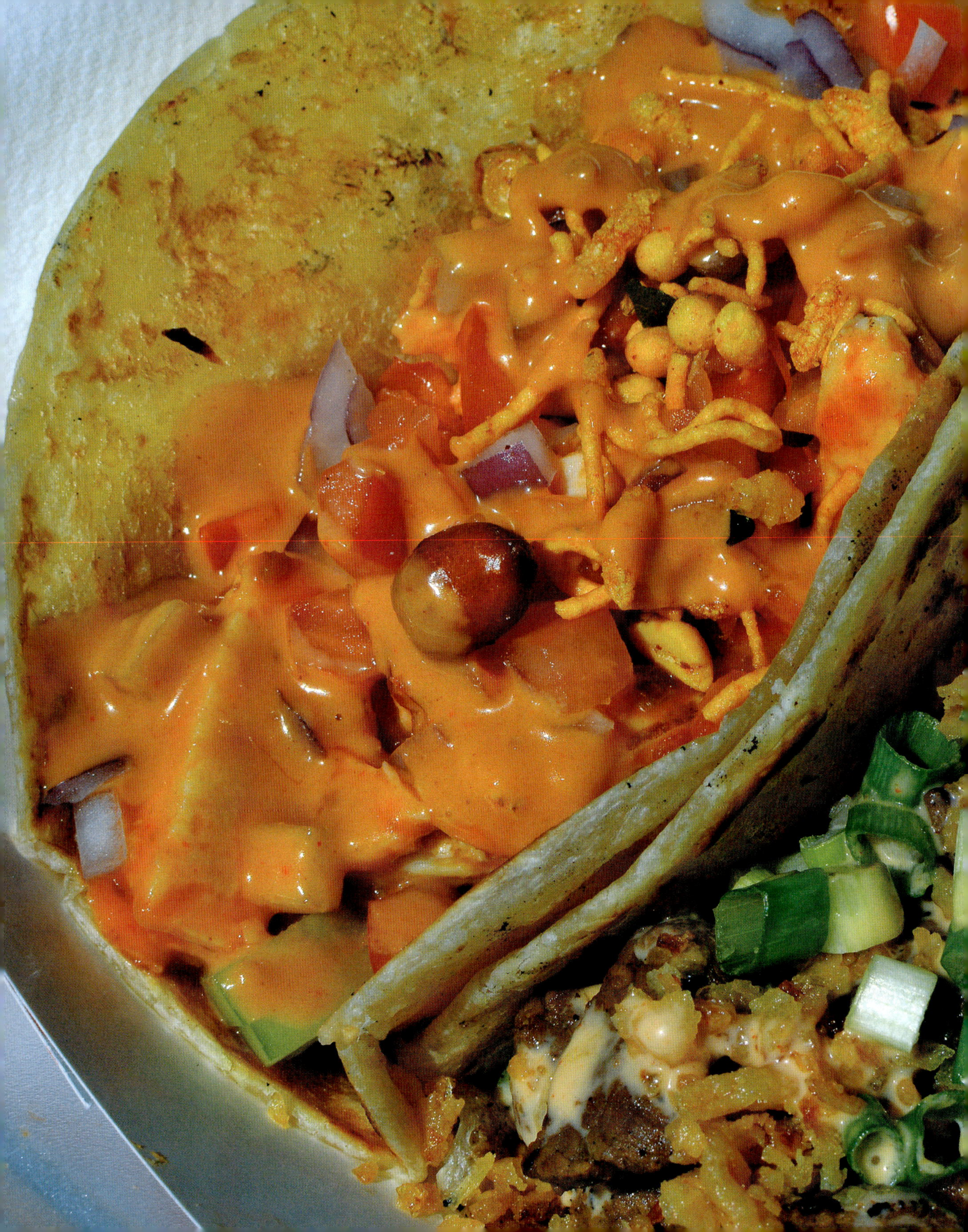

He met his wife, Tracy, while traveling in the Honduras, and she, being a native of Jacksonville, brought him here to settle down and start a family. Izzy's wanderlust inspired him to travel to seven different countries in Asia with his son to introduce him to the regional cuisines. They sampled a lot of street food and brought back even more food memories.

In 2012, Izzy started serving his globally inspired cuisine at the Riverside Arts Market. In November 2013, he bought the trailer from a fellow RAM food vendor who had built it before food trucks entered the Jacksonville scene but never used it. Izzy designed the logo and had the trailer wrapped at Atlantic Imaging. The trailer was completed in December 2013, and on January 25, 2014, Izzy launched Blue Pacific Grill and Taco Bar. His first outing was at Aardwolf Brewery in San Marco. When the Third Annual Jax Truckies Food Truck Championship came around in May 2014, Blue Pacific took top honors for Best Global Cuisine with its Malaysian Chicken Satay. Lucky readers, you get a recipe, you get a recipe, you get a recipe, everybody gets a recipe!

Blue Pacific's is one of those menus you want to explore every bit of rather than settling on one favorite and getting that every time. Malaysian, Japanese, Vietnamese, Thai, Indian and Mexican

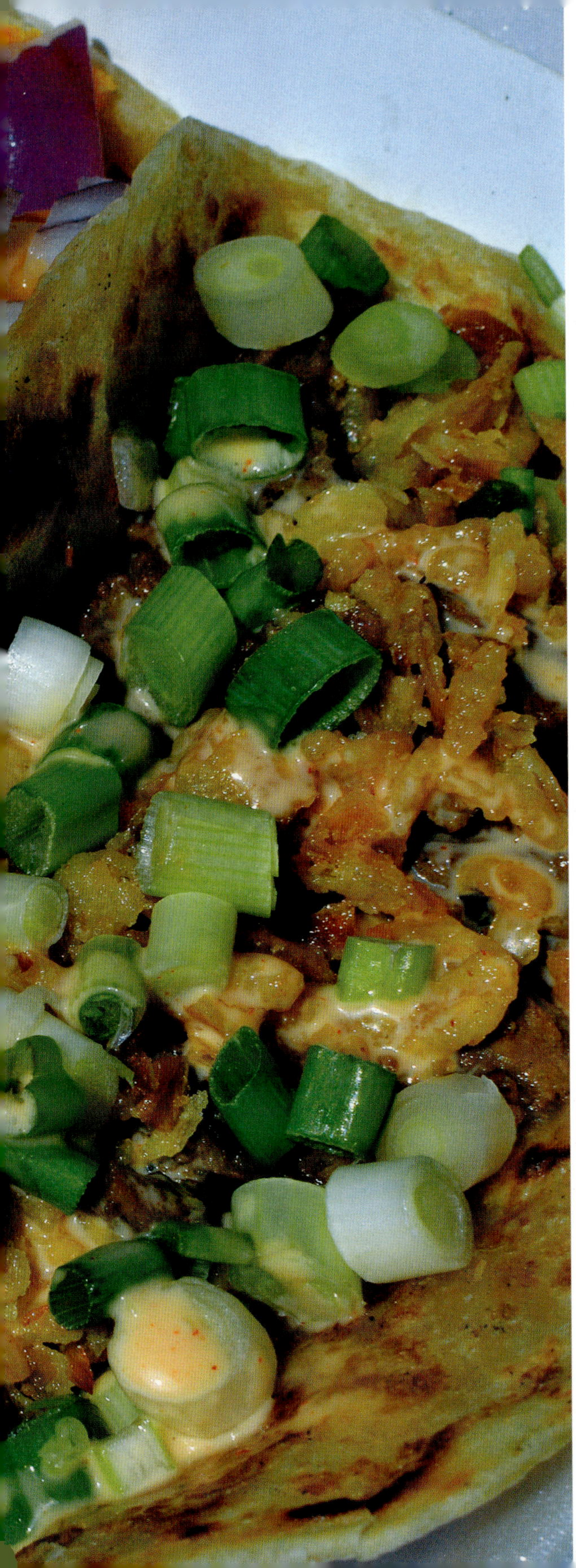

Tacos from Blue Pacific Grill and Taco Bar.

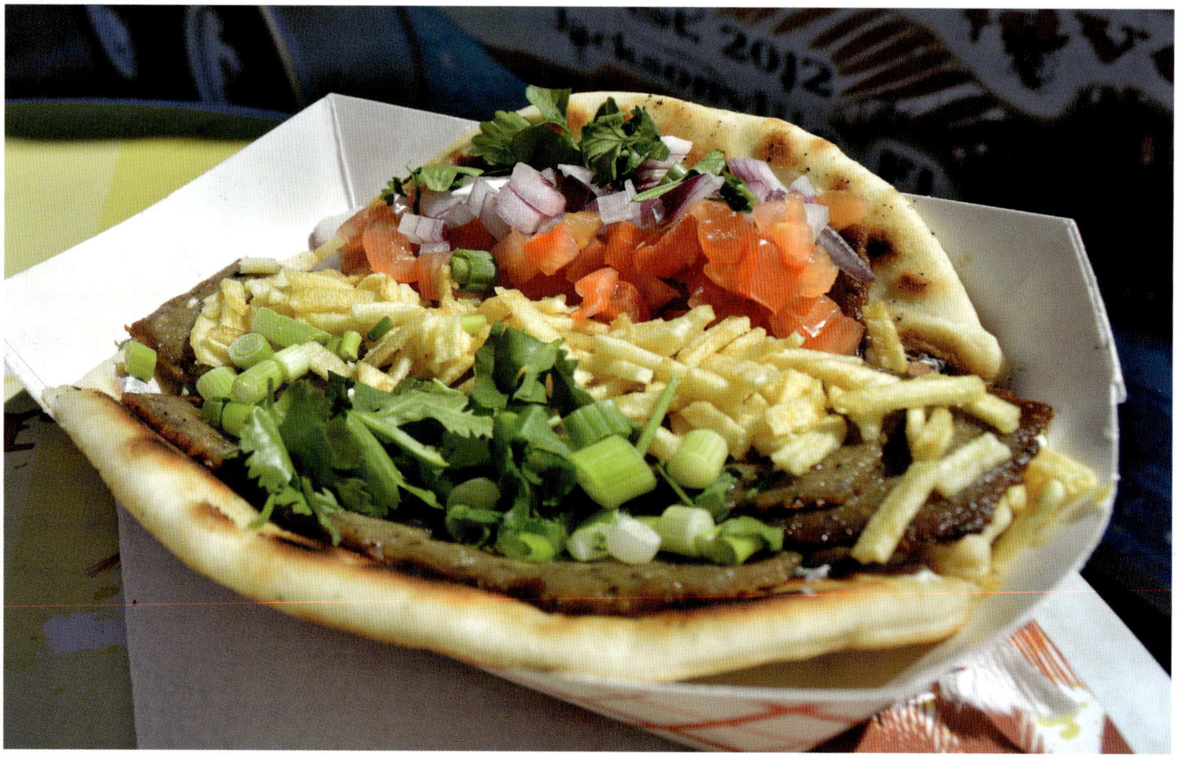

Lamb Gyro from Blue Pacific Grill and Taco Bar.

are just a few of the flavor profiles represented. Initially, there were nearly twenty selections, but the practicality of creating all of that food and housing it on the truck for service meant winnowing down the choices.

The global influence of his cooking results in dishes with complex tastes, colors and textures. Most are refined to accommodate milder palates. Tracy isn't a fan of spicy foods, so Izzy uses her as a bellwether for what Jacksonville's diners might enjoy.

Chicken Tikka tacos get loaded with chunks of marinated grilled chicken, lettuce, Bombay mix, tomato, red onion, cilantro and mango chutney sauce.

A local favorite, the Pulled Pork Taco is served with flour tortillas, coleslaw, slow-cooked pork, fried barbecue onions, potato straws, scallions and chipotle mayo. Like most of Izzy's tacos, the Pulled Pork Taco results in a symphony of taste, textures and temperatures.

The Japanese-influenced Teriyaki Steak Taco is enveloped in a scallion pancake and finished with cucumber, fried onions, sesame seeds, scallions and a generous drizzle of Izzy's Sriracha Yum-Yum sauce.

One of the non-taco items that has me dancing for joy is the Slow Cooked Chipotle Beef bowl: slow-cooked brisket roast and red onions, topped

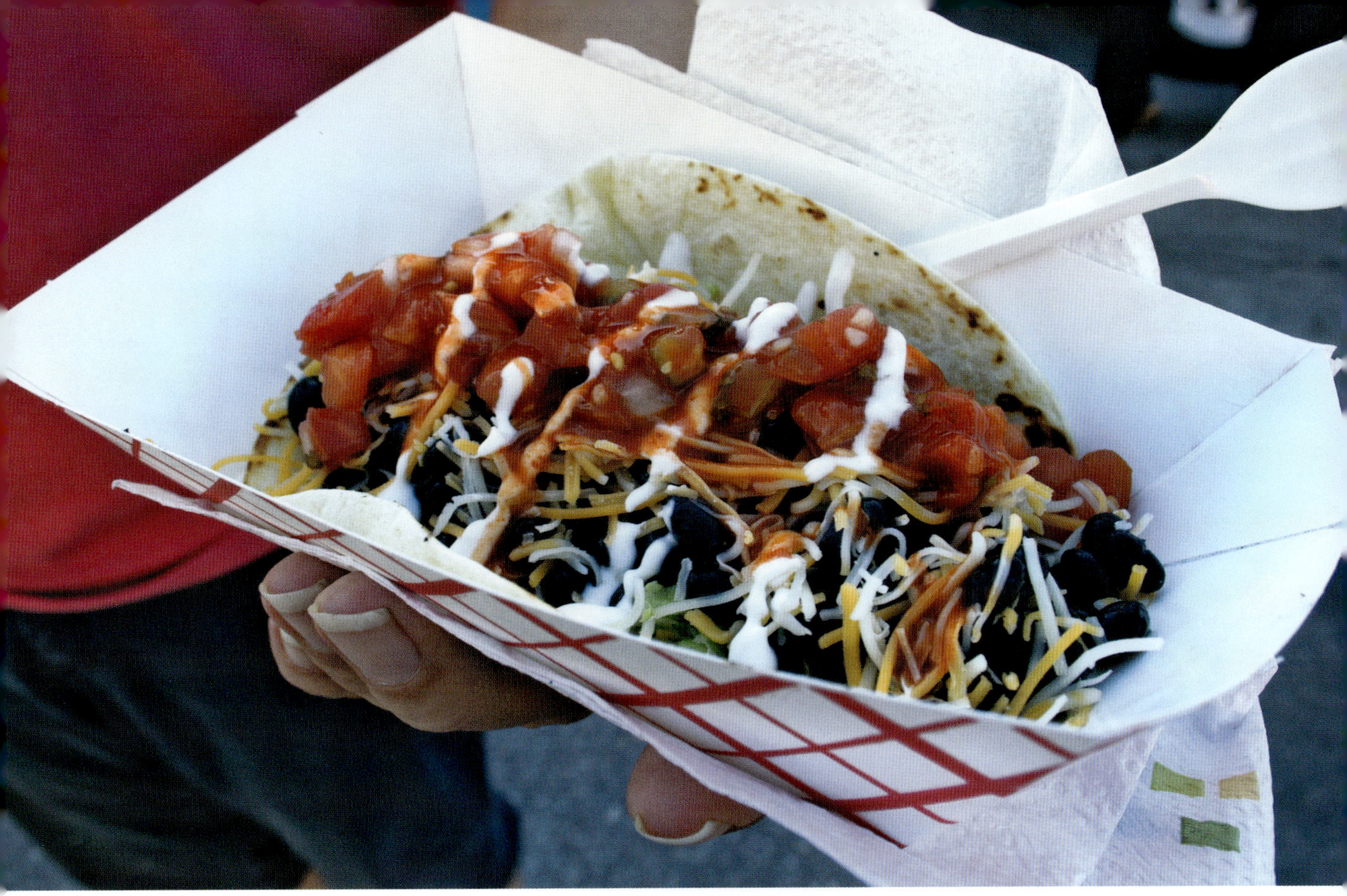

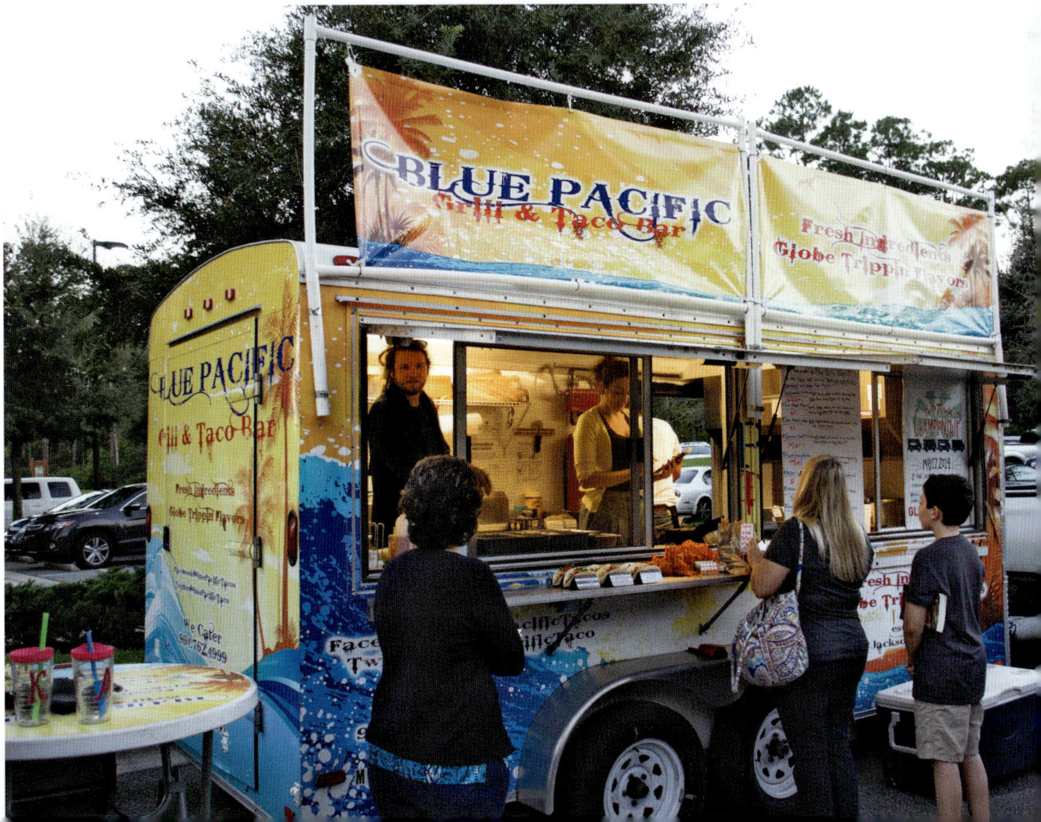

Above: Black Bean Taco from Blue Pacific Grill and Taco Bar.

Right: Blue Pacific Grill and Taco Bar.

with cilantro and chipotle mayo and served over Mexican yellow rice.

Speaking of beef, by now, Izzy should also be serving his gourmet handcrafted burgers. He announced them in late 2014. I can't wait to see the flavor combos he introduces with these!

The Angry Orchard Chili Con Carne is my fave when the weather gets crisp. It's a straightforward version with ground beef, beans and cilantro, topped with sour cream. It is served over Mexican yellow rice with a side of chips.

There is a rather substantial Lamb Gyro, for those who seek something more familiar. I loved this dish, which, like all Izzy's tacos, comes stuffed to the brim. It isn't easy to eat, but I rolled up my sleeves, leaned over one of the tall tables the crew puts out for diners and somehow got the entire thing in me without getting it on me!

An open note to the two lovely ladies who graciously shared their table space with me: I know you didn't expect your lunch to be invaded by a crazy woman or for your table to be turned into a photography studio. Thanks for sharing your space—it's one of the things I love about the food truck culture. It brings people together.

Vegetarians enjoy the loaded Black Bean or Chickpea Tacos, with lettuce, tomato, red onions, cilantro, shredded cheese and pico de gallo. My friend Chriss Brown of 927 Events ordered one during an event in Neptune Beach and offered me a bite. I was blown away by the depth of flavor they created with that combo.

Izzy's international travels are reflected in the variety of breads he makes fresh each week. Where most taco trucks start with tortillas, Izzy often builds his creations on Chinese scallion pancakes and Indian naan, chapatti and paratha (a fluffy, layered Indian bread that is ideal for holding heavy, saucy fillings).

You'll find Izzy's brightly decorated trailer at office parks throughout town and at all the major events. He loves serving at EverBank Field for Jacksonville Jaguars tailgating. He'll bring his globally inspired eats to your street, too. Ask him about catering your next event. Enjoy the globe trippin' flavors of Blue Pacific Grill and Taco Bar on Twitter @BluePacificTaco and on Facebook at BluePacificTacos.

BLUE PACIFIC'S AWARD-WINNING MALAYSIAN CHICKEN SATAY TACOS

Recipe from Izzy Tahil

1 pound boneless, skinless chicken breast
2 stalks lemongrass, or 1½ teaspoons lemongrass powder
3 small shallots
3 cloves garlic
½ teaspoon fennel seed
¼ cup water
2 tablespoons brown sugar
½ teaspoon ground cumin
½ teaspoon ground coriander
½ teaspoon turmeric powder
½ teaspoon galangal powder (find this in any Asian grocery)
1 tablespoon soy sauce
4 flour tortillas
1 cucumber, diced
1 onion, diced
1 tomato, diced
Satay Peanut Sauce (see below)

Cut chicken into ½-inch cubes. Set aside while you prepare spice paste.

Thinly slice bottom 6 inches of lemongrass. Place in blender with shallots, garlic, fennel seed and water. Process until smooth and then pour into a bowl. Add brown sugar, cumin, coriander, turmeric, galangal and soy sauce and mix well.

Add meat to spice paste and mix to coat. Cover and refrigerate for at least 2 hours or overnight.

Place marinated chicken cubes on a preheated oiled flat grill. Cook, turning meat over until seared, 2 to 3 minutes.

Warm the tortillas in a pan. In the tortilla, add the chicken satay, diced cucumber, red onions and tomatoes and top with Satay Peanut Sauce.

SATAY PEANUT SAUCE

Makes about 2 cups of peanut sauce

1 stalk lemongrass, or 1 teaspoon lemongrass powder
1 small shallot
2 cloves garlic
½ teaspoon ground cumin
½ teaspoon ground coriander
½ teaspoon turmeric powder
½ teaspoon galangal powder (find this in any Asian grocery)
½ cup water
1 cup roasted peanuts, or ¾ cup chunky peanut butter
3 tablespoons cooking oil
1 cup water
¼ cup packed brown sugar
½ tablespoon Sriracha
1 tablespoon soy sauce

Thinly slice bottom 6 inches of lemongrass. Place in blender with shallot, garlic, cumin, coriander, turmeric, galangal and ½ cup water. Process until smooth.

In a food processor, chop peanuts until they are very fine.

Place a saucepan over medium-low heat until hot. Add oil and swirl to coat sides. Add spice paste and cook, stirring until fragrant, 6 to 8 minutes.

Add 1 cup water, peanuts, brown sugar, Sriracha and soy sauce and stir until evenly blended. Bring to a boil. Then reduce heat and simmer, stirring frequently until slightly thickened, 4 to 5 minutes.

Serve with chicken satay

CHEW CHEW

Blake Burnett

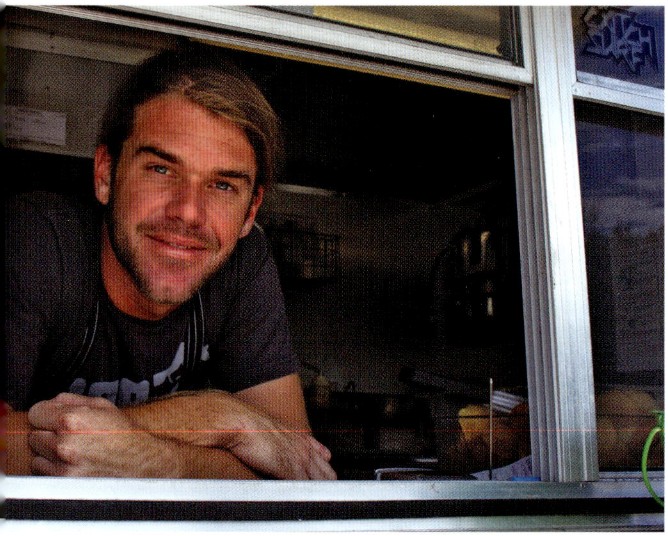

Blake Barnett, chef-owner of Chew Chew.

Skater, surfer, chef, food truck owner. Thirty-three-year-old Blake Burnett is possibly the most laid-back entrepreneur I've met. With his long blond hair, impossibly blue eyes and surfer's tan, Blake is the soft-spoken owner-chef and owner-operator of Chew Chew, a seriously fun truck, serving seriously good food.

Originally from Bradenton, Florida, Blake has worked in restaurants since he was sixteen, bussing tables, washing dishes and eventually getting some footing to work his way up the line. He went through the culinary program at Florida State College in Jacksonville (then Florida Community College of Jacksonville) and was part of the team that opened Eleven South Bistro and Bar in Jacksonville Beach.

He got some great experience working with talented chefs in high-end establishments until he felt confident he could go out on his own. He worked at Eleven South Bistro for about five years, including two college internships, before leaving with a friend, Nick Robson (now a chef-partner in 5Loaves 2Fish) to open the Speckled Hen on Philips Highway. A great menu but a bad location made that a short-lived proposition, and Blake moved on to Corner Bistro and Wine Bar in Tapestry Park.

In the spring of 2013, he was thinking of buying a truck, and his friend Richie from Super Food Truck offered him some practical experience and advice. He also introduced Blake to the folks at M&R Specialty Trailers, who have custom fabricated many of Jacksonville's favorite mobile kitchens. They helped him find a retired Wonder Bread truck. The whole fleet had just gone to auction, so Blake was able to buy Chew Chew for a reasonable price.

He hired friend and muralist Jessica Becker, known around Jacksonville for her beautiful mural of Día de los Muertos Virgen de Guadalupe at TacoLu in Jacksonville Beach, to

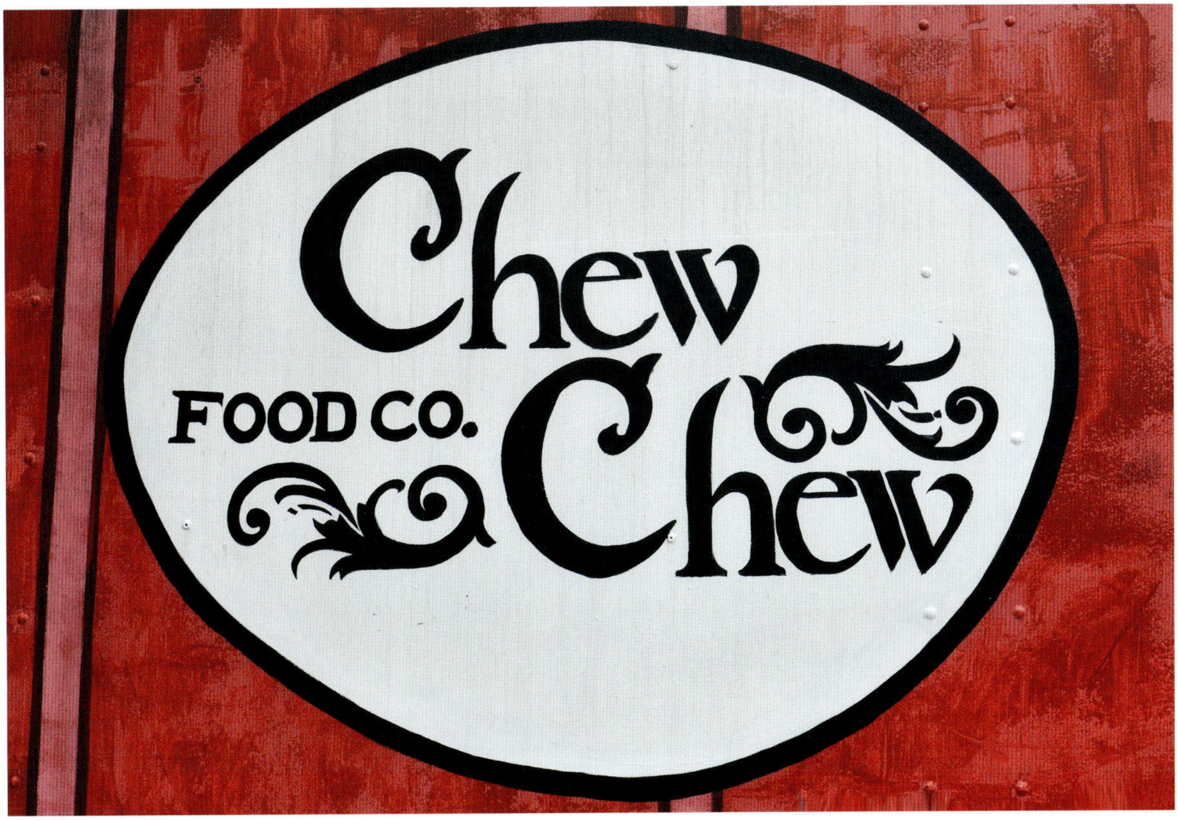

Chew Chew logo.

create the whimsical truck art. Her one-of-a-kind artwork has set Chew Chew apart from everything out there. Blake's original idea was to make the truck look like an old graffiti-covered boxcar. Friends helped him come up with the name Chew Chew. Jessica added the expansive Jacksonville skyline element, and her signature touches really set the truck apart from everything else out there.

From truck to build-out to custom artwork, getting Chew Chew on the road cost about $55,000. Blake worked with a restaurant consultant, Lawrence Yancey, to get his kitchen running right. When it came to planning a menu, he wanted to keep it small, something he could handle himself. He wanted it to be accessible, affordable and really, really good. He has managed all of this and more.

Last November at the Food Truck Block Party at the Landing, I sampled his Lobster Corndogs (yes, I did just say that) and a new seasonal menu item, Beer-Braised Oxtail Spring Rolls, served with a raspberry sweet chili sauce. The spring rolls were hot and satisfying, with just the right amount of crispiness outside

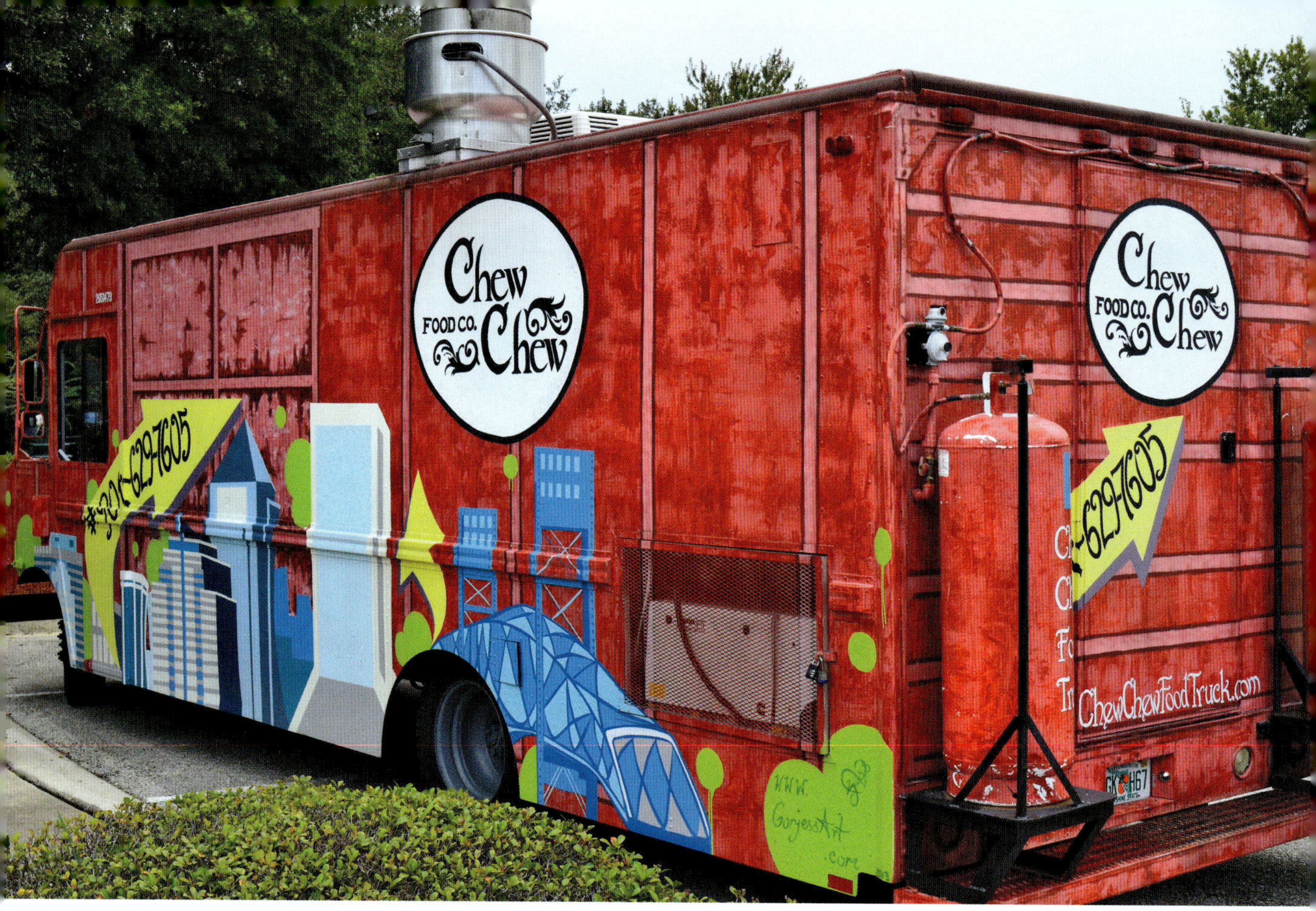
Chew
FOOD CO.
Chew
ChewChewFoodTruck.com

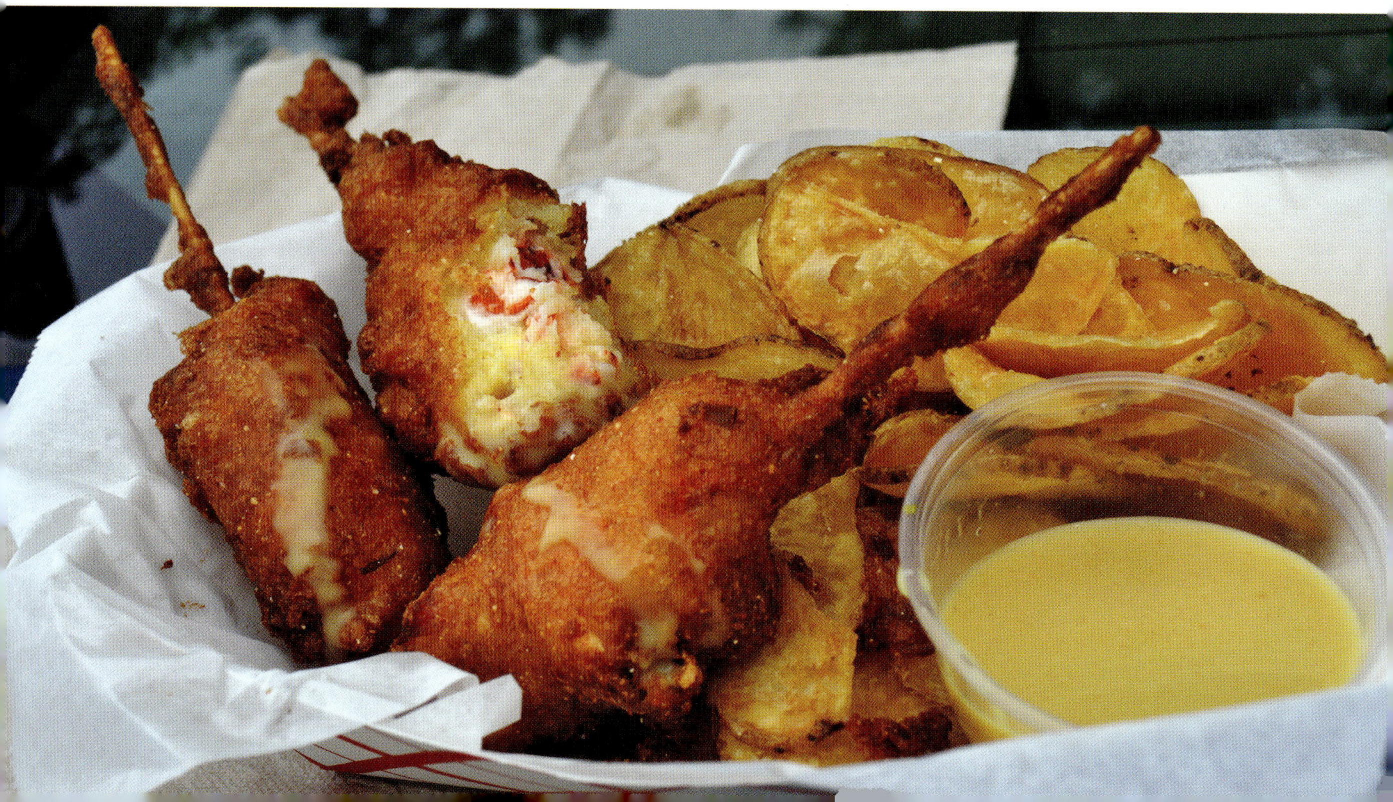

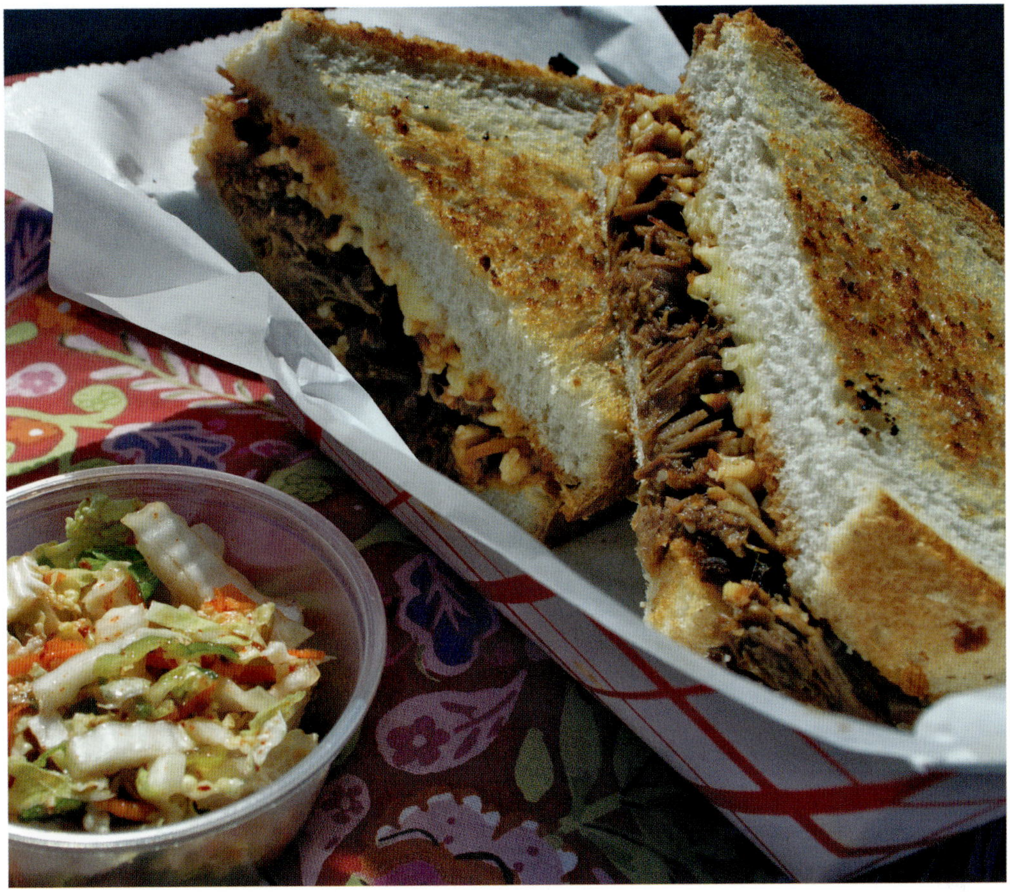

Korean BBQ Short Rib Melt with Kimchi Slaw from Chew Chew.

Opposite, top: Chew Chew food truck with custom mural by Jessica Becker.

Opposite, bottom: Lobster Corndogs from Chew Chew.

and a savory, melt-in-your-mouth filling. The spicy-sweet sauce was the perfect complement.

And then, hello, lobster corndogs, where have you been all my life? Blake told me he eats at least one a week, just for quality control. I would like to sign up for *that* job, thank you. Usually, I am not a corndog fan, but for these batter-dipped and fried hunks of perfectly cooked, luscious Maine lobster meat, I will make an exception. They come three to an order and are served with a lemon-honey Dijon mustard for dipping and/or drizzling. Trust me, it all just works.

The Korean BBQ Short Rib Melt is another top seller. Highlighting his Korean barbecue sauce, the meat is sweet and tangy from chili sauce and rice wine vinegar and spicy from Korean pepper paste. It is piled on sourdough with smoked Gouda and

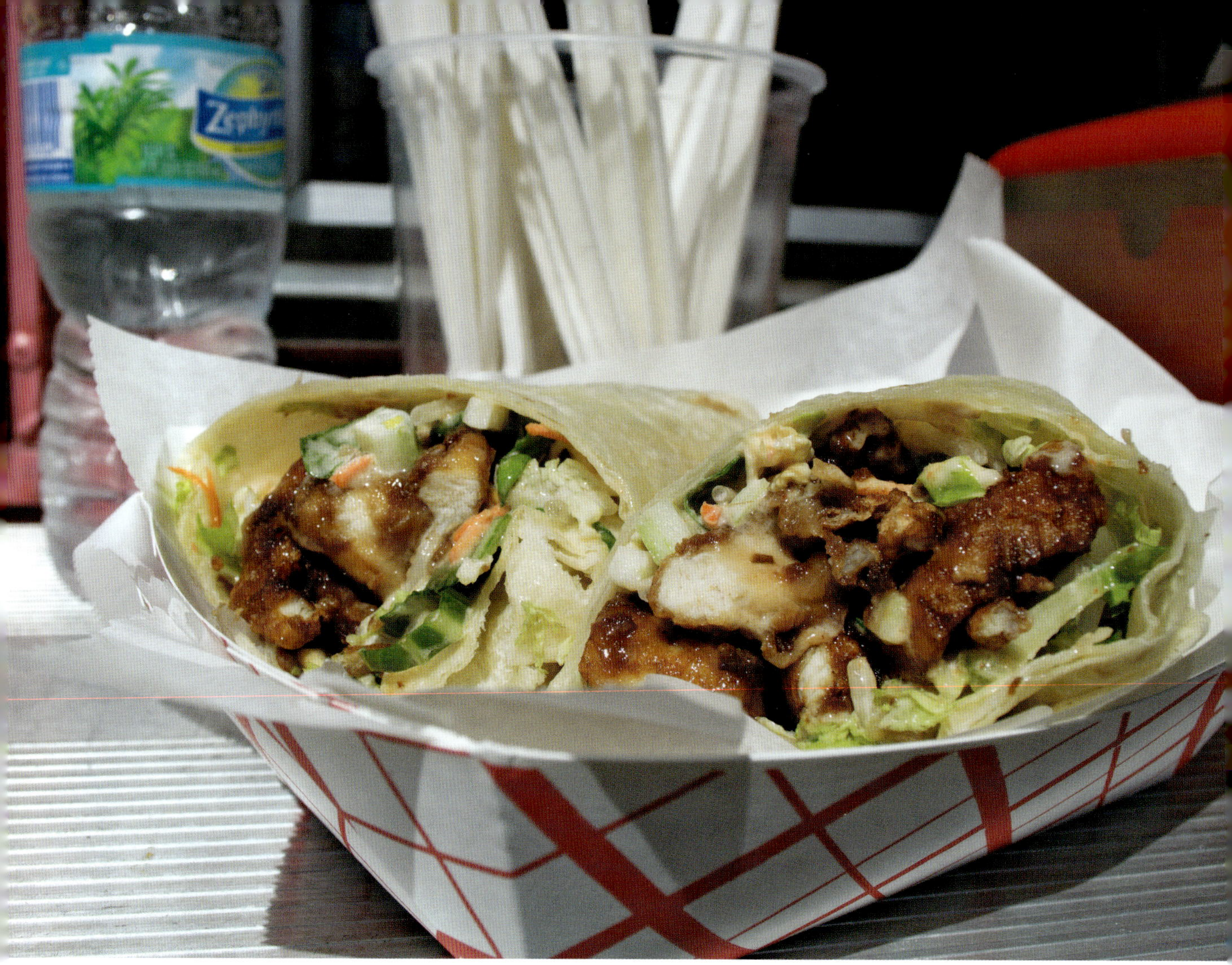

General Tso's Chicken Wrap from Chew Chew.

then grilled to a melty, smoky and toasty crunch. This monster of a sandwich is accompanied by a house-made kimchi slaw. Originally, he served the barbecue on a taco, but it was messy. He was considering scrapping it the day he tried it on a sandwich as a personal snack, and a classic was born. Blake has kindly shared his Korean barbecue sauce recipe here, and I have been slathering it on everything from scrambled eggs to grilled cheese to broiled chicken. Somebody had to taste test these recipes, right?

Some diners prefer the General Tso's Chicken Wrap; sometimes the Grilled Cheese wins the day. The Caprese Grilled Cheese is one of my favorites for summer. It is made with parmesan-crusted sourdough, and the mozzarella is marinated in a basil pesto and topped with super fresh sliced tomatoes. From the fragrant basil to the soft, gooey mozzarella and the toasty crunch of the bread, it's just crazy good.

Slider Burgers are another popular item. He keeps his menu selections fairly broad so that wherever he is serving, anyone can come up to the truck and find at least one thing on the menu about which they think, "Wow, that looks good. I think I'll get that."

It's fun to watch children interact with easygoing, soft-spoken Blake. He loves to see families come out to the truck and makes a point of taking the children's orders directly from them.

Chew Chew first chugged onto the streets of Jacksonville in September 2013, and since day one, Blake has been collecting tips to send his cat to ninja school. Sounds legit, right? Seriously, his is one of several fun and funky food truck tip jars around town, and everybody who has been to Chew Chew knows about Blake's ninja cat.

Blake's first few years in operation have been about finding a balance between working to make a living and working too much. Friends try to tell him he should get another truck going, but he likes the small scale of what he does now. He'll be the first to say he's not trying to get rich, he just wants to make good food, have something that he loves to do, feed people and not stress too much—and surf.

Blake's Ninja Cat tip jar at Chew Chew.

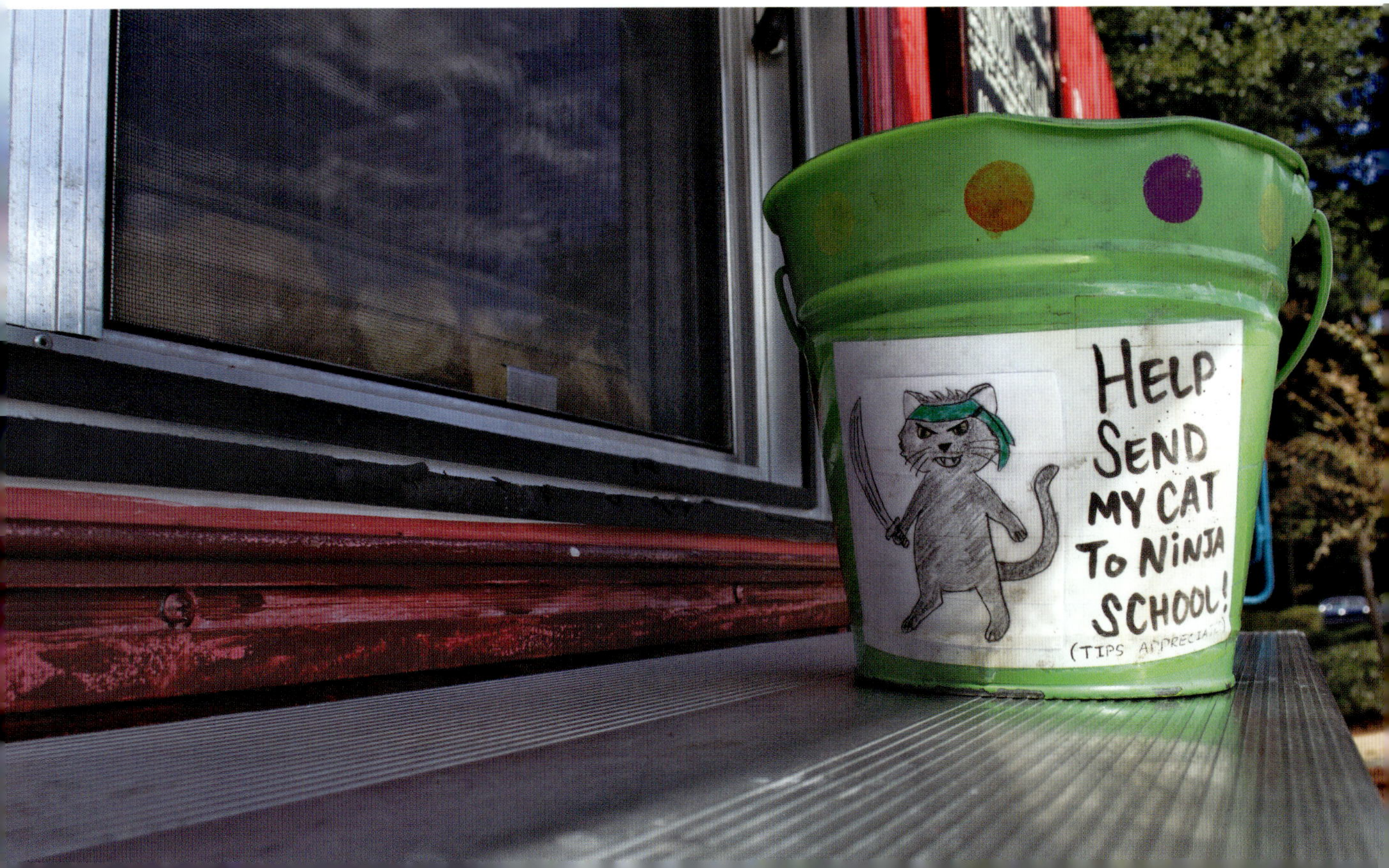

Blake doesn't put much stock in mobile food truck apps. Chew Chew has a set of established service spots every week that have earned him a loyal repeat customer base and plenty of new business. With that mobility comes a lot of extra work, however. On a typical day, Blake spends three hours on the road in addition to his service shift traveling to and from service spots and picking up produce, seafood and bread. If he could spend that extra three hours a day in one spot, it would be a lot easier, but right now, he likes serving customers all over town. Blake used to say he would never again work in a restaurant, but lately, as he has gotten more established with his lunches, he has started thinking about opening a lunch spot somewhere and keeping the truck for events. He's happy where he is for now, however, having fun with food.

Luckily for me, since I live at the beach, Chew Chew is often parked not far from Butler Boulevard, setting up frequently at 121 Financial at Gate and Touchton, Fanatics in Southpoint and Hodges at Sutton Park Drive. Chew Chew has also been a popular addition at festivals and events around the First Coast, at Food Truck Fridays at Nocatee Splash Park, at Jax Truckies Food Truck Block Party at the Jacksonville Landing and at Jaxsons Night Market in Hemming Park. You're likely to find Chew Chew just about anywhere people come together and share the food truck love. Find Chew Chew on Twitter @ChewChewFoodCo and like chewchewfoodtruck on Facebook. Then do yourself a favor and go try those Lobster Corndogs!

CHEW CHEW'S KOREAN BARBECUE SAUCE

Recipe from Blake Burnett

This sweet and tangy hot sauce is a key ingredient in our popular Korean Pork Melt. You can use it on any meat, as a marinade or a finishing sauce.

1 yellow onion, peeled and quartered
1 cup sweet chili sauce
2 cups rice wine vinegar
1 cup soy sauce
1 tablespoon sesame oil
1 tablespoon black sesame seeds
1 bunch cilantro, chopped
½ cup Korean chili paste

In a blender or food processor, purée onion, sweet chili and vinegar until smooth. Remove to a nonreactive bowl and whisk together the remaining ingredients.

CORNER TACO

Chris Dickerson

What is more American than to scrape together all that you have and fund your dream with little more than a mixture of passion, drive, courage and experience?

That's the question Chris Dickerson asked in response to an article in the November 25, 2011 issue of the *Beaches Leader* entitled "Jax Beach Boots Outdoor Food Vendor from Privately-Owned Shopping Center."

In his letter, Chris outlined his plan to create a one-of-a-kind food truck from a pristine used 1965 Airstream trailer he had combed the country to find. He outlined the costs of starting a food truck business compared to those of a restaurant startup and shared his thoughts on fair competition, customer loyalty and creating a unique brand, and he threw down the gauntlet to the restaurant owners who had complained that food trucks would create an unlevel playing field: "To restaurant owners who say food trucks are taking their customers: If your customers leave only because a food truck offers lower prices, then they were never your customers in the first place."

Chris grew up in Jacksonville and studied communications and prelaw rhetoric at Wake Forest. When his mother moved to Paris and entered the Grand Diplôme Program at Le Cordon Bleu, it started him thinking about what he wanted to do. Actually, he admits, he started thinking about

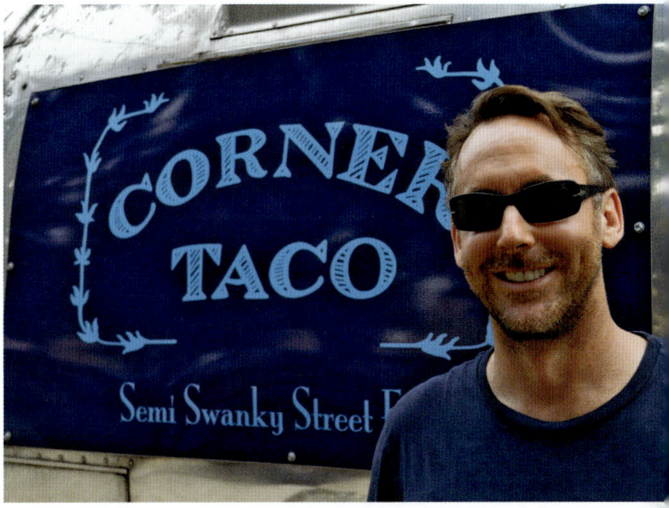

Chris Dickerson, chef-owner of Corner Taco.

what he *didn't* want to do first, and that eliminated about 90 percent of all jobs. Chris's mom, Katherine Ewing, received full degrees in both cuisine and pastry from Le Cordon Bleu and L'École de Gastronomie Francaise Ritz-Escoffier in Paris and trained at the Ritz Hotel there. When she returned to Florida, she put that classical training to work as chef-owner of Le Clos, a cozy, critically acclaimed café serving Provençal classics in Fernandina Beach.

Chris, too, knew he wanted to own his own restaurant. He was twenty-two, just out of college,

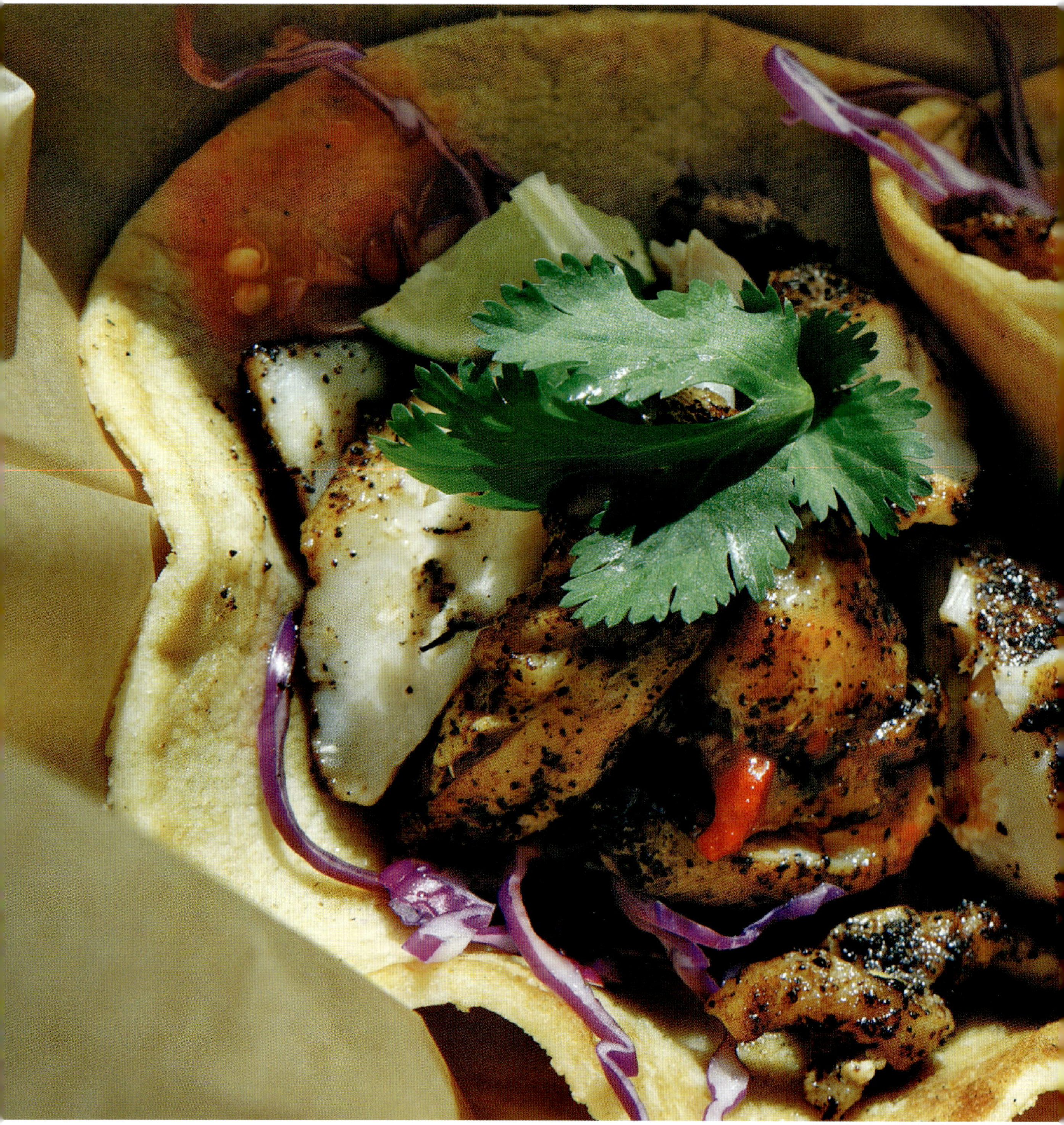

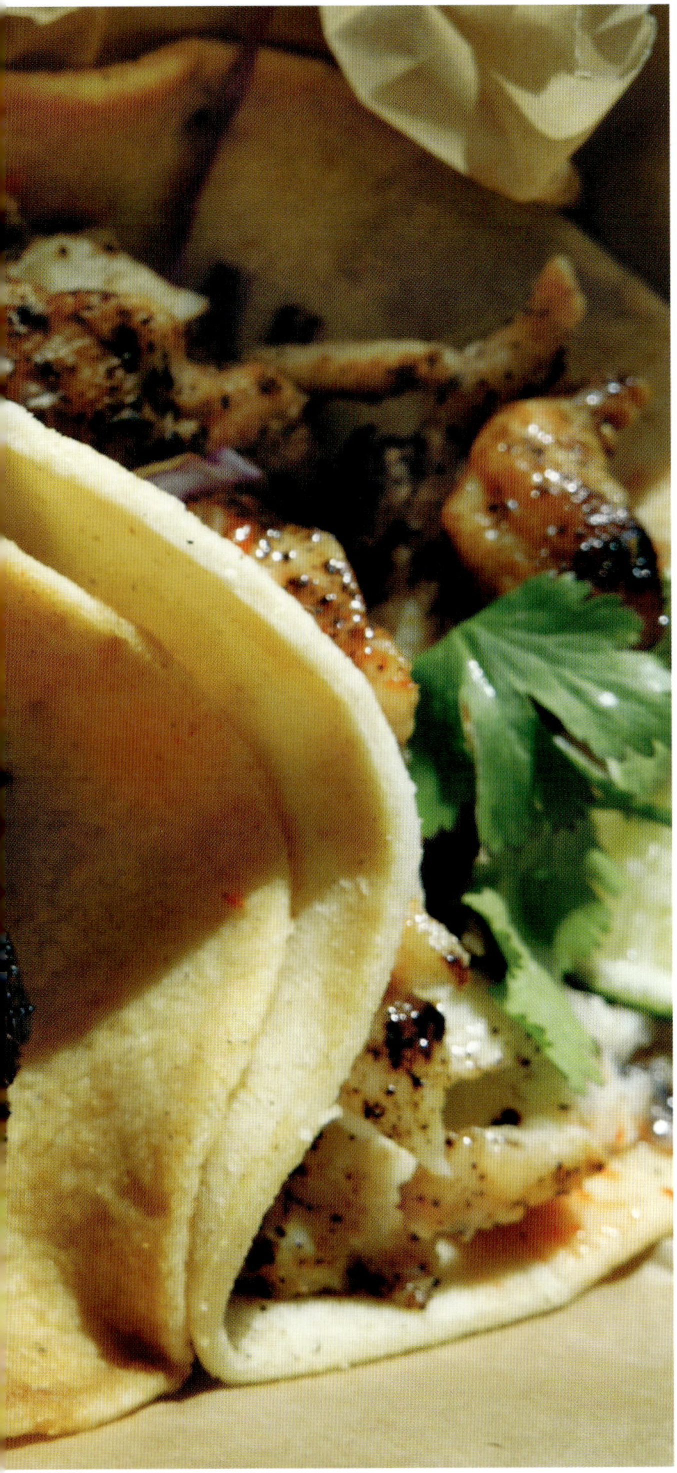

when he answered an ad in the *Florida Times-Union* for the prestigious Chef's Apprenticeship program at the Cloister at Sea Island, Georgia. It was tough going at first. Chris hadn't so much as chopped an onion when he walked in the door. He was thrown into the work, and it was sink or swim. He leaned in and got serious about learning and perfecting his craft, and by his second year, he was getting some prime assignments. Executive Chef Franz Buck saw promise in him and orchestrated introductions that opened doors. He enjoyed cooking alongside heavy-hitting culinary luminaries who came to town for events. He was invited to cook with the legendary Paul Bocuse, which was thrilling, and with James Beard award winner George Mahaffey, who invited him to come cook at the Little Nell in Aspen. He spent three seasons in the kitchen at the Little Nell and a season working the front of the house for Nobu Matsuhisa at Nobu.

Tiring of the pretense and fuss of fine dining and feeling the need to make more money, Chris moved to Washington, D.C., and spent ten years as a sales consultant for Sysco, North America's largest wholesale food distributor. He rose up the sales ranks and banked a ton of cash, much of which he invested in real estate and stocks and then promptly lost during the economic downturn.

Tacos from Corner Taco.

He moved to Buenos Aires for a while, but the more he was away from working with his hands and the more time he spent outside the United States, the further he was from finding his true self. Tired of travel and resolved to reset his career path, he returned to Jacksonville to pursue his American dream.

Chris worked in his mother's kitchen at Le Clos, bottling and selling fresh thyme vinaigrette dressing at the local farmers' market. He created a specialty foods company, Corner Natural Foods, to sell the dressing into retail outlets.

Then he made a deal with the owner of the Lemon Bar in Neptune Beach, where he built a kitchen and opened a "semi-swanky" taco stand. His food created a buzz at the beaches, and that irked some restaurant owners who were still smarting from the sour economy. The city responded by shutting him down. Remember that letter to the paper? That was Chris's way of announcing to the world that he and Corner Taco were hitting the road, and he was not going to let anyone get in his way.

He had already purchased the vintage 1965 Airstream Globetrotter, which he found online from a site called Vintage Campers. Friend and former partner Heather Douglas's uncle drove it to Florida from Indiana. They spent months refurbishing it. Chris designed the kitchen, his friend David Nissen fabricated it and, on January 14, 2012, Chris and Heather took it out to the streets of town.

The centerpiece of the Airstream's kitchen was a custom tortilla maker, a machine he purchased from Arizona. It allowed him to create dozens of fresh corn tortillas every day before his lunch shift. When they ran out of tortillas, they were done for the day.

Chris enjoyed getting out and meeting everyone during his days on the road, and Jacksonville's food truck enthusiasts flocked to the uber-cute Airstream setup, with its retro screen door and chalkboard menu featuring just a few, choice items. In addition to the tacos, the Dyno-Myte nachos made their debut on the truck: crispy corn tortilla chips dripping with white cheddar and Brie fondue, piquillo peppers and sliced grape tomatoes.

Chris's sweet spot was—and is—that he creates really good food but serves it in a casual, unpretentious atmosphere. He dubbed it "Semi-Swanky Street Food," and that label has stuck from the taco stand to the food truck and his brick-and-mortar business today.

Three short years later, if Corner Taco's Airstream isn't on the road, it is usually parked on the street near Corner Taco the restaurant, at 818 Post Street in Jacksonville's Five Points neighborhood. Chris can often be found taking orders from behind the counter, checking on the crew's

Opposite, top: Corner Taco's vintage Airstream.

Opposite, bottom: The Dyno-Myte from Corner Taco.

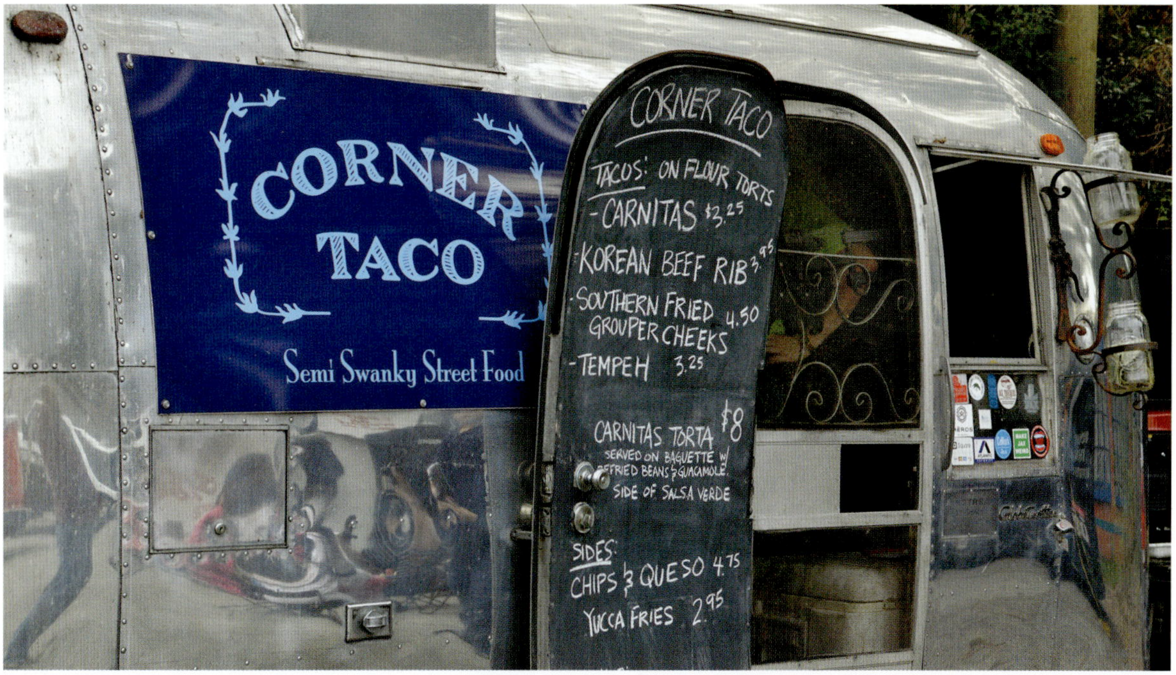
CORNER TACO
Semi Swanky Street Food
CORNER TACO
TACOS: ON FLOUR TORTS
-CARNITAS $3.25
-KOREAN BEEF RIB 3.95
-SOUTHERN FRIED GROUPER CHEEKS 4.50
-TEMPEH 3.25
CARNITAS TORTA $8
SERVED ON BAGUETTE W/ REFRIED BEANS & GUACAMOLE.
SIDE OF SALSA VERDE
SIDES:
CHIPS & QUESO 4.75
YUCCA FRIES 2.95

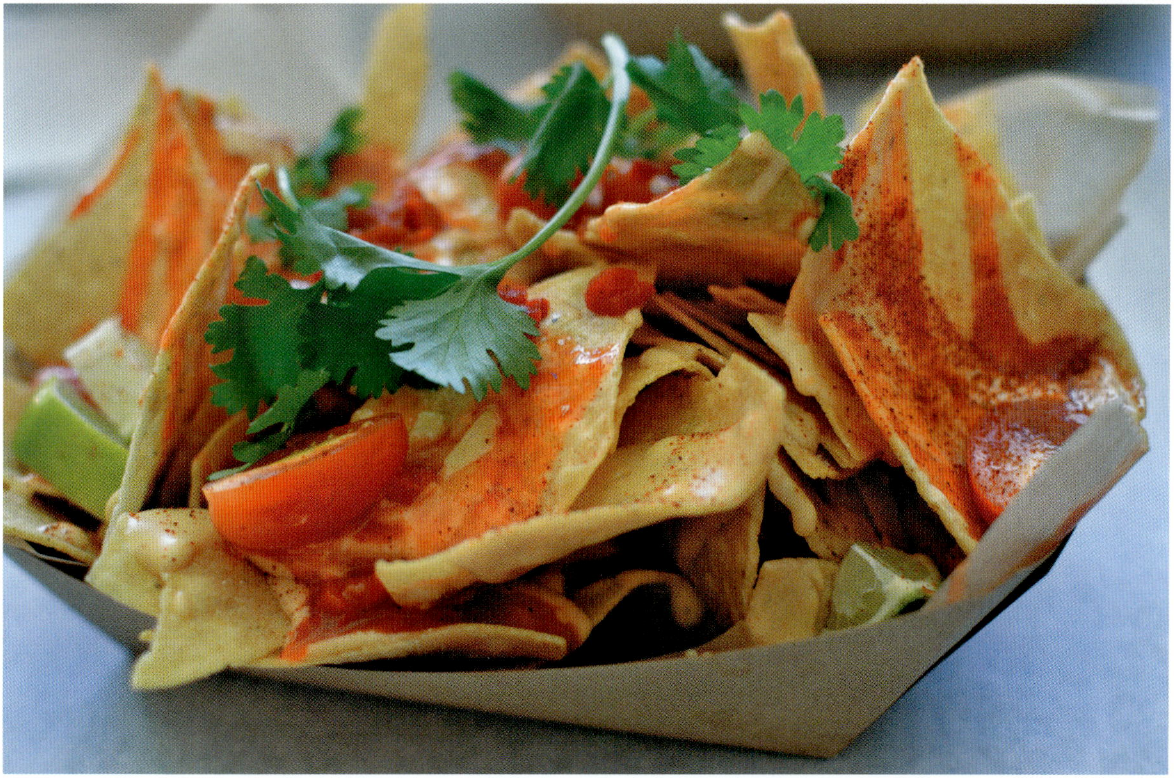

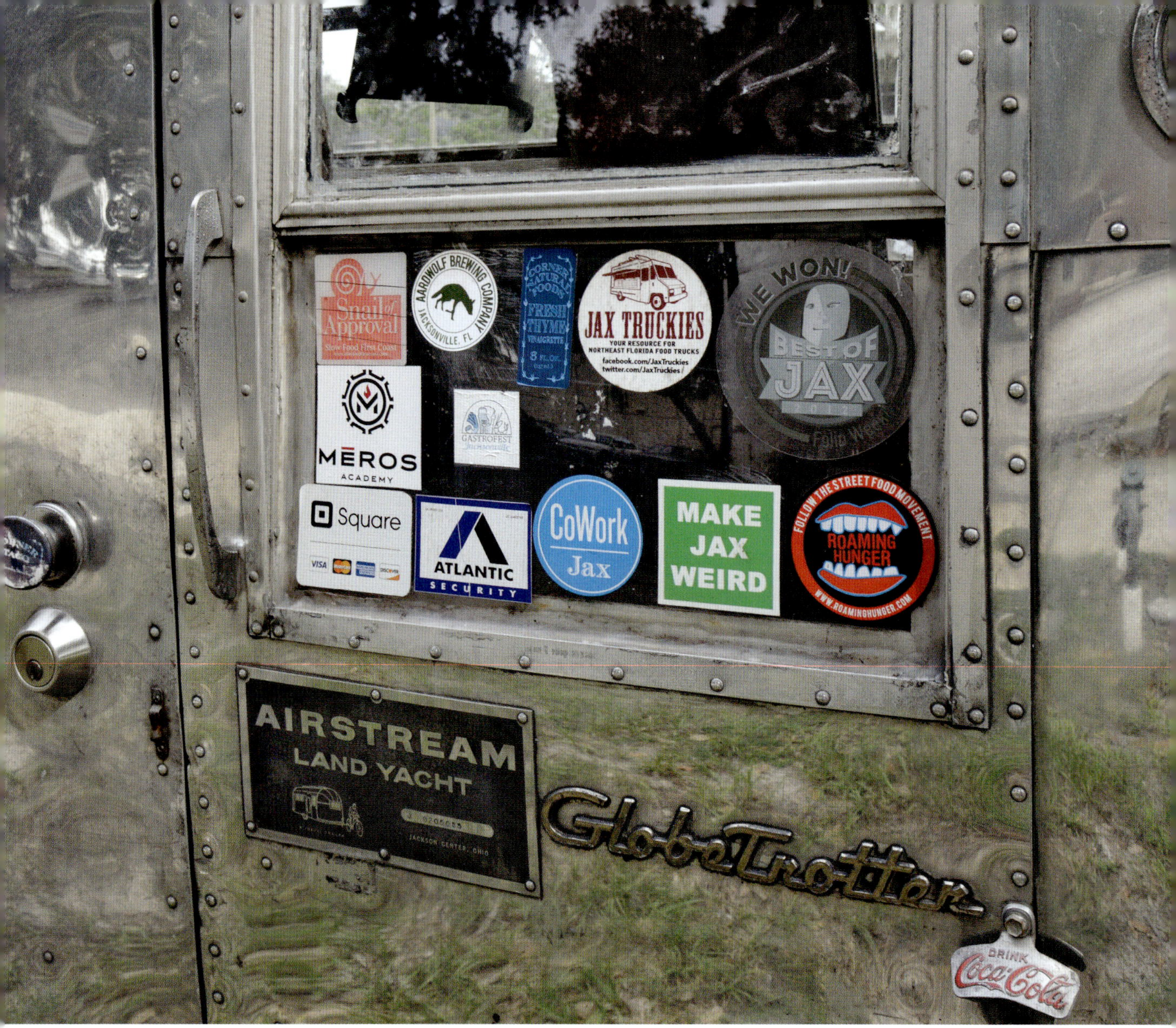

Corner Taco.

progress in the kitchen or buzzing around the dining room greeting customers. A line forms at the counter during peak lunch and dinner times, but it moves quickly.

In the restaurant, as with the food truck, Chris's food philosophy centers on building clean, fresh flavors "using ingredients you can pronounce." Most menu items are made fresh to order, and many are gluten free. Corner Taco's sustainable business practices and local sourcing earned Chris the Slow Food First Coast's Snail of Approval.

Fresh corn tortillas are formed in his custom-made tortilla maker and then dropped on the grill for a quick toasting. When they first opened the restaurant, they were averaging 500 to 750 tortillas per day. During the food truck days, he made 70 to 100 for a regular lunch shift.

The restaurant's mainstays include many of the food truck favorites, including tacos filled with carnitas, Dijon–buttermilk fried chicken or chicken marinated in his signature fresh thyme vinaigrette. All tacos are served on a freshly made corn tortilla, with fresh red cabbage, cilantro and lime. Side dishes like black beans and yucca fries have made it onto the permanent menu.

The first time I visited Corner Taco the restaurant, I opted for a few things I had enjoyed from the truck. The brisket taco features moist and savory beef. Chris told me it gets a flavor boost from steeping in a porcini mushroom broth and a mild, sweet heat from a dark red chili powder sourced from Chimayo, New Mexico. It imparts a rich, slightly smoky chili flavor. The Dijon–Buttermilk Fried Chicken Taco features juicy chunks of chicken in a light coating made super crispy with rice flour.

The Daily Fish Taco, last time I ordered it, was tender mahi-mahi, perfectly seasoned. A Grouper

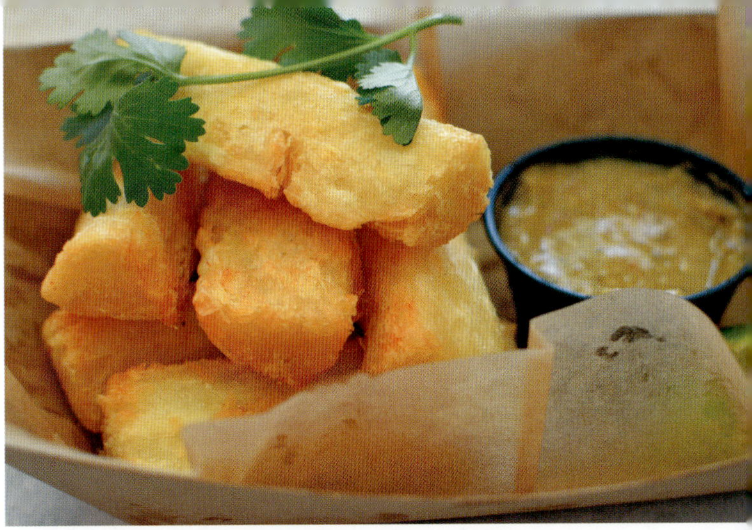

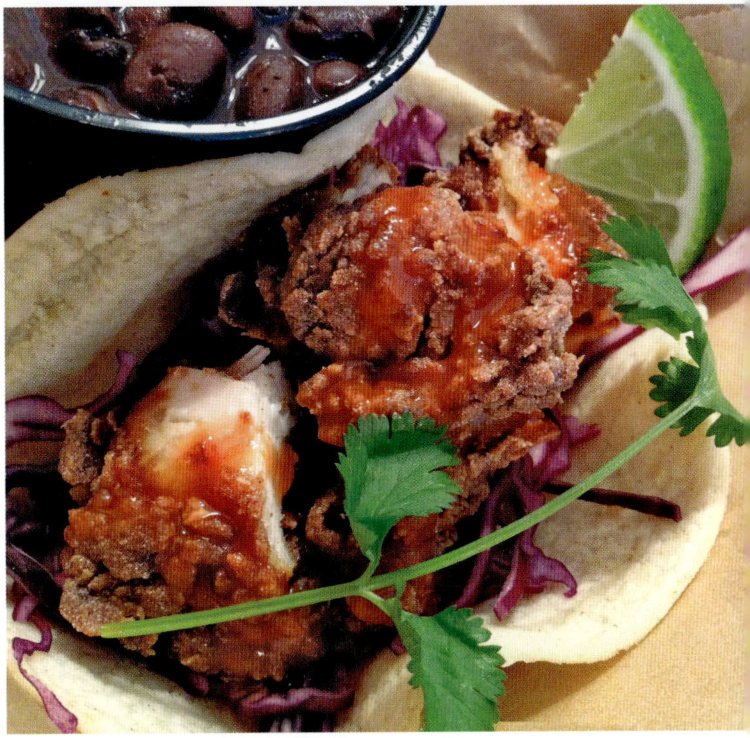

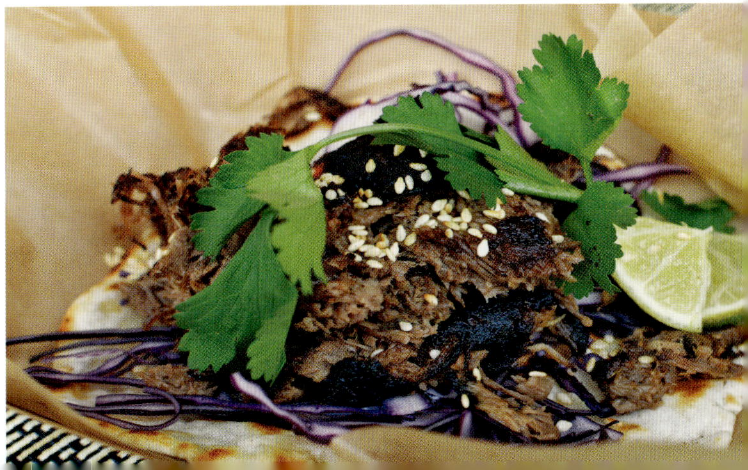

Top: Yucca Fries from Corner Taco.

Middle: Corner Taco's Dijon Buttermilk Fried Chicken Taco.

Bottom: Korean Short Rib Taco from Corner Taco.

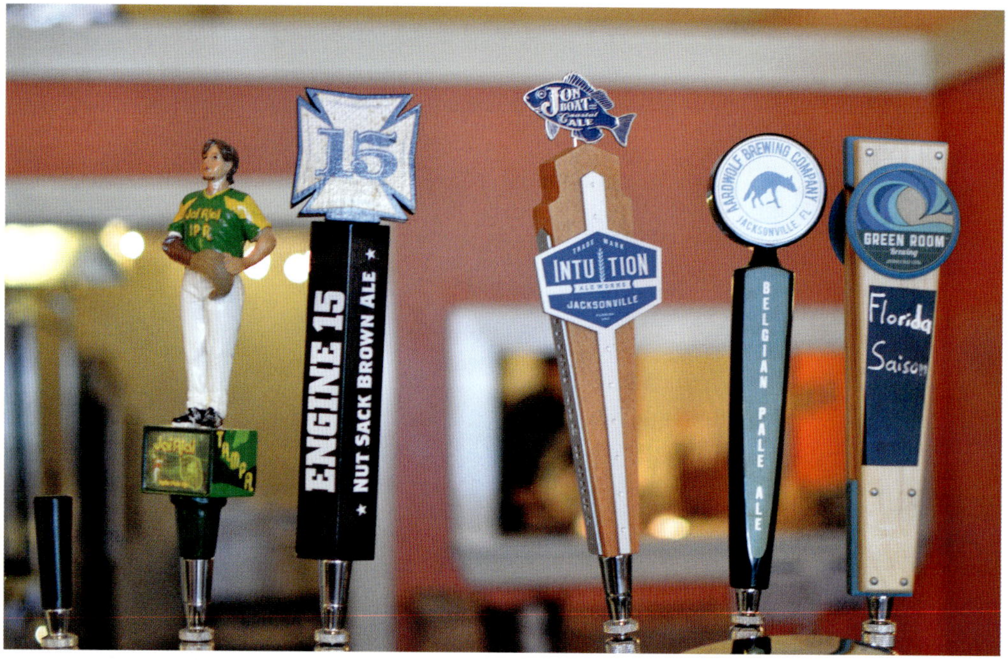

Local brews on tap at Corner Taco.

Cheek Taco has become a steady crowd favorite as well, and it gets a generous dollop of brightly colored house-made salsa verde.

Chris still loves to create new tacos and sauces, and he encourages his crew to do the same. Korean Short Rib Tacos have proven a crowd favorite. Inspired by Momofuku's pork bun, Chris created a pork belly taco, with hoisin pork belly, scallion and pickled cucumber. A Brisket and Brie Torta with Porcini-Flavored Jus was inspired by the great bread he received from a local bakery.

One of several vegan or vegetarian items on the menu, the Seared Asparagus Taco is filled to the brim with tender-crisp asparagus spears. A light dusting of Maldon sea salt flakes adds a fresh, briny note. General Tso's Tempeh and a "Whim Wednesday" special of roasted beets, arugula, chèvre, pistachio and Florida orange have been featured as well.

One of Chris's favorite dishes is the Fried Mayport Shrimp Taco with white corn purée and asparagus. It's fried lightly with rice flour so the flavors of the shrimp and corn purée shine through. After one taste, I knew that was the recipe I wanted Chris to share with you. It's so simple, but it coaxes great fresh flavors out of all the fresh ingredients. This dish says Jacksonville to me.

In the beverage department, I usually go for a blood orange San Pellegrino. Seasonal aguas frescas are also available, and some semi-swanky milkshakes, along with Mexican Coke, beer and wine. A selection of local

CORNER TACO'S FRIED MAYPORT SHRIMP WITH WHITE CORN PURÉE

Recipe by Chris Dickerson

Makes enough for 2 servings, plus some leftover white corn purée

FRIED SHRIMP

1 pound Mayport shrimp, peeled and deveined, tail on
1 tablespoon vinaigrette (such as Fresh Thyme from Corner Natural Foods)
1 teaspoon kosher salt
2 cups buttermilk
32 ounces (or enough to reach about 3 inches up the side of your Dutch oven) corn, grape seed or peanut oil
¼ cup rice flour

Combine shrimp with vinaigrette and kosher salt. Marinate for at least 1 hour and up to 24 hours. Soak in buttermilk for at least 1 hour and up to 24 hours.

Heat corn, grape seed or peanut oil in a Dutch oven or large pot with high walls (so it will retain even temperature and not splatter) to about 365 degrees Fahrenheit. The oil will look thin and loose. Test with a small piece of shrimp.

Place rice flour in a large bowl and dredge shrimp lightly just before frying. The shrimp will be golden brown and will float when cooked. Remove from oil immediately and place onto a plate lined with paper towels.

WHITE CORN PURÉE

(keeps for at least 3 days)
Makes about 1 cup

12 ears white corn
4 ounces heavy cream
½ cup water or chicken or vegetable stock
kosher salt, to taste
1 whole shallot (or small white onion), minced
2 teaspoons chopped fresh thyme
2 teaspoons cayenne pepper

Grate corn on the big eye of a box grater, making sure to extract the corn "milk" by grating close to the stalk.

Add the rest of the ingredients, except the cayenne. Bring to simmer and continue cooking for 5 minutes. Add cayenne and cook 1 minute.

Serve fried shrimp with white corn purée for dipping.

and regional craft pints on tap for just a few bucks per pour is evidence of the close relationship between the brewers and their independent food business counterparts.

Chris is looked up to by every newbie who opens a food truck business. He's their proof that the road they are on can lead to fulfillment of *their* American dream. He humbly represents all truckies as he focuses on building his business, mentoring his crew and turning out excellent, local, fresh food right here in Jacksonville, Florida. Find him at Corner Taco in Five Points and online at www.cornertaco.com. Follow @CornerTaco on Twitter for daily specials.

DANILO'S FAMOUS LUMPIA

Darryl Sayas and Gwendolyn McClelland

Darryl Sayas and Gwendolyn McClelland are partners in life and in business. They met working in the corporate world, never thinking they would one day leave their jobs and run a mobile food cart.

Named for Darryl's dad, Danilo Sayas, Danilo's Famous Lumpia was launched in September 2014 at the Beaver Street Farmers' Market. Sayas and McClelland could only sell frozen product there, but the couple was encouraged by customers' responses on a few occasions when they able to prepare them fresh, fried to order.

They took a gamble and invested in a small trailer they found on Craigslist, and with a few modifications, they were on the road. They made an appearance at Jaxsons Night Market, and in December, they joined the lineup at the newly opened Jax Food Truck Food Court.

The star of the show at Danilo's is the authentic lumpia, made from scratch from Danilo's original Filipino recipe and accompanied by sweet-

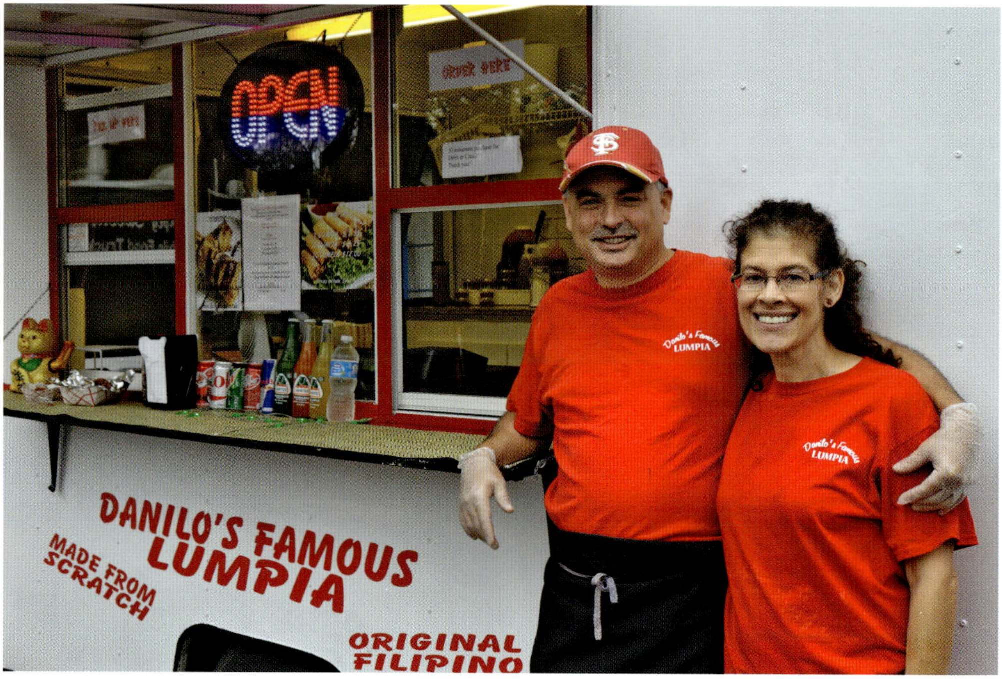

Darryl Sayas and Gwendolyn McClelland are owner/operators of Danilo's Famous Lumpia.

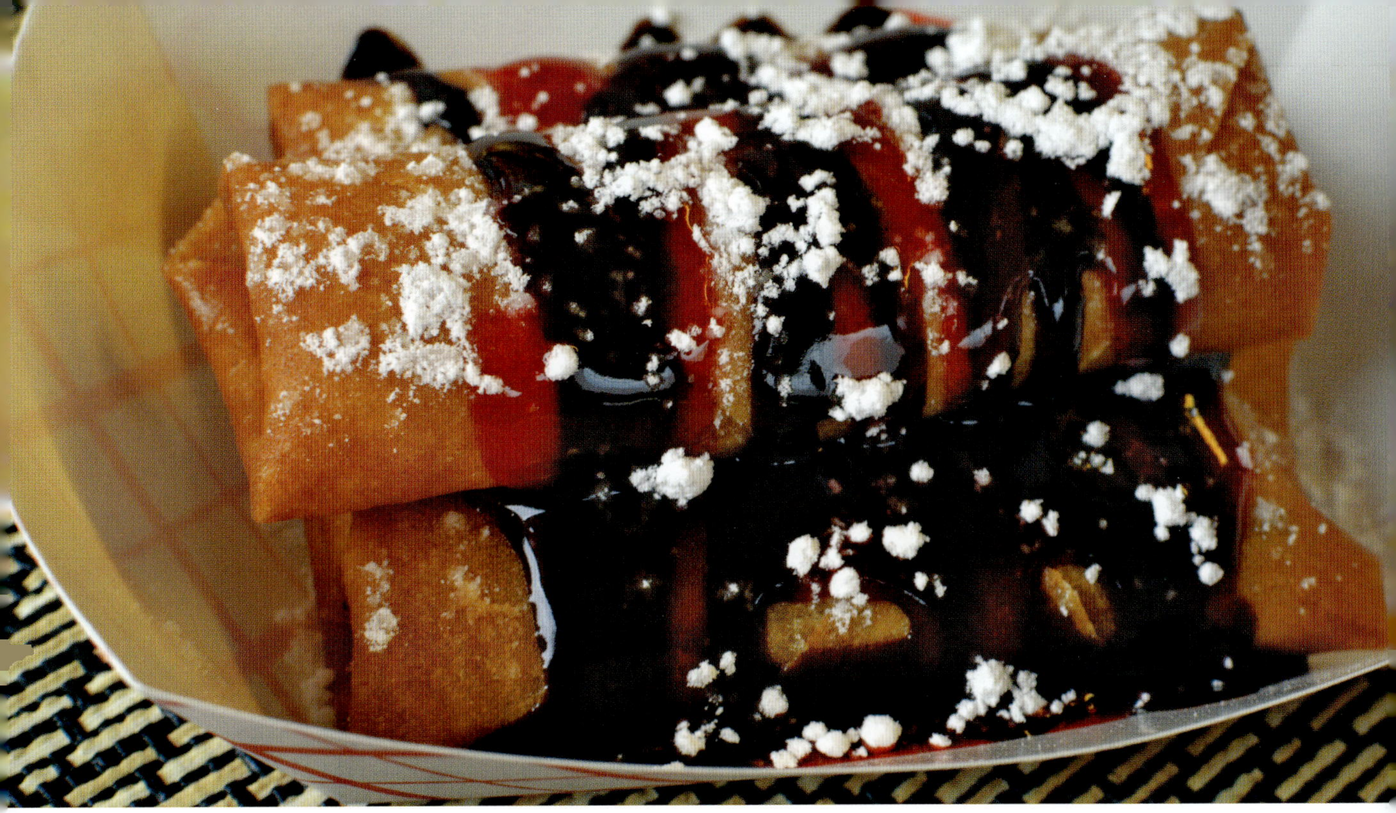

Danilo's Famous Lumpia offers an outstanding banana turrón for dessert.

and-sour or sweet chili sauce. They recently added a Pancit and Lumpia combo plate to their weekly menu, to rave reviews.

I love their lumpia hot and crisp from the fryer, but it is their dessert that draws me in every time. Banana turrón are my latest obsession. Hot, sweet, crunchy, soft and creamy all at once, they are pulled from the deep fryer, dusted with powdered sugar and drizzled with your choice of sauces.

I'm gonna tell you right now, as good as the chocolate, caramel and strawberry sauces are, the real deal is maple syrup. Just try it. Give it time to cool off a bit, or you're going to burn your mouth. It would be totally worth it, though. Find Danilo's Famous Lumpia at facebook.com/danilosfamouslumpia.

DRIFTWOOD BBQ

Patrick and Amy O'Grady

Amy O'Grady keeps a scrapbook of Driftwood BBQ's accomplishments in her office, and we had a great time going down memory lane when I asked her to tell me their story for this book.

She and husband Patrick juggle two full-time jobs, a growing barbecue business, one huge volunteer gig and two young kids and manage to make time for each other in the process. As I listened to the enthusiastic couple tell their story, it made perfect sense to me that they would end up running one of the most successful barbecue businesses in town.

Amy and Patrick didn't imagine themselves in the food business. She is the marketing manager for Charlie's Tropic Heating and Air in Mayport and president of a women's business networking group. He worked for an Audi dealership and is now also at Charlie's Tropic.

A home barbecue enthusiast, Patrick grew up watching the Food Network and learned to cook from his dad,

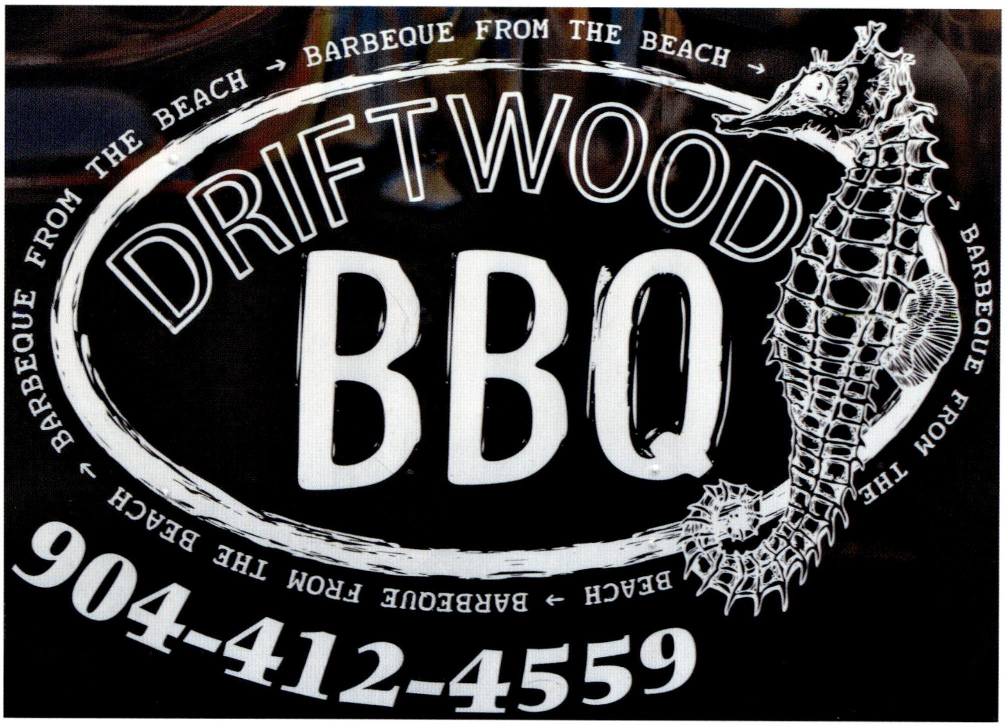

Driftwood BBQ logo.

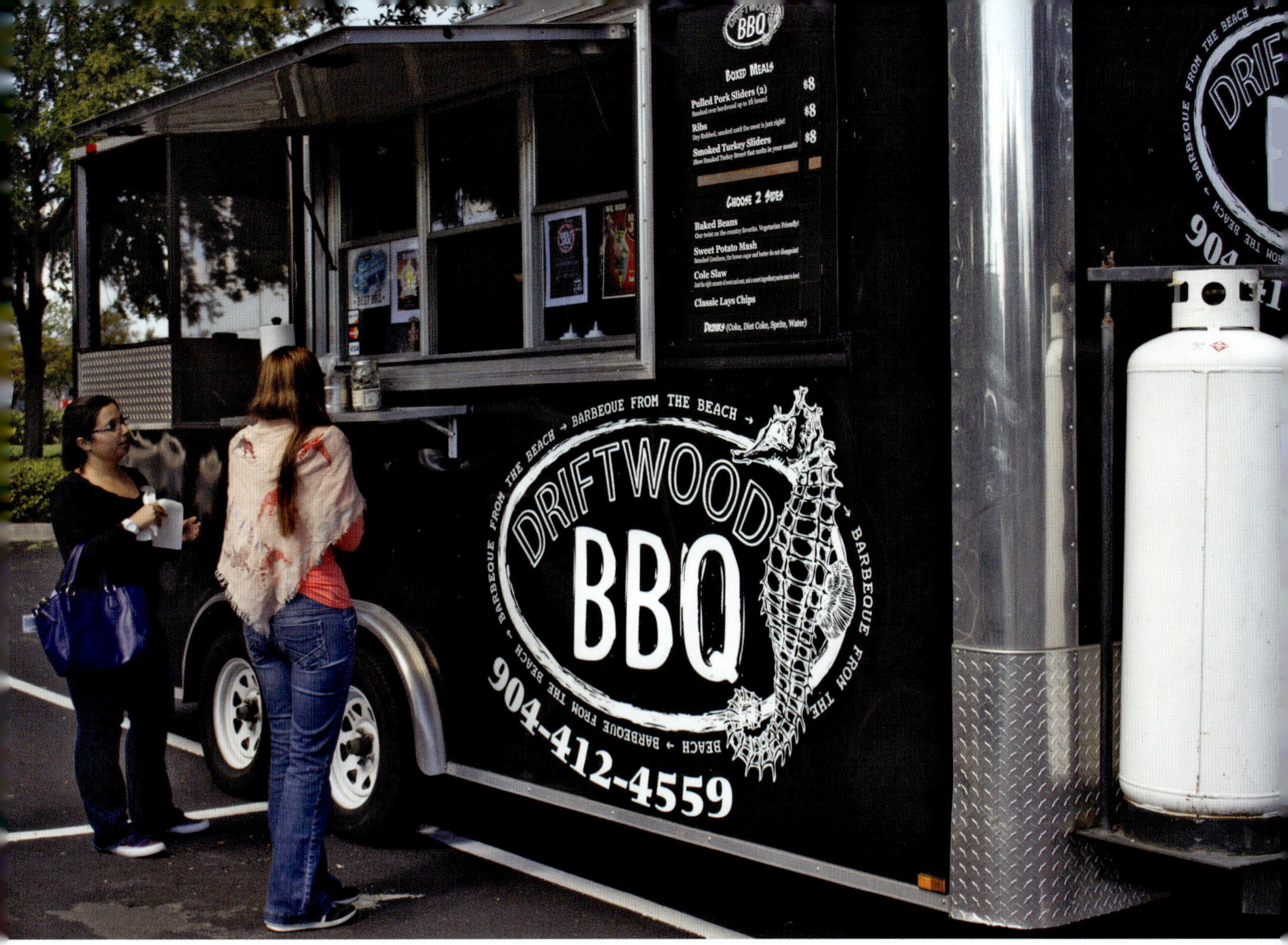

Driftwood BBQ.

who had been a chef at Kahuna's and Sliders at the beach. Amy's father's day gift of the Big Green Egg gave him the inspiration he needed to take his hobby to the next level of awesomeness.

They kept seeing this guy set up (illegally, they would later discover) on the side of the road, smoking meats. Patrick knew he could do the same thing just as well if not better. His dad was smoking whole hogs one Fourth of July, and that gave Patrick the idea to bring the ribs he was smoking over the weekend to the dealership. His co-workers served as his first taste testers, and their unanimous thumbs up stoked the fire. He got Amy on board, and together they jumped in the barbecue business.

During high school, Amy worked for Dave Wampler as a bus girl/expeditor at Jacksonville Beach's the Rite Spot. Her senior year economics project at Fletcher High was to research and report on the costs associated in starting a business, and she decided on a restaurant as her model. She credits that early experience and Dave's mentorship with giving her the confidence to say yes to starting Driftwood BBQ.

So here they were, planning to buy a food trailer and custom barbecue smoker, with absolutely no knowledge of the laws governing food businesses. They called Lynne Porter-Guitan at Blue Sky Consulting to help them review contracts, negotiate prices and determine the layout of their trailer. Her counsel saved the couple time and money, helped them find a commissary and gave them the foundation they needed to get off to a solid start.

M&R Specialty Trailers did the schematic and built the custom trailer. They didn't want fryers or griddles, but they did want air conditioning. No frying means less clean up, no grease disposal issues and more free time to spend with their family. Still, Amy admits if she had a second truck, it would probably be a French fry truck. Atlantic Imaging did their logo and supporting graphics in vinyl, and Spectrum Signs has fabricated a new metallic menu board for them. Amy searched online for black takeout boxes because white ones would be discolored by the smoke.

With one of the very first trucks on the scene, they started planning the business in April 2011, and September 7, 2011, was their first outing. Patrick loaded up the truck, drove around for an hour and a half and then happened on a spot at the side of the road, on Hodges at Sutton Park Drive South, in front of the Registry apartments. That was his first lunch service. They still set up there from time to time, and other trucks have discovered the spot as well.

Early on, they set up at Intuition Ale Works on King Street on weekday nights and the Riverside Arts Market on Saturdays. When their second child came along, Amy decided that RAM was too much work.

Being one of the first on the road, Driftwood had their share of scrapes with city officials. In their initial six months, they got about eight health inspections. Amy and the Jax Truckies crew attended the city council meeting when food truck permitting was voted in at Neptune Beach. Now trucks may operate there only for events and only with a special permit.

At first, they were focusing on pulled pork sliders and really piling on the meat. Patrick thought, "Get 'em talking," but when Amy took samples to a businesswomen's luncheon, she noticed the women were removing half the meat. Her business acumen kicked in, and they revisited all their menu items for food cost and sensible portions.

They started making potato salad from scratch and other items that required extensive prep, and then they decided to switch to sweet potatoes, which, in addition to being super easy to make, have the added benefit of being healthier. One thing that hasn't changed much since day one is Patrick's coleslaw recipe. It gets a little extra crispness from the addition of jicama and just the right amount of sweet and tart from—well, see

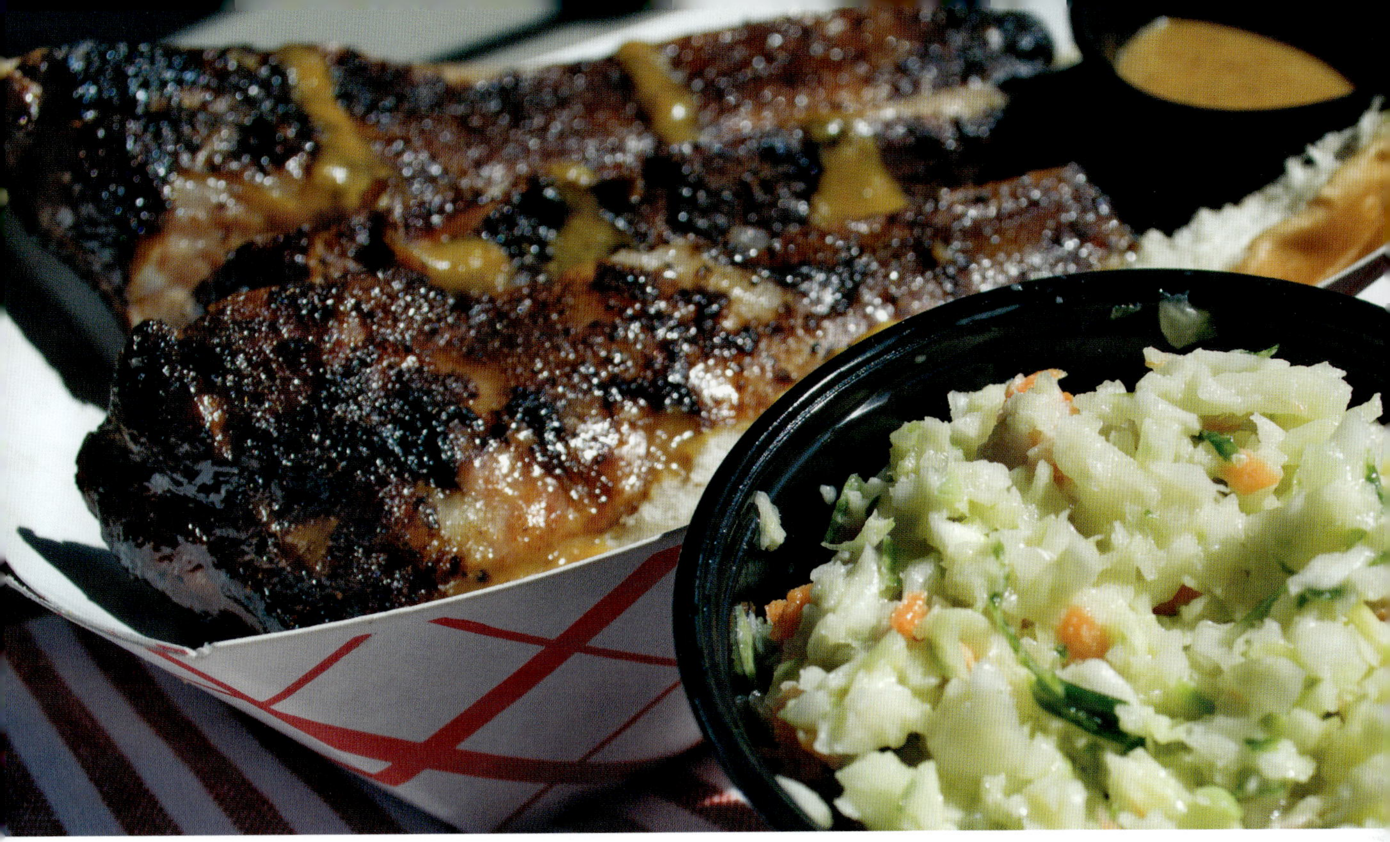

Driftwood BBQ's Ribs and Coleslaw.

for yourself. After much coaxing, he shared his top-secret recipe with us on page 63.

Patrick's barbecue is a mix of North Carolina and Texas styles: dry rub, low and slow, with mustard sauce. "Tell her about the sauce debacle," Amy urges Patrick, and he obliges. You can tell they get a kick out of telling this story. Initially, Patrick offered only one sauce. He was trying to convert everybody, one person at a time, to his favorite (mustard-based) sauce. A debate ensued, and friends of the couple explained the relative virtue of pleasing more customers by offering the locally preferred tomato-based sauce and a hotter version for those who expect a little heat. Reluctantly, Patrick took their advice and created three sauces. Which is the top seller? Patrick admits it's the red sauce. The meat is served without sauce, though, so the diner can taste the rich, smoky meat first and then decide which and how much sauce he or she wants.

Big surprise—the man on the side of the road selling ribs made it look a hell of a lot easier than it is. Something I've heard from virtually every truck operator I've met is how physically exhausting this work can be. For barbecue businesses, there's another element to consider. You've got to fuel the fire, literally.

After years of hunting for and chopping their own wood, they discovered they could purchase a seemingly endless supply from Swamp Man firewood sales off of Girvin Road. "Swamp Man" Sydney Smith

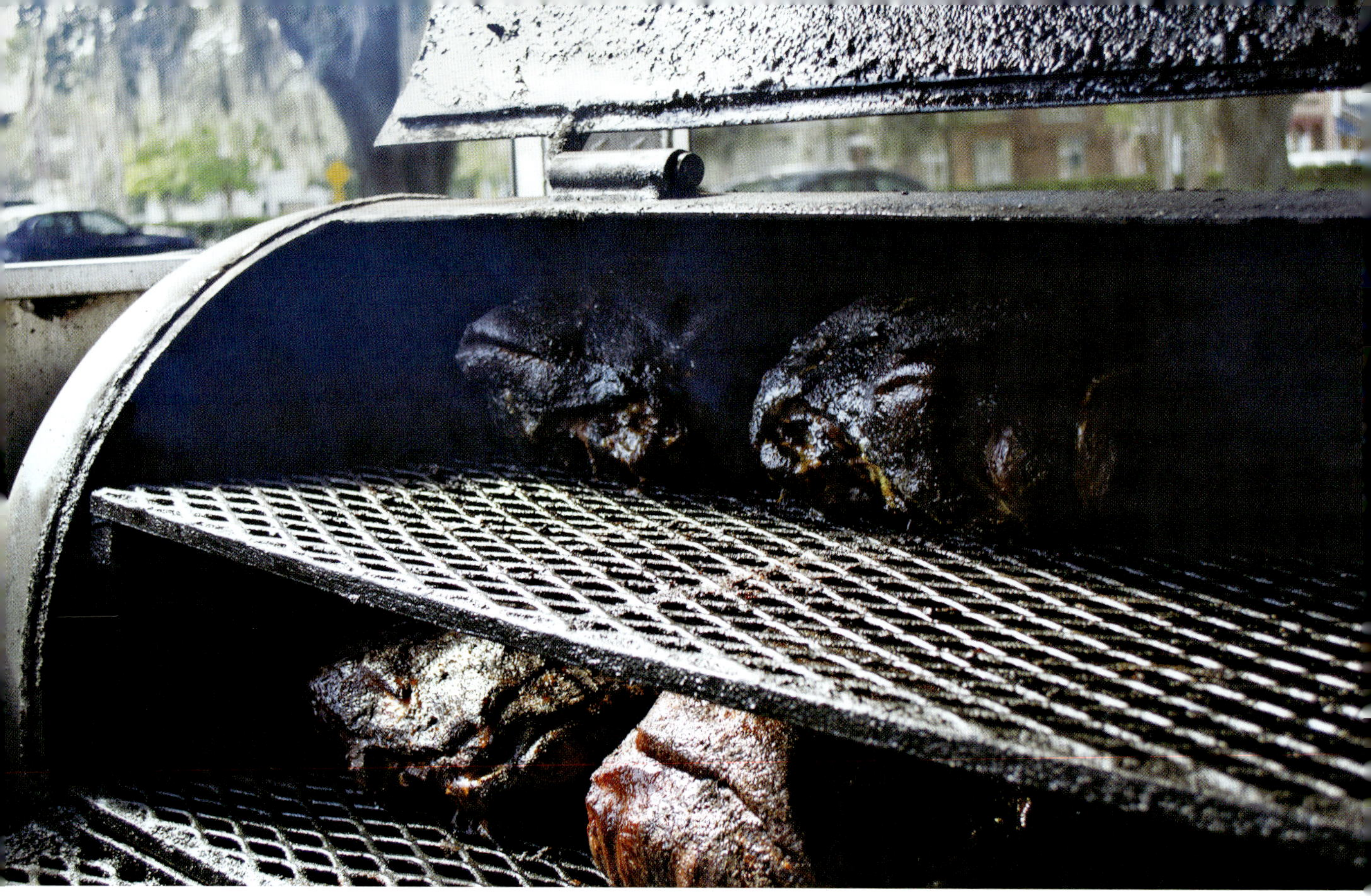

Smokin' it old school at Driftwood BBQ.

and his wife, Effie May, supply many of the barbecue companies in the area. Talk about buying local! The trees come from developers and tree surgeons who would rather drop them off with the Smiths than pay to dump them. In his late seventies, Smith says cutting and stacking wood the old-school way keeps him in shape.

Patrick gets his workout slinging pork butts and racks of ribs onto the smoker. The routine used to be that the meat went on the fire at 11:00 p.m. each night, with hourly additions of wood, so it would be ready for lunch the next day. They eventually got the hang of scheduling the cooking so it didn't consume their sleeping hours. Up at 5:30 a.m., Patrick will throw the meat on at 6:00. While they are serving, the meat is cooking, low and slow, in the smoker on the back of the truck. Patrick pulls it off at 8:00 or 9:00 p.m. If it is an event weekend, he may get home at 11:30 or midnight. "Days off" are spent shopping for ingredients, prepping for the next week's menu and cleaning everything.

For a year and a half, Patrick worked the truck solo for lunches, taking the hottest part of the summer off. Then they were able to hire their first employee, a son of a friend who was a culinary school student. Another young man, Hunter Stocks, was hired as lead chef. They taught him how to drive the rig in the huge parking lot at Academy Sports.

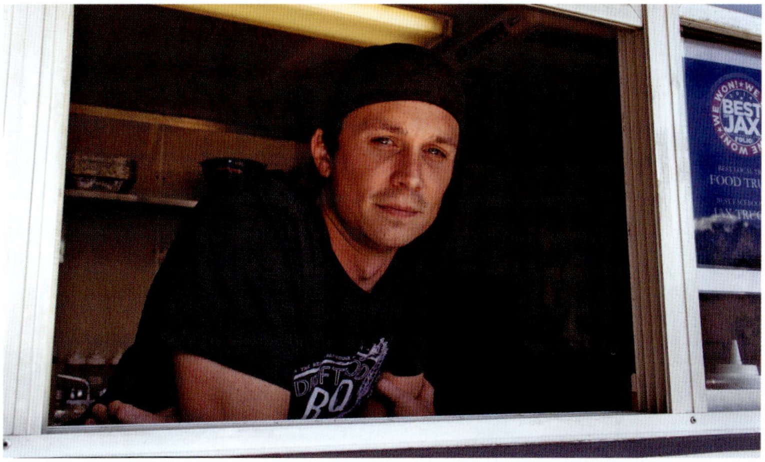

Patrick O'Grady, co-owner and pitmaster of Driftwood BBQ.

Patrick also works at Charlie's Tropic, and Amy manages Jax Truckies, the area's first and largest food truck advocacy and support group. I'm not sure where they find so many extra hours in each day, but I suspect neither of them have slept more than two hours straight in the last four years.

When sons Conor (five) and Devlin (three) see a food truck, they point and say "Dad's trucks!" Family comes first to the young couple. Each gig Driftwood BBQ accepts has to meet the criteria that the potential earnings are enough to be worth the time away from the kids. These days, lunch is served at AvMed on Fridays and Orange Park during the week.

Have a special request? Need your barbecue fix? Just want to tell them to have a nice day? Find Amy and Patrick online at www.driftwoodbbq.com and check Jax Truckies to find their smokin' trailer!

DRIFTWOOD BBQ'S COLESLAW
Recipe from Pitmaster Patrick O'Grady

1 head green cabbage, finely chopped
3 bunches green onion, finely chopped
3 carrots, peeled and shredded
1 small jicama, peeled and shredded
¾ cup white sugar
pinch salt
⅓ cup vegetable oil
1½ tablespoon seasoned rice vinegar
1 cup mayonnaise

Wash all vegetables and set aside to dry. In a medium bowl combine sugar, salt, oil, vinegar and mayo together and set aside. With a food processor finely chop the cabbage and place in a large bowl. Hand chop the green onion and add to the cabbage. Peel and shred the carrots and jicama and then mix all the vegetables together. Pour half the sauce over the vegetables and mix thoroughly. Add the sauce a little at a time to achieve the desired consistency.

5LOAVES 2FISH

Chef Toben Stubee and Chef Nick Robson

Fresh, Never Frozen, Made With Love

A glance at the culinary careers of the two young partners behind 5Loaves 2Fish food truck reads like a list of some of the First Coast's most notable fine-dining restaurants. Their beginnings were a bit more humble.

Toben Stubee started cooking at age sixteen. He worked at Outback Steakhouse full time while he studied mechanical engineering at the University of North Florida (UNF), but he wasn't feeling like that was his future. So he quit school and moved to Miami. He went to work in an Italian restaurant and learned cooking the old-school way. That's where he fell in love with the kitchen life. He honed his craft at the Culinary Institute of America at Hyde Park, where he graduated as class valedictorian in 2005. Back in Florida, he landed a plumb job at Opus 39 in St. Augustine. Toben was

5Loaves 2Fish.

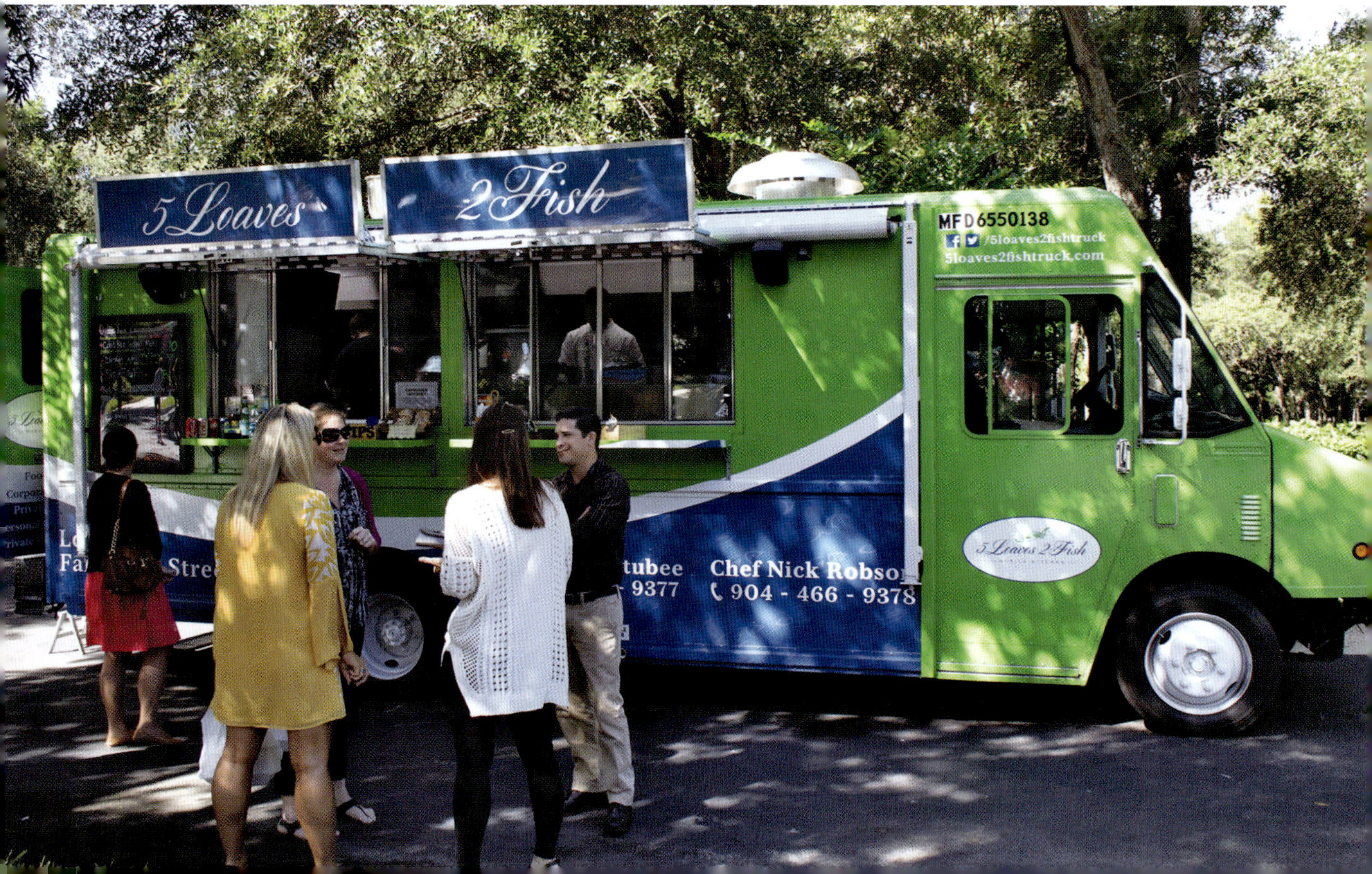

chef de cuisine at the thirty-five-seat fine-dining restaurant, working with a five-course tasting menu that changed daily. Here he met Nick Robson, and the two enjoyed working together. After a few months, Toben left St. Augustine to open Eleven South Bistro in Jacksonville Beach. A year later, he brought his old friend Nick in as sous chef. He also hired a young upcoming chef, Blake Barnett (now chef-owner of Chew Chew).

The next rung in the culinary ladder for Toben was a stint at Matthews, a San Marco fine-dining restaurant owned by Chef Matthew Medure. He appreciated his time there, but again, it wasn't his ideal job. So he started thinking of ways he could enjoy his style of cooking and be more in control. In August 2008, he found his niche as a personal chef for the Stein family (think Stein Mart), a post he held for six years. The work was rewarding, if solitary. Most days, it was just Toben in the kitchen watching CNN all day. He enjoyed traveling with the Steins from time to time. It was a good fit, but he knew it wasn't going to be for forever.

Nick Robson started cooking at fifteen at Winn-Dixie and then Steak and Ale. He went to Outback, where he learned a lot about speed and discipline. He attended culinary school at Johnson and Wales in Charleston, South Carolina, and during that time, he worked at a couple independent fine-dining restaurants. He scored a great gig as an intern at Commander's Palace in New Orleans, and he hung out there for a year just enjoying life in the city. When he returned to Florida, he came to work for CIA alumnus Michael McMillan, who was starting Opus 39. When Michael opened the Tasting Room, Nick moved there as chef de cuisine. He was loving life and learning a lot about running a restaurant.

Eventually, Toben called him to join the crew at Eleven South, where he worked for about three years. He ran the kitchen as executive chef before venturing out with a friend to open the Speckled Hen, a Southern casual dining restaurant that, despite a great start, suffered from a bad location and eventually folded. Back at Eleven South, Nick was looking for a deeper purpose in his life. Toben invited him to attend his church, and the two began talking about working together again.

They missed collaborating in the kitchen, and they started tossing around ideas of how they could cook together again and still have nights off to spend with their young families. One day, Toben was driving to work at the Steins' house and saw his friend Blake round the corner in his big red food truck Chew Chew on the way to Restaurant Depot. Toben had been watching the food truck trend take place, and he took this as a sign. He pitched the idea to Nick, and they just knew they had to make the leap. They wrote a business plan, called some potential backers, talked with a few banks, even tried to do a Small Business Association loan. Persevering though doors weren't opening to them, they

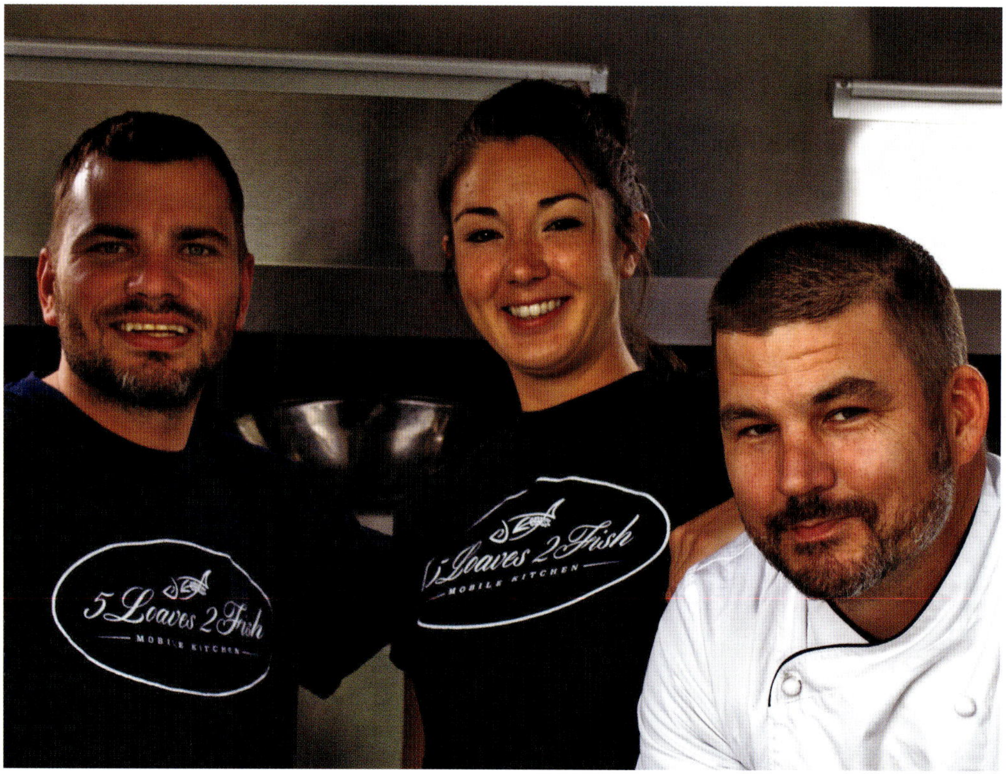

(Left to right) Nick Robson, Gina Corbin and Toben Stubee serve lunch from 5Loaves 2Fish.

tried Chase bank, which had just started growing its presence in the Jacksonville market. The Chase financial advisors were impressed with their business plan and with the talented duo, so they wrote them a loan.

Nick and Toben found their truck—a Freightliner MT45—online in Miami. Concession Nation of Fort Lauderdale did the build-out. They thought the truck was pretty solid, but over the first few months they were on the road, many of its systems needed to be replaced. Matt the Mechanic has become a great local resource for Jacksonville's truckies, and he's on speed dial at 5Loaves 2Fish.

On June 26, 2014, they opened for business, and now the two friends work together again—a *lot*. Nick's wife, Stacey, helps out with social media, and Jax Truckies has been great for generating leads getting them into bigger events.

They love planning the menu, which they change completely every week in keeping with their fine-dining passion. They are like kids in a candy store, wheeling their carts through Fresh Fields or the farmers' market, seeing what great ingredients are available and then getting creative. I asked if they would share a recipe

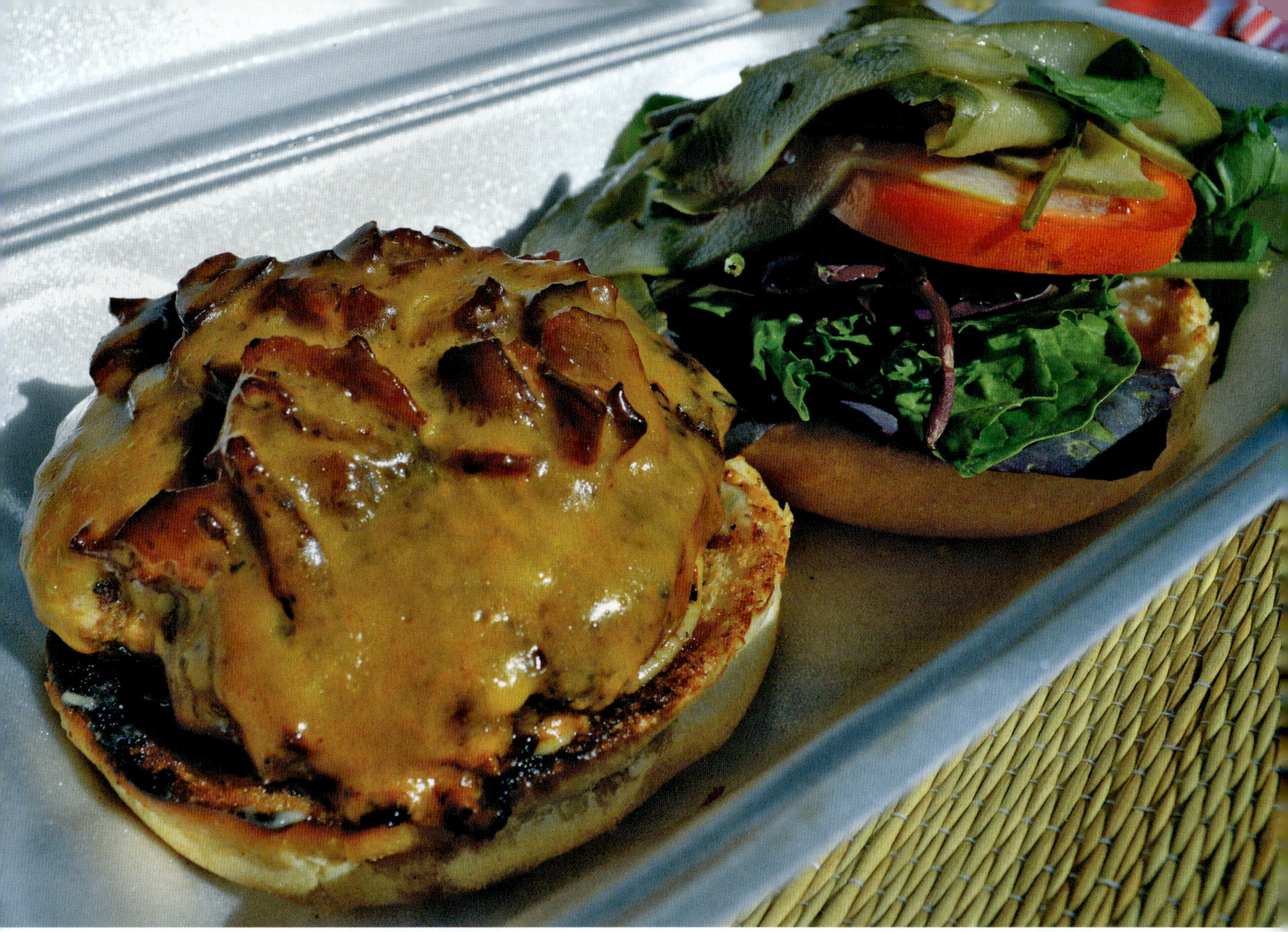

Grass-fed cheeseburger from 5Loaves 2Fish.

with us, but they admitted they don't use them!

When they started, they sourced some things from Twinn Bridges herb farm and other local farms, and they still purchase a lot of produce locally. They support local sources whenever possible and donate to Second Harvest food bank. When their young business begins to make a profit, they intend to give back to the community.

The grass-fed burger is their top seller. It comes with their house-made pickle on a great toasted brioche bun. I like it bacon-cheeseburger style, with melty cheddar and bacon jam. My sister ate this one, and she said it was the best cheeseburger she has ever eaten!

If you like salads, this is your truck. How about a grapefruit glazed–shrimp, heirloom baby tomato panzanella salad, sprinkled with micro basil? If you didn't like them before, how do you like salads now?

The Fried Green Tomato BLT and the Shrimp and Grits are popular choices. Locally sourced fish sandwiches have a steady fan base as well.

Besides sandwiches, Nick and Toben serve entrées like shrimp scampi on farfalle, braised short rib on potato hash and sliced grilled pork

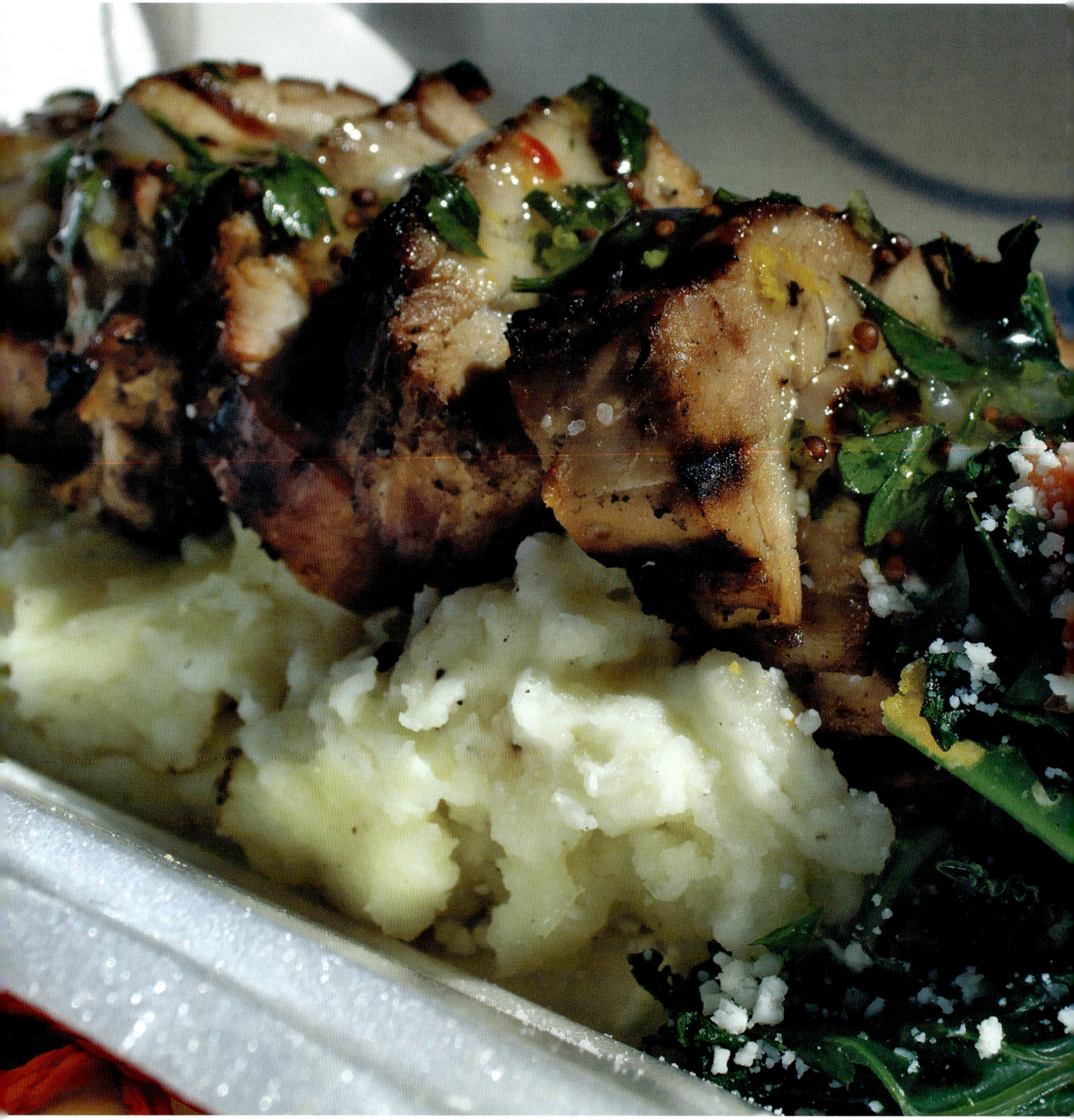

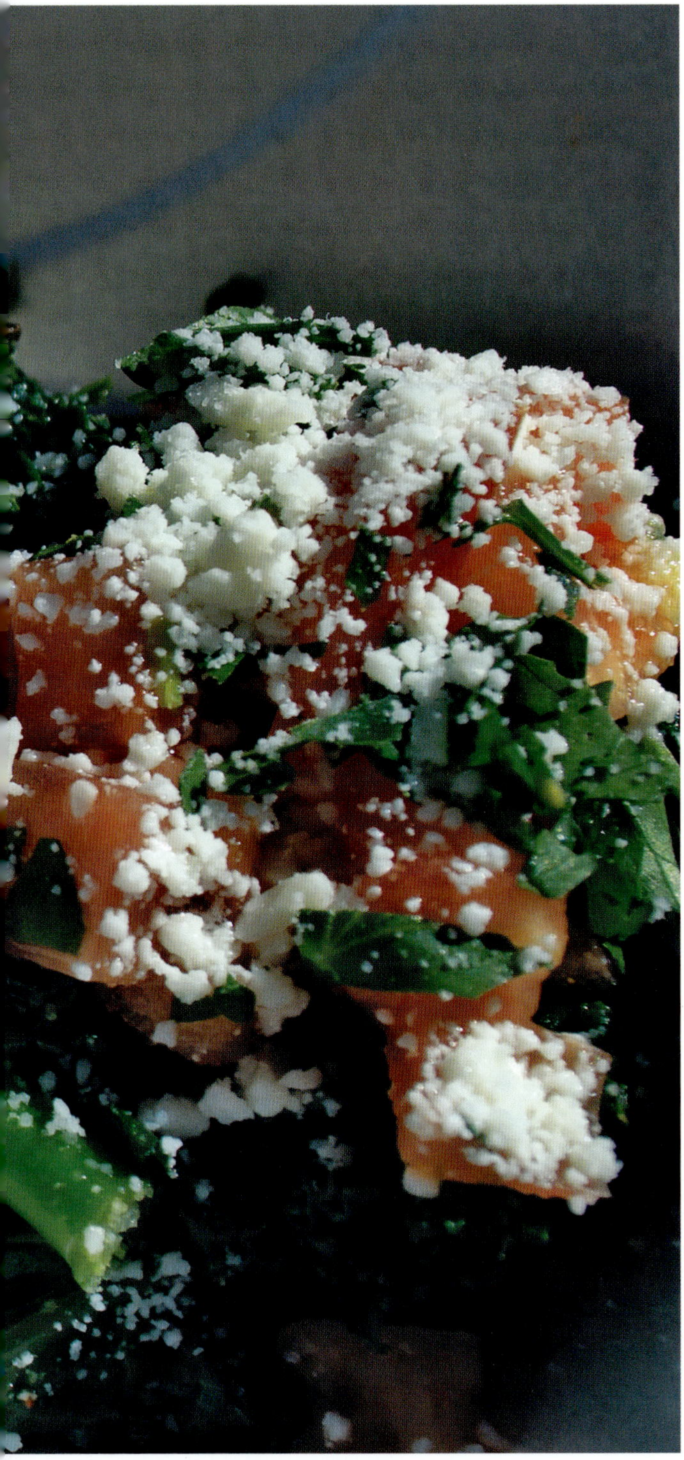

tenderloin on creamy mashed potatoes with a fresh kale salad.

It's not easy being the blue and green truck. They know they're going to have to pay their dues, and they freely admit that their fine-dining menu won't be for everyone. Their style of food, in other cities, is more prevalent and more heavily supported. When you check out 5Loaves 2Fish, I urge you to skip the fries and try one of their delicious custom sides if they are on the menu, like crispy Brussels sprouts or thinly sliced fried yucca chips.

They are finding their niche in serving different areas of town. In areas like Riverside, diners are open to higher-end options. On the Southside, it's all about the burgers, according to Nick. Jaxsons love pork, and 5Loaves 2Fish went through six sides of pork belly feeding the masses at Jaxtoberfest,

Which reminds me, I asked them how they felt Jacksonville diners have responded to their name being a biblical reference. Toben said some people refer to 5Loaves 2Fish as "the Jesus Truck." He is quick to remind them that when Jesus fed the masses, it was a farm-to-street operation, and so is theirs.

The two were surprised at the trouble they had finding service spots at first. They wish Jacksonville would work with trucks a little more and open up a block for trucks to park at lunch.

Pork tenderloin with mashed potatoes and kale salad from 5Loaves 2Fish.

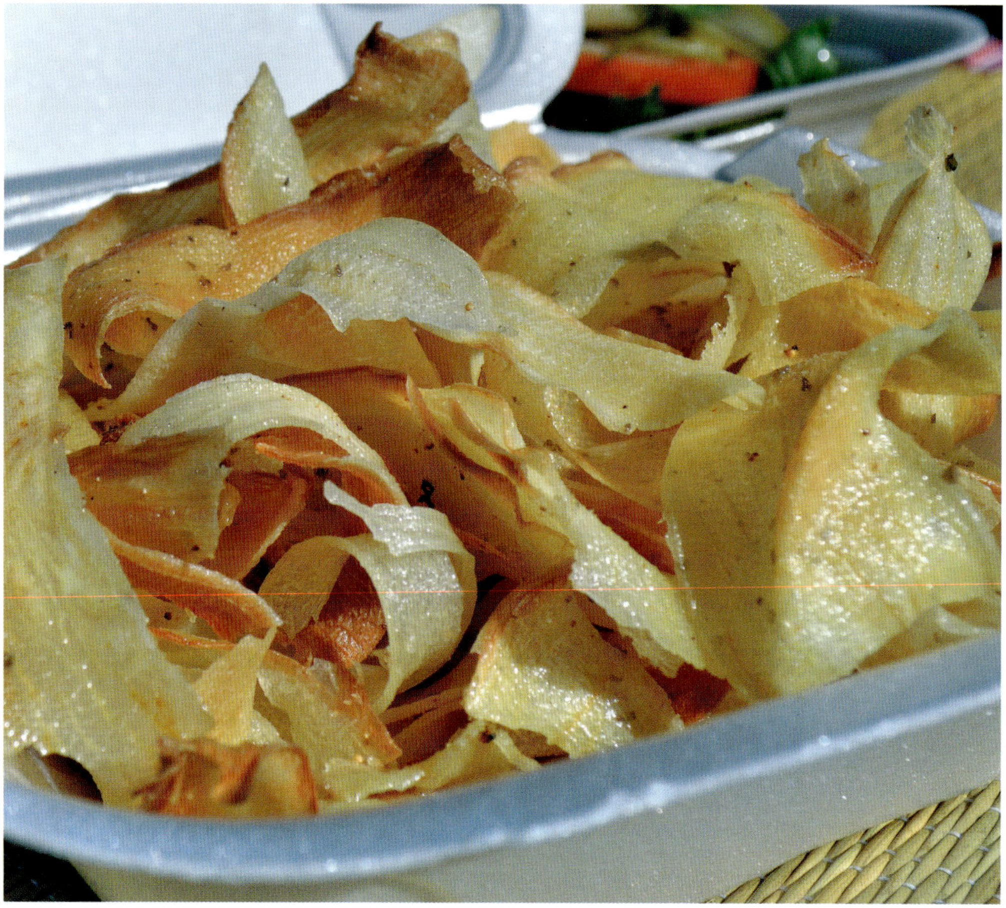

Yucca chips from 5Loaves 2Fish.

They got into a regular Friday lunch slot at EverBank Plaza and Thursdays at Acosta. They have served private lunches for the Jacksonville Jaguars and Deutsche Bank, and they were a hit at First Coast Magazine's one-year anniversary party. Christ's Church does Food Truck Sundays, and they have enjoyed serving there.

What's next? Pop-up dinners sound like fun to them, on or off the truck. They were working on finding venues and looking into the logistics when we spoke. The heat was incredible during the height of August, and next year, they hope to take the summer off and enjoy some of their newfound freedom. Look for 5Loaves 2Fish online at www.5loaves2fishtruck.com, or follow them on Facebook and on Twitter (@5Loaves2FishTrk).

FUNKADELIC

Jerry and Amanda Asker

Jerry Asker fell in love with the kitchen life in his family's restaurant, Jerry's Sports Bar, at Atlantic and Hodges Streets. He was called in to pinch hit as a chef and wound up teaching himself and learning from co-workers along the way. Amanda was waiting tables at Jerry's when she met her future husband and business partner.

The two decided they would open a restaurant at the beach, but they couldn't find anything suitable in their price range. Amanda suggested a food truck, only halfway jokingly, but when Jerry's mom said the same thing a couple months later, the idea stuck.

They bought a step-van, a former bread truck, in Orlando. They gutted it and took it to M&R Specialty Trailers in Macclenny, where they designed an efficient kitchen.

Jerry had the vision to incorporate music and art in the truck's theme. Funk music offered the fun, happy, energetic vibe they were looking for, hence the

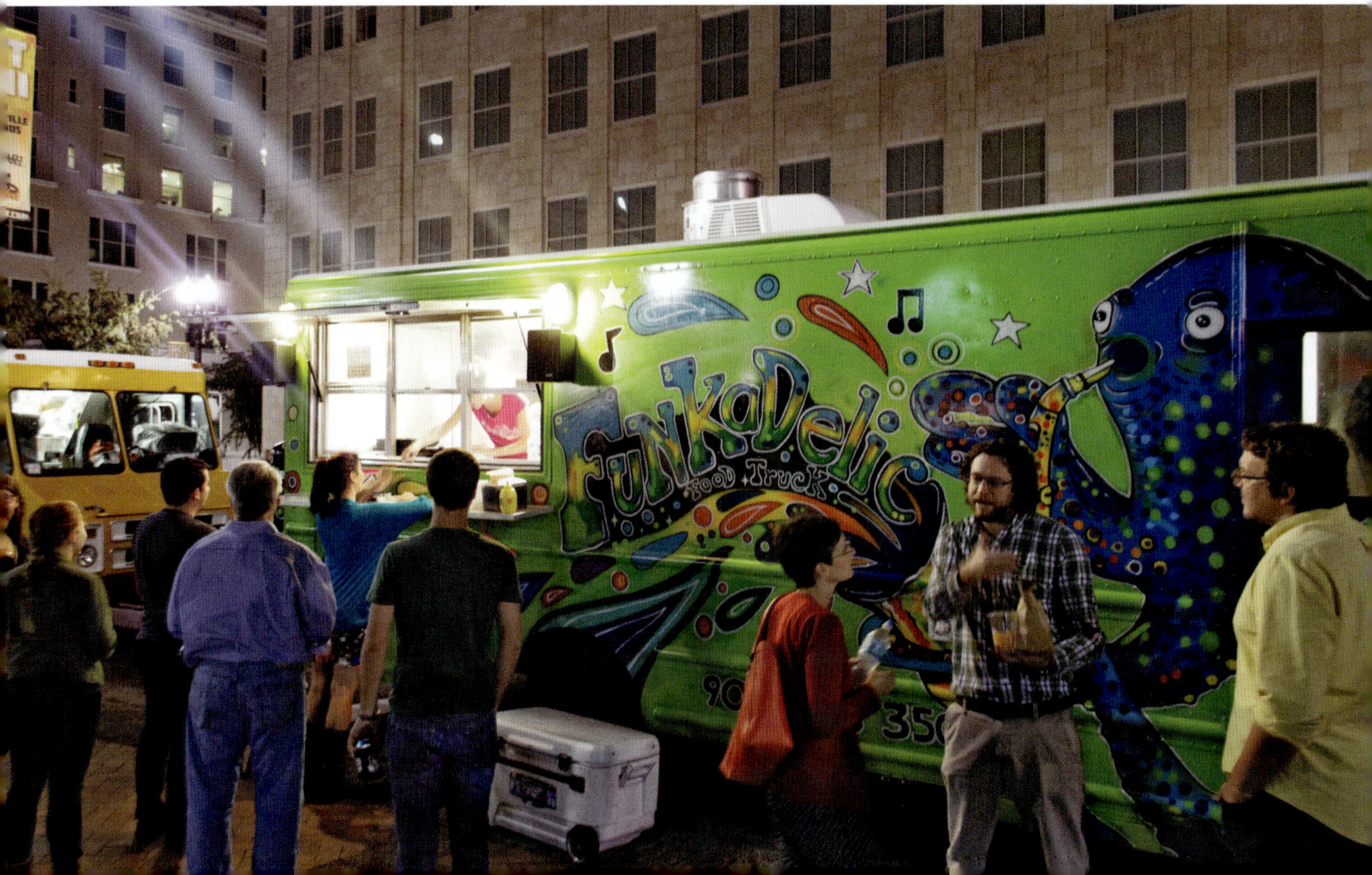

Funkadelic draws a crowd at Jaxsons Night Market.

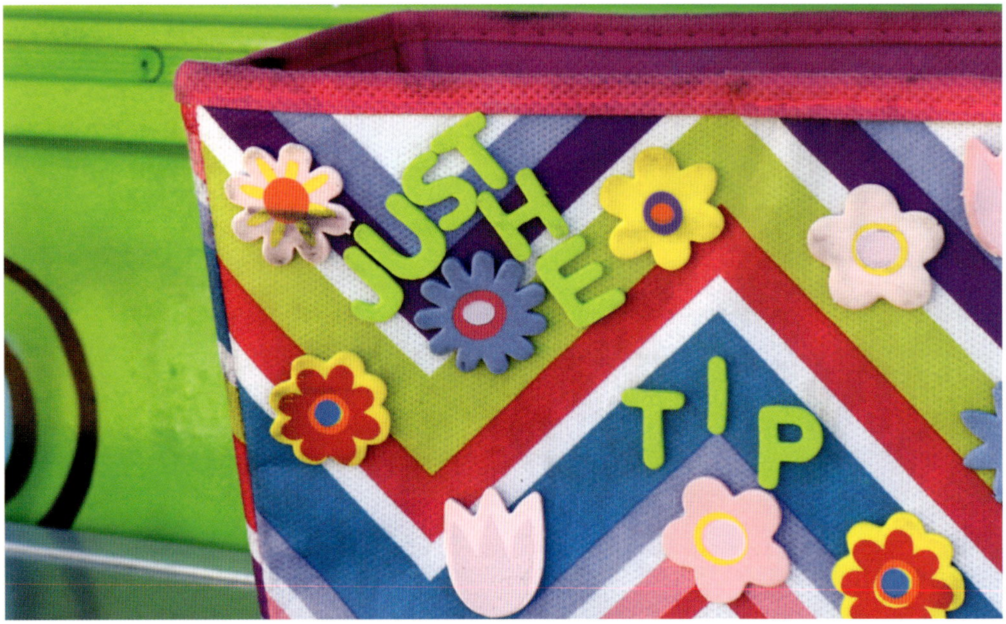
JUST THE TIP

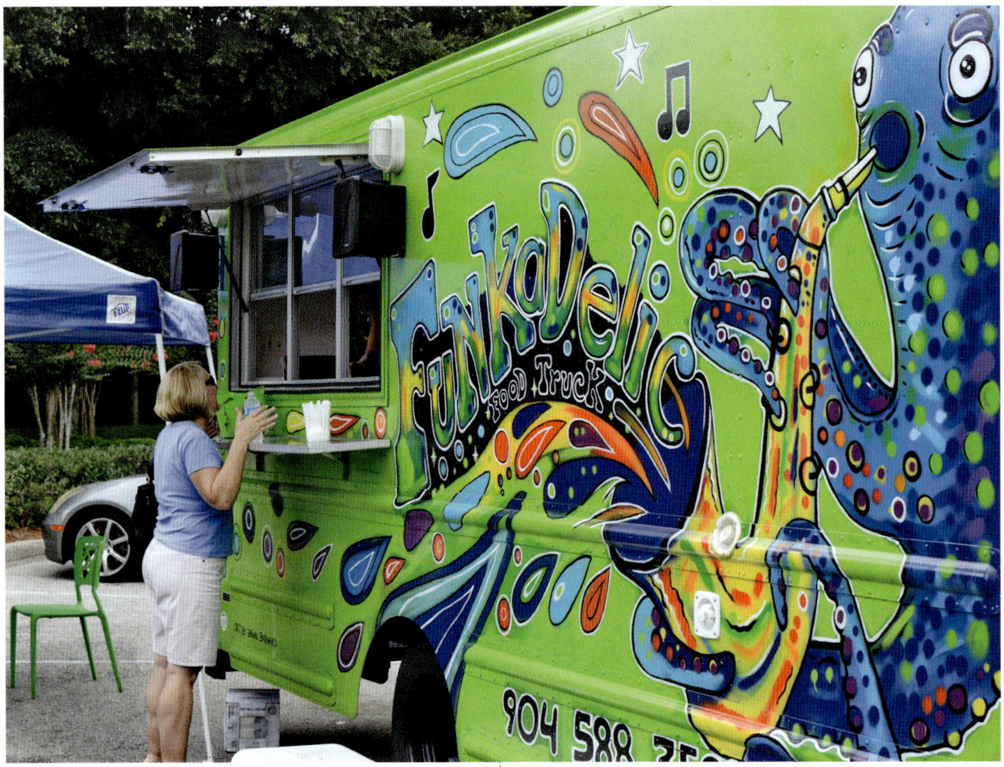
FunKaDelic
Food Truck
904 588

name Funkadelic. It has struck a chord with local diners, too. Amanda told me that a group of loyal customers have taken to calling themselves the Funkateers. Sign me up!

Artist and friend Brian Barnard of Fernandina Beach was commissioned to paint the truck. With bright blues and greens; trippy, playful graphics; and a funky sea creature playing a saxophone, the truck is very fresh, fun and one of a kind.

Jerry is all about the food—menu planning, prep and cooking. The menu Jerry created was a mix of things he dreamed up that just sounded good to him, dishes he researched online and some things he liked that trucks were doing in other states.

Their first service date was December 14, 2013. Jerry told me he had never even tasted a few of the dishes until they started serving them! He has tweaked things a few times since that opening day, and their menu is the purest expression of this talented chef's vision. It evolves with the seasons and the availability of fresh ingredients. This summer, I had a fantastic blackened sockeye salmon filet special with ripe mango and Sriracha slaw, drizzled with soy caramel. It was visually stunning, and the taste was what my mom would call "out of this world good."

The inspiration for Funkadelic's addictive Roasted Beet Home Fries came from Paul Key, winner of *Top Chef Austin*. Jerry loved the idea, played around with the recipe, made some tweaks and created his own sauce. He roasts his beets fresh. In fact, the entire menu is made from scratch on the truck. It's not the easy way, but it's the only way they want to work. They don't carry ketchup or mustard. Jerry wants everything in their own special sauces. The last time I got the beets, they were being served with Funk Sauce. Don't ask me what's in it. Even if I knew, I wouldn't tell. Some things are best left a delicious mystery.

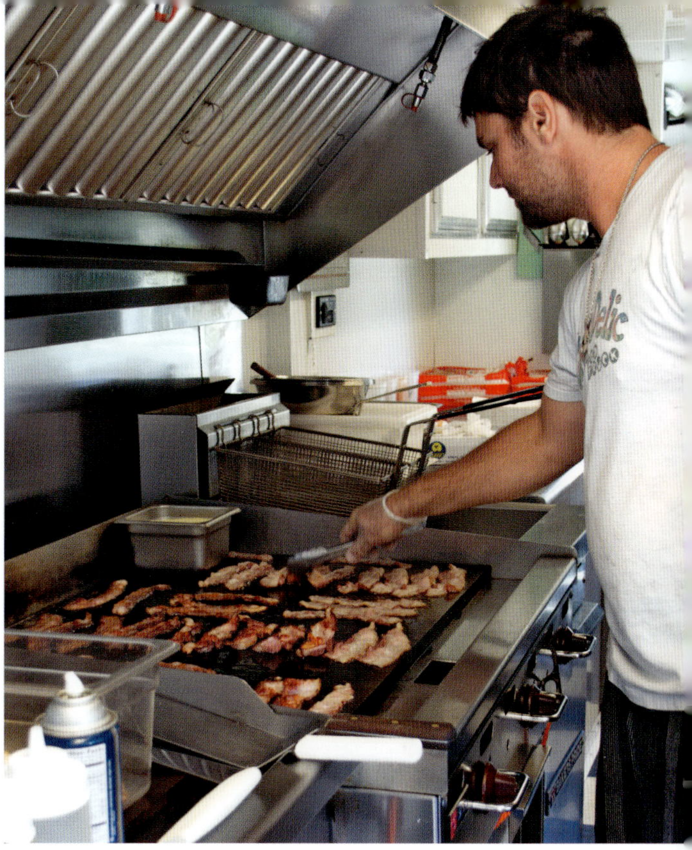

Funkadelic's Jerry Asker cooks bacon.

Opposite, top: Funkadelic's funky tip jar.

Opposite, bottom: Funkadelic's bright graphics make it easy to spot from the street.

The Beer-Cheese Soup is a thing of beauty—simple, silky and altogether satisfying. I was so excited when Jerry

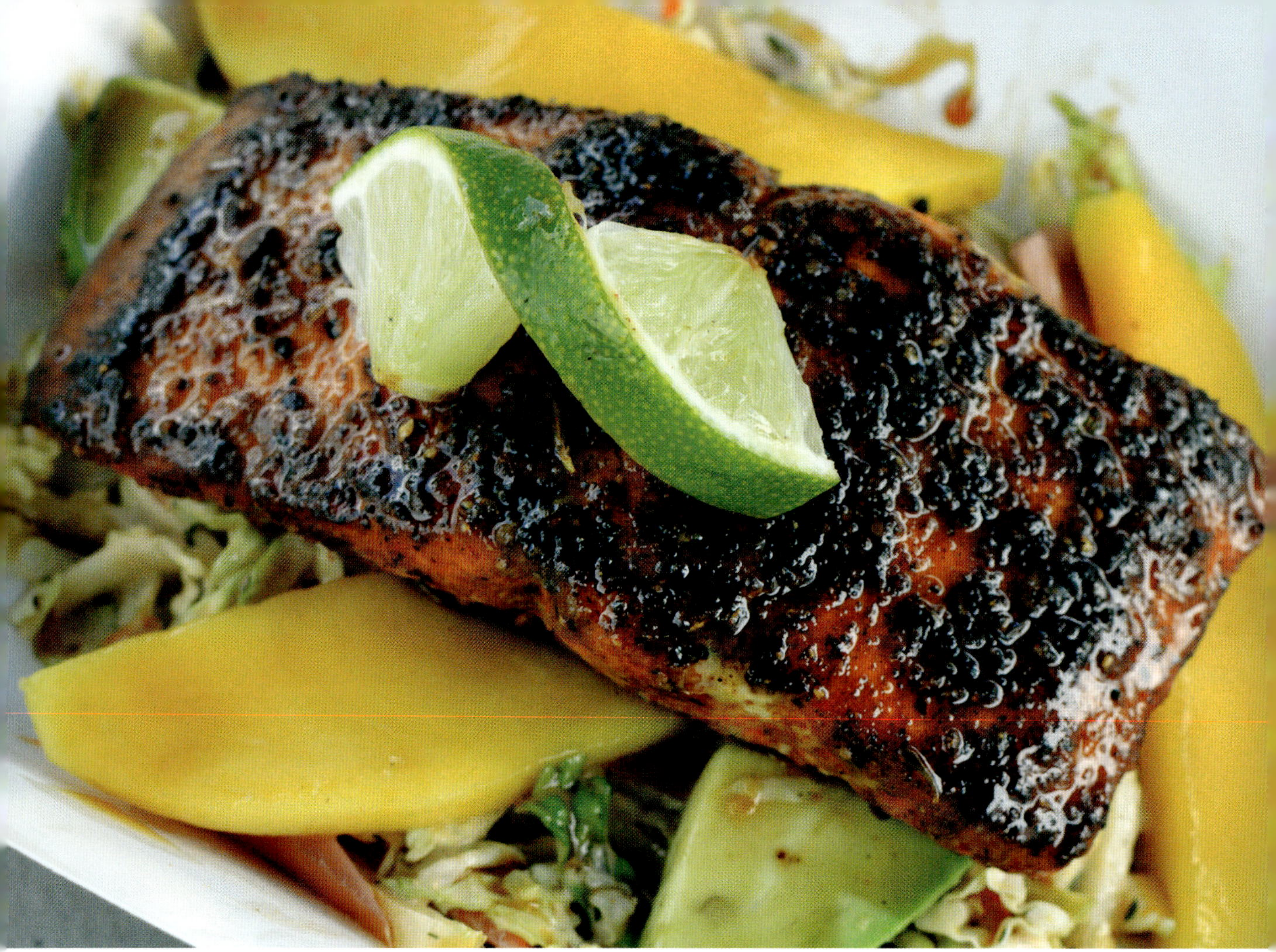

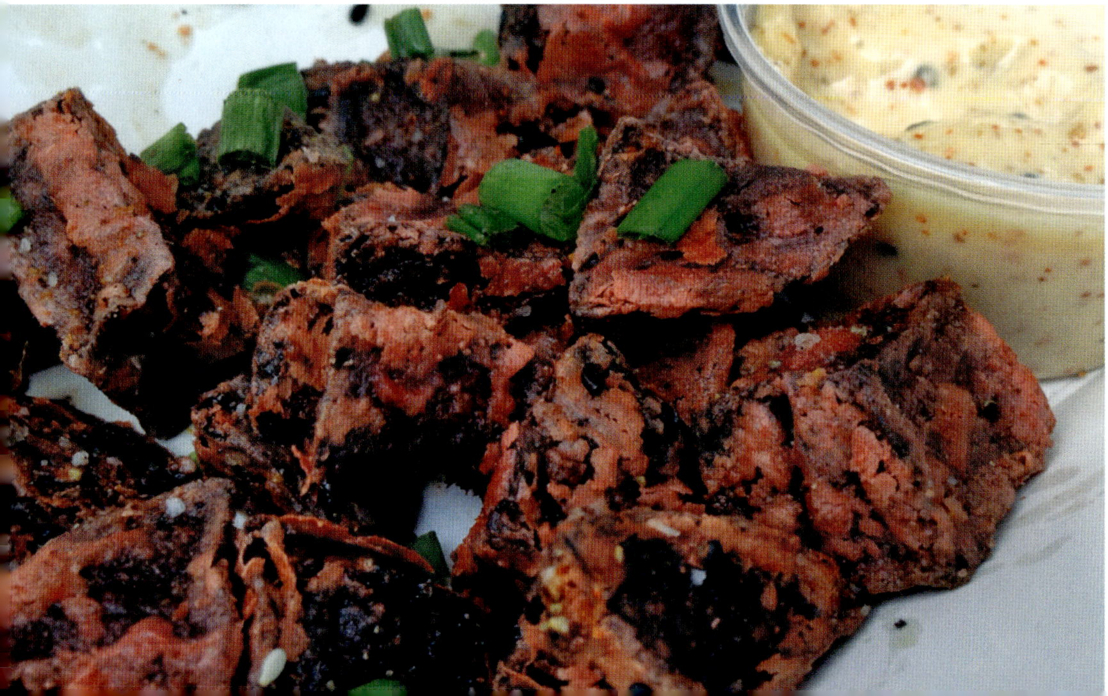

Above: Sockeye Salmon with Sriracha Slaw from Funkadelic.

Left: Funkadelic's addictive Beet Fries.

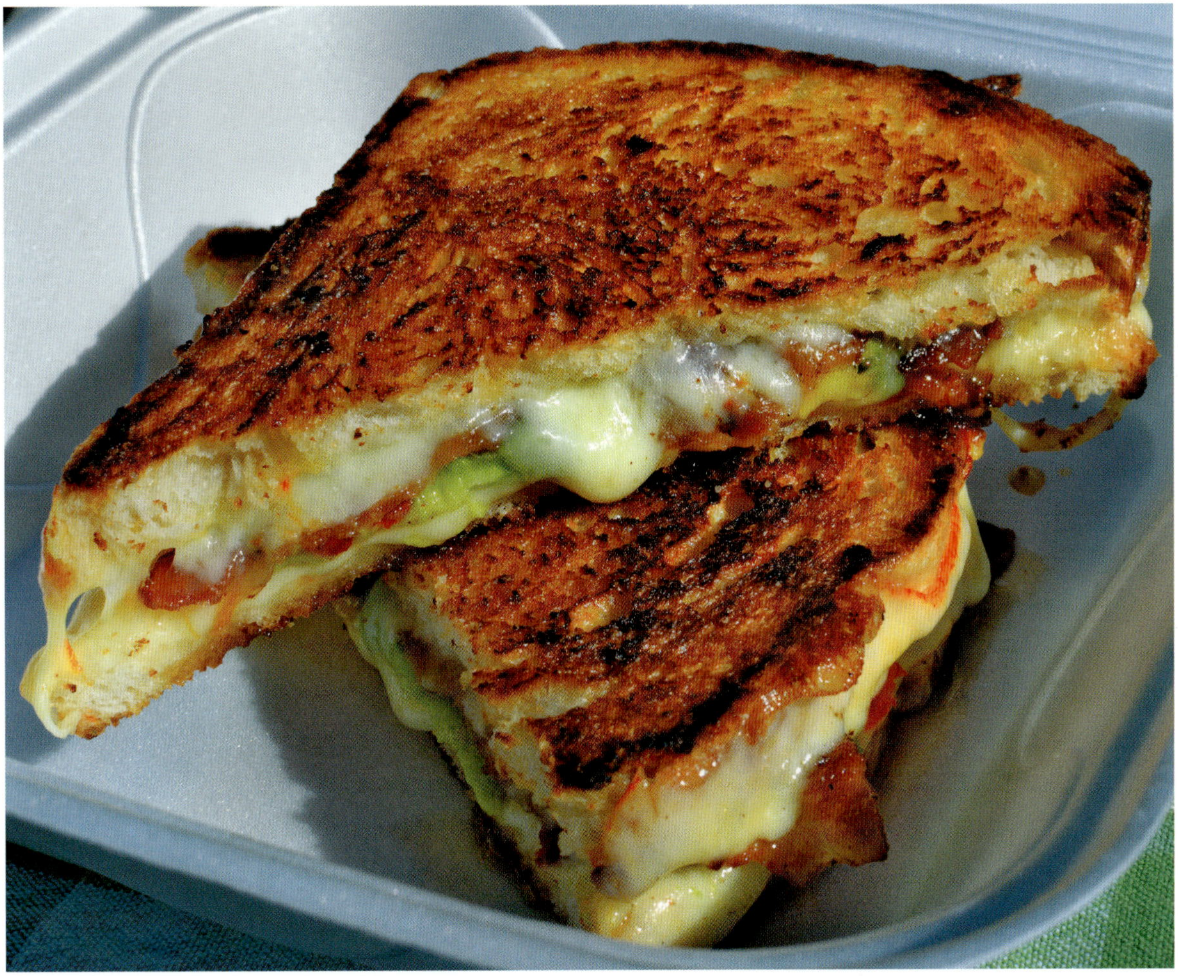

Funkadelic's Gourmet Grilled Cheese with Datil Pepper Jelly.

sent me the recipe to share with you here! You can thank me later, friends. If you're not the cooking type, just go get this at the truck, if it is in season. If not, I'm sure they'll have an equally awesome soup in its place.

OK, here it goes. I know a grown woman should not wax poetic about a grilled cheese sandwich, but I cannot help myself. I saw a couple enjoying the Gourmet Grilled Cheese for lunch at the Food Truck Food Court, and I made a mental note to order it the next time out. The next time turned out to be the next day because you know I obsessed over that sandwich all night! Here's the thing. This bad boy starts with the best grilled bread, Muenster cheese, avocado and Applewood smoked bacon slices, as well as, wait for it, Datil pepper jelly. Sweet, hot and salty, the sandwich is excellent: the melted cheese mingles with that pepper jelly, crunchy bacon and smooth avocado, all between the crisp, perfectly grilled bread. I kid you not, if they are serving this right now I suggest you stop whatever you are doing and get over there before they run out! Sometimes a sandwich is more than just a sandwich, am I right?

Amanda, in addition to the service window, handles the business end—the booking, scheduling, bookkeeping, marketing and promotion. She knows being an owner gives her a different perspective on customer service, and she's passionate about making sure everyone is having a positive experience. She and Jerry have worked some pretty big events, like the Imagine Music Festival in Atlanta, Spirit of Suwanee and Blackwater Music Festival in Live Oak and the First Coast Music Fest in downtown

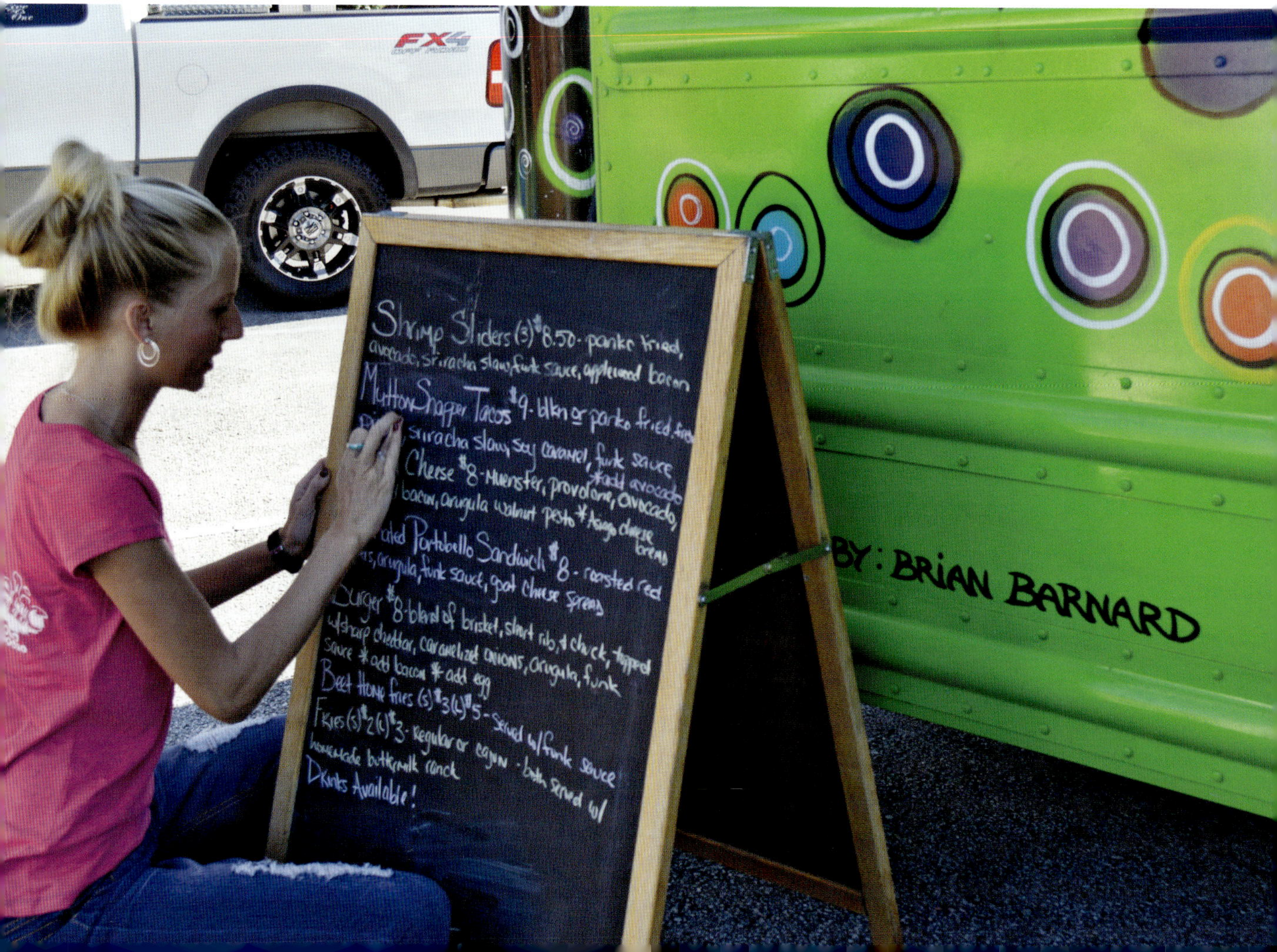

Amanda Asker, co-owner of Funkadelic, prepares for the lunch rush.

Jax. Funkadelic's brand of funk, food and fun is a natural fit with the festival crowds. The truck killed it at One Spark, Jacksonville's original crowd-funding festival, and Jerry and Amanda regularly bring "da Funk" to Art Walk, Jaxsons Night Market and the local breweries. They have a regular Thursday lunch gig at 121 Financial Credit Union on Touchton, and they frequently do two-a-days with a lunch one place and dinner service somewhere else.

Amanda's plan is to eventually move on to running her own business as an event planner. She loves party planning and wedding coordinating, and she got a taste of it in May 2014 when she and Jerry tied the knot at the Ribault Club. Their wedding coordinator even suggested bringing the truck, but Amanda insisted they wanted to be far away from it—at least for the day.

Jerry and Amanda are moving forward nonstop. There's never a day off (unless it's your wedding day). There is always maintenance, phone calls, booking, paperwork, shopping and menu planning to be done. They both agree that the truck has been the perfect way to get their name and reputation out there, and they keep the atmosphere light and fun. Jerry jams on the grill while Amanda smiles her mega-watt smile in the window, and they crank up the tunes and power through even the longest lines.

It's not all music and laughter, though. There was the day last year,

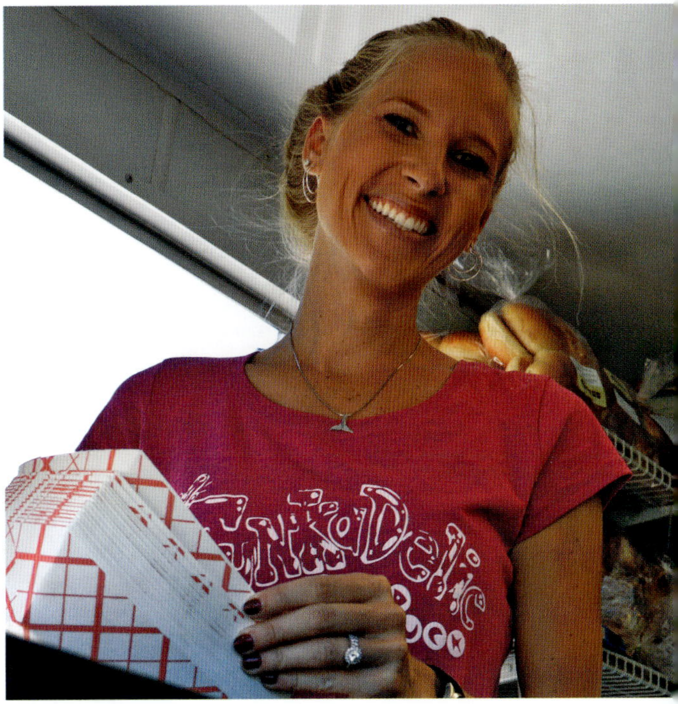

Amanda Asker.

for instance, when they were headed to a lunch service and the truck broke down just before they reached the top of the Matthews Bridge. Amanda was steering, and Jerry and crew were pushing the giant truck uphill on the bridge in heavy traffic. *That* day, the idea of owning a brick-and-mortar restaurant was looking pretty good to them.

Jerry pictures them in a small restaurant with a small revolving "chalkboard" menu and an exhibition kitchen so people can watch their food being prepared. He is encouraged by the success of fellow truckie Chris Dickerson's Corner Taco. Funkadelic

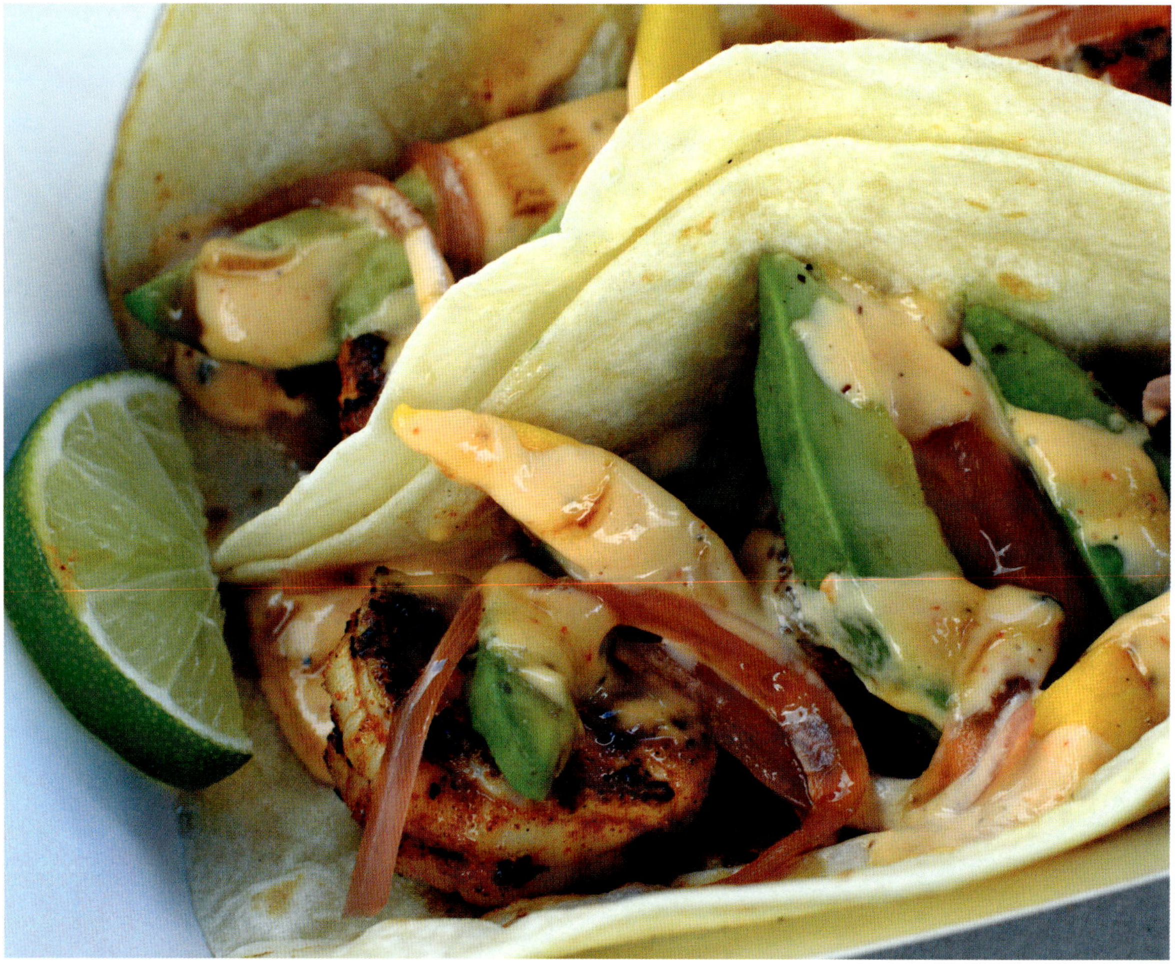

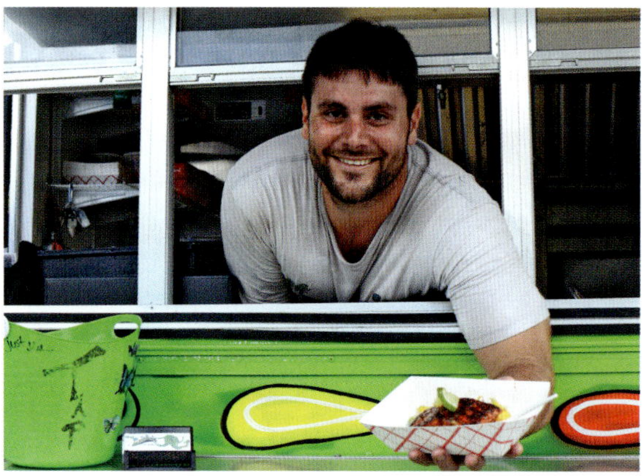

Above: Shrimp Tacos from Funkadelic.

Left: Jerry Asker, co-owner and chef of Funkadelic.

is booked in several big moneymaking events in the coming year. The Askers hope to roll that success into a restaurant, at which time, Jerry admits, the Funkadelic food truck might just be available for sale to the next enterprising chef. Get your funk on, Jacksonville!

FUNKADELIC'S BEER-CHEESE SOUP
Recipe provided by Chef Jerry Asker

½ gallon chicken stock
½ quart heavy cream
1 quart whole milk
½ pound unsalted butter, plus ⅛ pound
1 large carrot, chopped
1 medium onion, chopped
3 stalks celery, chopped
¾ to 1 cup flour
2 tablespoons Dijon mustard
15 ounces flat amber ale (such as Fat Tire)
¼ pound Muenster cheese, freshly grated
½ pound sharp white cheddar, freshly grated
½ pound original Velveeta, cubed
kosher salt, to taste
freshly ground pepper, to taste
thyme powder, to taste

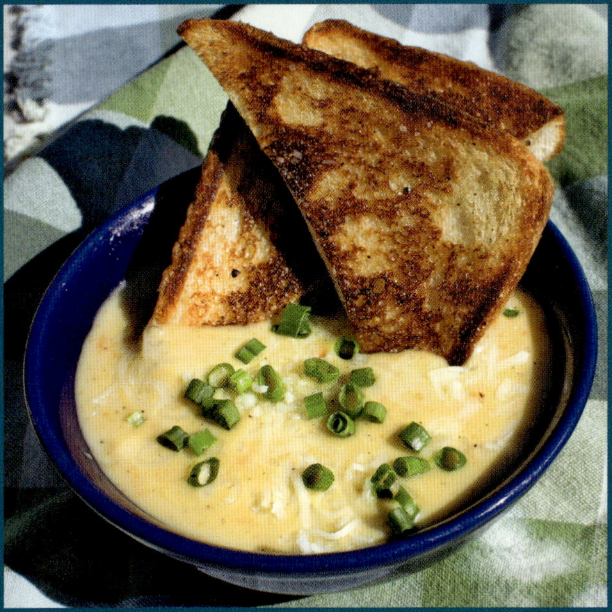

Funkadelic's Beer Cheese Soup.

In a medium saucepan, pour chicken stock and heat until warm. In a second medium saucepan, combine heavy cream and milk on medium heat, being careful not to let the mixture come to a boil.

In a large stockpot on low heat, melt ½ pound salted butter. Add the carrot, onion and celery (mirepoix) and cook until tender. Strain the remaining butter from the mirepoix mixture and set aside. Add the cooked vegetables to a food processor and purée.

Add the reserved butter back to pot with the extra ⅛ pound. Add the flour to make roux. (There should be enough flour to make the roux very thick, without sticking to the bottom of the pot.) Cook the roux on low heat for about 10 minutes, stirring and watching carefully—do not let it burn! Stir Dijon mustard into roux, and then quickly whisk in the hot chicken stock—it will thicken ***very*** fast. Once the mixture is smooth, add the hot milk and heavy cream and whisk until smooth. Now is the time to add the beer! Let all ingredients come to slow boil. Add the mirepoix purée and all cheeses. When cheeses are all melted, season with salt, pepper and thyme powder. When the soup comes to a slow boil again, you're done!

Transfer the soup to a container and place in an ice bath in the sink until properly cooled.

Enjoy!

FUSION

Chef Ashley Amin

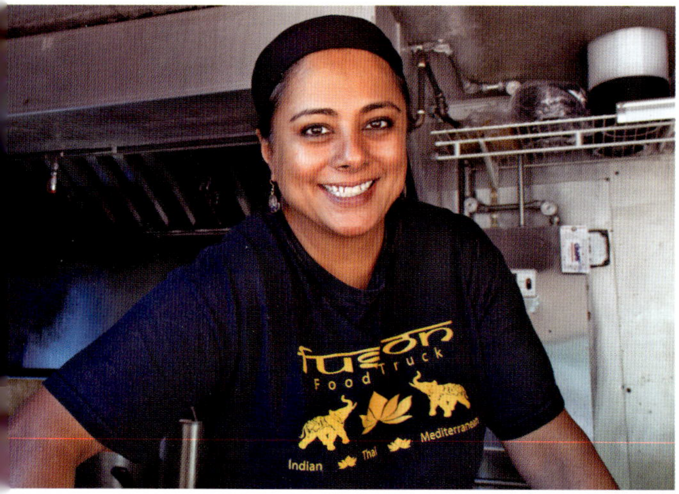

Chef Ashley Amin of Fusion.

Chef Ashley Amin has cooked for the Dalai Lama, the king of Jordan and famous Indian singer Jagjit Singh, but on this day, her black-and-gold Fusion food truck was parked at EverBank Field, where she and husband Dee were feeding the players and staff of the Jacksonville Jaguars. The next day they would square off against "her" San Diego Chargers, and Ashley took some good-natured ribbing as they saw her photograph in her chef whites on the truck and learned that she was an award-winning chef from San Diego.

Ashley's story didn't start in San Diego. She was born in East Africa to parents of Indian descent. She grew up in England and attended London Business School. When her parents moved to the States, her brother followed shortly afterward. He opened a small frozen yogurt store called Cool Corner in the Hillcrest area of San Diego, and Ashley came over two years later to help him run the business.

They started selling their mom's home-cooked garbanzo curries, rice and samosas, and when the Indian food outsold the frozen yogurt, a new business was born. Over the next few years, the brother and sister duo opened several restaurants, from fast casual fusion to fine-dining Indian cuisine. San Diego's critically acclaimed Monsoon Group included Monsoon Fine Cuisine of India, Bombay, Royal India, Masala Spices of India, the Sapphire Room and Monsoon Group Catering. Ashley was executive chef for all the Indian restaurants, creating all the menus and managing front-of-house operations.

In 2012, the young restaurant exec took stock of her life and decided to switch gears. Her mind set on marrying a nice man and settling down, she met her husband, Dee Amin, on an Indian matrimonial website. Dee was working in Jacksonville as a trainer at Verizon, so Ashley left the restaurants and family behind and found work here as a business analyst at Merrill Lynch and then at Florida Blue.

Soon Ashley informed Dee that she had the itch to open a restaurant. Inspired by the couple's

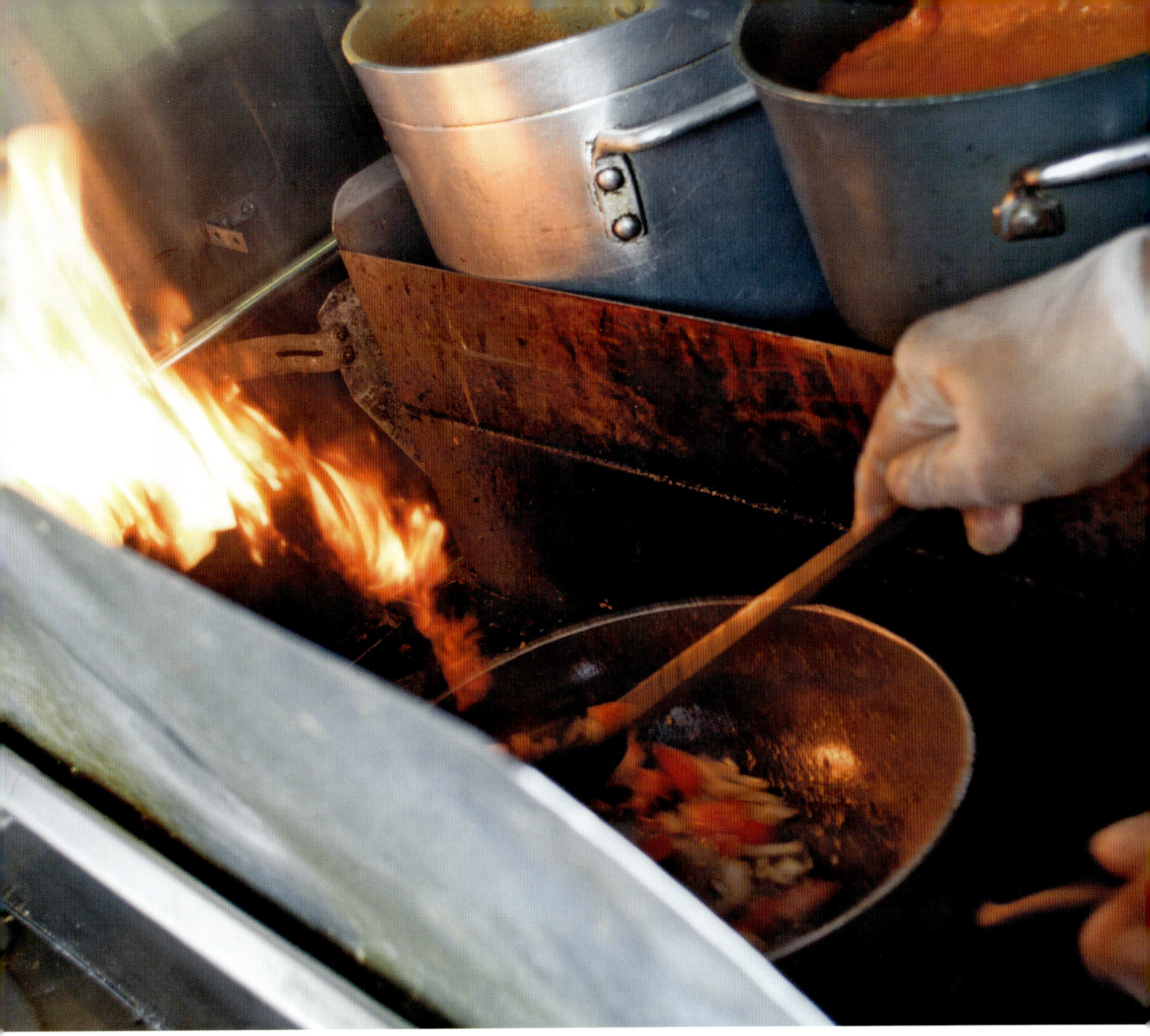

Ashley sautés spices and aromatics for Madras Curry.

friend Anthony Hashem of the Happy Grilled Cheese, she began researching the costs and sketching out her concept for a food truck.

While Ashley is a planner, Dee is more of a doer. One day, she came home from work to a surprise—the 1987 Chevrolet food truck he had bought for her that day on Craigslist.

Finding a truck that had some basic kitchen equipment ready to use made it easier to get it on the road, and with a little effort and TLC, Fusion was soon good to go. While Ashley was trying to decide what day and location would be best to start, Dee informed her he had booked her truck for a private event at a

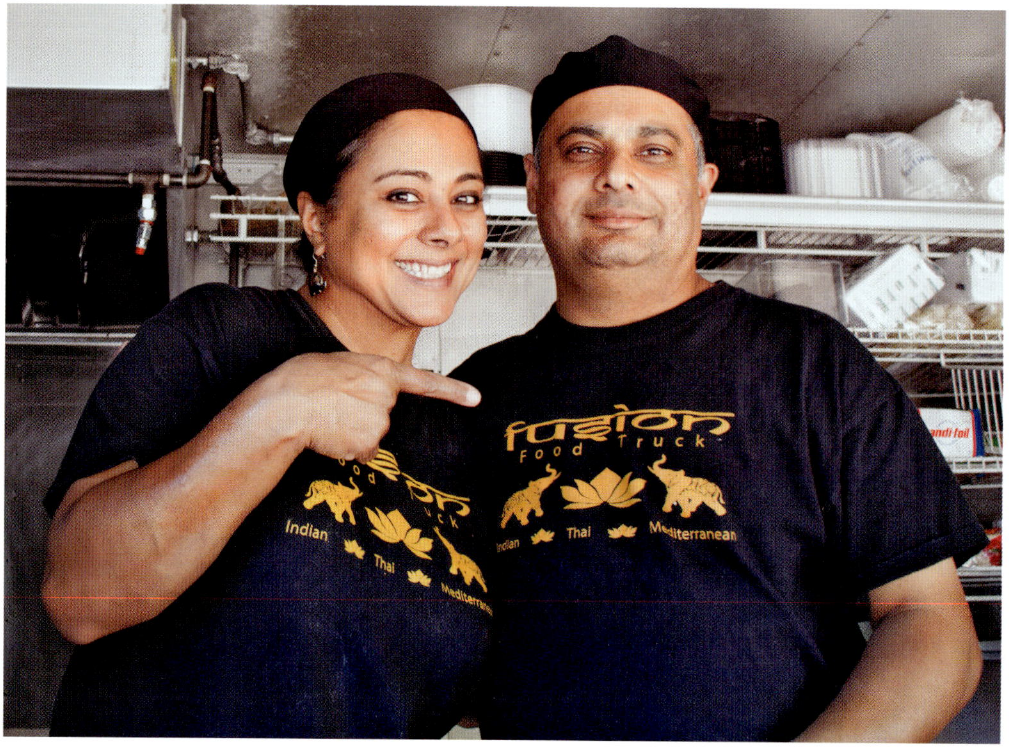

Ashley and Dee Amin, owners of Fusion.

church *the next day*. After the shock wore off, they grabbed their groceries, started prepping at the crack of dawn and, on February 8, 2014, Fusion hit the street. They hadn't even done a test run in the kitchen yet. Once they started taking orders that first day, they found out their fryer didn't work! A pot of oil was pressed into service on the stovetop, and of course, they were slammed with orders for samosas and other fried items all day.

The next step was to call property managers and ask for bookings. It took a few weeks to get a full weekly schedule going, but her hard work paid off. After that initial two weeks, they were facing a consistent six-day week, frequently running lunch and dinner bookings on the same day.

After just a few months of operation, Dee again surprised Ashley when he quit his job at Verizon and came to work with her on the truck full time. They had factored in two people to help with the workload, and Dee decided to fill one of those positions so he could be there to help Ashley with the day-to-day running of the business. Of working together with her husband, Ashley says it was a little rocky at first, but it's much better now that Dee knows his way around the truck's kitchen. He is a very patient partner and a hardworking guy.

Fusion is one of a handful of genre-specific trucks that doesn't specialize in

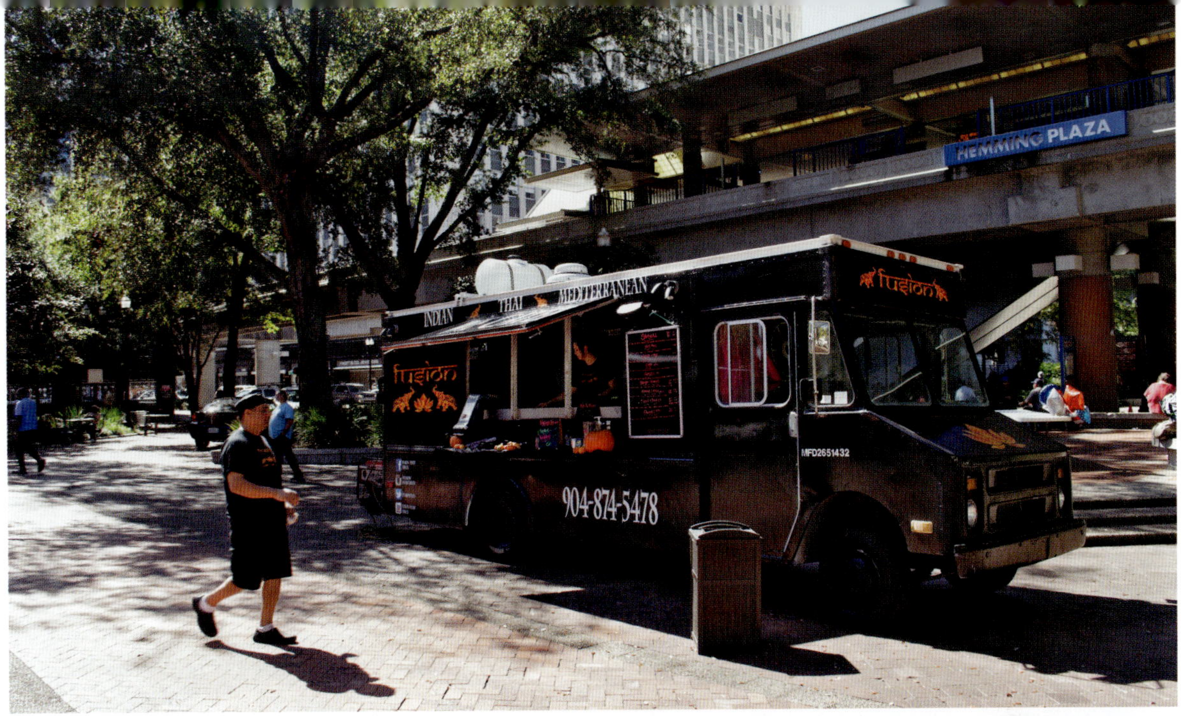

Above: Dee Amin of Fusion rushes through Hemming Park at the end of a lunch service.

Right: Fusion's menu rotates frequently, so there's always something new and delicious.

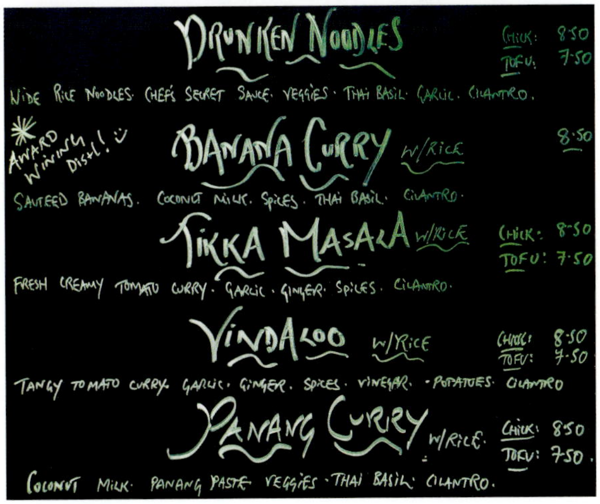

barbecue or burgers. Indian, Thai and Mediterranean dishes are all represented here. Their menu consists of five staple items and five specials, in rotation from a repertoire of over one hundred dishes.

I have tried just about all of their Indian and Thai curries, and I love it when I visit the truck to find another dish in the rotation that I haven't yet tasted. Thai is one of my favorite cuisines, and Ashley's Panang Curry is one of the best I've eaten anywhere. Thai Drunken Noodles are a big seller, and Indian classics like Chicken Tikka and Vindaloo are soul-satisfying choices.

Vegetarians win big here, too. Most of Fusion's dishes can be prepared with tofu as the protein, and the rotating menu always features one or two classic vegetarian dishes, including Potato Samosas and my newest obsession, Channa Bhatura, a chickpea curry (Channa Masala) served with Bhatura, a puffy deep-fried leavened bread from North India.

Ashley has slowly been introducing new dishes to North Florida diners and is encouraged by how readily they are accepted, even sought out. One night during a Jax Truckies food truck rally, her Banana Curry sold out in record

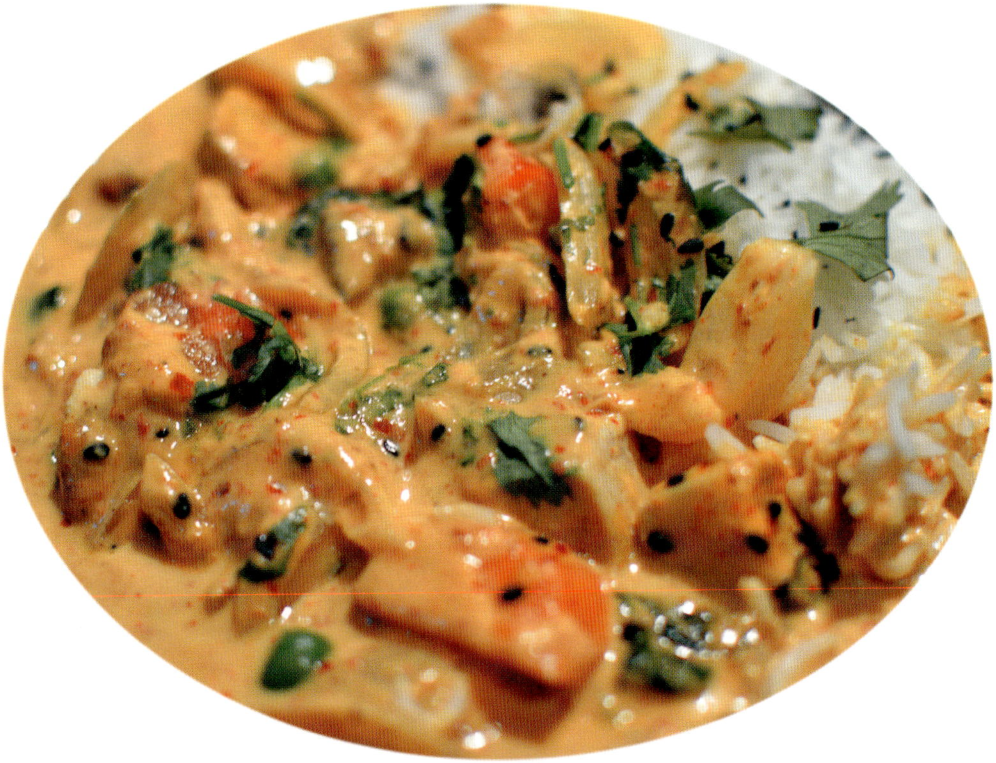

Fusion's menu features both Thai and Indian curries.

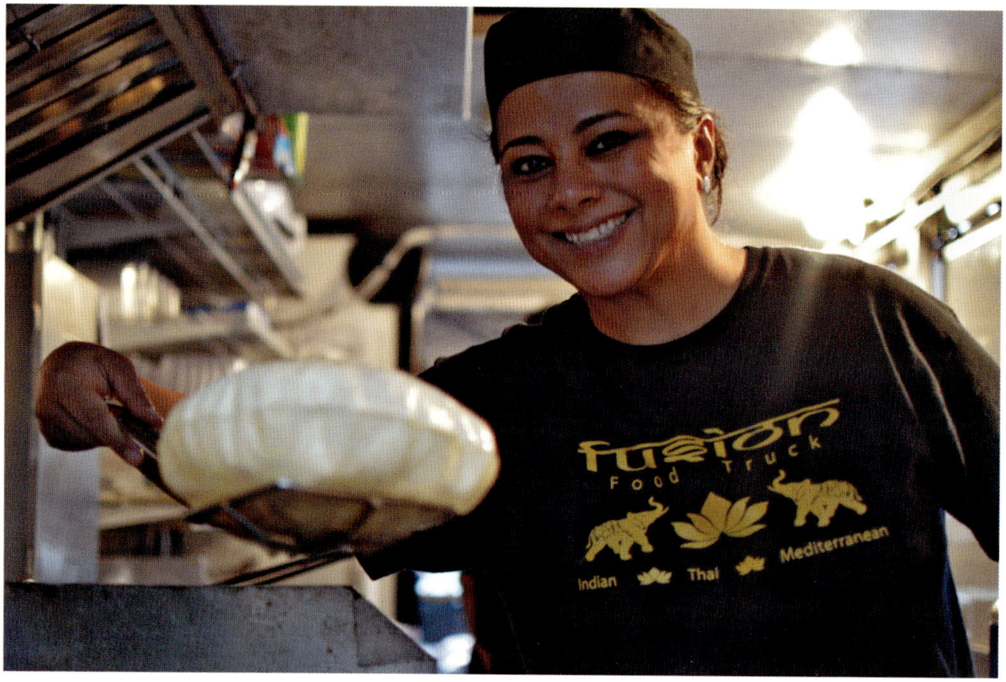

Chef Ashley fries puffy Indian Bhatura.

time. She asked someone how they came to order it, and they told her they saw Caron from Jax Truckies and *Folio Weekly*'s Bite Club eating it, and she told them they *had* to get some too. Ashley issued an open invitation to Caron to come eat by her truck every night!

Ashley's inspiration for the Banana Curry was an early childhood memory of a dish her mother made with the whole banana, skin on. She would cut the banana into three pieces, slit it open and stuff it with a masala paste, then sauté the pieces with onions, garlic and tomatoes. Ashley's version has the same base as her Panang Curry, a little sweeter than her mom's, and she peels the banana before it hits the skillet. I love the combination of sweet and salty, and I most definitely like it hot.

Fusion had only been on the scene for three months when the Third Annual Jax Truckies Food Truck Championship rolled around in May 2014. A growing fan base came out in support of the charismatic young chef, and Ashley's Banana Curry took the prize for Most Innovative Dish.

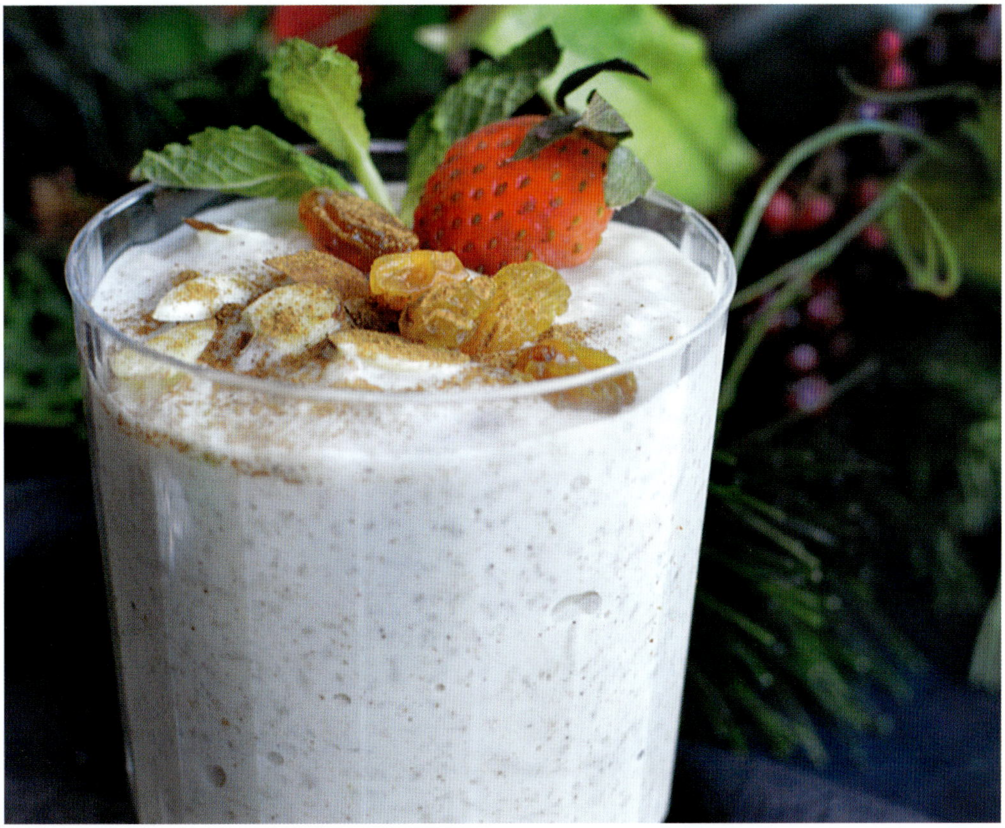

Kheer from Fusion.

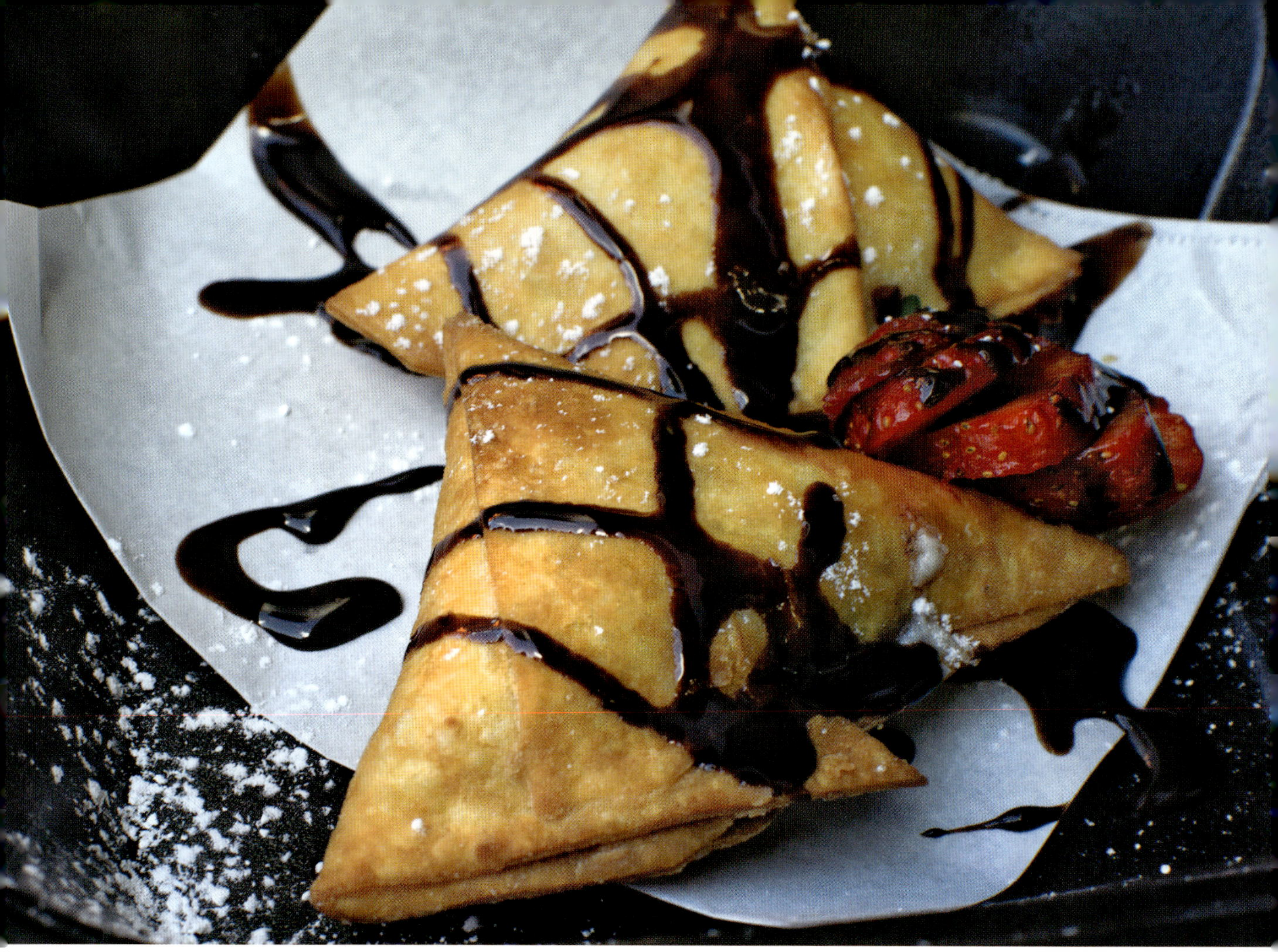

Chocolate Cheesecake Samosas from Fusion.

Speaking of sweets, Fusion's menu always has a few dessert options, and I have made it my duty to sample all of them for you. You can't go wrong with the crowd-pleasing sweet and light Mango Mousse, but I encourage you to try a new one each time.

Kheer is a rice pudding, made on the truck and served warm. Subtly flavored with cardamom, this creamy comfort food is studded with golden raisins and topped with roasted almond flakes and a sprig of fresh mint. It's like a grown-up version of the rice pudding my mom used to make for us kids.

Ghirardelli Chocolate Cheesecake Samosas made their debut as a Valentine's Day special and have been a fan favorite ever since. They have everything going for them—bite into the hot fried samosa shell and the creamy cheesecake filling oozes out, filling your mouth with happiness. The rich chocolate sauce and sweet powdered sugar mix in there as you eat, giving that sweet and slightly tart filling a run for its money. They come two to an order. I take mine to go, and I confess that so far, I have yet to reach the house with both of them intact.

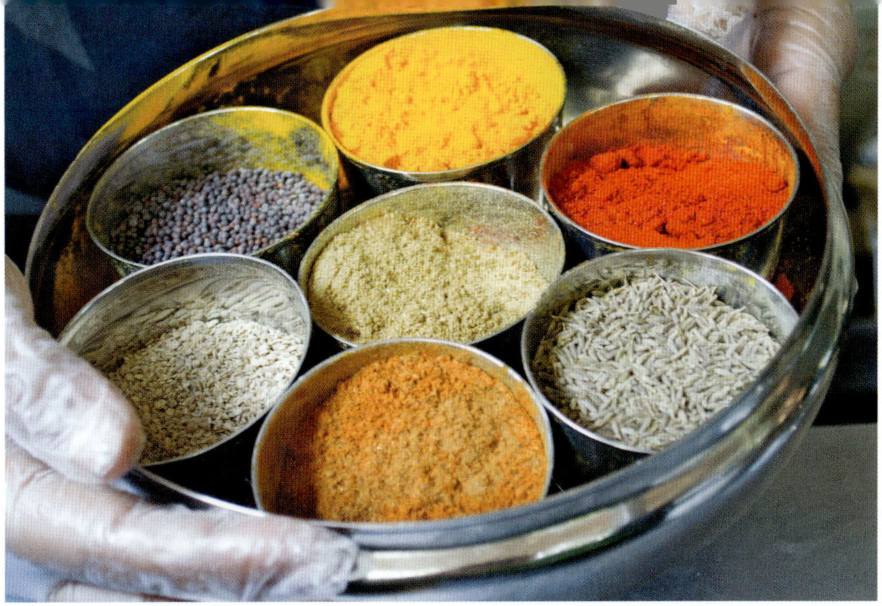

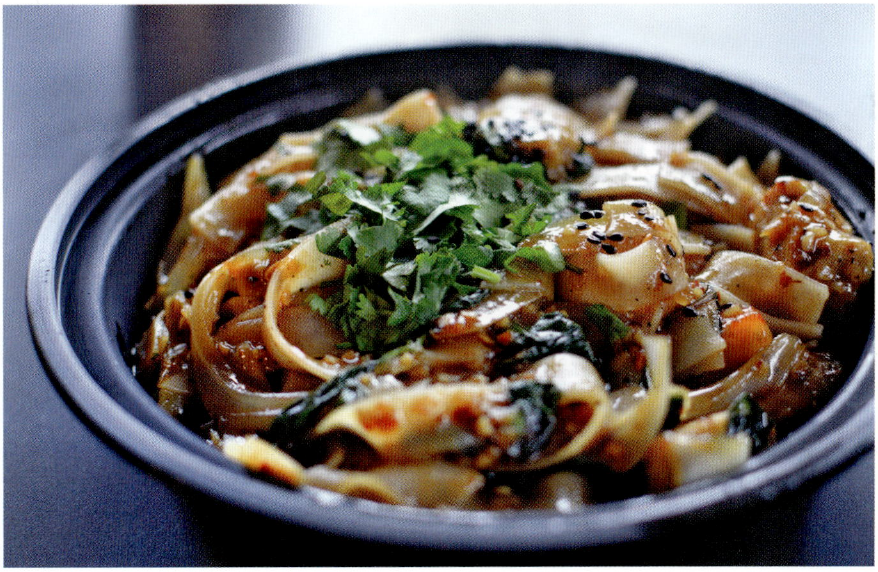

Top: Chef Ashley's spice box.

Bottom: Fusion's Drunken Noodles are Chef Ashley's personal favorite.

A question Dee and Ashley hear a lot is whether or not a dish is spicy. If you're worried about the heat, don't let that stop you from trying something new here. Their dishes can be ordered to any degree from not spicy at all to "Thai spicy," featuring Thai bird chilies. Indian dishes are full flavored with masala—the range of spices that make each dish a masterpiece of flavor and aroma, but Ashley can control the heat level in your dish without sacrificing taste, just by altering this mix. If, like me, you're all about the hot stuff, you're in luck, too.

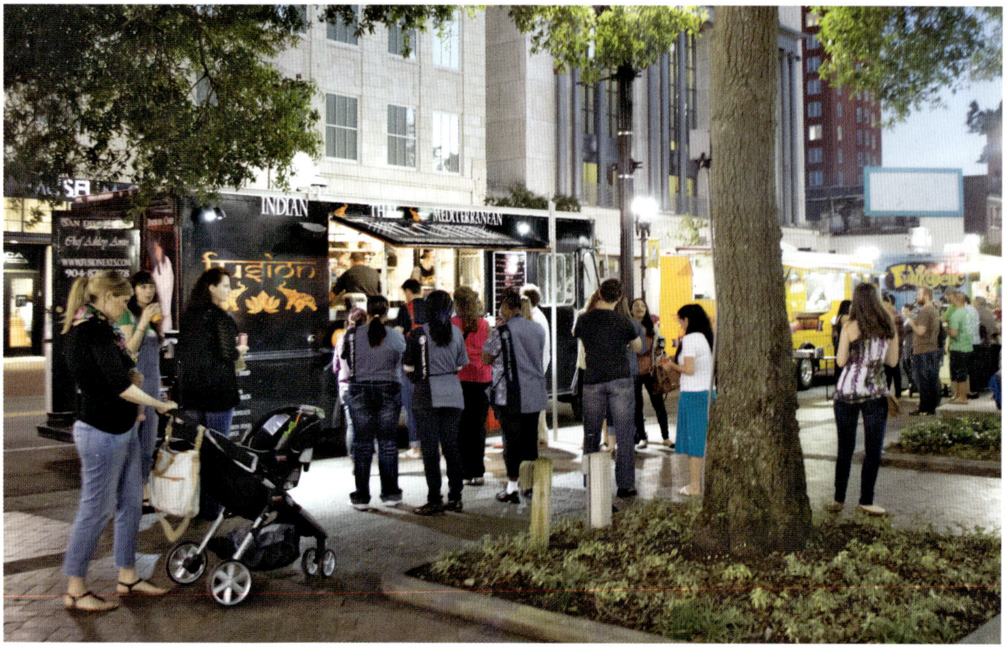

Bottom: Fusion at Jaxsons Night Market in Hemming Park.

Ashley's original design concept was a vividly painted truck with a Bollywood feel, brightly colored in purples, pinks and yellows, but in the interest of reigning in costs, she and Dee decided on a simple black-and-gold wrap from Above Paint. Now she's more than happy with the classic look. She does wish for a six burner, though (in case Dee is reading this and wondering what to get her for her birthday).

A regular lunch slot at Deutsche Bank has been a great fit, as a large number of international workers are stationed at the campus. They also serve lunches at Acosta and McKesson Streets on the Southside, AvMed and St. Vincents in Riverside, Hemming Park downtown, Nocatee for Food Truck Fridays and many more locations. Fusion frequently returns to EverBank Field for NFL tailgating food truck style. Festivals, fundraisers, catered affairs—Fusion has it covered.

I asked Ashley what advice she would give to prospective food truck owners. Her answer was this: "This is not a hobby—a food truck is a business. To become successful you need to be all in. Unlike a restaurant, you're moving around all the time, meeting new people. Return customers and repeat locations will contribute to your success."

Ashley is happy to share her recipe for one of her favorite dishes—Chicken Madras. I was beyond honored when she made it to order for me one evening during Food Truck Friday at Nocatee. It's one of my favorites now, too.

FUSION'S CHICKEN MADRAS
Recipe from Chef Ashley Amin

I grew up in England, home to some of the best Indian food you could ever eat. I remember eating Chicken Madras at our local curry house every other weekend. Mum never allowed us to eat chicken at home, being a strict vegetarian, so Dad used to take us out to get our chicken curry fix. I love cooking this curry, as it's quick and easy compared to other Indian curries. You can pretty much add any protein you like or simply cook it with vegetables. I like to cook this dish with fresh Thai chilies, but that's because I like it hot. Enjoy!

Serves 4

20 bite-sized cubes of chicken (about 1½ pounds), boiled and kept aside
2 tablespoons cooking oil
½ teaspoon cumin seeds
½ teaspoon black mustard seeds
3 whole cloves
2 cardamom pods
1 cinnamon stick
2 large curry leaves
1 teaspoon minced garlic
1 teaspoon grated ginger
2 medium brown onions, diced
2 medium-sized tomatoes, diced
2 teaspoons tomato purée
2 green chilies, chopped for extra heat
½ teaspoon turmeric powder
1 teaspoon madras curry powder
1 green bell pepper, diced
1 teaspoon lemon juice
½ teaspoon salt
½ teaspoon black pepper powder
1 teaspoon fenugreek powder
8 ounces water
1 small bunch cilantro, finely chopped

Heat up 2 tablespoons of oil in a large wok. Quickly add cumin seeds, mustard seeds, cloves, cardamom pods, cinnamon stick and curry leaves. You will see that everything is splattering. Do not burn the spices. As soon as you have dropped in all these spices, add minced garlic and ginger, remove from heat and cook for 30 seconds. Place back on heat and add onions. Sweat the onions till they are slightly brown.

Add tomatoes and cook on medium heat covered for about 4 minutes. Add tomato purée and simmer for 2 minutes on medium heat, covered.

Add the chicken, green chilies, turmeric powder, madras curry powder, bell pepper, lemon juice, salt and pepper. Stir all ingredients well. Simmer for about 5 minutes, covered. Add water and bring to a boil. Reduce heat and cook for another 5 minutes. Finally, add fenugreek powder and cilantro, stir and simmer for 2 minutes. Serve with hot basmati rice and your favorite Indian bread. Garnish with fresh cilantro leaves.

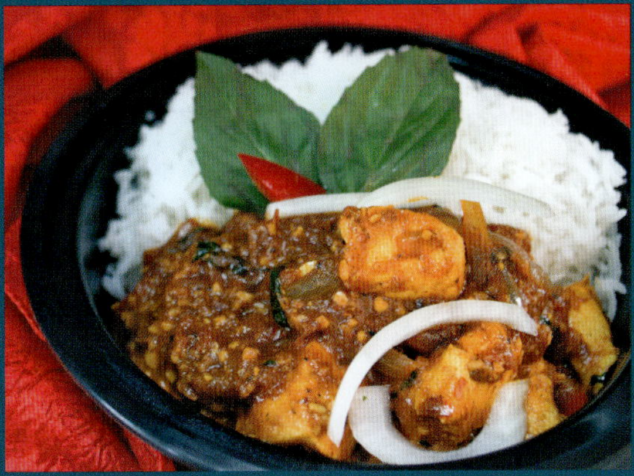

Chicken Madras Curry.

GOURMET AVIATOR

Alex Montanez

With a well-worn copy of the book *The $100 Hamburger: A Guide to Pilots' Favorite Fly-In Restaurants*, aviator Alex Montanez found himself seeking out great restaurant food around the country. While based in St Louis, he would take orders around the airport and then fly to a favorite restaurant, pack the plane with ribs and bring them back to his co-workers. Over time, he developed his own line of sauces.

Being in aviation, he was surprised to discover that no one had brought to market a wing sauce with an airplane theme, so he created his own "Aviator" Wing Sauce. Then he bottled a barbecue sauce that won an award and added a third sauce that won another. He marketed through home grilling parties and sold out almost every time. He resolved to scale up his business, and in 2007, he opened an online store to do just that.

Alex worked for Bell Helicopters and then took a contracted position at Northrop Grumman for a year, after which he was laid off. Heeding the call of friends who had always encouraged him to open a restaurant, he decided to start with a food truck.

He spent a year designing and building out the truck, which he bought from a junkyard next door to Northrop Grumman. Being a hot-rod enthusiast, he restored everything on the truck. He developed a business plan and got an Small Business Assocation loan to get the kitchen and get on the road. He designed the kitchen himself and hired M&R Specialty Trailers to fabricate it. Corr Digital designed the wrap, paying homage to the golden age of aviation. He equipped his truck to the same standards as a restaurant, making it a self-contained kitchen/prep/storage facility.

Gourmet Aviator was one of the original ten trucks opened in Jacksonville in 2012. Alex appreciates everyone who supported the trucks through the process of legislation and defining the appropriate level of regulation for trucks to operate downtown, as well as at the beaches.

The road wasn't always smooth for the frontrunners in Jacksonville's food truck scene. Hired by Florida Theater for a film festival, Alex was violently confronted by the owner of a nearby restaurant. The police got involved, measuring tapes came out, and the Gourmet Aviator was found to be parked just a few inches too close to his door based on the ordinance in place at the time. Most restaurant owners have embraced the truck scene, Alex points out.

Last year, the Travel Channel came to town for its *Grilled* outdoor cooking competition. Someone sent Alex a link and suggested he apply for the show, and out of 250 contenders,

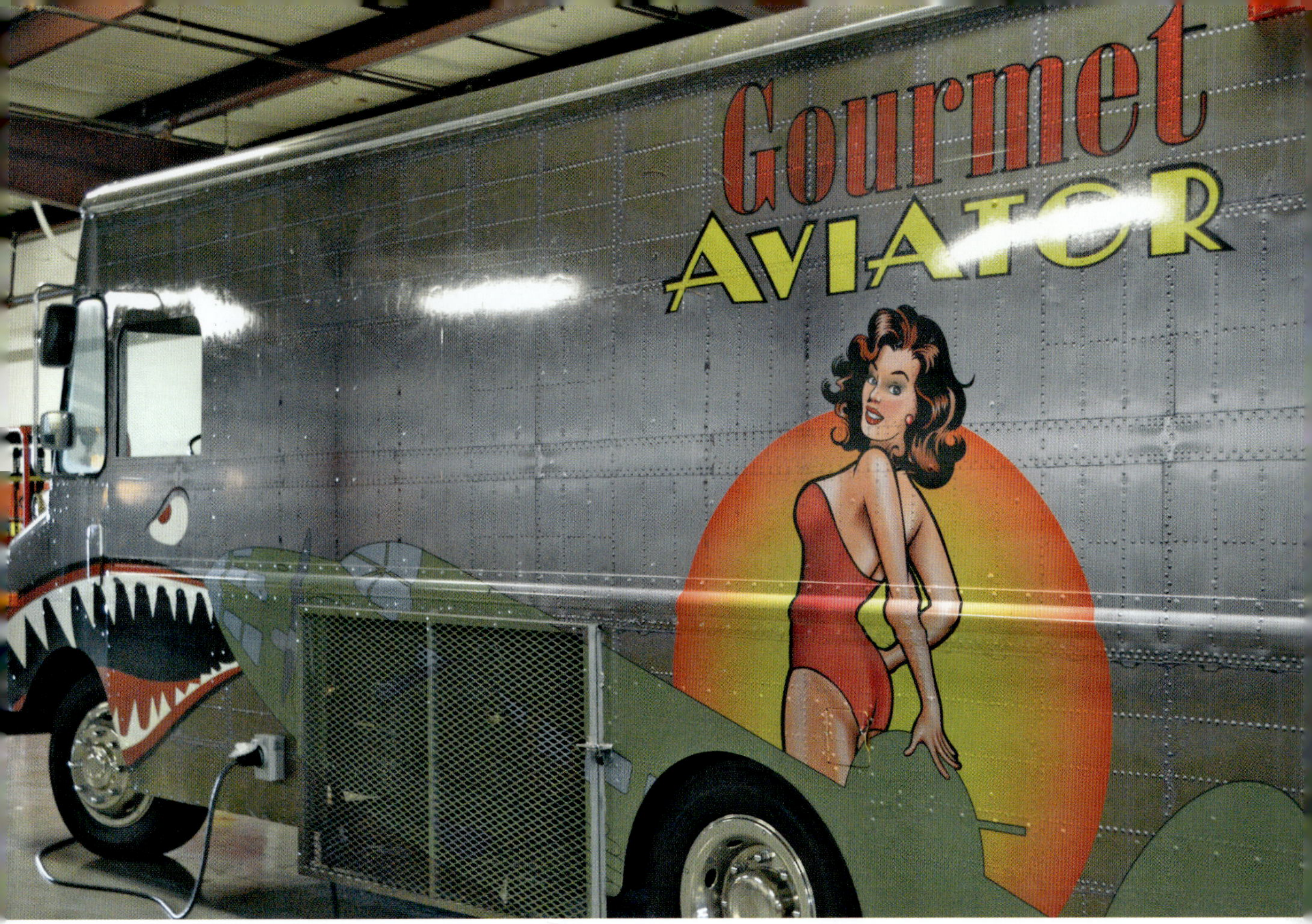

Gourmet Aviator.

Alex was one of the four who made it to the final competition. After three days of on-air outdoor competition and post-interviews, Alex came out on top, winning bragging rights as Jacksonville's Grill Master. He's incredibly humble about his big win. He admits he had a great time doing the show, and when we met last year, he was hoping to get a call for the championship.

Alex is one of the organizers of Jacksonville Food Trucks (JFT), a mentoring and lead-generating group for trucks. Its JFT Warehouse on Powers Avenue (next to Restaurant Depot) provides parking and dry goods storage, trash service, pest control and more. His JFT partner, Tom, helps truck operators with configuring their kitchens and does some build-out and restoration on site.

Alex taught a continuing education class at Florida State College in Jacksonville to help prospective food truck owners bridge the gap between expectations and reality. In his class, he covered every aspect of owning and operating a truck. He heeds his own advice, too, changing his menu depending on the venues and providing the food customers are

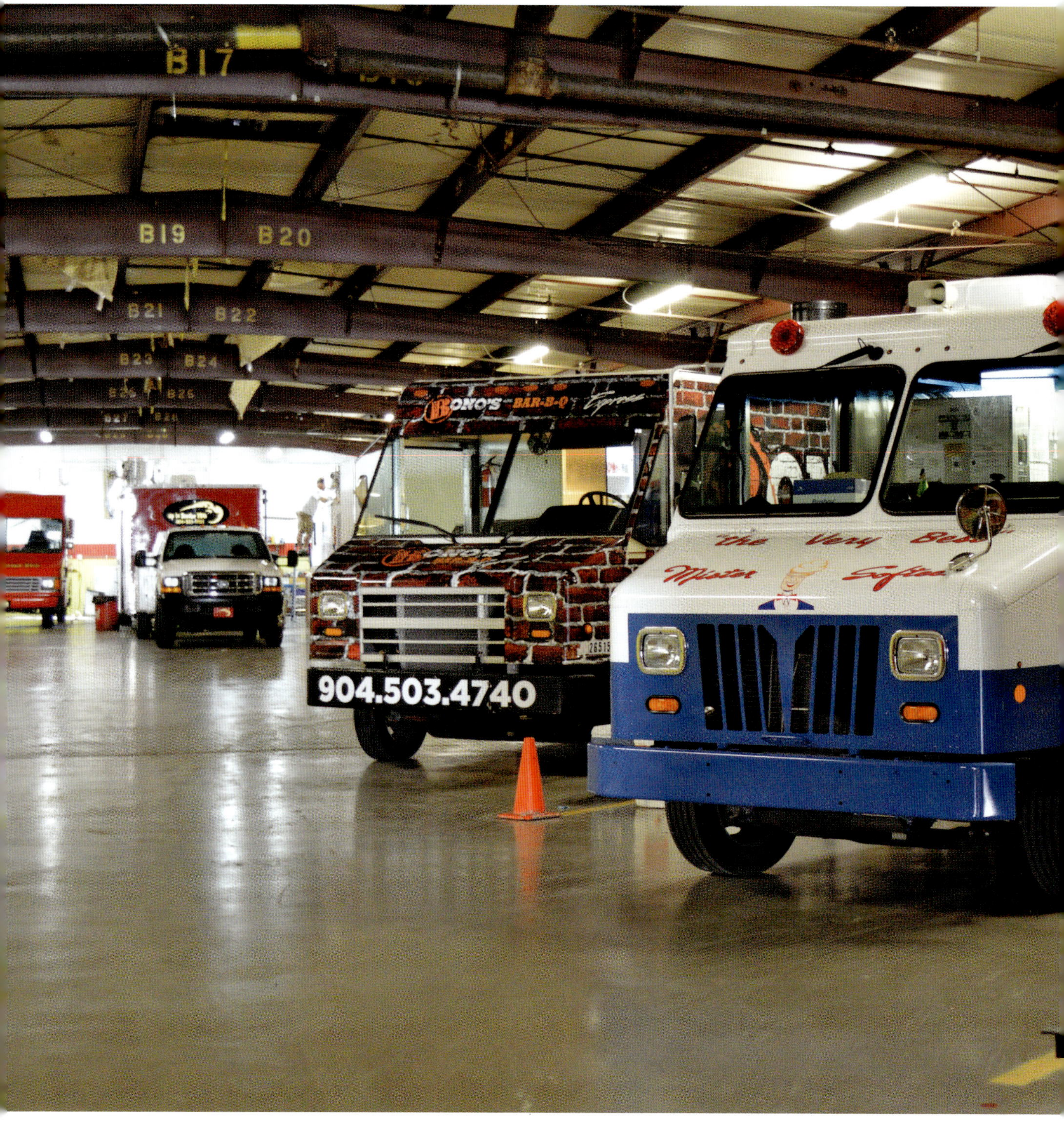
B17
B19
B20
B21
B22
B23
B24
B26
BONO'S BAR-B-Q Express
904.503.4740
the Very Best
Mister Softee

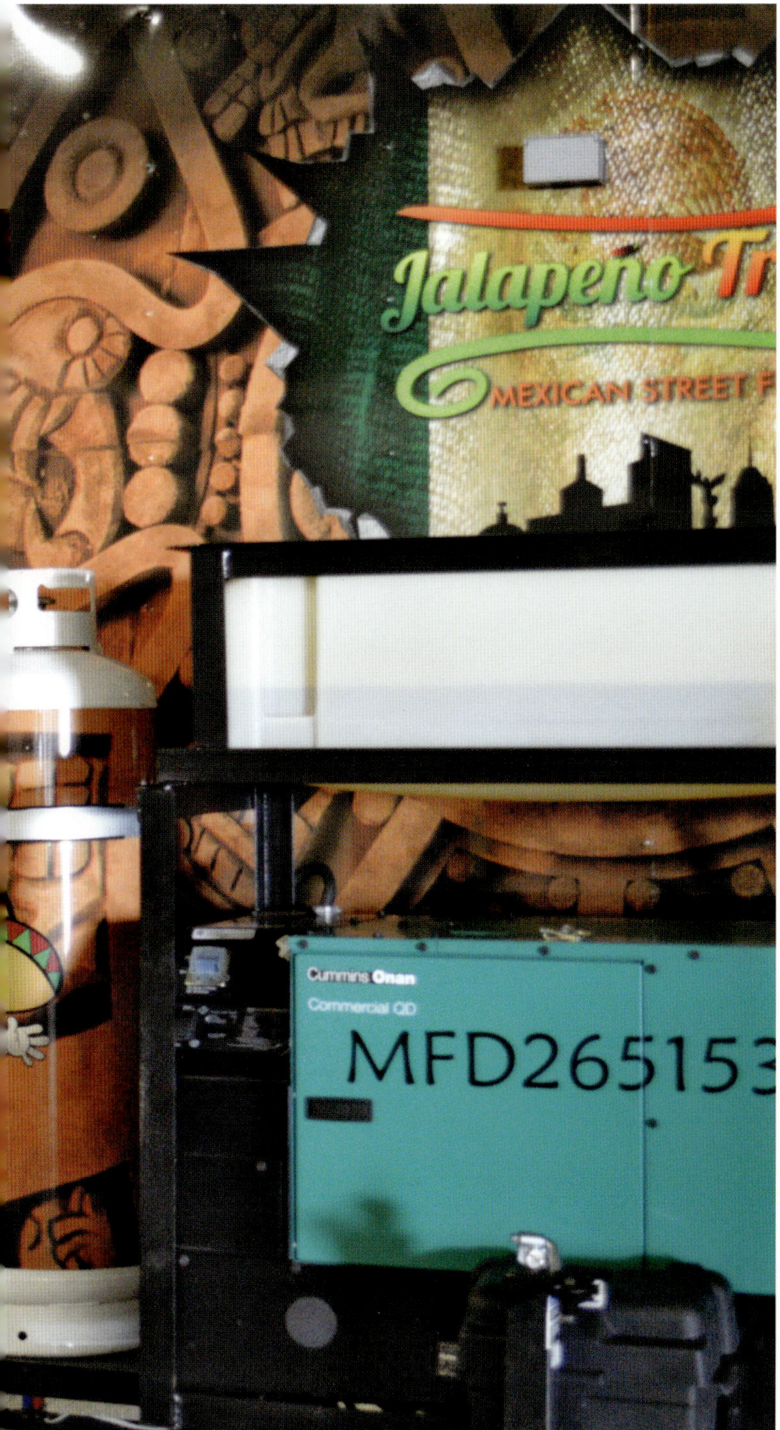

seeking. He didn't want to sell burgers at first, but the customer who wants a burger can get one from his truck now, along with the more exotic Plantain Sliders, inspired by the classic El Jibarito sandwich. Tostones are topped with roast pork, Alex's signature Aviator BBQ sauce, a made-from-scratch cilantro-ranch slaw and Aviator Mayo. About that pork, he roasts it with Puerto Rican spices for twelve hours, low and slow, until it is fall-apart tender.

All of his sauces are made fresh. A beer-based barbecue sauce is made with local brew. He makes compound mayos, such as the spicy Aviator Mayo and (with his Mexican Corndog) a Mayo-Ketchup, his version of a popular Puerto Rican condiment. Even the simple hamburger gets a cilantro-seasoned compound butter.

Nutella Empanadas are filled with Nutella hazelnut spread and sliced bananas, fried to a crisp, melty golden state and served with caramel sauce for dipping.

Vegetarian dishes include a great Fried Green Tomato Slider, topped with arugula and Alex's signature sauce.

Jacksonville Food Trucks Warehouse.

Alex's love and respect for food and its place in our culture stems from his childhood in Puerto Rico. His grandfather had a small farm with hogs and chickens, and one of his strong memories was every year during the holidays, when the large extended family would participate in butchering hogs and breaking them down for the feast. Everybody had a task. He left at seventeen, but these early memories—like grilling fish right on the beach and building a makeshift rotisserie to cook a turkey on a spit—are experiences he wants to pass on to his son, Javier, who is just starting to develop an interest in cooking and food.

Alex dreams of owning a restaurant that would continue the aviation theme on a grand scale, not unlike the Ninety-fourth Aerosquadron. But it would have to be near the water so people could fly their seaplanes in. He envisions a massive room with an airplane inside and a museum-like design with aviation memorabilia and merchandise like flight jackets.

Alex readily admits this business is a labor of love. He is selective about when and where he works. He often sacrifices margin to participate in larger events like the Jacksonville Jazz Festival, which netted him far, far less than the cost of entry. He gets calls for catering assignments and private events based on the exposure, though, so the sacrifice has paid off for him. He competes in Food Truck Wars when they come to St. Augustine and, so far, has placed in the top two or three out of over eighty trucks—he is, after all, Jacksonville's Grill Master.

Follow Gourmet Aviator on Facebook to find out where he will be serving his award-winning food. For more information, a full catering menu and contact information, visit Alex online at www.gourmetaviator.com.

THE HAPPY GRILLED CHEESE

Anthony Hashem

One of a kind. That's how I would describe the Happy Grilled Cheese (HGC) truck, and the same definitely goes for its iconoclastic owner, Anthony Hashem.

Jacksonville native and self-proclaimed "Sultan of all things CHEESY," Anthony grew up working in his family's restaurant, the Desert Sand Sandwich Shop on Beach Boulevard. He worked in several restaurants from childhood through college, but he made his career in cellphone sales and service. One day in late 2012, he decided his necktie had become more of a noose, and he walked out the door. In November 2012, he started fixing up an old cafeteria truck, and on February 27, 2013, the Happy Grilled Cheese was on the road.

The truck itself is a rolling work of art. The original, hand-painted orange, red and white graphics were created by local muralist Jessica Becker, who also painted Chew Chew. With Jess's whimsical hand-painted art on the outside, and a hardworking, fun-loving crew cranking out toasty, melty goodness inside, the Happy Grilled Cheese is on a mission—to provide quality, fresh food at great prices to every corner of Northeast Florida.

Anthony purposely kept his cheese choices more mainstream, to keep food costs in check and give customers something familiar they can relate to. There are seemingly endless variations on the regular menu, however, plus more on the daily specials board. Rumor has it there are even a few "secret menu" items that regulars can coax them to create from time to time. They do house-made soups and fresh-cut potato chips.

My first HGC sighting was in June 2013, during the Second Annual Jax Truckies Food Truck Championship at the Burrito Gallery in downtown Jax. The Crunch Melt (a grilled cheese sandwich with homemade chips, mac 'n' cheese, grilled onions and tomato soup) won HGC the award for Most Innovative item at that outing. I'd love to say I tried it, but the lines were so long I decided just to snap a few photos, chill out and enjoy a local brew from presenting sponsor Intuition Ale Works with Cari Sanchez-Potter.

I finally caught up with the popular truck one Saturday afternoon in the heat of July when it was parked in the lot at the Winn-Dixie shopping center at the corner of San Pablo and Beach Boulevards. The Intracoastal area has played host to a few trucks since, primarily in the parking lots of offices off San Pablo near the Mayo Clinic.

My first taste of the HGC turned out to be a great choice. Since I was born in San Diego, I went with the California Melt, a colorfully layered

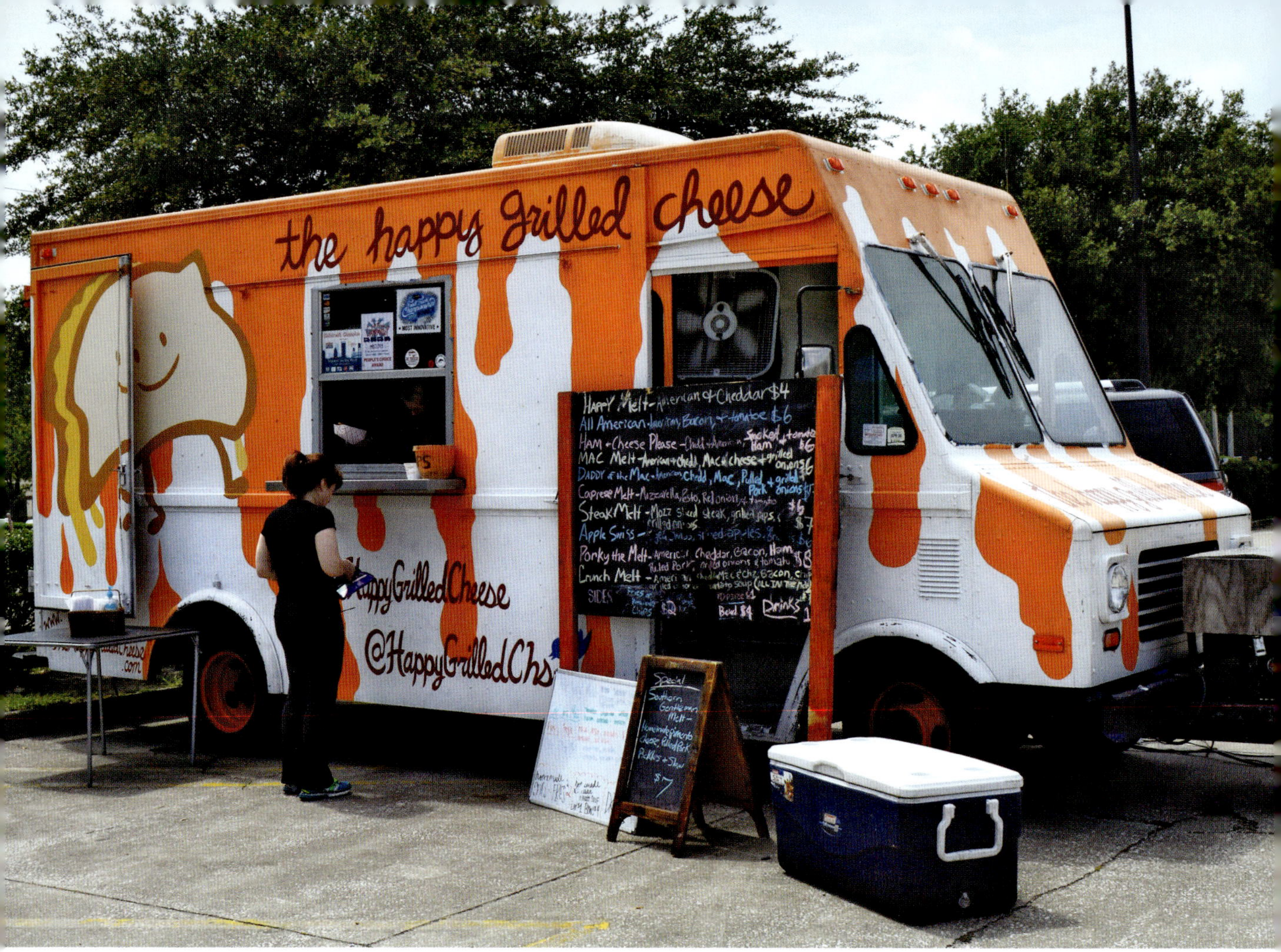

The Happy Grilled Cheese.

Opposite, top: The California Melt from HGC.

Opposite, bottom: HGC's Apple Swiss Melt.

concoction of American and cheddar cheeses, sliced turkey, avocado, tomato and bacon. It delivered exactly the flavor and textures I expected. Oh, and as a bonus, their house-made chips were the bomb! They are sliced and cooked in small batches on the truck. Get some if they have them when you go.

Probably their most popular sandwich is the All American Melt, with American cheese, bacon and tomato slices. Another top seller, the Mac Melt, features homemade mac and cheese and grilled onions, along with melty American and cheddar cheeses. Yes, this is a grilled cheese sandwich with mac and cheese *inside*. If you think that's wild, meet the Daddy of the Mac Melt. Think Mac Melt and then add some pulled pork to that bad-boy! Now who's your daddy?

My new favorite is the simple Apple Swiss Melt: Swiss cheese, chopped Granny Smith apples, grilled onion. It's great when you want something full flavored yet vegetarian.

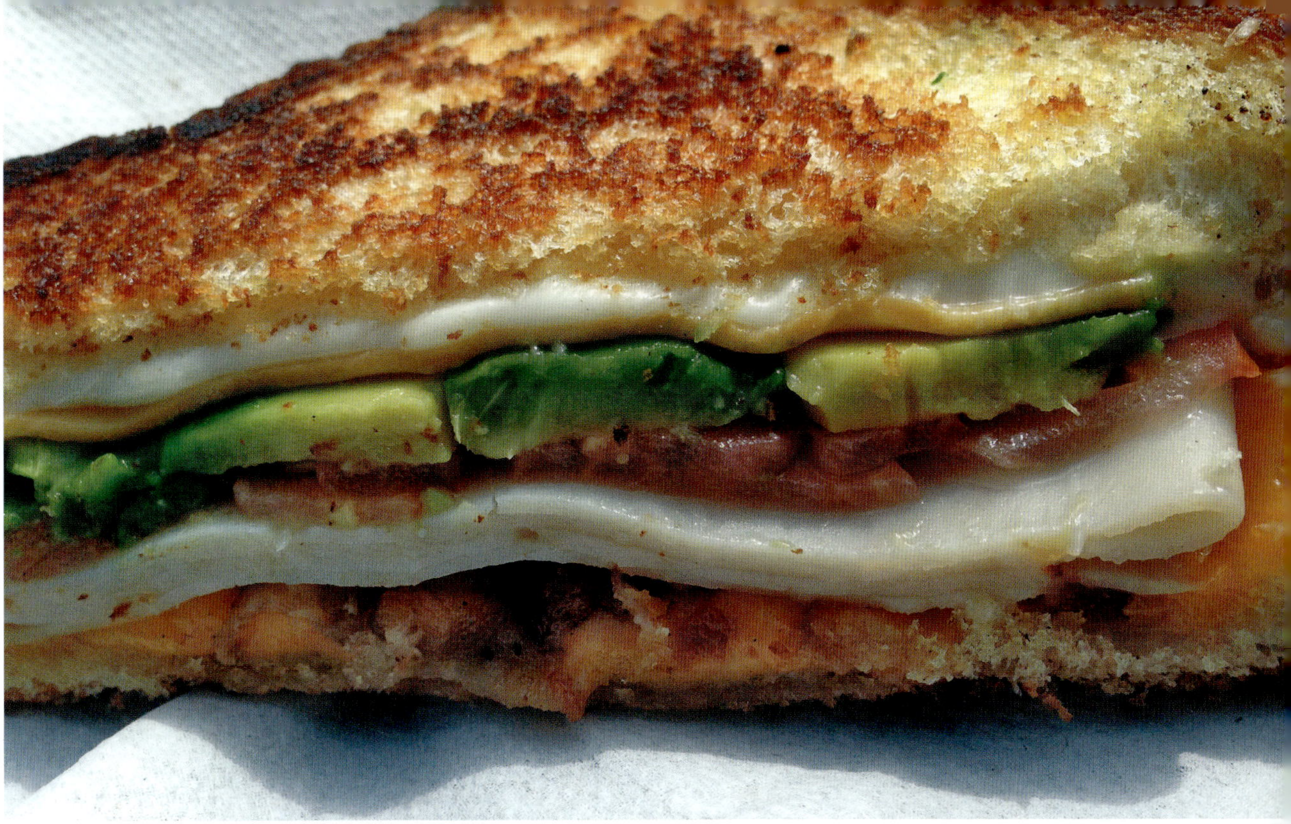
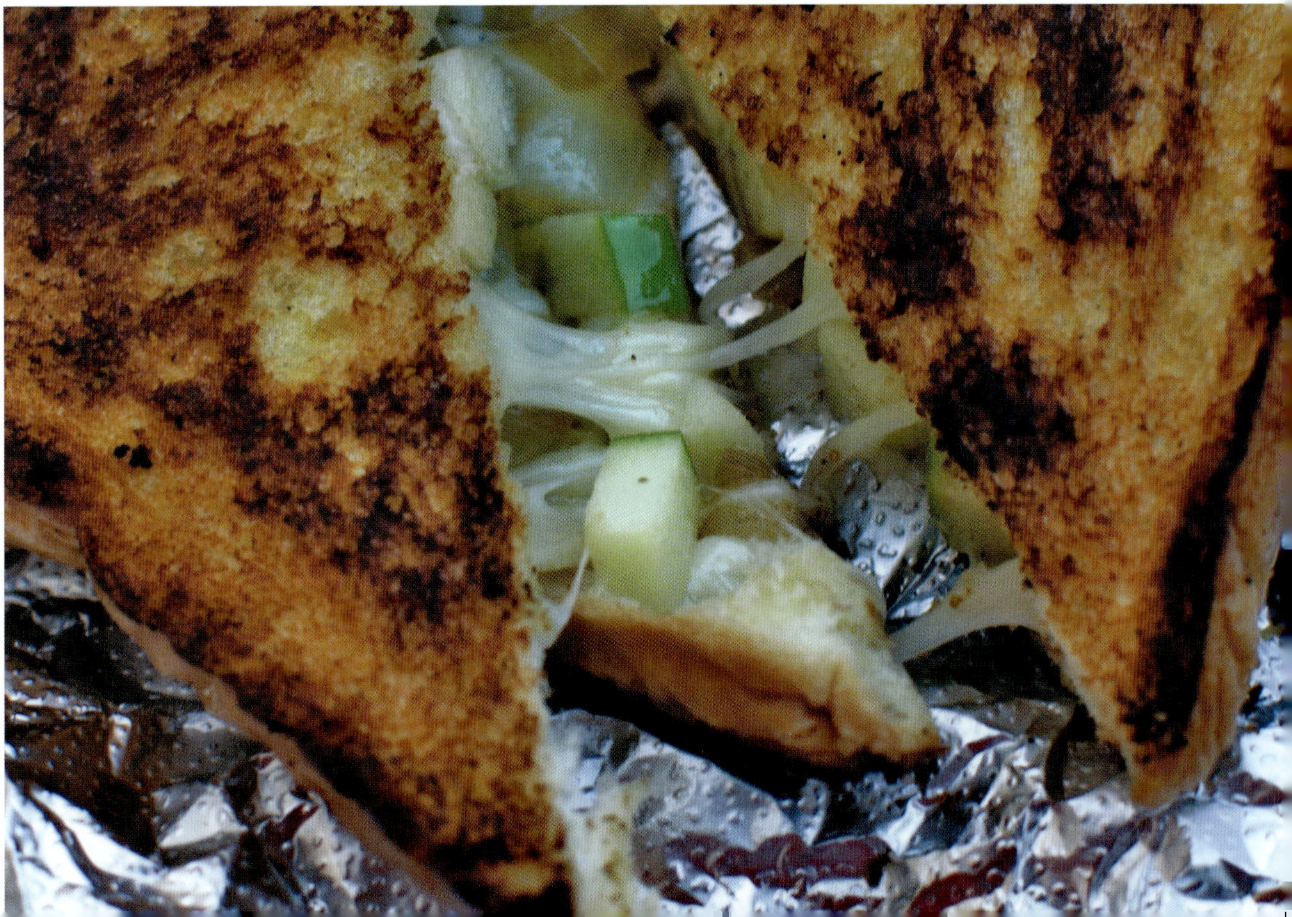

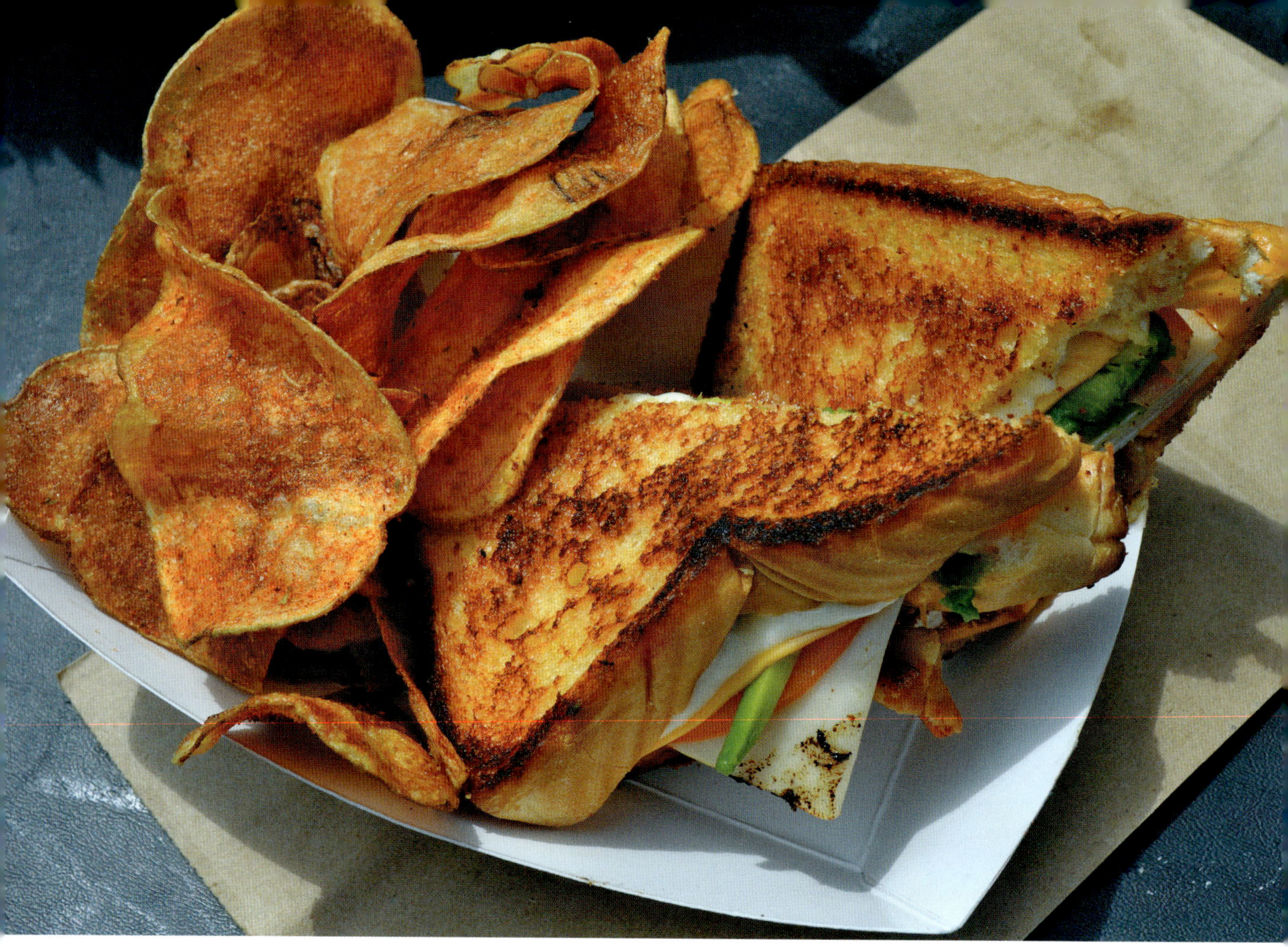

California Melt and house-made chips from HGC.

Anthony tells me he has never been happier or felt more successful in his life. That having been said, there was a point where the pace of his business picked up so quickly he just had to hold on for the ride. He wanted to run a food truck business—bam, he had one. He planned to own a restaurant, and it is happening. He has secured a prime storefront location in Five Points, and current estimates are that Happy Grilled Cheese the restaurant will open in the spring of 2015. Plans are to have the same basic items as the truck, plus many more.

In the "it's a small world" department, Anthony went to high school with Jax Truckies founder Mike Field, and worked for a certain wireless carrier with Dee Amin from Fusion Food Truck. In fact, Ashley (Fusion's chef and Dee's wife) told me Anthony was instrumental in helping them make the decision to get trucking. I suspect there are more than a few others Anthony has inspired and mentored. In fact, he is so well connected in the food truck world I good-naturedly refer to him as the

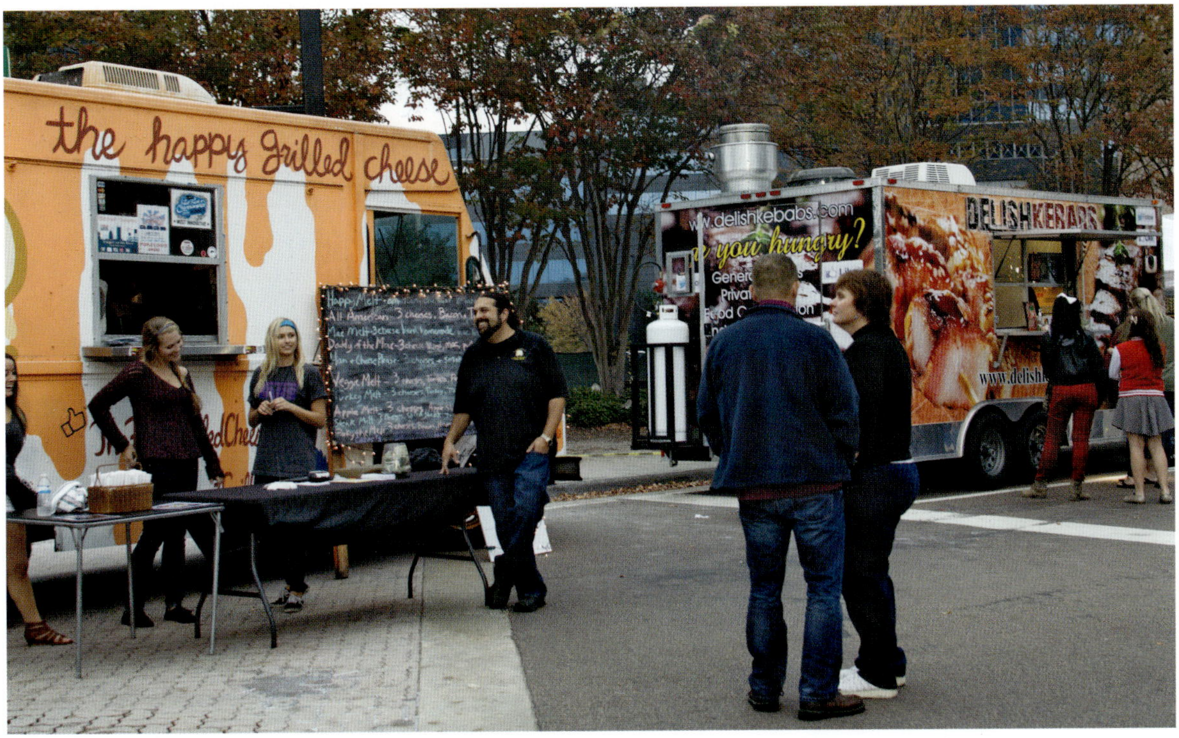

HGC at the Jacksonville Landing.

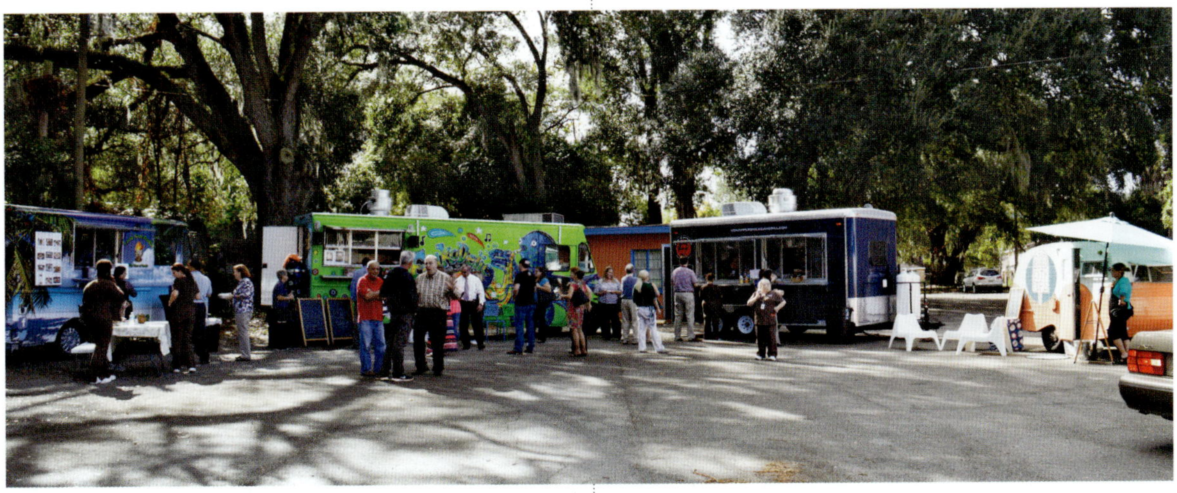

Jax Food Truck Food Court.

"Godfather of Grilled Cheese." His truck crew operates without him on board most days now while he works on the next big thing.

When he learned that the Beach Boulevard property his family had owned for decades was going to be sold, Anthony pitched an idea to the family to reinvent it as a venue for food trucks. He had seen similar business structures in Austin, and he was thrilled to have the opportunity to both help save a piece of their family's history and build a new business that his parents and uncle could operate.

Jax Food Truck Food Court opened on December 1, 2014. Hosting a rotating roster of three to five trucks per day, with a variety of cuisines and at least one dessert option (for all sweet-

Danilo's Famous Lumpia at Jax Food Truck Food Court.

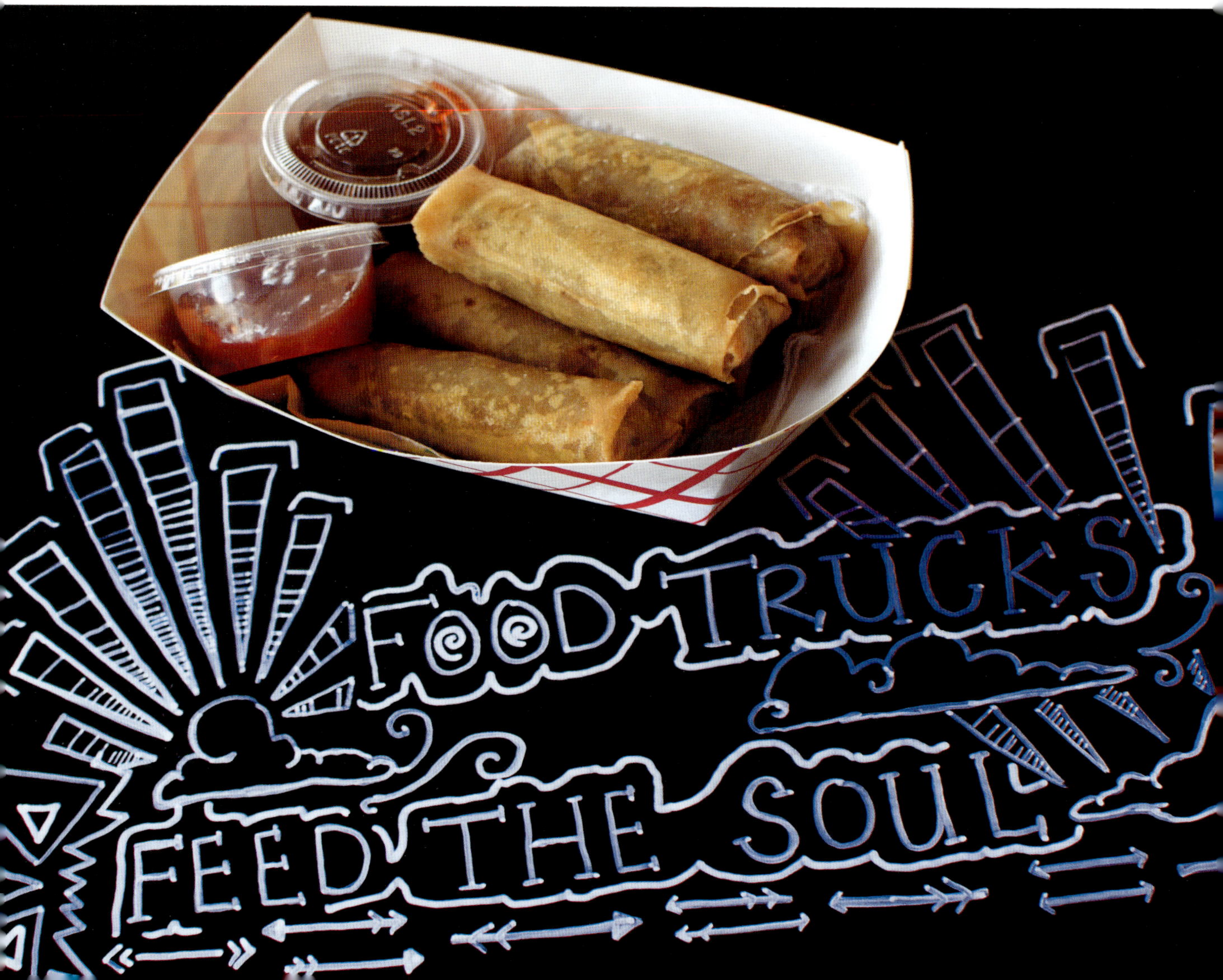

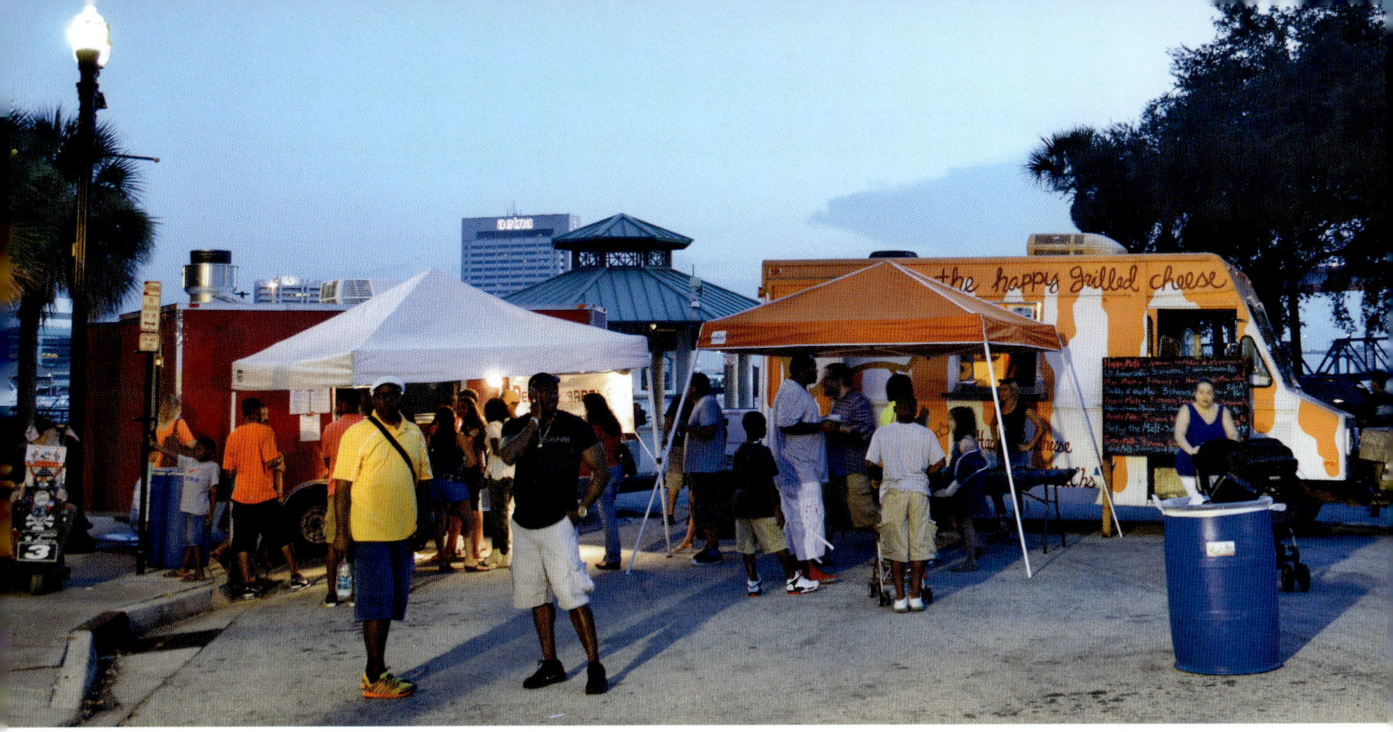

Delish Kabobs and the Happy Grilled Cheese parked near the St. Johns River for Jax Truckies Block Party at the Jacksonville Landing.

toothed readers out there). There is ample parking, a good selection of food truck fare at great prices and plenty of outdoor and climate-controlled indoor seating. It's a great way to check out new trucks. Jax Food Truck Food Court is open weekdays during lunch hours at 3814 Beach Boulevard next to Kuhn Flowers.

Anthony invested in the development of Food Truck Finder U.S.A., a GPS-based mobile application that helps hungry diners find their favorite trucks. It was a slow start getting local trucks onboard, but every month, we see a few more joining the party. Download the app for free from iTunes or Google Play.

Look for HGC at office parks, local craft breweries, festivals and fundraisers. The bright orange-and-white truck is a regular sight at the Jax Truckies Food Truck Block Parties at the Jacksonville Landing. It is a family friendly truck, with familiar food kids and adults love. HGC loves doing catering gigs too and is down for everything from children's parties to wedding reception noshing.

Keep it cheesy, Jacksonville! Follow @HappyGrilledChs on Twitter and Facebook and find the truck's service locations with Food Truck Finder or on Jax Truckies Facebook page.

JALAPEÑO TRUCK

Kerri Dennis and Hector Carrichi

Walk to the window at the massive Jalapeño Truck, and you'll most likely be greeted by a petite blonde with a great big smile.

Kerri Dennis got the idea for a food truck when she started reading about the trucks in LA. Having traveled extensively in South America, she knew she wanted to go with a Latin theme. She knew it was beyond her scope, with no restaurant experience, and she'll be the first to tell you it was her partner of three years, Hector Carrichi, who made the Jalapeño Truck possible.

Hector learned to cook from his mother and grandmother in Mexico City. He has worked in several restaurants and is familiar with many cuisines, but of course, he loves Mexican best.

Kerri and Hector shopped around for a used truck or trailer, and not

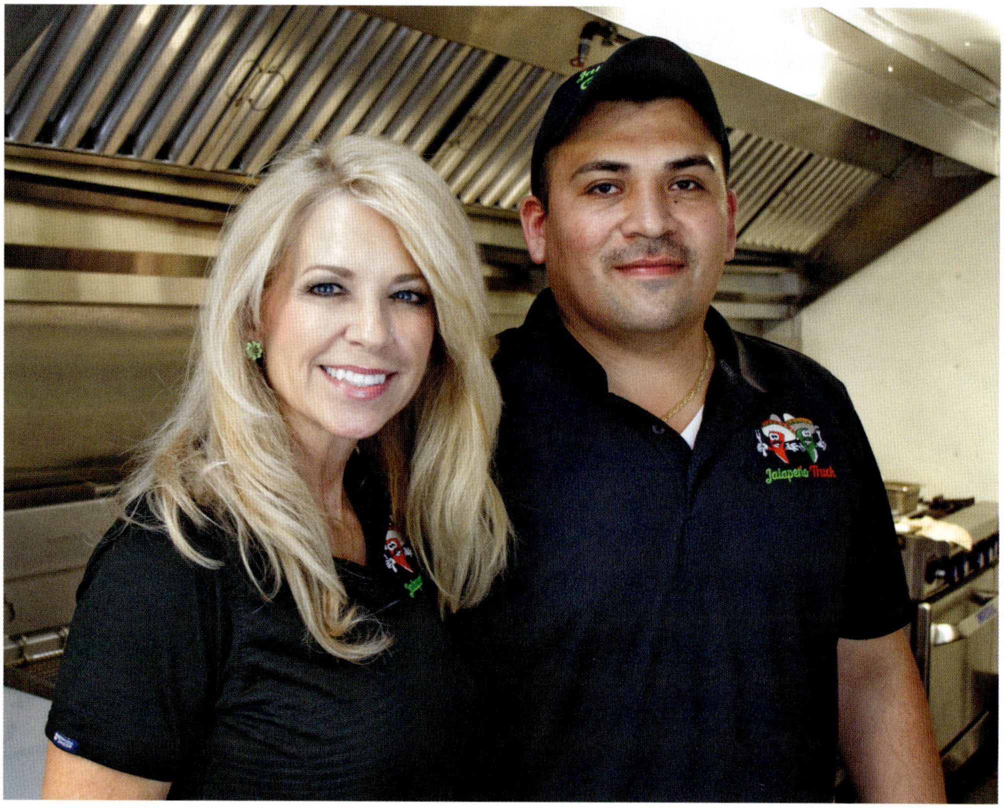

Partners Kerri Dennis and Hector Carrichi of the Jalapeño Truck.

finding anything that suited them, they decided to have one built. They took masking tape to the floor of their garage and out onto the driveway and drew pictures on cardboard for the appliances, placing them in various configurations until they had their workflow planned. She says they probably drove the folks at M&R Specialty Trailers crazy, calling to check on the trailer constantly. Corr Digital did a great job creating the wrap design. They placed the order in February and picked up the trailer in early July 2014. From Kerri's initial

Jalapeño line in progress.

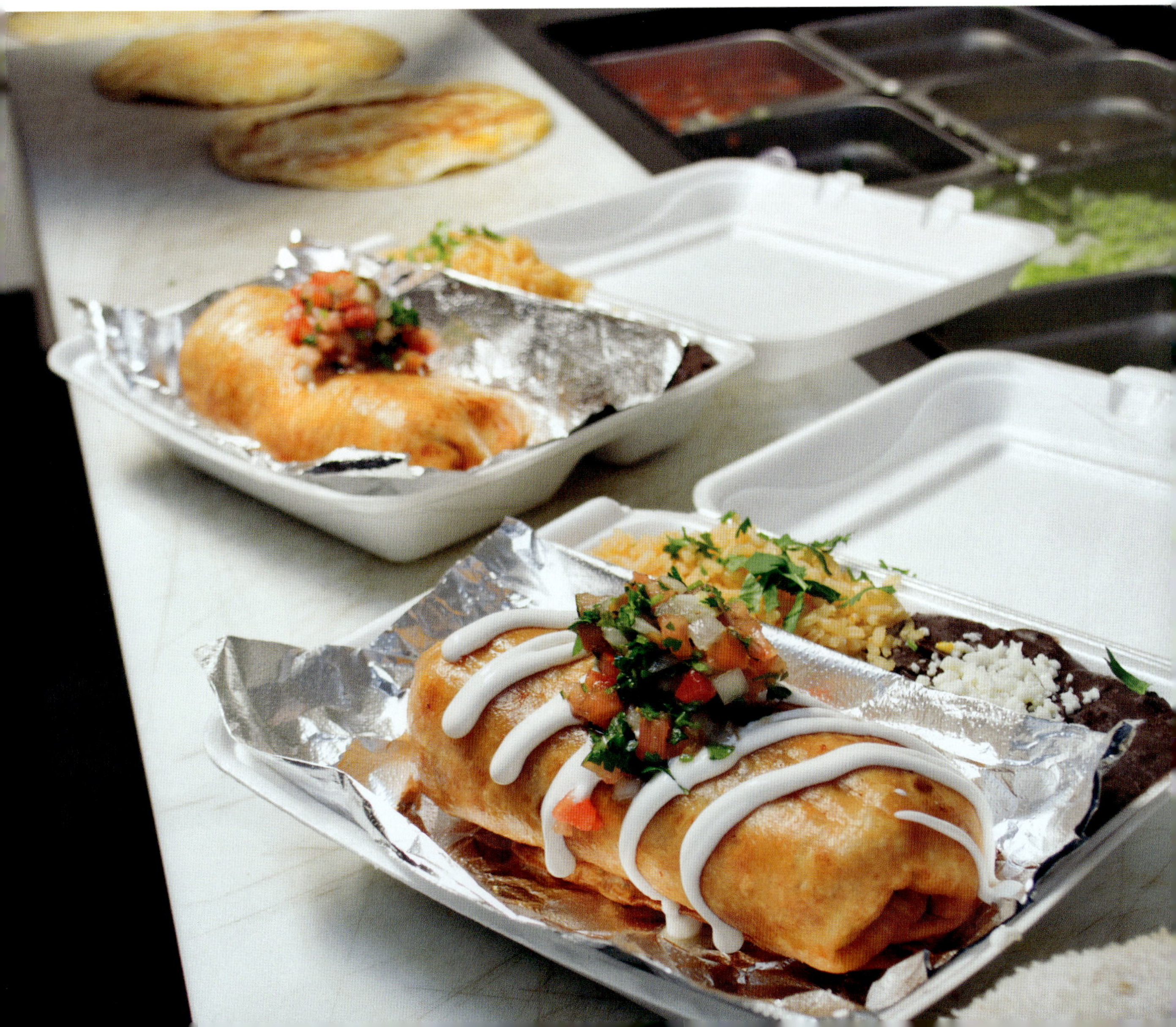

idea to wheels on the street was, all told, about five or six years.

Kerri has a solid business background. She is constantly analyzing, planning and strategizing. As a founding partner of the biggest flight training school in the country, she understands complying with regulations and licensing and managing a business. She does a great job on social media. Beyond sharing their locations, she is creating a community of regulars who love the truck and love seeing themselves in the pictures she posts on Instagram. She tries to project fun, lightheartedness and love. Their philosophy is that everybody is important, every interaction matters. They want to make everyone's day brighter, both by their interaction with them and by what they feed them.

And then there is the food. Hector, Kerri and their crew are making real-deal, authentic Mexican street food on the Jalapeño Truck: huaraches, pombazos, tlacoyos, sopes, tortas. They make all their own seasonings, their own chorizo from fresh-ground pork and fresh salsas on the roomy, well-organized truck.

Early on, friends who are also Mexican restaurant operators warned them they wouldn't succeed selling traditional Mexican dishes and that they would have to "Americanize" everything. Ironically, when these same friends visit the truck, they buy the authentic Mexican dishes. I do, too. In fact, when I visit the Jalapeño Truck, I usually ask Kerri what I should get. She hasn't steered me wrong yet.

They do offer some more basic things to cater to crowds. There are burritos, chimichangas and even jalapeño poppers. They also offer a quesadilla that they call "la Gringa." Whatever they make, they keep the flavors authentic and the preparation fresh.

The first time I waited in line for goodies from the Jalapeño Truck was at a food truck rally at Best Bet in Orange Park on one of the hottest days in August. I didn't realize at the time that they had been on the road for just a few short weeks. I told Kerri I was thrilled to see an authentic Mexican menu and asked her to decide what I should have. After some deliberation, she decided I needed to try the Pombazo, a massive sandwich on a Telera roll that is dipped in brick red guajillo pepper sauce and then seared on the grill. The filling options are spicy chicken, papas y chorizo or pollo a la mexicano. It was so delicious and full flavored, and the freshness of the ingredients really came through. I had to circle back after I ate it to tell them how much I enjoyed it and thank them for keeping it authentic.

The most recent time I visited they were parked downtown in front of Interline Brands. They invited me on the truck, so I got to watch my lunch being made. I could see firsthand the attention to detail and the quality ingredients they put into each and every dish.

The tacos are a basic Mexican style, with simple, fresh flavors. They usually

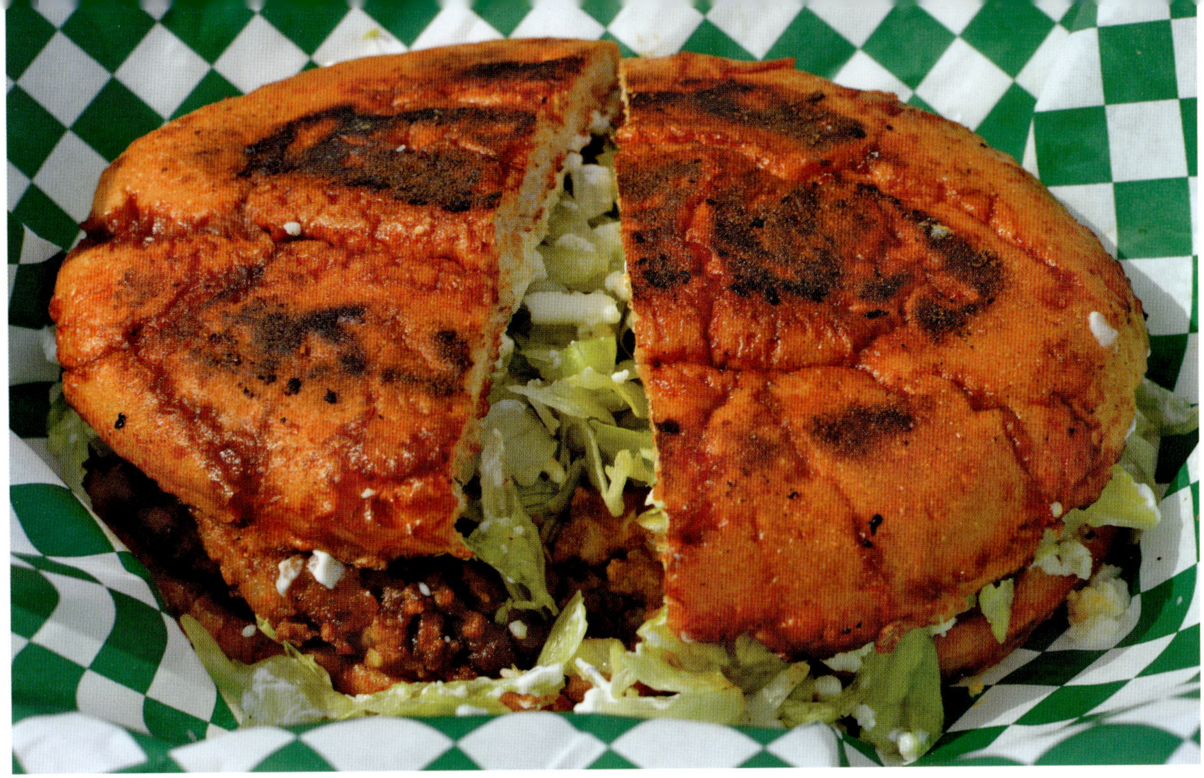

Above: Pombazo from Jalapeño Truck.

Below: The Machete from Jalapeño Truck starts with a fresh-griddled masa shell.

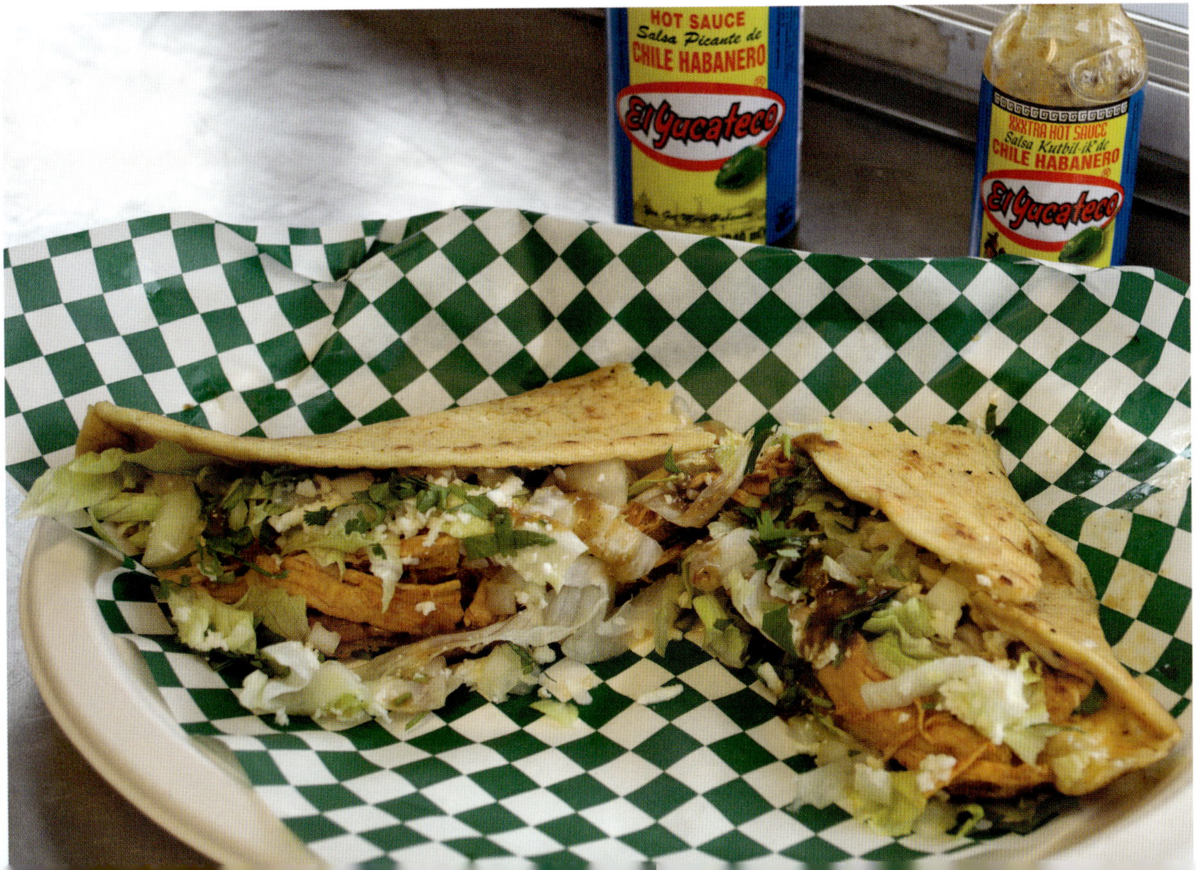

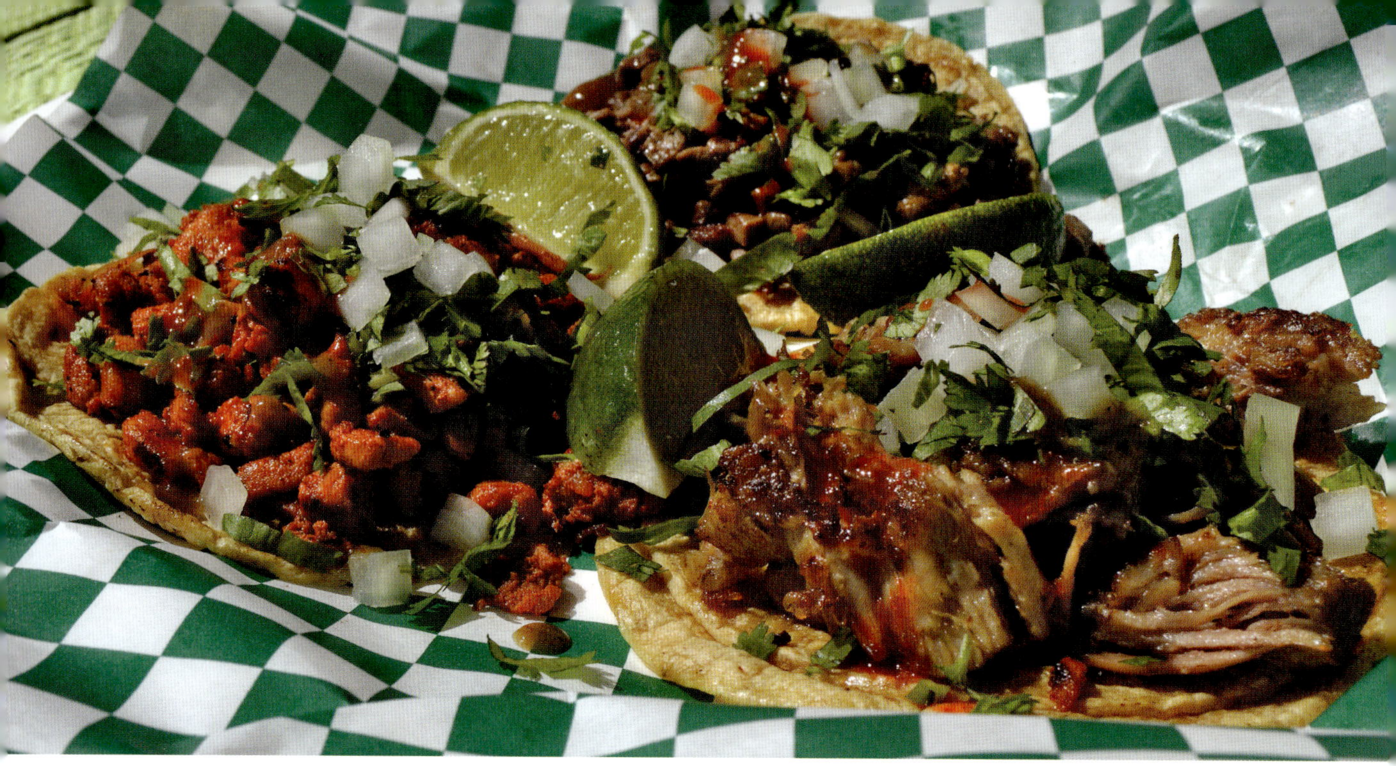

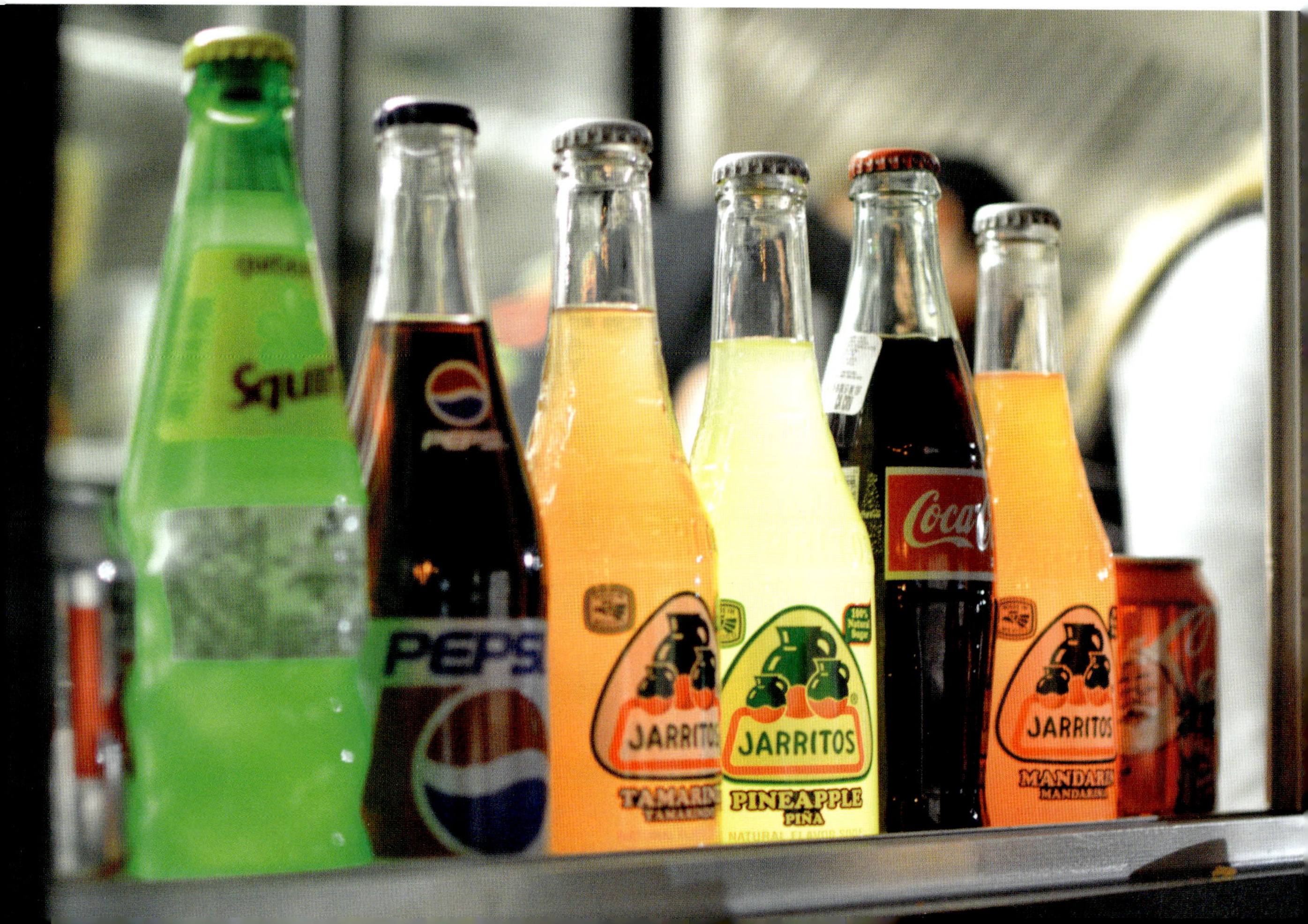
JARRITOS
JARRITOS
PINEAPPLE
PIÑA
JARRITOS

have chorizo, carne asada, el pastor and some of the best carnitas you'll find out there. There are familiar brands of bottled hot sauces on the back ledge of the trailer, among them my favorite, El Yucateco, a habanero sauce from Oaxaca.

The cuisine of Mexico is very seasonal. Kerri tells me the menu board at the Jalapeño Truck will include more hearty classical dishes when the weather gets cooler, with lighter fare in the summer. They like to create "not so secret" specials, too.

Their setup includes several tables and chairs for diners. Another truck operator saw her lugging them onto the truck one day and suggested she would soon tire of the extra work. Kerri says the opposite is true. They love having their customers chill out and enjoy their food. She believes that if everyone concentrated on the basic human comforts, the world would be a better place. Kerri loves to call Hector out of the kitchen to watch people gathered at the truck, enjoying their food. She and Hector love feedback from their customers. They are in this business for the love of it.

A slave to the gym for years, these days Kerri feels the burn tackling fifty-pound bags of onions, lifting them up into her cart and onto the truck. She knew the business would

Opposite, top: Tres Tacos from Jalapeño Truck.

Opposite, bottom: The beverage selection on the Jalapeño Truck.

Kerri takes a lunch order at Jalapeño Truck.

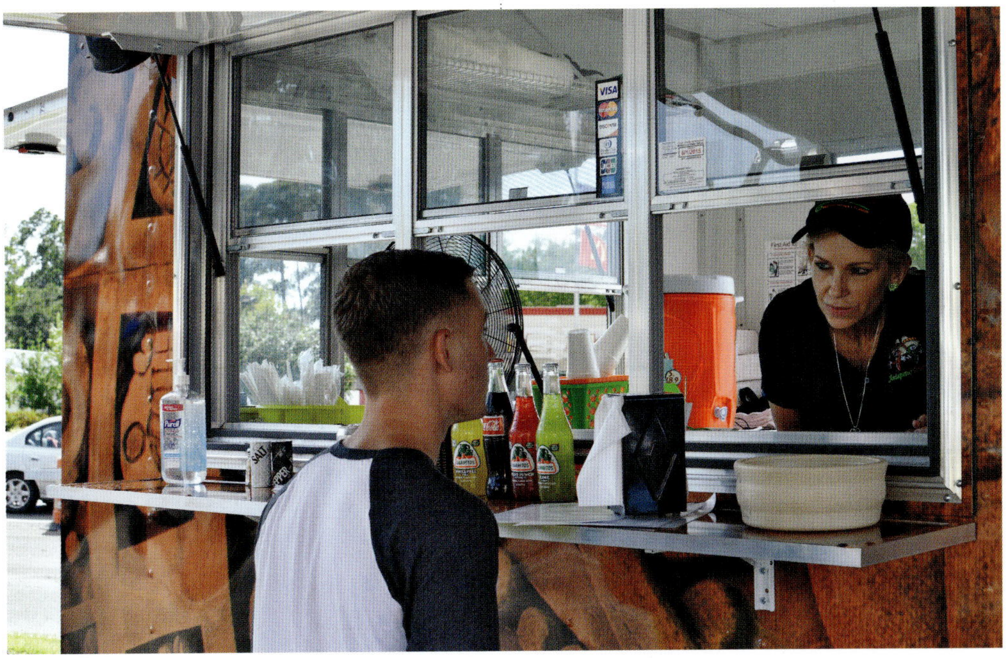

be physically demanding and time consuming, but there were certain things she promised herself she was not going to sacrifice—her hair, her nails; however, once she was working on the truck in one-hundred-plus-degree heat, she cut herself some slack. After the weather cooled down, she went right back to being her neatly put-together self.

When Kerri started looking for trucks in town, she found Alex at Gourmet Aviator. She asked him for advice, and he was more than willing to share his knowledge. In fact, Kerri says the people she has met along the way in this industry have all been extremely supportive despite essentially being in competition with one another. In her previous business environment, competition was more cutthroat. The truck operators, she observes, are all banded together, but they are also fiercely independent and completely in charge of how they do things. That suits her style. She confesses to having a streak of anarchy in her, and I don't doubt it.

Kerri isn't hoping for a brick-and-mortar restaurant like so many truckies, but some day, she would just like to find a nice rustic setting where she and Hector could park the Jalapeño Truck full time and continue to serve the great food their customers crave. Until then, if you want to chomp down on some of the best Mexican food in Jacksonville, book them to cater your next big gig or just check out their menu, you can find them via their website, www.jalapenotruck.com; Facebook page, JalapenoTruckJax; and Twitter and Instagram @JalapenoTruck.

THE LOVING CUP

Matthew Lennon

It was Fourth of July weekend 2013. A group of friends were hanging out; dinner was done and the wine was flowing. The next day, they would head to Sarasota Springs to catch up with the Phish tour. They were joking about making back their ticket money to the three-day show by selling shots of wine online when someone suggested they sell coffee, and as it turned out, that was exactly what Matthew Lennon had in mind.

Matthew (his friends call him Matty) was the manager of the Starbucks on Third Street in Jacksonville Beach at that time. His dream was to fuse his love of music with his growing appreciation for coffee. He wanted to open a mobile coffeehouse, travel the country, work all the tours, have a blast and rake in the cash. It sounded like a great plan.

The trailer had been purchased, and the next logical step was to select a name for the fledgling business. The enthusiastic friends reviewed several options, and the consensus was that if Phish played Loving Cup that weekend, their friend would *have* to make that the name of his new business. The plot was hatched.

As luck would have it, the song was nowhere on the set list—that is, until the last number of the last day. Matthew Lennon's new coffee business had the perfect name. A call to a local graphic artist, Karen Klefman, yielded a logo design. AB Signs created the vinyl, and soon the Loving Cup was on a roll, figuratively speaking. In fact, the very day the logo was applied to the truck, Matty got a call from a prospect who would become one of his biggest regular customers.

He got the idea then about owning a mobile coffee bar, and as luck would have it, one of his regular customers at Starbucks was Chris Dickerson from Corner Taco. This was at the time when Chris was at the peak of his success with his Airstream taco trailer and getting ready to take the step up to brick and mortar. Chris served as both inspiration and sounding board while Matty charted his future.

He had been searching for a truck that would allow for a double-line system, where you order from one window and pick up at another, but he couldn't find anything like that in his budget. The trailer he ended up purchasing was a former T-shirt and college game day merchandise sales trailer. The truck was on eBay when Matt found it and started negotiating with the owner. After four weeks, he sealed the deal at just $5,000, and in July 2013, he pulled it home to Jacksonville. At this point, it was simply an empty, solid white shell. He worked on it a little at a time and kept his Starbucks job.

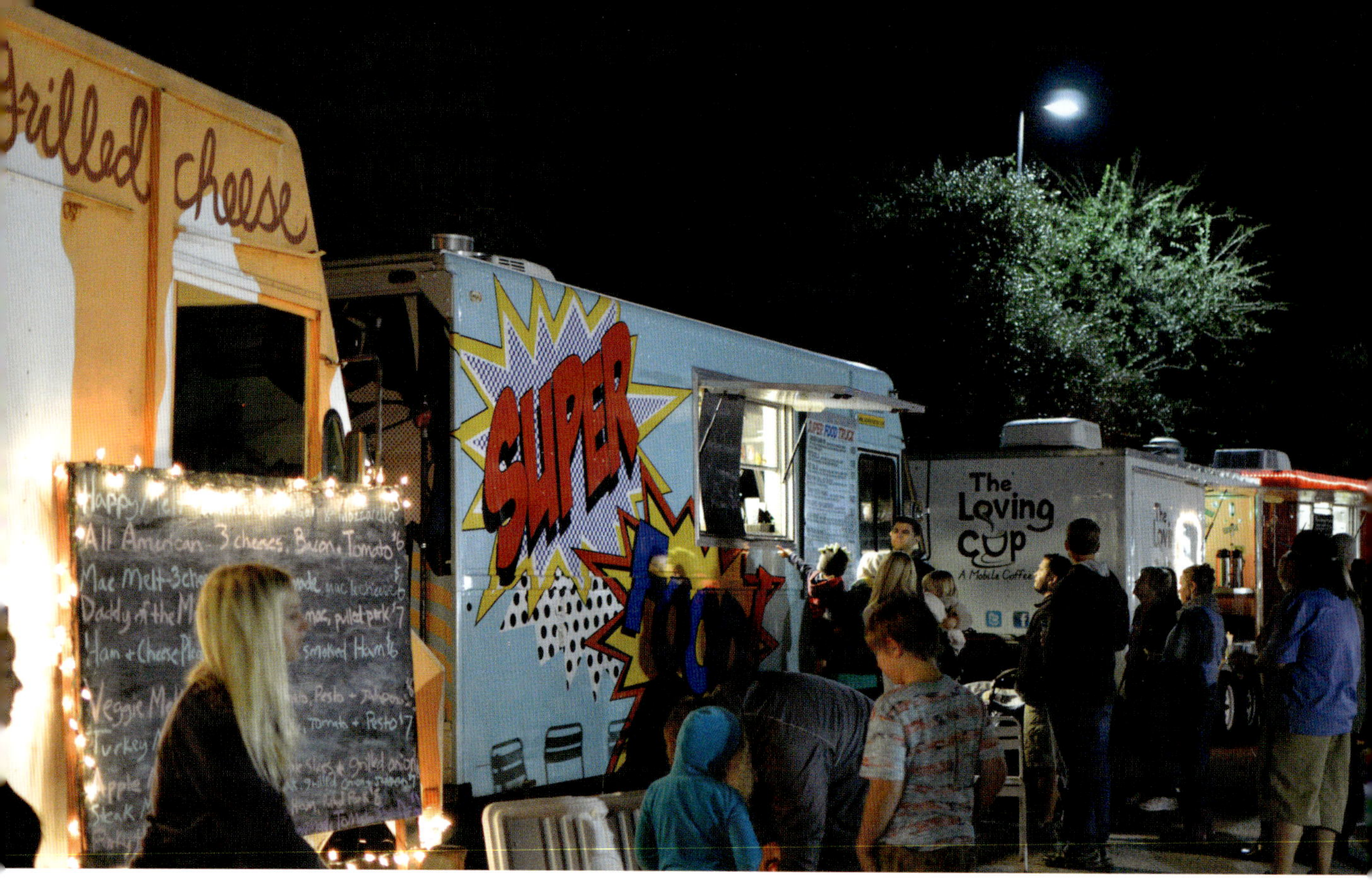

Food trucks line up at Nocatee.

At the same time, a friend called offering to sell him all the equipment from his coffee shop in Savannah. Then it was a matter of roughing out the space, plumbing and electric, logo, signs, menus, commissary, licensing and registration. He had two older Champion generators, which he laughingly refers to as "scare the children" loud. Now he uses Hondas, which run much quieter. All told, the cost to bring the Loving Cup to the road was around $25,000.

Matty has been in the hospitality business since before age eighteen, first as a busboy, cook and dishwasher. He worked front and back of the house with Bonefish for over eight years, opening stores in Jacksonville Beach, Augusta and Savannah before returning to Florida in 2009 and moving to Starbucks. He knew little about coffee at the time, but he knew a lot about people. He trained at the St. Johns Town Center location, at Neptune Beach and then at Third Street in Jacksonville Beach, where he worked four years to the day. It taught him a lot about coffee and cultivated a passion. When he was at Bonefish, he thought of himself as a "wine geek," and now he classifies himself as a "coffee geek."

On December 28, 2013, the Loving Cup made its Jacksonville debut on a rainy Saturday at the now defunct Bartram Park Farmers' Market. Matty's girlfriend came along to

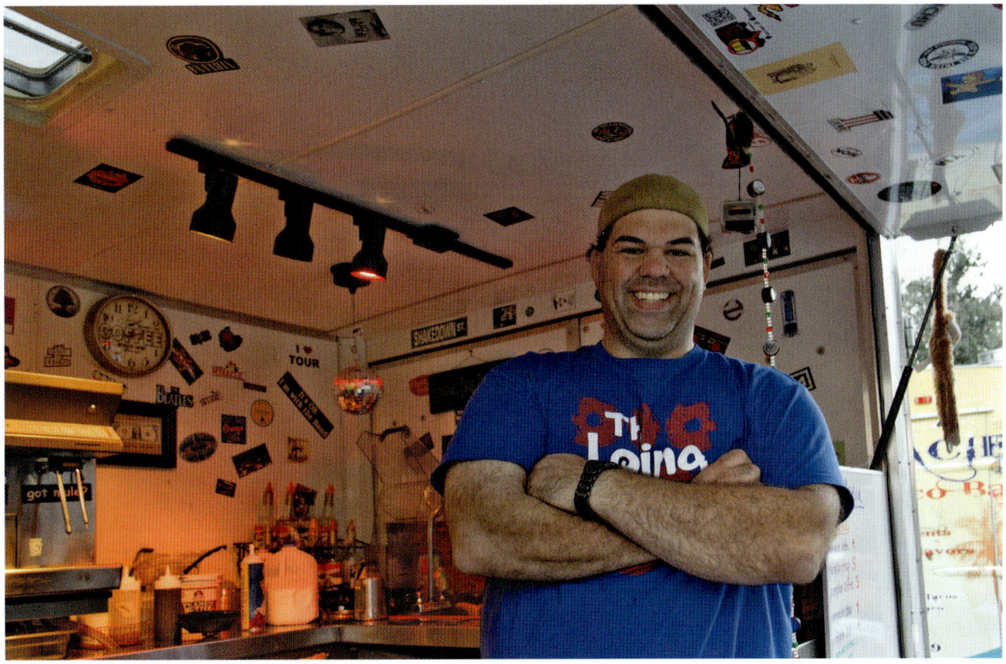

Matty Lennon and The Loving Cup.

help on the truck, and together they made all of twenty-eight dollars, three of which came from his mother. Everyone was happy to see the trailer, so he didn't care that it was a slow start. He had a clear path in mind, and he was on it!

Music festivals are Matty's happy place. He had been to quite a few of them where he saw lots of coffee vendors and lots of customers. Breaking into the festival market was tough until he got his first gig, and then, once he had proven he could manage that, he was invited to many more. Friends have come along to help out on the music tours and festivals, where lines can get very long. Matty loves the festival crowds, though. He says everyone is chill. It's like they are on vacation, so it's just fun serving them, all day and all night.

Creating a fun mobile coffeehouse atmosphere was a cinch for Matty. He put a few band stickers up inside the trailer and hung a disco ball in one corner. At night they put lava lamps out on the fenders and occasionally run a strobe light as well. The crowds have embraced the Loving Cup, too. Matty says now his customers will often come by and add their own stickers to the trailer walls. They feel a connection with the Loving Cup and with the gregarious Matty.

The Loving Cup's coffee menu goes beyond the basics. Oh, sure, you can get your espresso, Americano, latte, cappuccino, teas, chai, mocha, macchiato—you know the drill. If

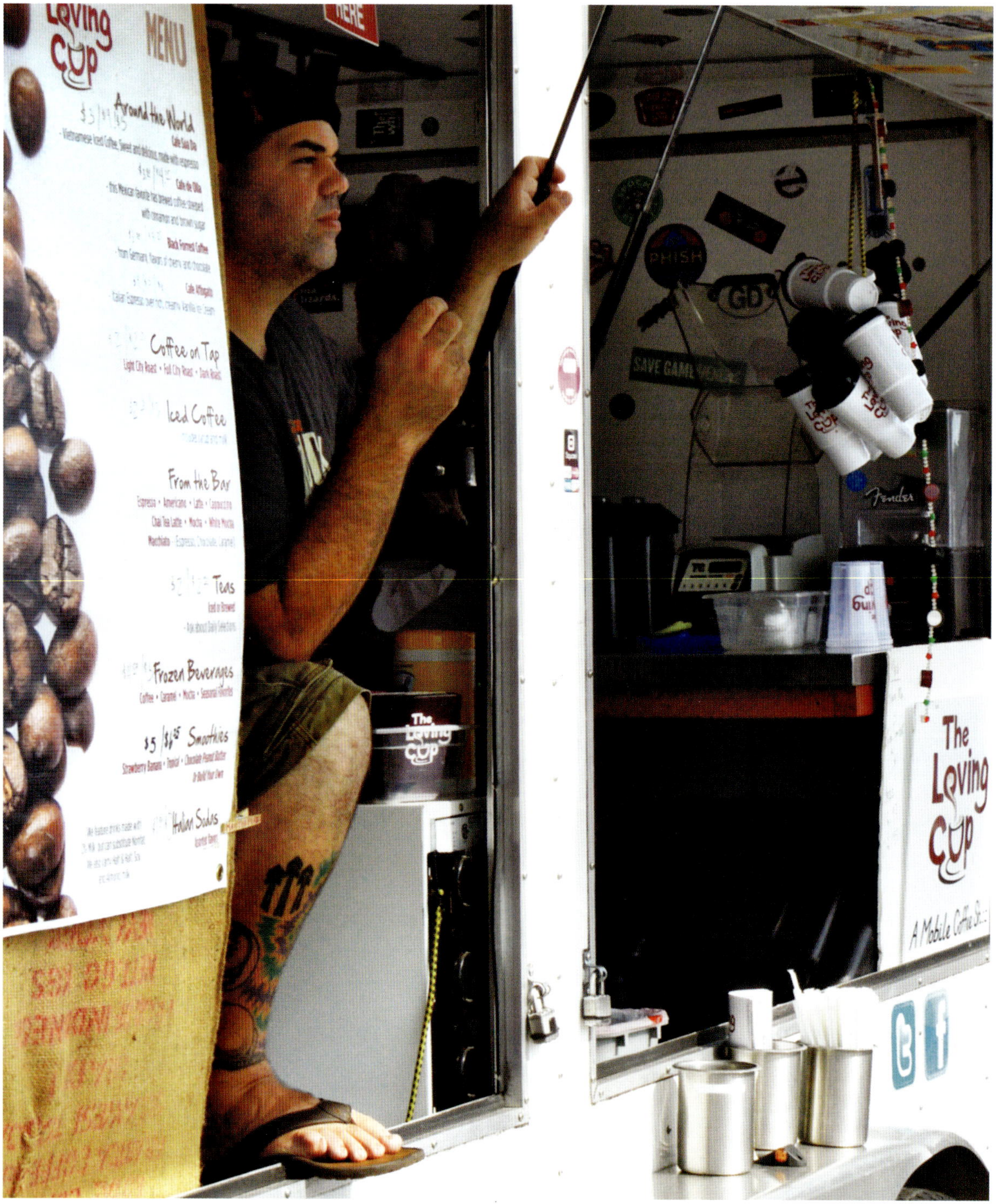

A rare quiet moment.

you want a more "trippy" coffee truck experience, try one of the Loving Cup's "Around the World" coffees. Café Sua Da is a classic Vietnamese iced coffee, an espresso-based drink made sweet and creamy with sweetened condensed milk. I loved this one when I tried it at Nocatee during one of its Food Truck Fridays events. The trouble is I am such a sweet tooth I could drink three of these! Black Forrest Coffee tastes of chocolate and cherries in a playful nod to the classic Bavarian Black Forrest Cake, and the decadent Café Affogato tops rich, creamy vanilla ice cream with dark Italian espresso. In the Mexican Café de Olla, the coffee is steeped with cinnamon and brown sugar. It has the rich, cinnamon flavor notes of traditional Mexican coffee. Matty has given us a home-kitchen version of his Café de Olla, and I can't wait for you to try it.

Matty loves to create specials, and one of his most popular to date is his Butterbeer Frappuccino, made with caramel, toffeenut and whipped cream. This is the drink that won Matty the Sweet Tooth Award at the Third Annual Jax Truckies Food Truck Championship in 2014. I'm also a fan of the Fluffhead Frap, which swaps out the caramel for marshmallow.

Of course, the menu also includes teas and several flavors of Italian Soda. He makes a wide array of smoothies as well as frozen coffee and other seasonal beverages.

Matty will head back out on the road when festival time comes along. The Loving Cup has already been invited to work Coachella in 2015 and has signed on with a large catering and concessions company out of San Diego to get into several more major festivals.

Lift your cup to The Loving Cup! Find them on Facebook, and at www.thelovingcup.coffee

THE LOVING CUP'S CAFE DE OLLA
Recipe from Matthew Lennon

When brewing a pot of coffee, add three cinnamon sticks and one cup of brown sugar to your pot. Brew coffee right over the top of the cinnamon and brown sugar. Let it steep for 4 minutes. Drink it like you would any coffee, add cream or soy milk, if you prefer. I recommend trying it first to test sweetness before adding more sugar.

What a beautiful buzz!

MAMA'S FOOD

Natalia Lorincz

Natalia Lorincz loves to cook and throw big parties. These days, she's doing that just about every day on her big purple and blue food truck, Mama's Food.

When Natalia moved from Washington, D.C., to St. Augustine to be closer to her parents, it was hard to find work at her previous income level, even with ten-plus years of experience. She took a part-time position as an administrative assistant.

Natalia's dad, Paulo Lorincz, loved having his two grandchildren close by, and he saw his daughter working hard to make ends meet. Then he made a suggestion that would change all of their lives. With his hospitality industry experience and her love of cooking, why not open a food truck? Paulo happens to be the banquet manager at the Tournament Players Club (TPC) Sawgrass in Ponte Vedra. He talked to some contacts in the industry and put the plan in place, and the whole family rallied behind the idea. It was he who named the truck Mama's, after Natalia's mom. Most of the things they cook are based on Mama's family recipes from Argentina.

Concession Nation of Fort Lauderdale created the Mama's Food truck kitchen. Natalia found the company online and worked with it to create her vision of a fun truck with bright, rich hues to make it colorful but not too crazy. Her dad helped with the kitchen layout. Inside, her truck features a full-sized griddle and a full oven. Tom from Up in Smoke and the Jacksonville Food Trucks helped rearrange the working space, adding a second fryer and enlarging the prep area. They have two steam tables, a full-sized refrigerator and a freezer.

Mama's Food first hit the road in the hottest time of the year, August 2013. Its first outing was a lunch service at Baptist Hospital in downtown Jacksonville. The truck parks at the JFT Warehouse, and Natalia is thankful for the great friends she has met there. Their guidance and generosity have made it possible for her to stay on the road. Monthly meetings of Jacksonville Food Trucks have been a great source of networking, leads and business advice. Tom and Jen from Up in Smoke have been so helpful to the single mom turned food truck entrepreneur. Jen has given her marketing advice gleaned from her years running their successful barbecue catering business. Alex from Gourmet Aviator loaned Natalia a generator when Mama's Food's failed. He has even stepped in to help out on the truck when it has been short staffed.

Natalia was surprised at first that people often label her food as Mexican. She doesn't work too hard to correct them, though. Once people try the food, they love it. When people

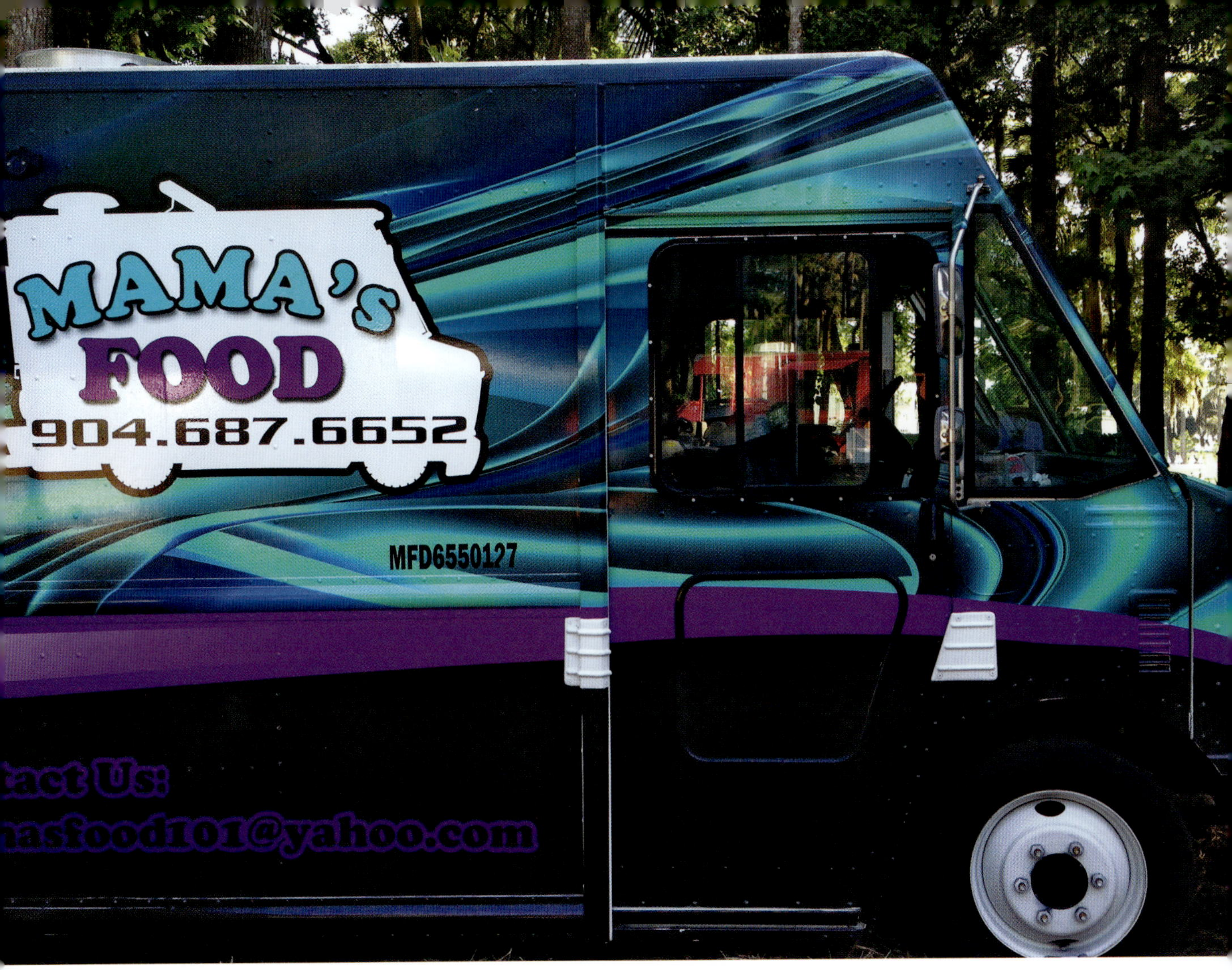

Mama's Food.

encounter Mama's Food for the first time, they are likely to ask at least one question—is it spicy? The answer is it really isn't. The red pepper that forms the base for its chimichurri is more sweet than hot. The next question she hears is what is chimichurri? Of course, the short answer is it's a green sauce for grilling meats with origins in Argentinian cooking. In Natalia's case, it's a red version, based on her grandfather's recipe that has been passed down through the generations. I tried to convince her to share the recipe with us, but she's not coughing up any trade secrets. She does occasionally sell it by the jar, though.

Originally, she was planning to bake her empanadas, but when she couldn't find the custom dough she needed, she turned to frying them. When she first started serving them, more than a few people had to ask what they were. She started sharing samples with people as they perused the menu, and now these flaky, meaty little packets of dough are among the top sellers. She began with

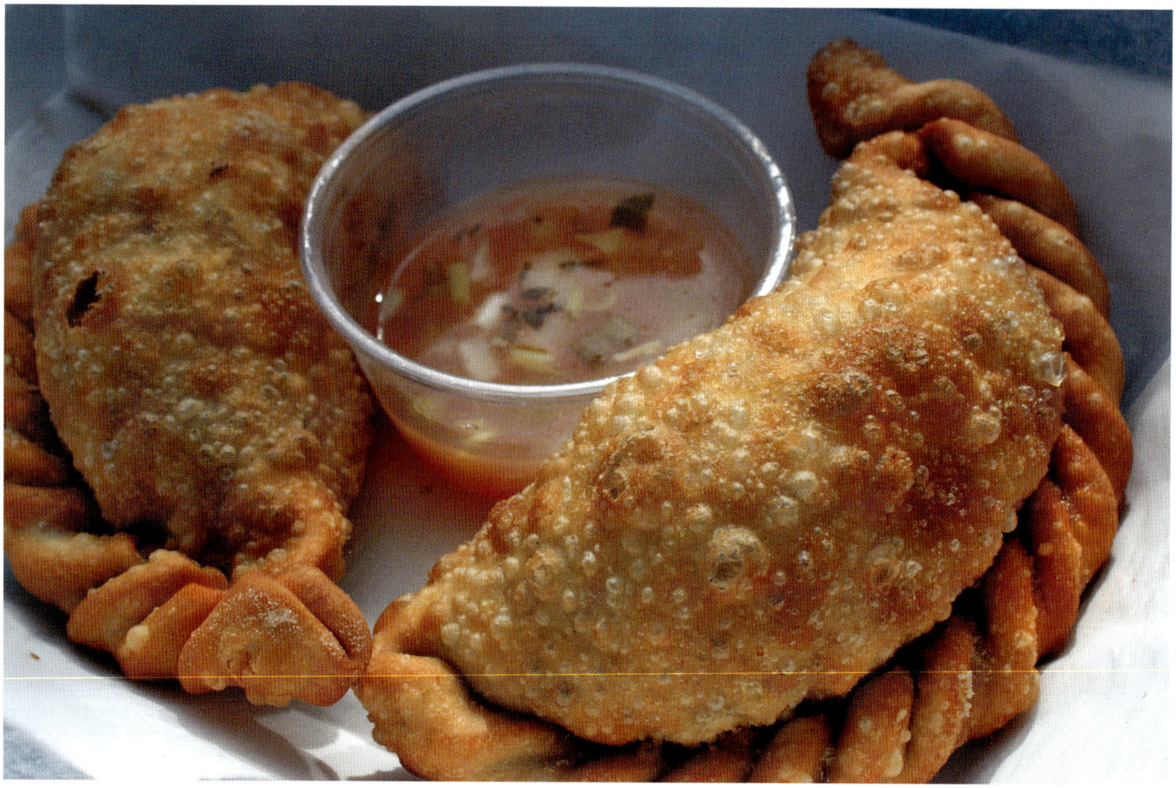

Mama's Empanadas.

Opposite, top: Mama's Philly Cheesesteak.

Opposite, bottom: Mama's Quesadilla.

beef but now also offer chicken, as well as vegetarian options with spinach and cheese.

When Mama's Food is booked for family-friendly events, Natalia adds crowd-pleasing, kid-friendly items such as chicken tenders, burgers and fries. Never fear, the empanadas are safe. Natalia has promised she will never remove them from her menu. She has made some minor adjustments to the menu board, however. For instance, when she changed the name of her "Chimichurri Steak Sandwich" to "Grilled Steak Sandwich," the overstuffed, tasty, toasty sandwich became a big hit, and people started asking what that great flavor was! Another menu item that is taking off is the Chicken Quesadilla. The chicken is marinated in the chimichurri, and she puts chimichurri mayo in the sandwich to help meld the flavors. There is a massive amount of melted cheese—the salty, stringy, melty, gooey kind.

Natalia drives the business and the huge truck. On busy days, she is assisted by Sarah (a friend), her aunt, a sister in Miami and her brother. Natalia's mother is usually with

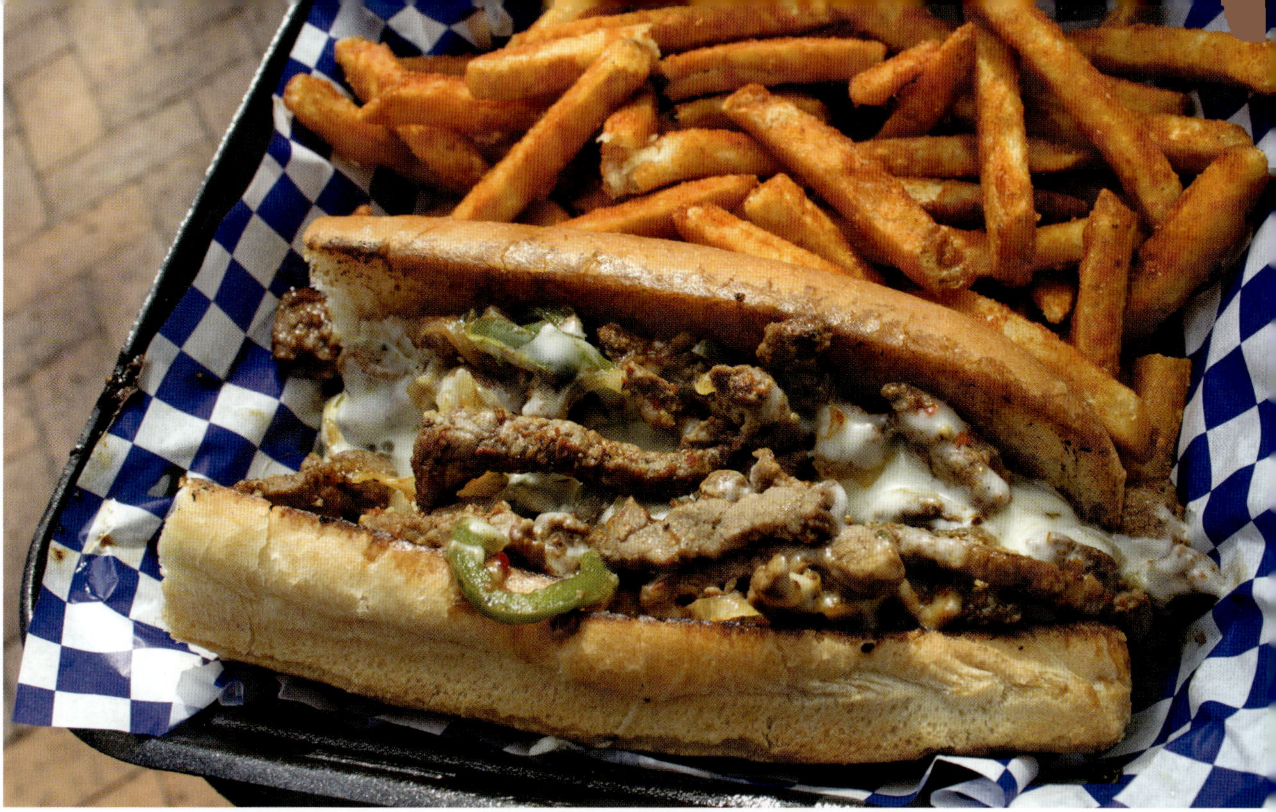

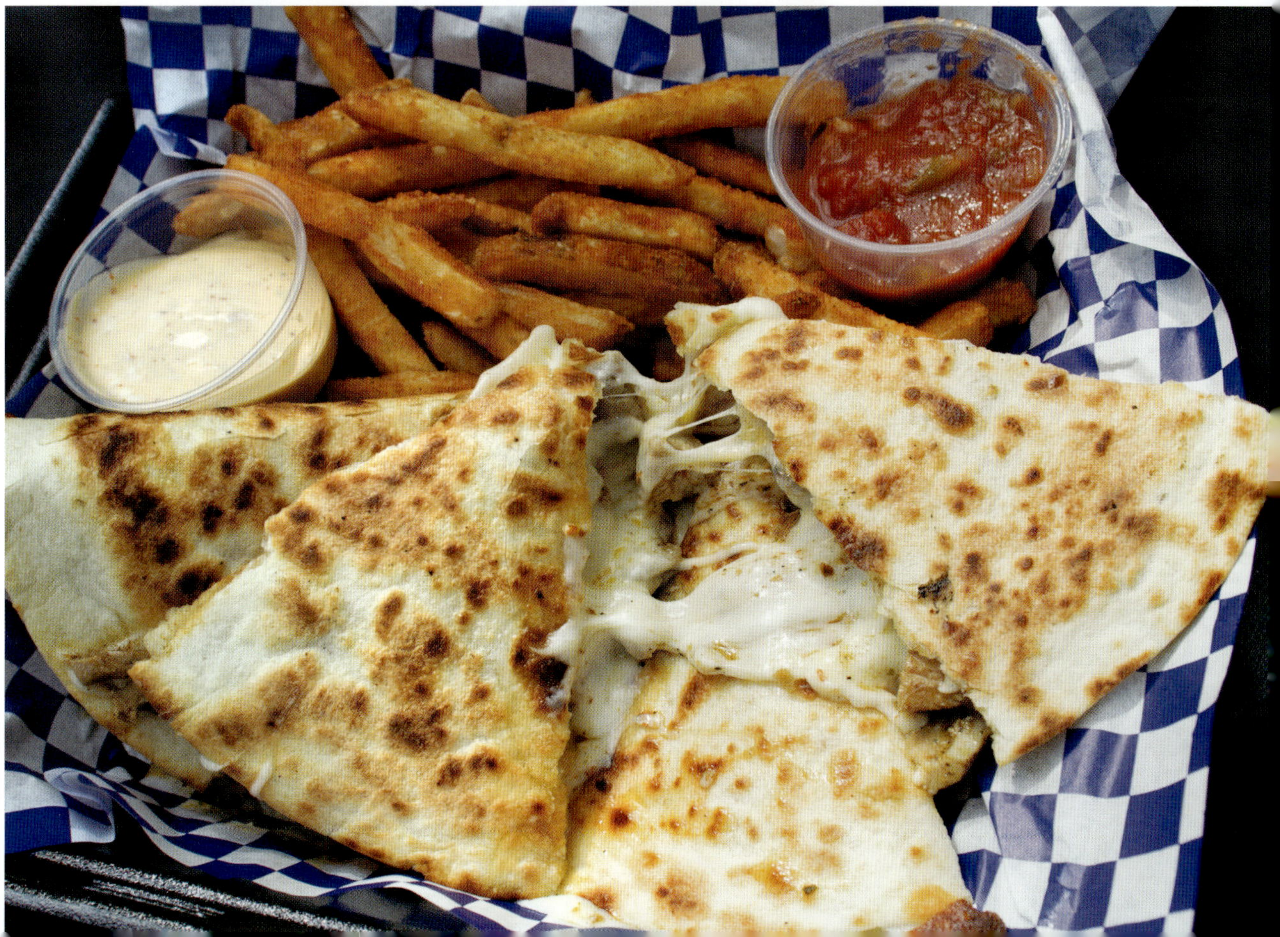

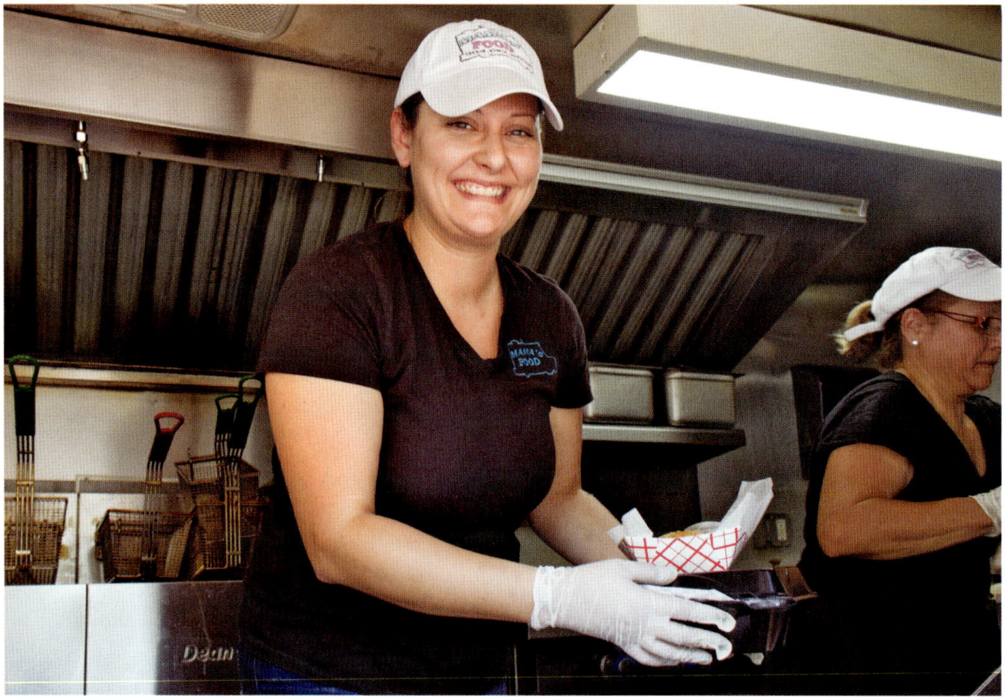

Natalia Lorincz of Mama's Food.

Natalia's children while everyone works on the truck.

Running her own business means putting in long hours and missing her children, ages nine and six. The upside is when they can come out and see their mom working on the truck at an event. Serving at the big events is the fun part for Natalia. Some are quite successful, and the trucks can make a lot of money if everything goes as planned. At the Web.com Tour event at TPC Sawgrass last year, Mama's Food rolled in packed to the roof and sold out of everything on the truck the night of the concert.

It's a tough business, running a food truck. The sheer amount of physical labor, planning and time—for sourcing, prepping and serving—was a surprise to Natalia, but she has taken it all in stride. There are nights she gets home exhausted, looks back at her day and realizes how hard she has actually worked. She plans to take it easy with her kids during the summer and then work hard the rest of the year, bringing her own brand of Argentinean cooking to the streets of Jacksonville. Come to Mama's and check out Natalia's daily specials at www.facebook.com/MamasFood101.

MOTHER TRUCKIN' PIZZA

Mike and Kellie Rice

Mother Truckin' Pizza is owned and operated by Mike and Kellie Rice.

Featuring fresh, hot pizza by the slice; subs; toasted ravioli; and other Italian crowd pleasers, the big brown truck can often be found during lunch service at the Greystone office park off Deerwood Parkway. Kellie has also begun making the trek up to Heckscher Drive to feed the hungry crowds at BAE Systems.

The truck is nicknamed Dolly, a nod to its former life as a bakery delivery vehicle. M&R Specialty Trailers did the restoration. The bold, colorful wrap—one of my favorites—was designed and produced by the talented team at Corr Digital.

The first pizza rolled off the truck in March 2014, and their first real gig was the following month. Since then, ardent fans, referred to as "Mother Truckers," have been spreading the word about the hot new pizza truck.

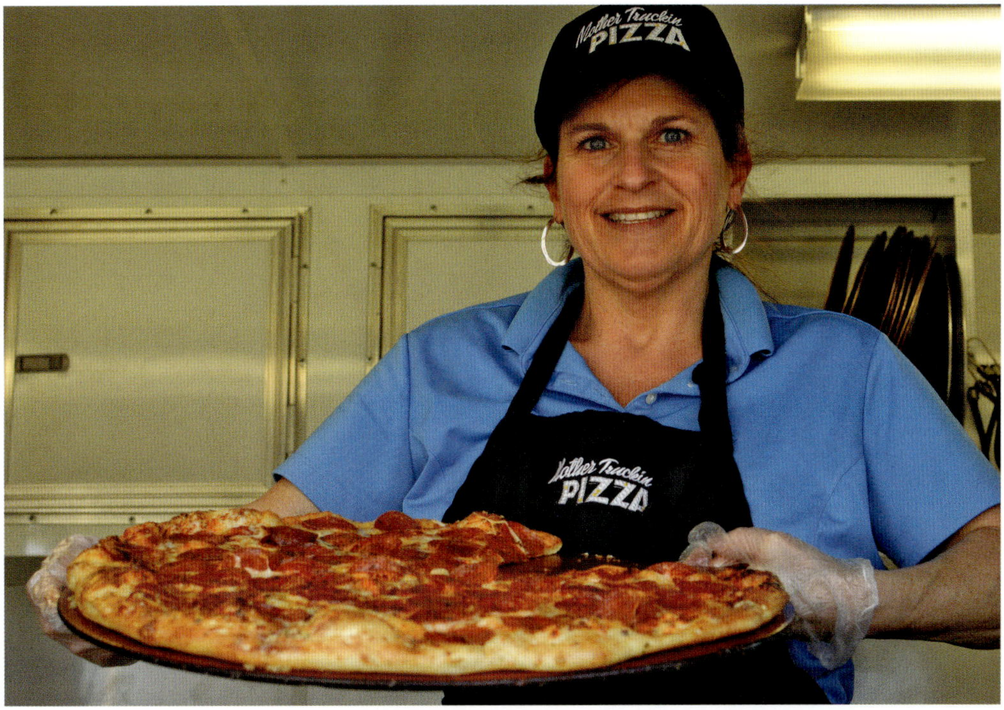

Kellie Price and her husband, Mike, own Mother Truckin' Pizza.

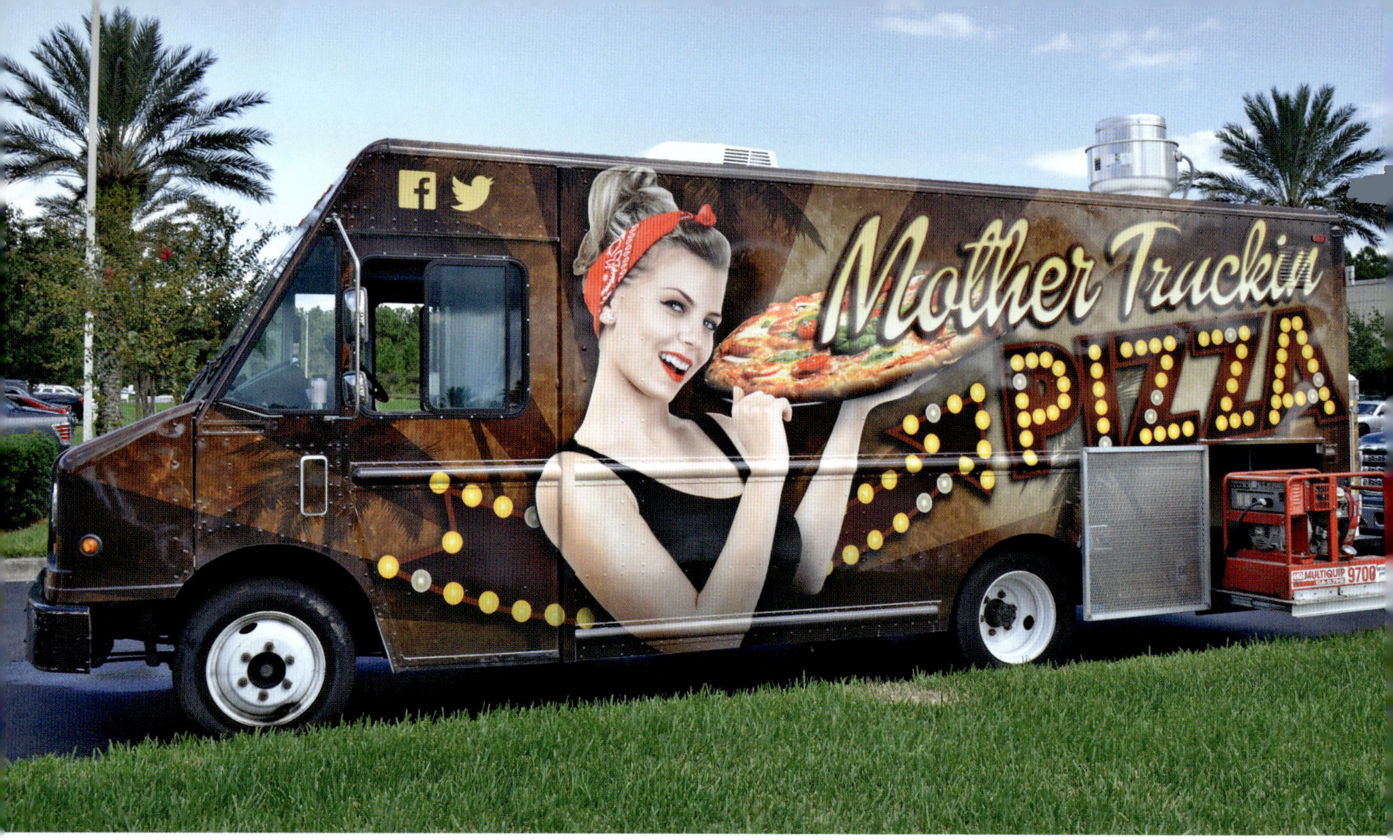

Mother Truckin' Pizza's bold graphics were designed by Corr Digital.

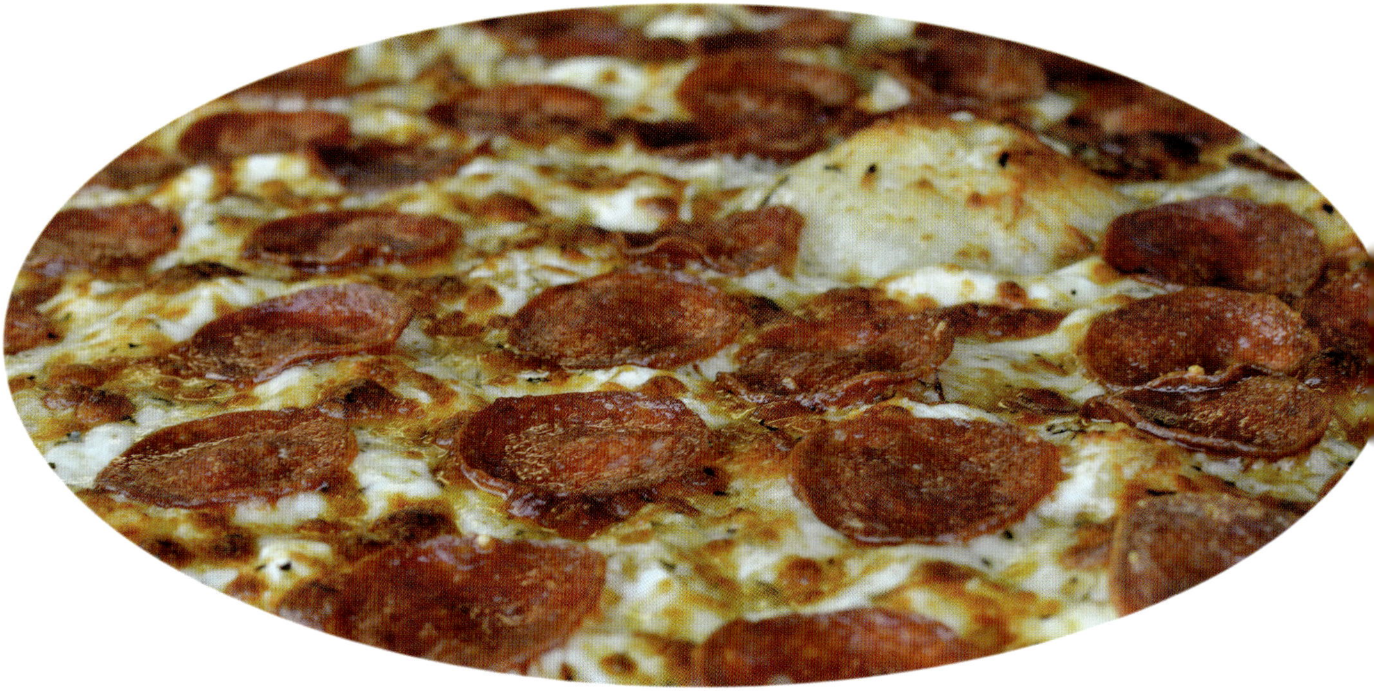

The White Pizza from Mother Truckin' Pizza.

They have been seen around town at Everbank Field's Food Truck Alley, AutoBahn Indoor Speedway, the Historic Springfield Main Street Cruise, Country Music Fest, Beaches Octoberfest and Fletcher High School's class reunion Block Party at the Beaches Museum & Pablo Historical Park.

Kellie says they love being part of the food truck community in Jacksonville. Alex from Gourmet Aviator in particular was very encouraging and answered questions for them when they were just getting started and had no idea where to turn. "It's nice to see other truck owners at events—we work together and share a lot of valuable info we learn along the way."

They are available for private parties and events, so grab a slice soon! Find Mother Truckin' Pizza online at mothertruckinpizza.com.

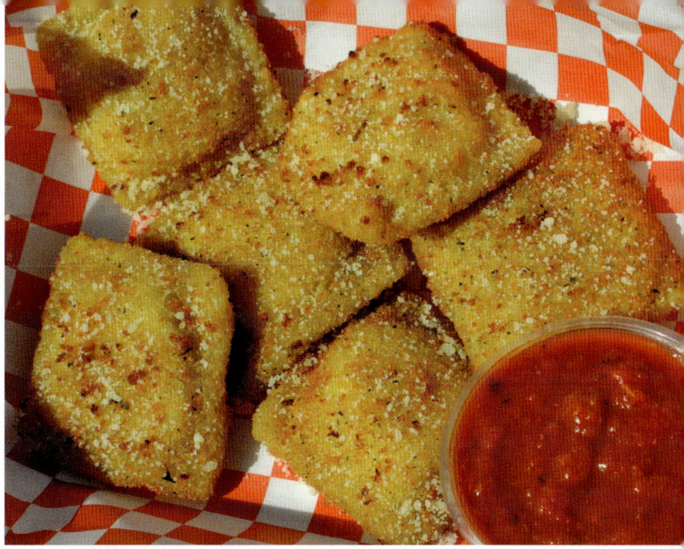

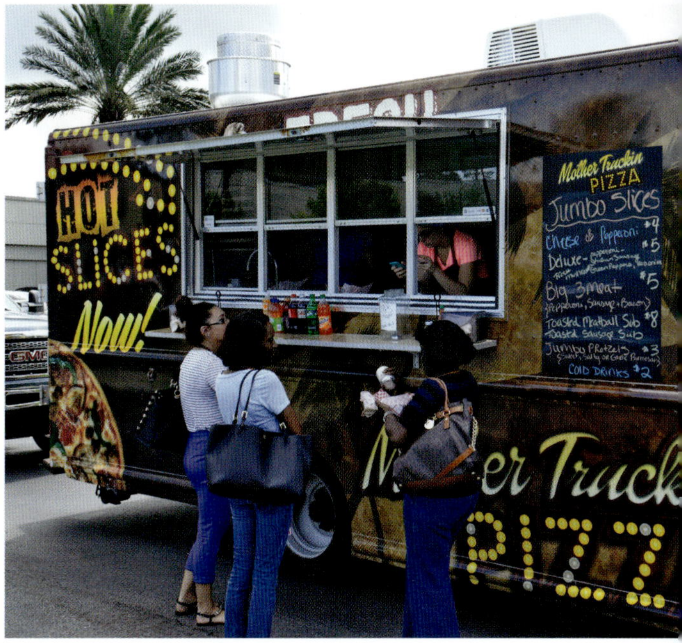

Top: Mother Truckin' Pizza's Toasted Ravioli with marinara dipping sauce.

Bottom: Mother Truckin' Pizza serves the lunch bunch at Greystone Business Park.

MUZZI'S MADHOUSE

John Scaramuzzi

The youngest son in a large Italian family, John Scaramuzzi grew up on the south side of Chicago.

Muzzi, as his friends call him, was a self-taught cook—except for what he learned from his mother and grandmothers as he was growing up. He had a career in finance for fifteen years, but any time family or friends were having a party, he was the one who did all the cooking.

When the concept of opening a restaurant started to take shape, Muzzi and his wife, Jackie (she's also from Chicago), took six months to research what that would look like. The consensus was the food truck route, with its lower capital investment, was the more attractive option.

With that decision made, the culinary direction of the truck was addressed. An Italian upbringing made that choice a fairly straightforward one. They homed in on their favorite, Chicago-style Italian, since it was not already well represented in Jacksonville.

They thought about keeping their jobs and operating the truck on weekends only, but when he and

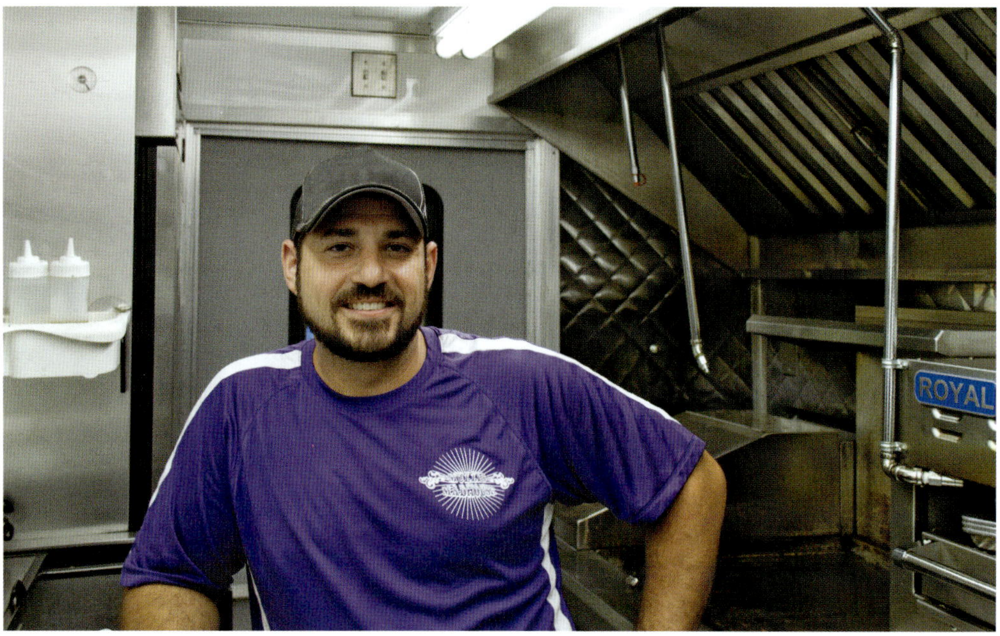

John Scaramuzzi, owner of Muzzi's Madhouse.

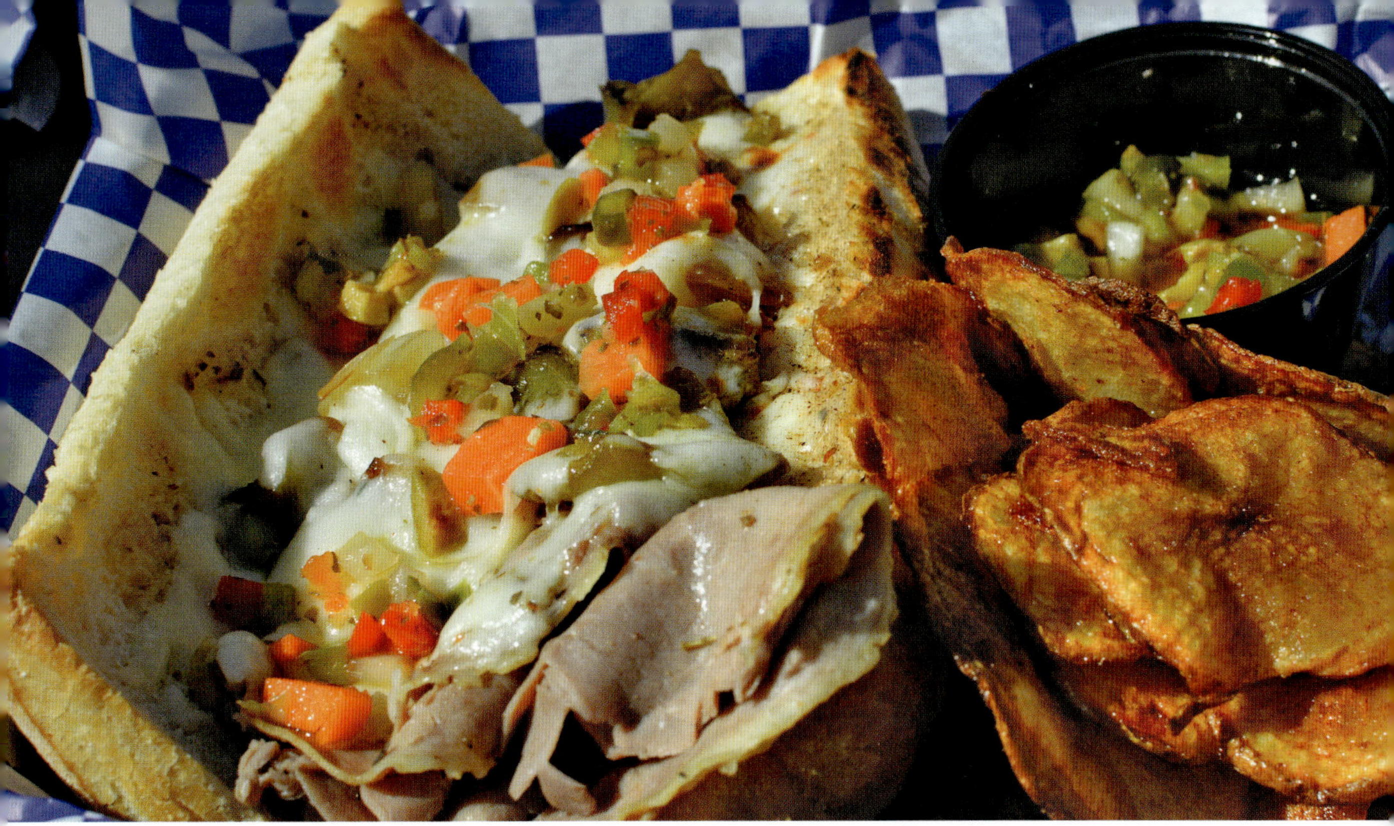

Muzzi's Chicago Style Beef Sandwich.

Jackie both got laid off from different companies on the same day in February 2014, Muzzi knew the time was right. With an ample severance package for a cushion, and with a business plan in hand, they sought and were approved for financing. Food Cart USA in Miami sold them a retired Aramark uniform delivery truck, gutted it and custom fabricated everything from the inside out.

Finally, after about three and a half months and somewhere between $50,000 and $80,000, the "Purple People Feeder" rolled up I-95 and hit the streets of Jacksonville in June 2014. First things first—it's pronounced MOO-zeez, not MUH-zees, Madhouse. It took me a while to get the hang of that, but I'm on board now.

The big purple truck with the Chicago skyline in silhouette is a work of art inside and out. The gleaming kitchen is both efficient and ample. Since they melt cheese on most of their sandwiches, they have a salamander, something of a rarity on trucks here. Muzzi's parks at the Beaver Street Commissary's Food Truck Lot, and John does his prep and cooking on the truck. Air conditioning helps keep the temps out of the triple digits on hot Florida summer days. A two-burner stove is enough to get them through most of the time. Monday is gravy day at Muzzi's, though, and the stovetop gets a workout.

For much of Italian cuisine, the sauce is the most important element.

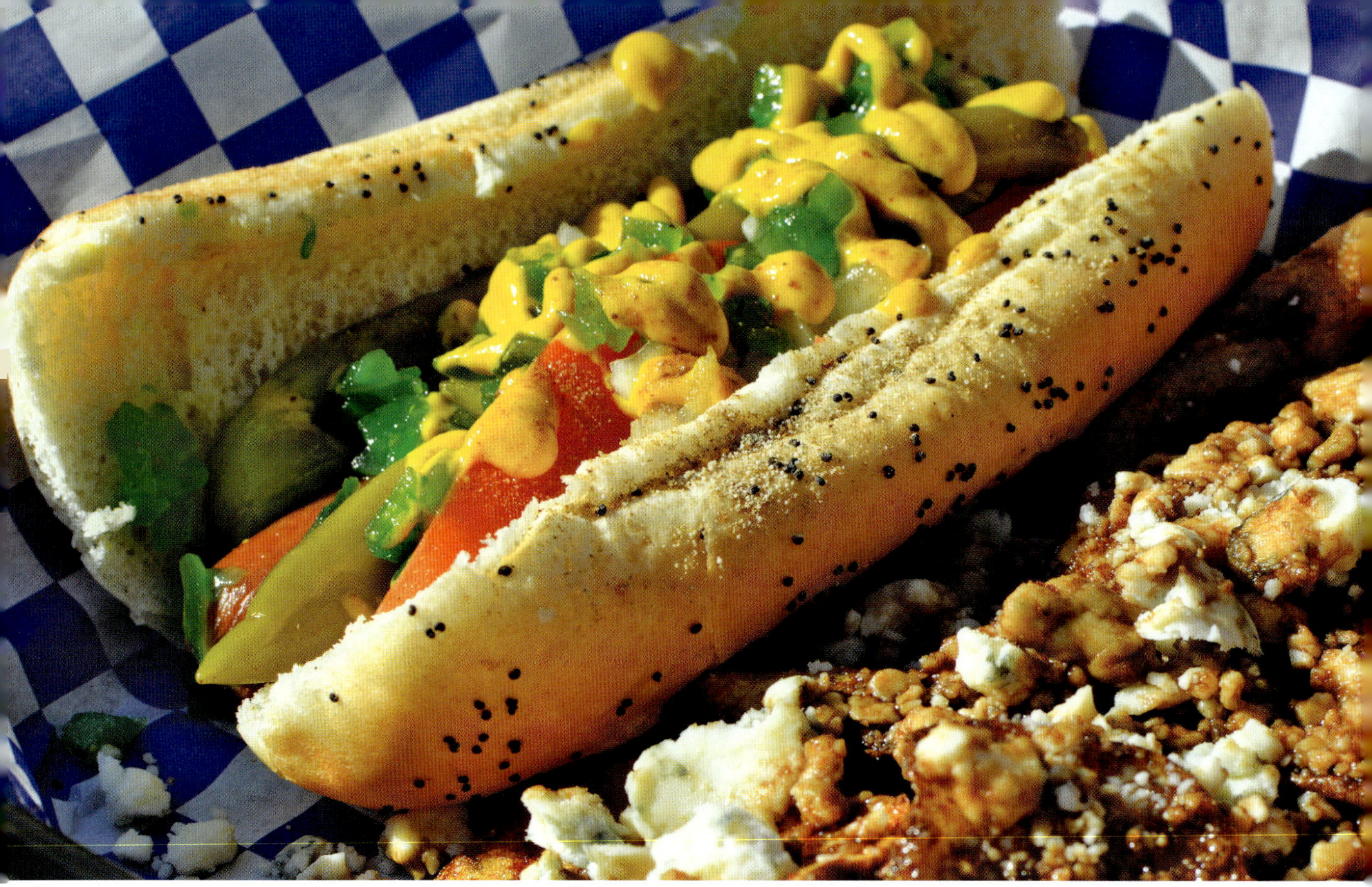

Muzzi's Chicago Dog.

Muzzi's "Sunday Gravy" is no exception. It's his own recipe, based on the one he learned from hanging out in the kitchen watching his mom and grandma cook—or, as they called it, causing trouble.

A six-hour sauce, the gravy is started Monday morning. They cool it down Monday night, store it and load it on the truck. Then they heat it on the stove and store it at temp in steam tables during service. There is no meat in the sauce, so they can use the same base for vegetarian options. Balsamic vinegar gives it a hint of sweetness. He purées it, mainly because his kids, Vincent and Adriana, weren't fond of seeing large chunks of peppers or onions, so he found that if he puréed them, no one would know they were there. A temperature-controlled steam table helps ensure the sauce doesn't burn or get too dark.

He prides himself on keeping a gleaming, clean truck, which means daily scrub downs after a long lunch service.

Before they opened for business, John and Jackie researched lines and ticket times at other trucks during events, and they did some relay testing to make sure they could keep their ticket times low.

Muzzi's mission is to provide a piece of John's heart, soul and zest for life into every dish he serves. I don't know the exact recipes, but I do know that transplanted Chicagoans rave about his traditional Chicago-style Italian Beef sandwich. Roasted Italian Beef thinly sliced, dipped in jus, served on a wet roll, with sautéed green peppers, onions, melted provolone and mozzarella cheeses and Madhouse Magic—homemade Giardiniera, a spicy Italian relish that accompanies many of Muzzi's dishes. Hearth-baked rolls are sourced from the Windy City's legendary Gonnella Baking Company.

Muzzi's Chicago Style Hotdog is the old-school classic—a Vienna dog, served on a poppy seed bun, topped with tomatoes, a pickle slice, sport peppers, onions, green relish, mustard and celery salt. They make their own potato chips, and a favorite snack of mine is these crunchy gems loaded

Jackie works Muzzi's window during an event.

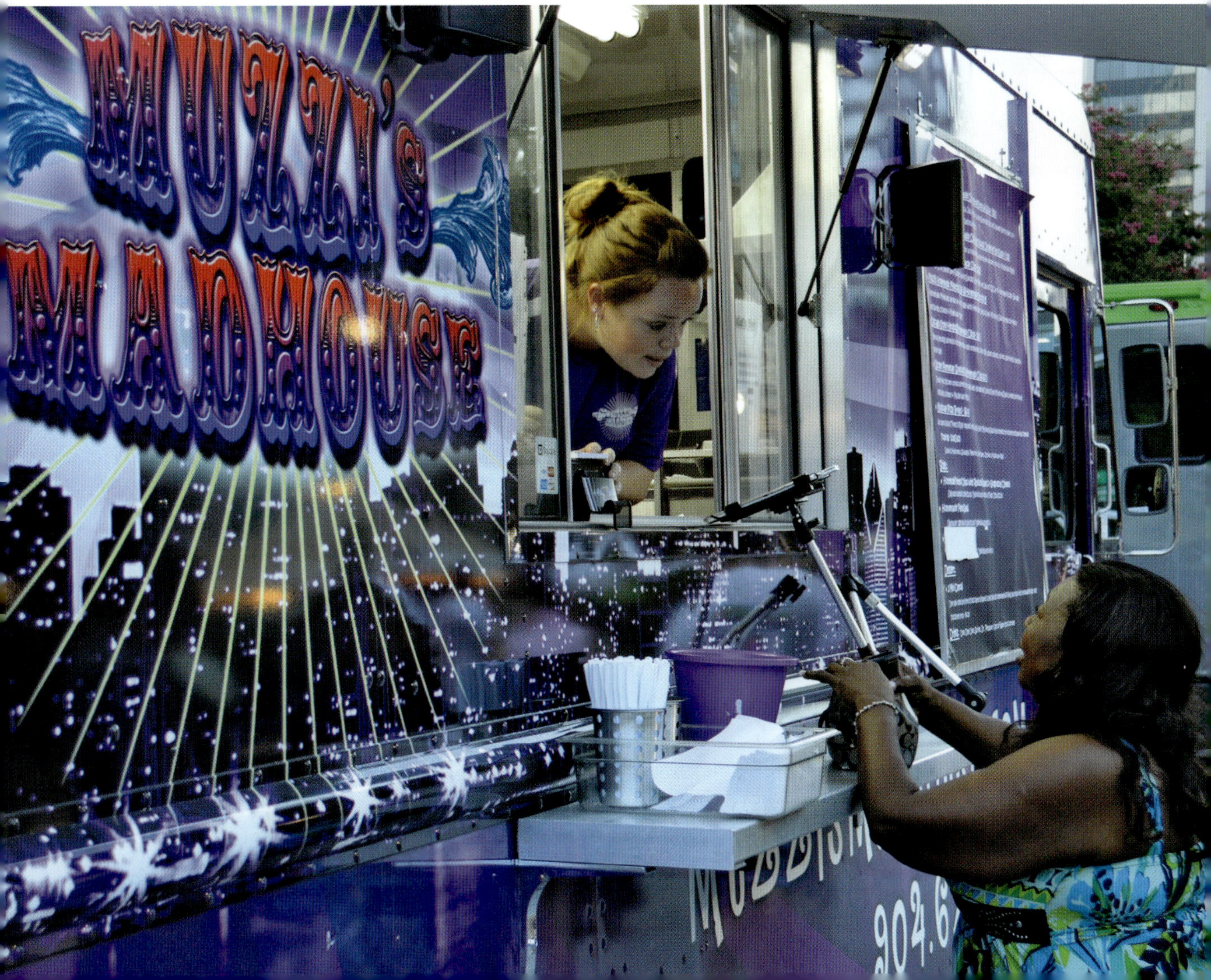

with melty Gorgonzola and drizzled with balsamic vinegar.

Specials in development include crêpe manicotti and baked penne with vodka sauce.

For dessert, there is usually a pair of mini cannoli, one plain and one chocolate dipped, with house-made filling and topped with powdered sugar and chocolate syrup. Then there is the occasional wild card creation, like the infamous S'mores Brownie. Yes, you heard me. Every bit as good as it sounds.

Muzzi's Madhouse is a popular truck at the big events. John has done most of them. Tailgate alley at the Everbank Field for the Jacksonville Jaguars home games, Jaxsons Night Market, the Block Party at Jacksonville Landing and Food Truck Fridays at Nocatee, to name a few. Everyone seems to love the hearty, meaty, cheesy, saucy Italian fare, and the truck usually sells out of the most popular items before the night is over. John likes working all over town to get the word out and earn a larger customer base. Eventually, he'd like to expand, either with a second truck, in a small takeout-delivery place or in a restaurant. I'd make my reservations early if I were you. Find Muzzi's Madhouse on the Food Truck Finder app and online at www.muzzismadhouse.com and on Twitter @MuzzisMadhouse.

ON THE FLY SANDWICHES AND STUFF

Chef Andrew Ferenc

Jacksonville may have come late to the national food truck party, but when we arrived, Andrew Ferenc of On the Fly Sandwiches and Stuff was one of the lead drivers. His simply equipped white panel van made its debut in late June 2011. These days, he keeps pace with a much bigger field.

If you're hungry and need food fast, Andrew is the guy to call. Of course, Andrew's wife, Kelly, is probably the one who will answer. Kelly manages everything on the business end of their food truck and catering businesses, and Andrew handles everything culinary. Kelly also has her hands full with the couple's two young boys, Cash and Colby.

Andrew found his niche when his parents made him get a job at age fifteen. His first culinary gig was as a dishwasher at Tijuana Willie's in Inverness, Florida. He thought it was the coolest thing, how the cooks could come together, communicate and put out all that food without skipping a beat. One day TW's chef went on a binge and didn't show up for work for three days. Andrew volunteered to step up. He got a

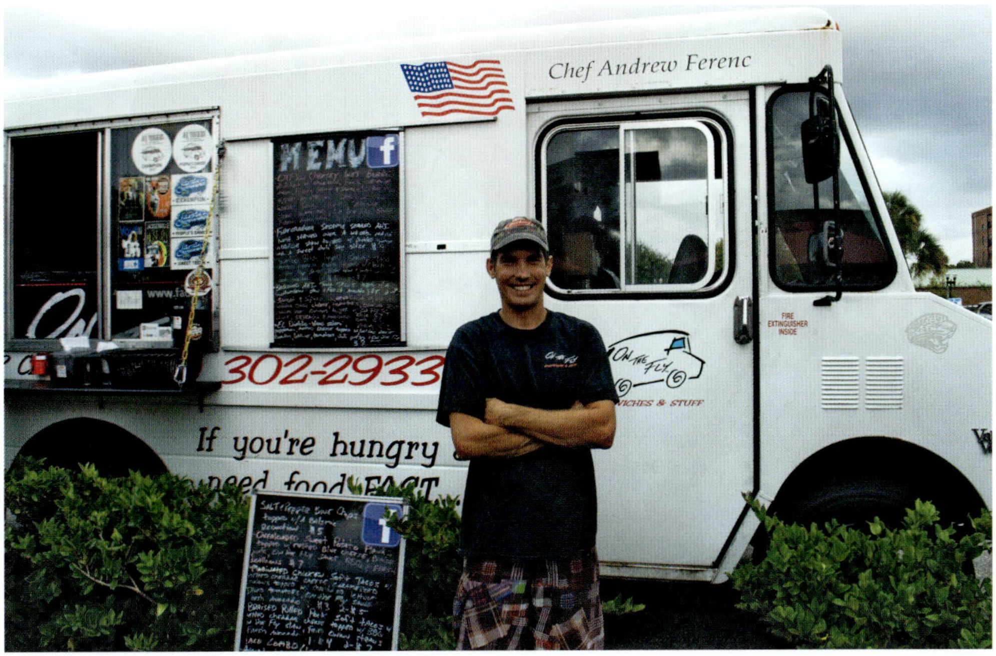

Chef Andrew Ferenc, owner of On the Fly.

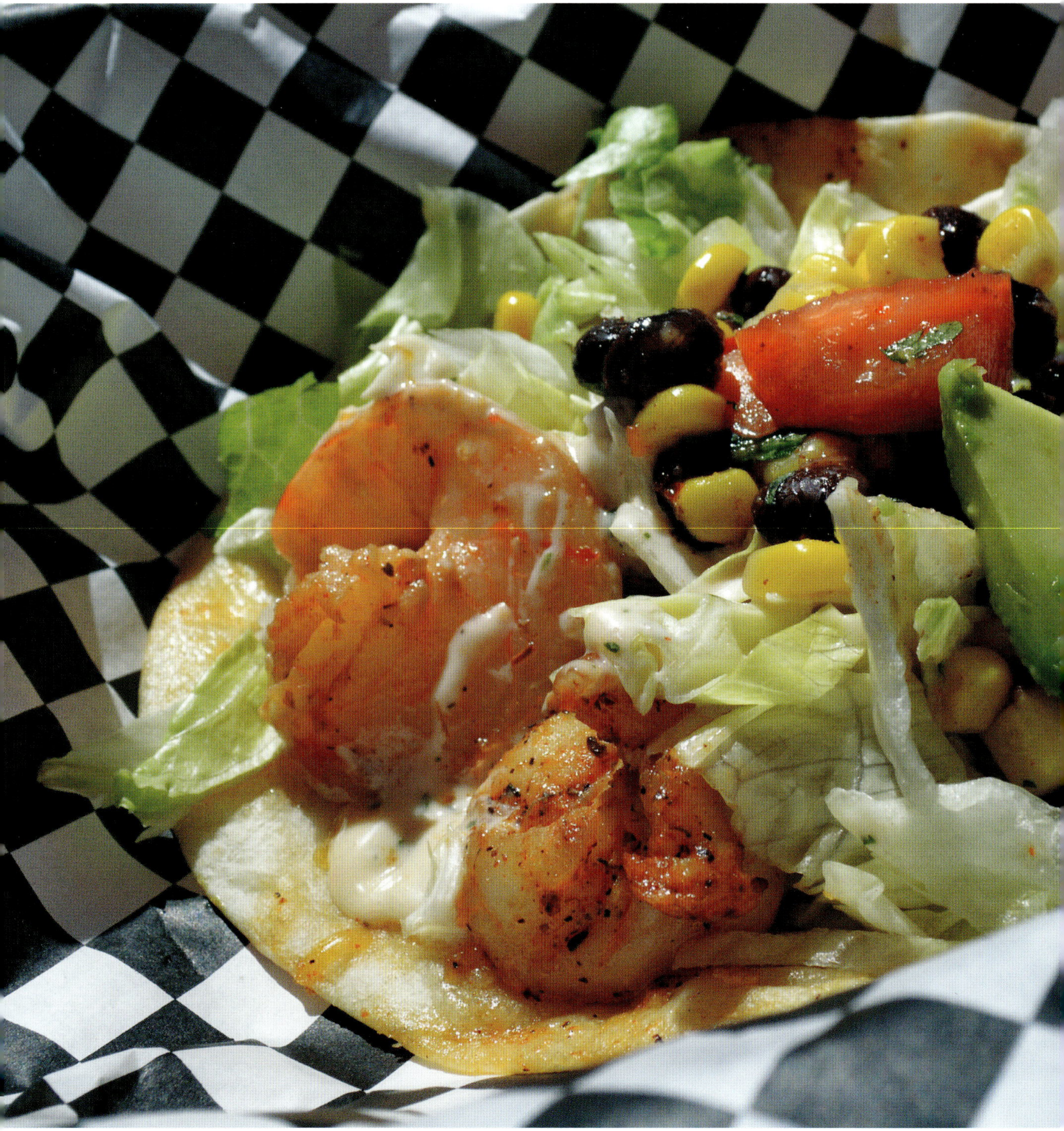

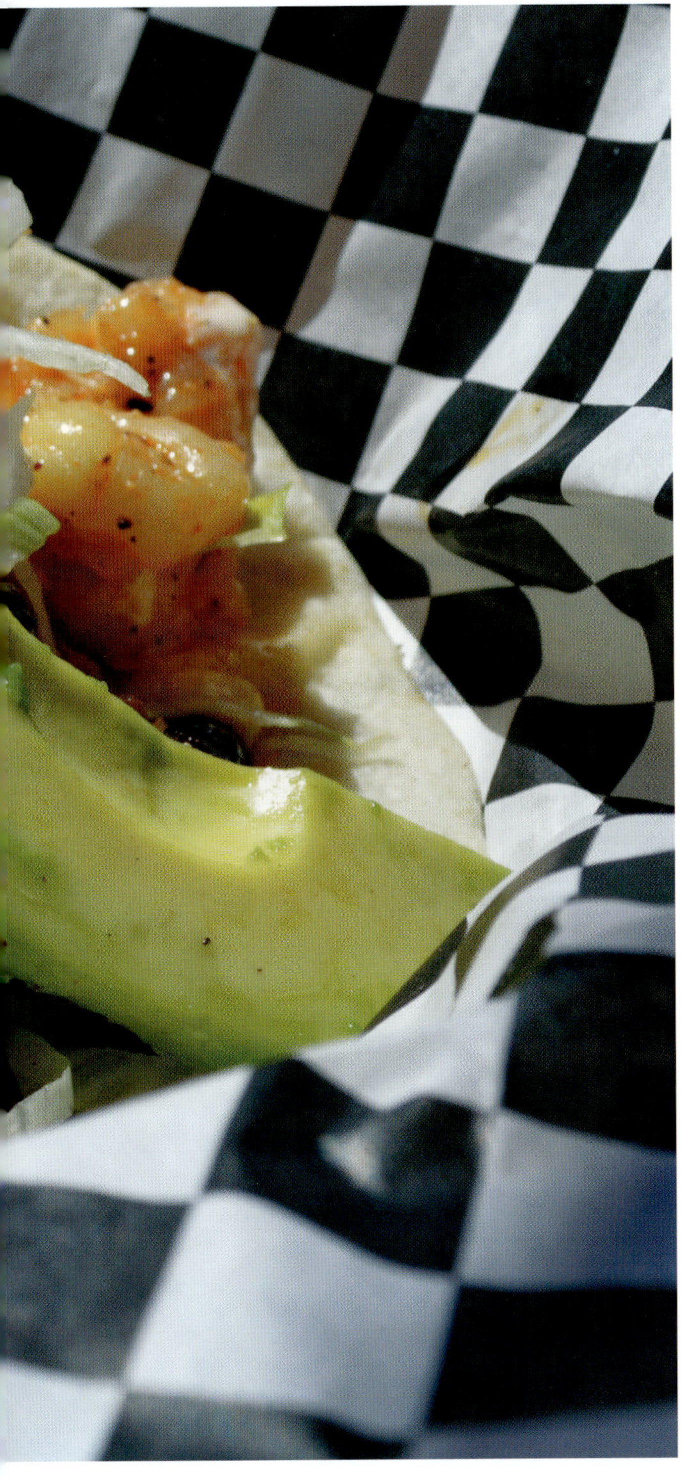

place on the line and worked his way up from there.

His parents suggested he attend the technical institute, finish high school and study cooking there, which he did. Then it was on to American Culinary Academy at Lakeland, Florida, where he got his associate's degree. While there, he did an internship at the Terrace Hotel, where he got to cook for visiting celebrities.

While visiting his sister at the University of North Florida, he fell in love with Jacksonville. He moved to town and got a job at First Street Grille, an upscale oceanfront restaurant and bar. He moved with owners Kathy and Malcom Marvin when they took over the old Homestead on Beach Boulevard (now TacoLu). Andrew also worked in Ponte Vedra at Aqua Grill, the Comfort Inn in Jacksonville Beach and Selva Marina in Atlantic Beach. He prides himself on his professionalism and has maintained good working relationships with all his former employers.

When his son Cash was born, Andrew was working such long hours that he hardly got to see him for the first year of his life. He decided enough was enough. He could either leave restaurant work or start his own business. Little did he know that starting On the Fly would make him busier than ever, but important family events are on his calendar. He was there for Cash's first

Tiger Shrimp Taco from On The Fly.

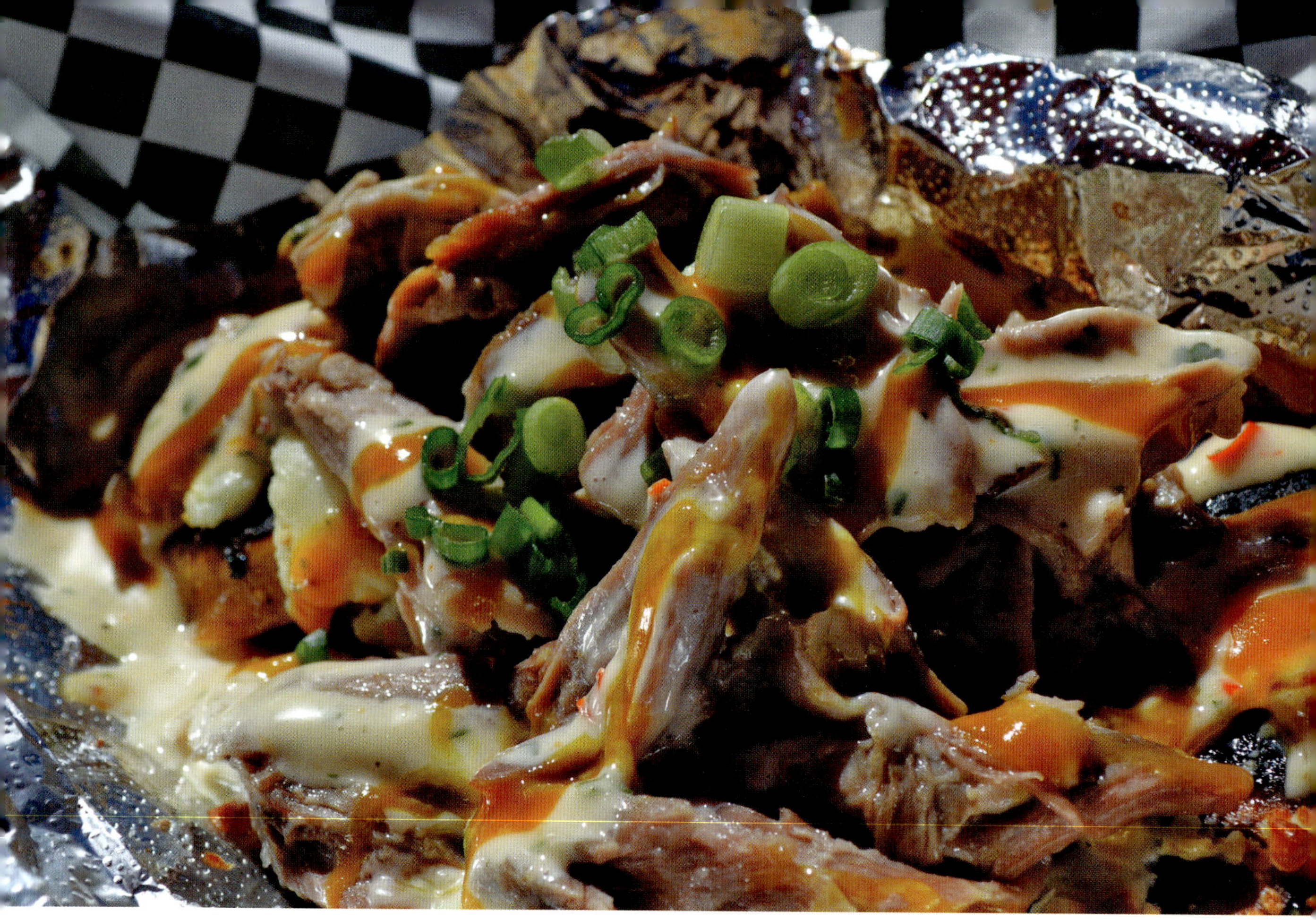

OTF's Sweet Potato Planks.

baseball game and didn't have to ask anyone but himself for the time off. The newest addition to the family, son Colby, will see a lot more of his dad.

He researched the food truck scene. Other than Bus'in Your Chops and a catering truck operator known as Sweet Pete who served ravenous crowds in the streets of San Marco at 1:00 a.m., nobody had the gourmet food truck thing going in Jacksonville. Andrew found the truck on Craigslist—an empty shell of a former ice cream truck. A relatively modest build-out allowed him to hit the ground running without going into debt. His simple logo with the sketch of the truck was a napkin drawing; the lettering for "On the Fly" is Andrew's own handwriting. The kitchen, which he designed, is the smallest he has known in fifteen years of cooking, but it is easier to clean and maintain. The kitchen runs on 100 percent electricity, no propane. His griddles are big box store–bought electric models, and he doesn't use a deep fryer.

When developing his menu, Andrew heeded the advice of a former employer, Dan (of Dan's Clam Stand in Homosassa Springs), who impressed upon him the economic wisdom of serving large volumes of simple, good food, fast. In the beginning, Andrew changed his entire menu weekly, but when returning patrons were disappointed when their favorites weren't listed on the board, he settled on a regular set of items, with occasional specials. Andrew calls it "high-end street food—freestyle."

He does his own twist on traditional dishes, like tacos with fresh-grilled jumbo black tiger shrimp, topped with iceberg lettuce, black bean and sweet corn salsa, On the Fly Sauce and avocado.

Blue cheese chips are topped with balsamic glaze, and quesadillas are filled with banana peppers, caramelized onions, tomatoes and chicken, pork or shrimp. He keeps everything fresh and prepped daily.

Sweet Potato Planks are topped with crumbled Gorgonzola cheese, loads of braised pork, On the Fly Sauce and fresh scallions.

The positively addictive crème brûlée with mini peanut butter cups was not on the original menu, but when he makes it, he only has to post a picture on Facebook—it will sell out within the hour. I managed to get him to hold on to one for me long enough to photograph it for this book, and lucky me, I got to eat the photo prop when we were done. Then he shared the recipe so we can make it at home! I don't know about you, but I've been

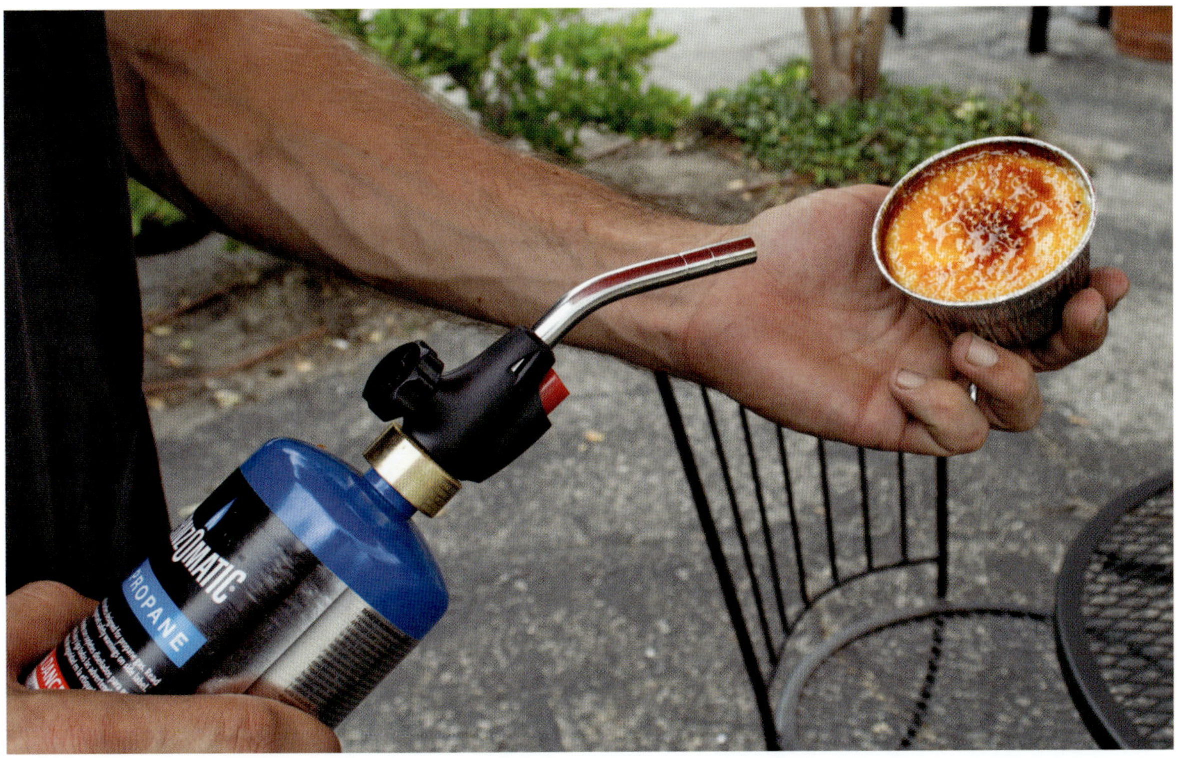

Andrew caramelizes the sugar top of a Crème Brulee at On the Fly.

looking for a good excuse to buy a blowtorch. Thanks, chef!

Like many early truckies, Andrew forged an alliance with a local craft brewery. The Green Room at Jacksonville Beach offered him a spot in its back lot to feed its hungry patrons. Although there was a law on the books that said you couldn't sell food to the public from a vehicle, Andrew felt this arrangement existed in a "gray area" since the truck wasn't catering to walk-ups, just brewery patrons, and it was parked in a closed-in area on private property. He operated there for five months before local authorities stepped in and sent him packing. The resulting uproar started a dialogue that eventually helped spur Jacksonville and Neptune Beaches to revisit their codes and allow food trucks, albeit with certain restrictions.

These days, On the Fly has a permanent parking spot downtown in a small, privately owned lot at the corner of Adams and Jefferson Streets, a few blocks from the new Duval County Courthouse. There is a steady stream of regulars, downtown workers who walk a few blocks and wait in line to grab something to take back to the office and others who devour their gourmet

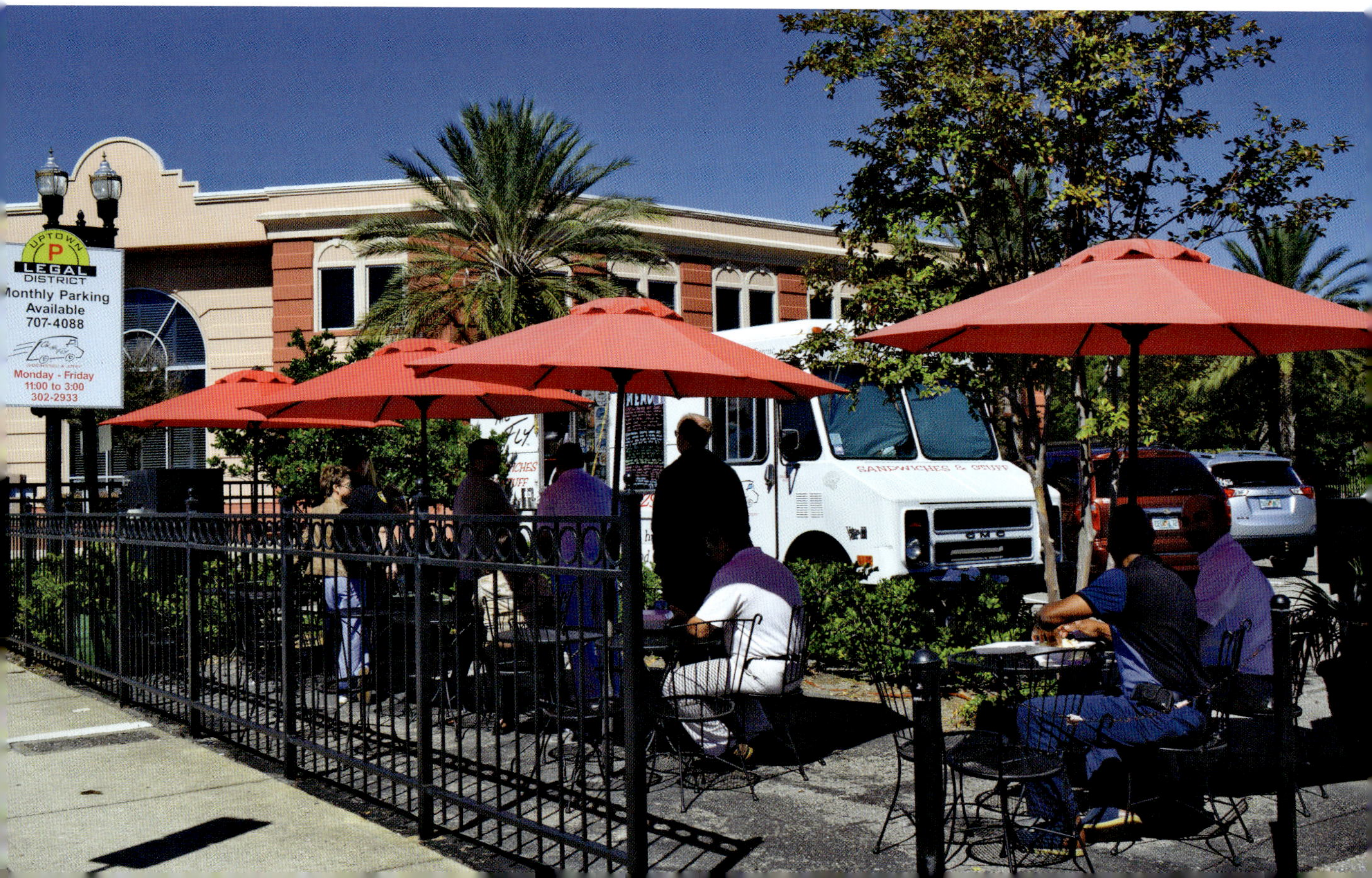

On the Fly's permanent location at Adams and Jefferson Streets is downtown near the courthouse.

goodies at one of the many shaded tables on the outdoor patio. OTF is there every weekday from 11:00 a.m. to 3:00 p.m., subject to change due to weather or special events (little-league games, for example), and it offers catering service in the evenings.

Jacksonville does love its food trucks, and On the Fly is a particular favorite. Last year, a few die-hard fans even had the image of the OTF truck tattooed on their forearms. On the Fly was voted Best Food Truck in the 2012 *Folio Weekly* Best of Jax readers' choice awards. The Food Truck Championship 2012 and 2013 garnered the truck both Judges' Choice and People's Choice Awards, and in 2013, Andrew's Chocolate–Peanut Butter Pretzel Bar won in the Food Truck Championship Sweet Tooth category. Newbie trucks took the honors in 2014, and Andrew resolved to up his game next year.

Andrew gives his crew due respect, but he also knows that he bears the ultimate responsibility for his own reputation. He doesn't take that for granted. His hand is on everything that comes out of his truck, and he doesn't send the crew out without him. He enjoys a large repeat following, largely because he knows he has to grab a diner's attention with his or her first dish and keep that diner happy every time with the same quality experience.

Will there be a day when On the Fly morphs into a brick-and-mortar location? Possibly. If so, Andrew would do breakfast and lunch and keep his nights open for family. And he wants it to be downtown, so he can keep his same loyal clientele. You can find On the Fly in his lot at Adams and Jefferson Streets or online at www.ontheflyjax.com and, of course, on Facebook.

ON THE FLY'S REESE'S PEANUT BUTTER CUP CRÈME BRÛLÉE

Recipe from Chef Andrew Ferenc

Our crème brûlée is a popular desert item that sells out quickly on our food truck. Our menu consists of traditional foods with a twist, and that's what we wanted to do with a dessert. You will need ten four- or five-ounce ramekins and a propane gas torch.

Serves 10

1 quart heavy whipping cream
3 whole vanilla beans, split and scraped, or 1 teaspoon vanilla extract
1 cup granulated sugar, plus additional ½ cup for brûlée topping
10 large egg yolks
1 bag Reese's Peanut Butter Cup minis, broken or chopped into small pieces

Preheat oven to 350 degrees. In a saucepot, add heavy cream, vanilla and 1 cup sugar. Stir and bring to a boil. Turn off heat. In a separate mixing bowl, whisk egg yolks. Add the cream mixture to the egg yolks a little at a time (tempering), stirring continually.

Continued on next page

Disperse Reese's Peanut Butter Cup pieces into crême brûlée ramekins. Pour egg and cream mixture over Reese's Cups until about ¾ full. In a deep cake or roasting pan, position dishes and add water to fill halfway up the sides of the ramekins.

Bake 20 to 30 minutes or until custard is set. Remove ramekins from pan and refrigerate for at least 2 hours. Remove the crème brûlée from the refrigerator 30 minutes prior to browning the granulated sugar on top.

Divide the remaining ½ cup of granulated sugar among the ramekins and spread evenly on top of each. Using your propane gas torch, melt the sugar so that it forms a crispy top. Let the top cool briefly and serve.

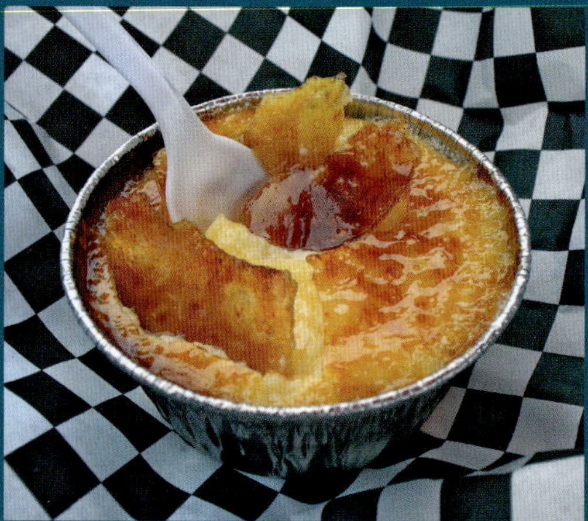

On the Fly's Reese's Peanut Butter Cup Crème Brulee

SMOKE IT UP BARBEQUE

Kelham Stephenson

One of my personal favorite barbecue operations is Smoke It Up Barbeque, run by a relatively young chef with a strong work ethic and a passion for excellence.

Kelham Stephenson got his first kitchen job at age thirteen. After working his way up the line at various restaurants, he attended culinary school at Johnson and Wales in Providence. He also got an early education in barbecue production from family friend Elaine Murphy working at her roadside barbecue trailer, True Blue, in Kingston, Massachusetts.

Although he started with culinary studies in Providence, Kelham ended up earning a bachelor of science in hospitality management at the Denver campus of Johnson and Wales. After graduation, he took a job with Westin Hotels. While in Denver, he helped a few friends get their food trucks up and running. When a bad motorcycle accident provided the young man some perspective, he decided to invest in his future and create a catering business. Getting off to a rocky start

Smoke It Up's house-made Pickles and Pickled Onions.

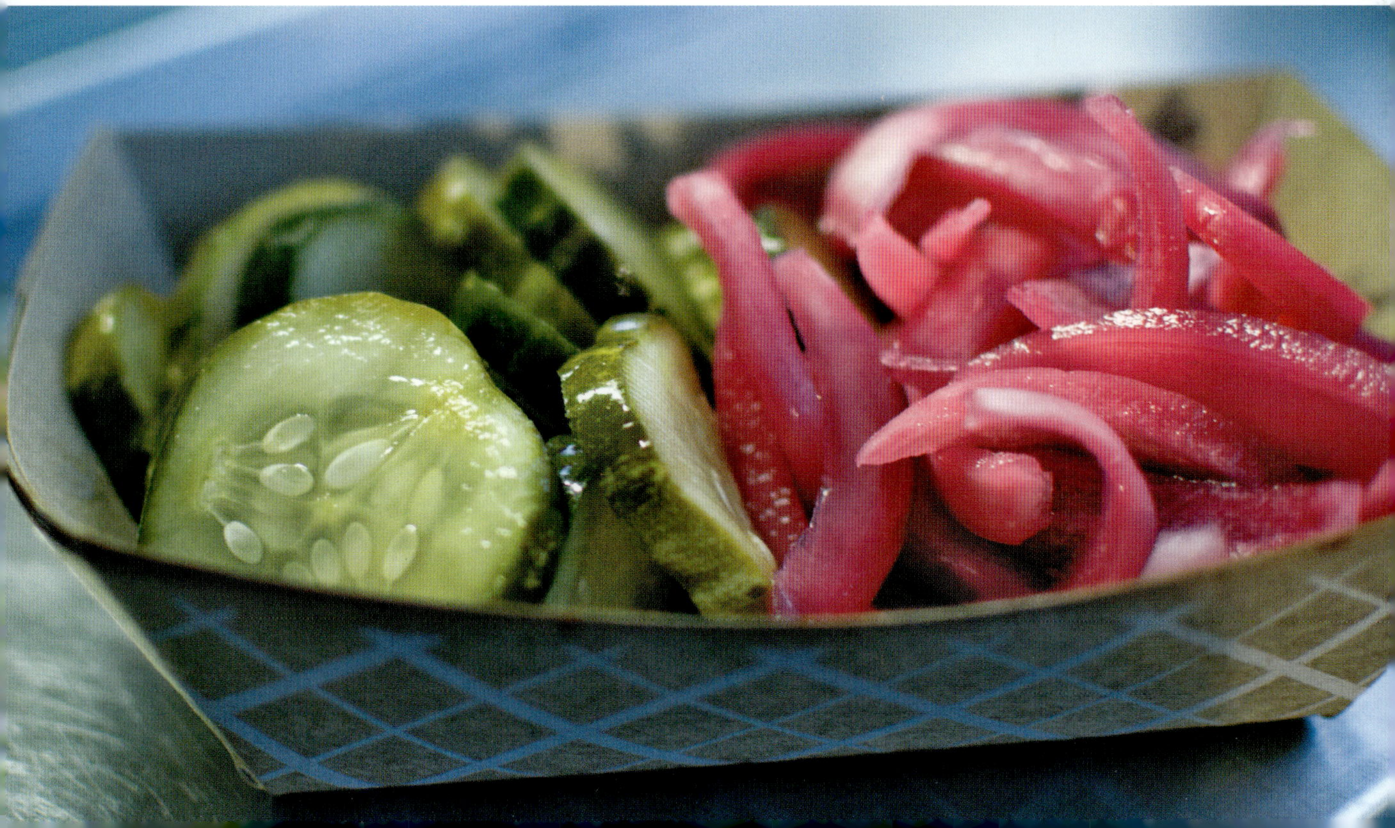

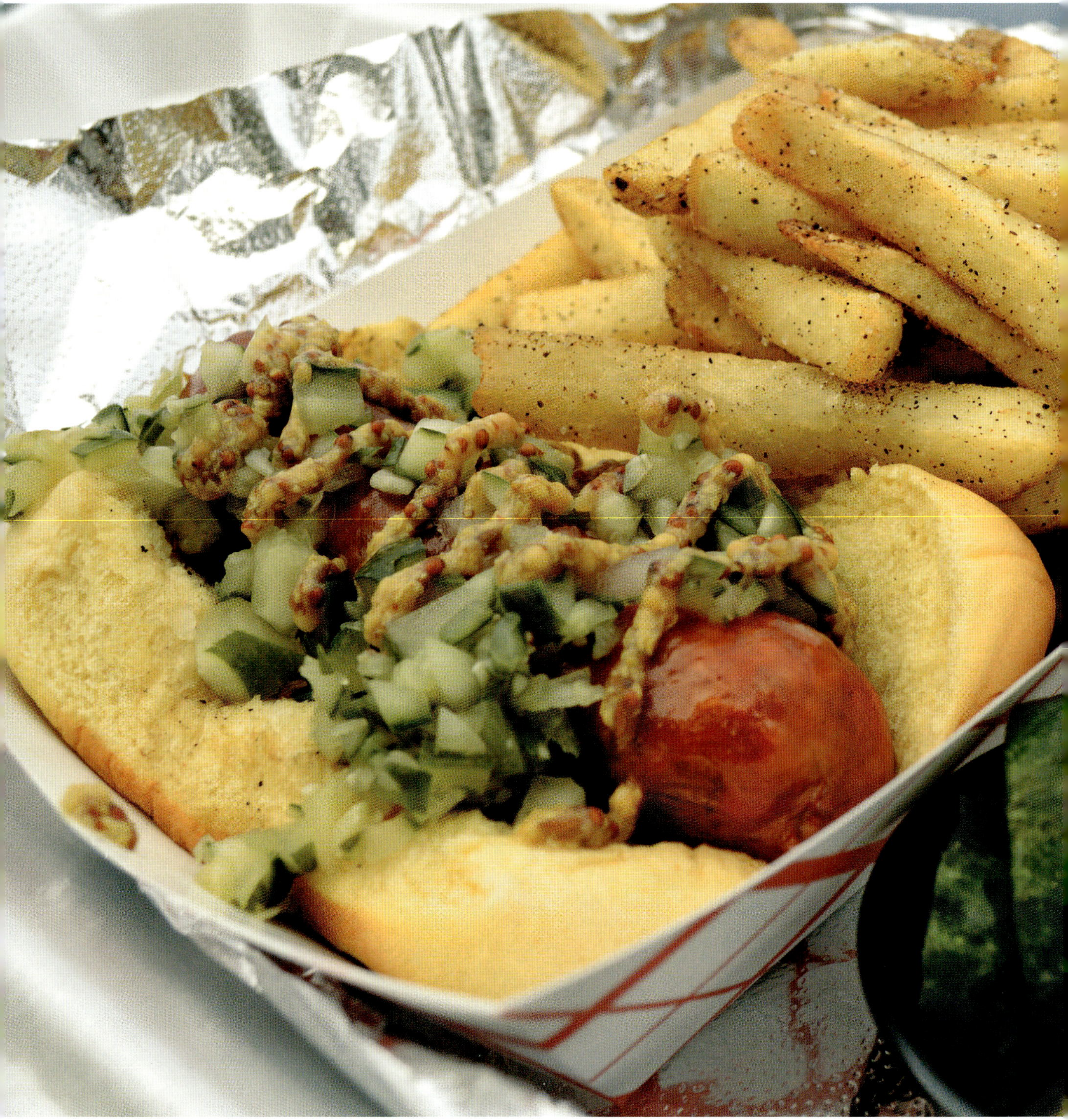

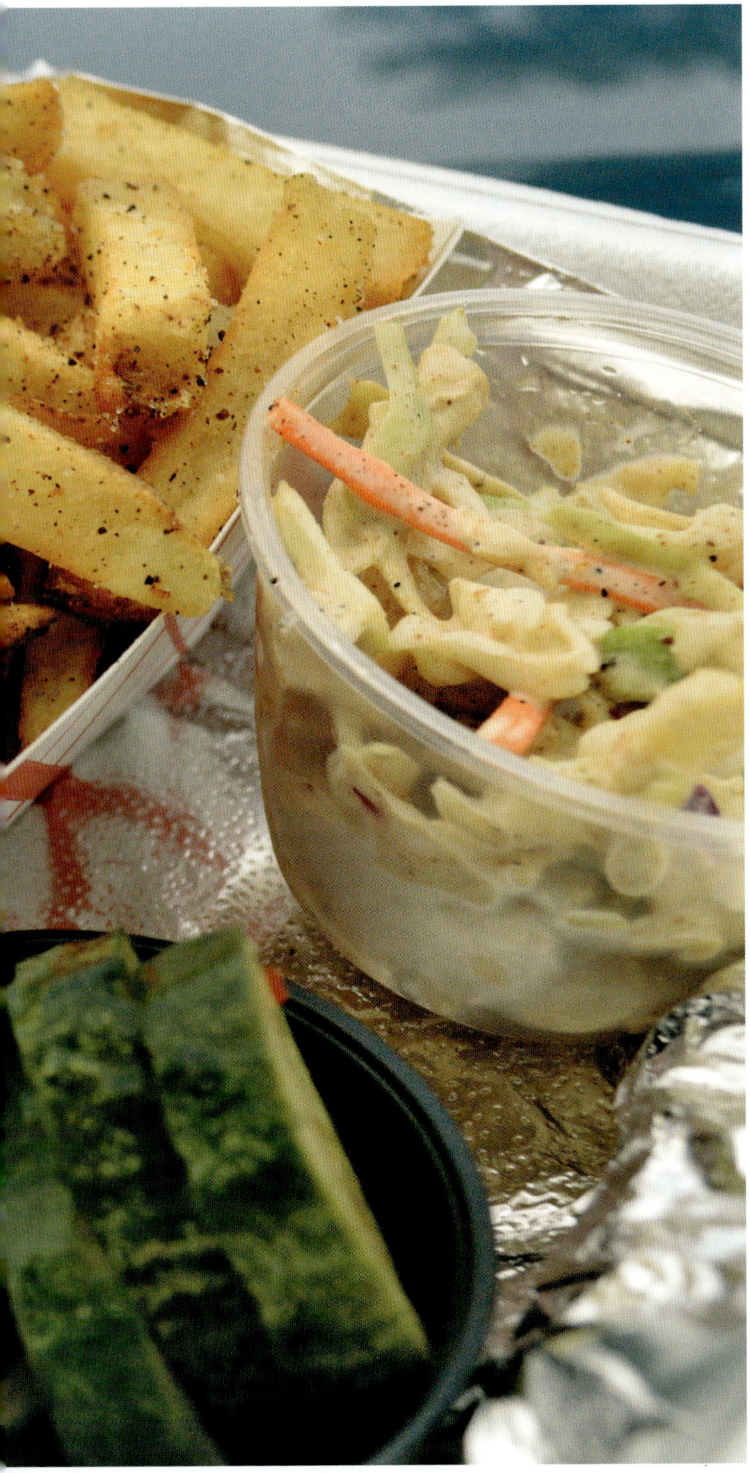

in Denver, he eventually headed to Jacksonville, where his girlfriend was working for the Jacksonville Jaguars, his sister was attending Flagler College in nearby St. Augustine and the food truck scene was heating up.

The outlook for food trucks in Jacksonville encouraged Kelham to create a gleaming new mobile kitchen. Beaver Street Commissary operator Chriss Brown helped him navigate Jacksonville's regulations and licensing requirements, and friends and family pitched in to help get Smoke It Up Barbeque on the road.

The sleek black, white and red truck and trailer features a large, bright open kitchen with lots of windows. A wood-fired Lang Smoker is the workhorse behind the scenes. While meats are cooked low and slow, on the truck the service is fast, and the crowds are embracing Kelham's straightforward style. Maybe they want that firsthand interaction with the people who have created the food, or they just want to be part of the scene. Whatever the reason, business has been steady for the trucks like Smoke It Up that are providing a consistent quality product.

Smoked Sausage Sandwich with pickles from Smoke It Up Barbeque.

Kelham cooks everything in the mobile kitchen except for the meats, which are smoked on the wood-fired smoker. At Smoke It Up, the focus is on the simple flavors of the meat, letting diners add sauces as they care to. Kelham's first choice is always to source local, organic, freshly farmed produce.

Smoke It Up makes about twelve gallons of each sauce fresh each week. An array of house-made pickles takes four to eight days in the refrigerator before they are ready to serve. When the truck works with local breweries like Aardwolf, it will feature the brewery's beer in its house-made mustard.

Pulled pork is the top seller at Smoke It Up Barbeque. Pork butt is smoked for thirteen hours over hickory, cherry and pecan wood. Once off the smoker, the fat cap is removed and hand shredded into tender pork. It's great in a slider or a sandwich, but I like it on its own, with just a drizzle of the house-made North Carolina vinegar-based barbecue sauce and a side of fresh coleslaw, which Kelham makes with chili-lime mayo.

Sausages made in house are my personal favorite. There's a firm snap to the bite, and the juicy, smoky pork is perfectly seasoned. I like mine loaded with the house mustard, chopped pickle and plenty of vibrant pink pickled onions. It's salty, sweet, tart, savory, crunchy, soft, juicy, spicy and oh, so delicious.

People expecting brisket or ribs might find them during a dinner outing, but the labor involved isn't practical for Smoke It Up's lunch operation. For the most part, the meats are smoked in the morning and served the same day.

Chicken wings, for example, are brined for twelve to twenty-four hours. Then they get an hour and a half on the smoker, and after cooling, they are loaded on the truck. As ordered, they are dropped in the fryer to crisp the skin and tossed in a paprika-based rub. The result is a juicy, smoky, full-flavored wing. I like to dip them in the Kansas City–style sweet sauce as I eat them.

Finding locations to serve has become easier as Smoke It Up got the word out through events like the Jax Truckies Block Party at the Jacksonville Landing and the Food Truck Alley at the Jaguars games. Lunches at Key Buick and McKesson on the Southside and evening service at Aardwolf Brewery in San Marco have helped the truck grow its customer base. Catering events and parties has become a big part of the business, too.

Fellow food truck owners have been there for Kelham when he needed guidance along the way. As he soon discovered, while they are his competition, they are also a welcoming community. His advice to new owners is "Don't be afraid to reach out to this great network of truckies, who are more than happy to share their knowledge and lend a hand up."

It's possible that by the time you're reading this, Kelham may be opening

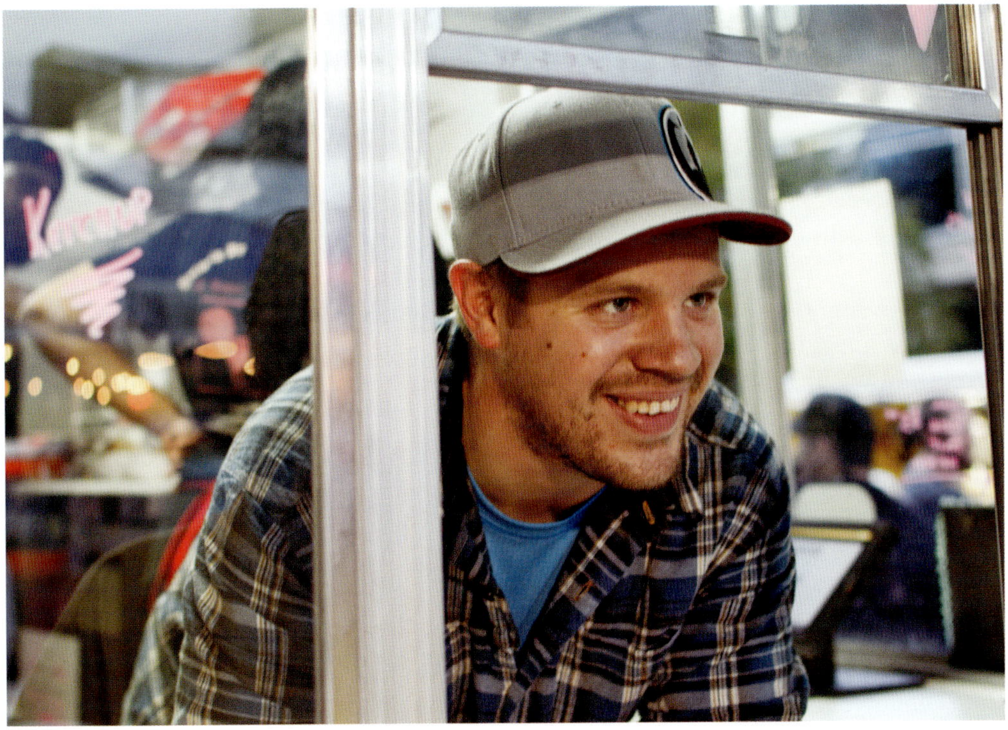

Kelham Stephenson, owner of Smoke It Up Barbeque.

a restaurant. Wherever you find it, Smoke It Up Barbeque is worth the trip. Find the truck online at www.smokeitupbbqkitchen.com, follow him on Twitter @SmokeItUpBBQ and check out Kelham's drool-worthy feed on Instagram @smokeitupbbqkitchen.

SON OF A BUTCHER

Randy Leibl and Danyelle Smialkowsky

One of the most popular trucks to hit the streets late last year, Son of a Butcher came to be because co-owner/operator Randy Leibl was hungry for a good Philly cheesesteak.

Randy spent most of his life in the restaurant business. Born in Winnipeg, Canada, he moved to Clearwater–St. Pete with his family at age fifteen and got his first job at the Double H (for hotdogs and hamburgers). He attended Florida State University, and at age twenty, he got his first heavy kitchen experience working the nightly dinner cruise for Starline Cruises. By 2006, he owned controlling interest in three restaurants in Ohio and partial interest in three more. He had already become successful in the business when he realized that it wasn't what he wanted to do. He sold his restaurant holdings and swore he'd never return to the food biz. He moved to Biloxi, Mississippi, where he helped with post-Katrina cleanup, tried to break into the real estate business and flexed his muscle as a semi-professional poker player in the casinos for a few years.

Back in Florida, he did some research on the food trucks in Jacksonville and felt there was room for a real, straightforward sandwich. Real and straightforward could also describe Randy himself. He's an immensely entertaining and genuine guy, but one thing he isn't is the son of a butcher. His wife, Darla, actually came up with the name, playing on the slightly irreverent and fun tone he wanted to establish with their brand.

Enter Danyelle Smialkowsky, a first-class Philly cheesesteak cook from Baltimore, as well as Randy's niece and business partner. She had been in the restaurant business for ten years, working on the line, when Randy invited her aboard to help run the business.

Randy found a guy in the Tampa area who had rescued a rusted-out, former ice cream truck, a 1990 model with only thirty-one thousand miles on it. More cute than functional, it was bright yellow outside and sported a very small kitchen inside, with a two-foot grill and fry baskets. He bought it on sight and hauled it back to Jacksonville, and they started working on it. Randy and Danyelle rolled up their sleeves, installed the refrigeration unit and did the sheet metal work to reconfigure the truck themselves.

Randy knew Danyelle had a strong work ethic, but initially, he had no idea how instrumental she would be to the success of the operation. But he absolutely did refer to her as a beast in the kitchen—in the best sense of the word, of course! She has seemingly boundless energy and enthusiasm, and no matter how hot it gets in the small kitchen, she just leans in and gets it

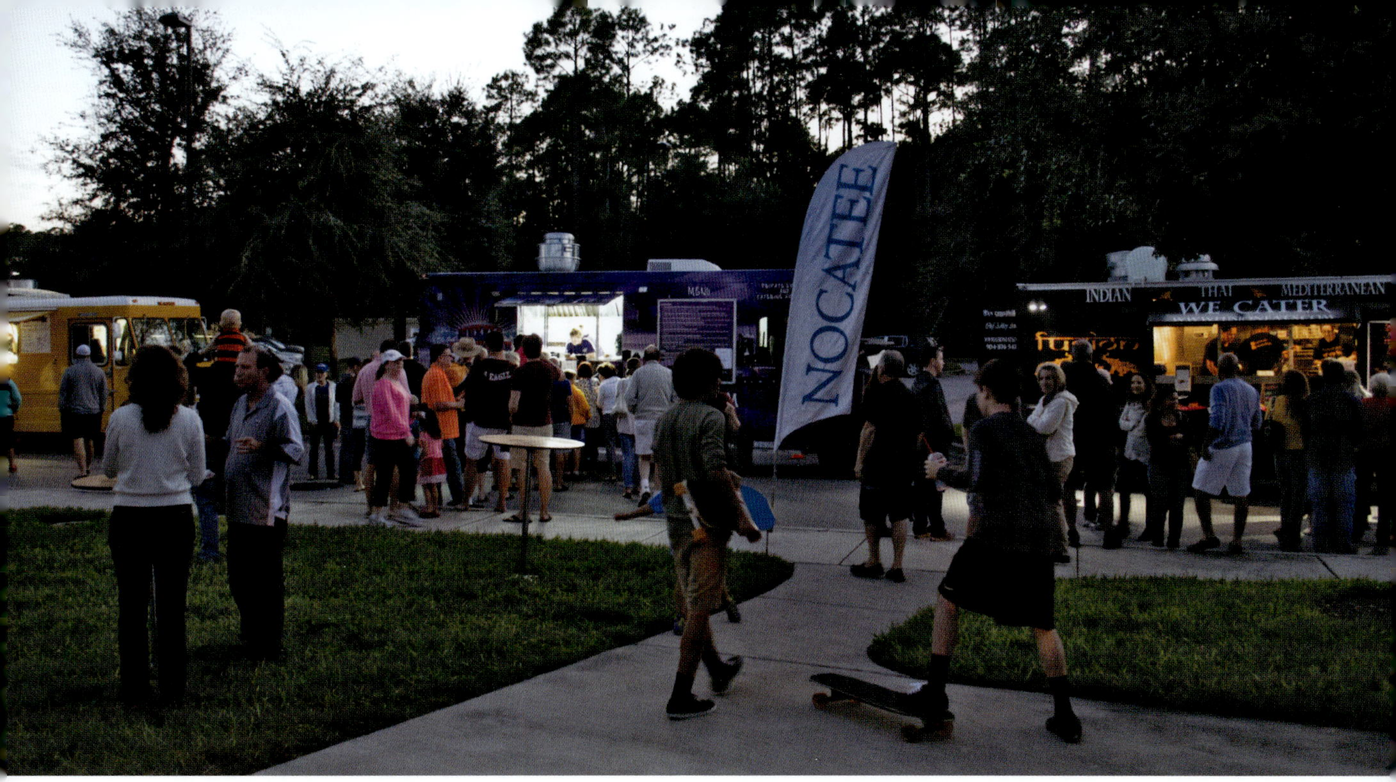

Families turn out for Nocatee Food Truck Fridays.

done. The two have developed a rhythm working together in tight quarters to crank out orders and entertain their loyal and growing customer base.

Their first day of service was September 1, 2014, at the grand opening of a dance studio on Beach Boulevard. The first customer in line was fellow food truck aficionado Mark Ballinger. Randy says he was waiting there when the window opened. An hour later, Jax Truckies founder Mike Field showed up and ordered the Chocolate Elvis (fresh-baked bread grilled with Nutella and sliced banana). Then he invited them to attend Food Fun(d), an event he organized to support local startups.

Randy and Danyelle are very much about concept, having a great time and plating a great product.

The cornerstone of their menu is the Original-Style Philly: fresh-baked bun and thin-sliced grilled rib-eye steak, with lettuce, tomato, grilled onions and peppers and, of course, cheese whiz. Want Provolone? You got it! Watch Danyelle work the grill, chopping and seasoning the steak for this monster of a sandwich, and you know it's gonna be good.

It was Danyelle's idea to add grilled fresh Mayport shrimp to create the Mayport SOB.

In my not-so-humble opinion, our fresh Mayport shrimp—sweet, plump and pink—is the best food resource local to north Florida. But if your shrimp isn't fresh, fuggedaboutit! As Randy says, it doesn't matter how you season it, or how you prepare it, you have to start with the best available fresh ingredients. When figuring the food costs for the Mayport SOB, the

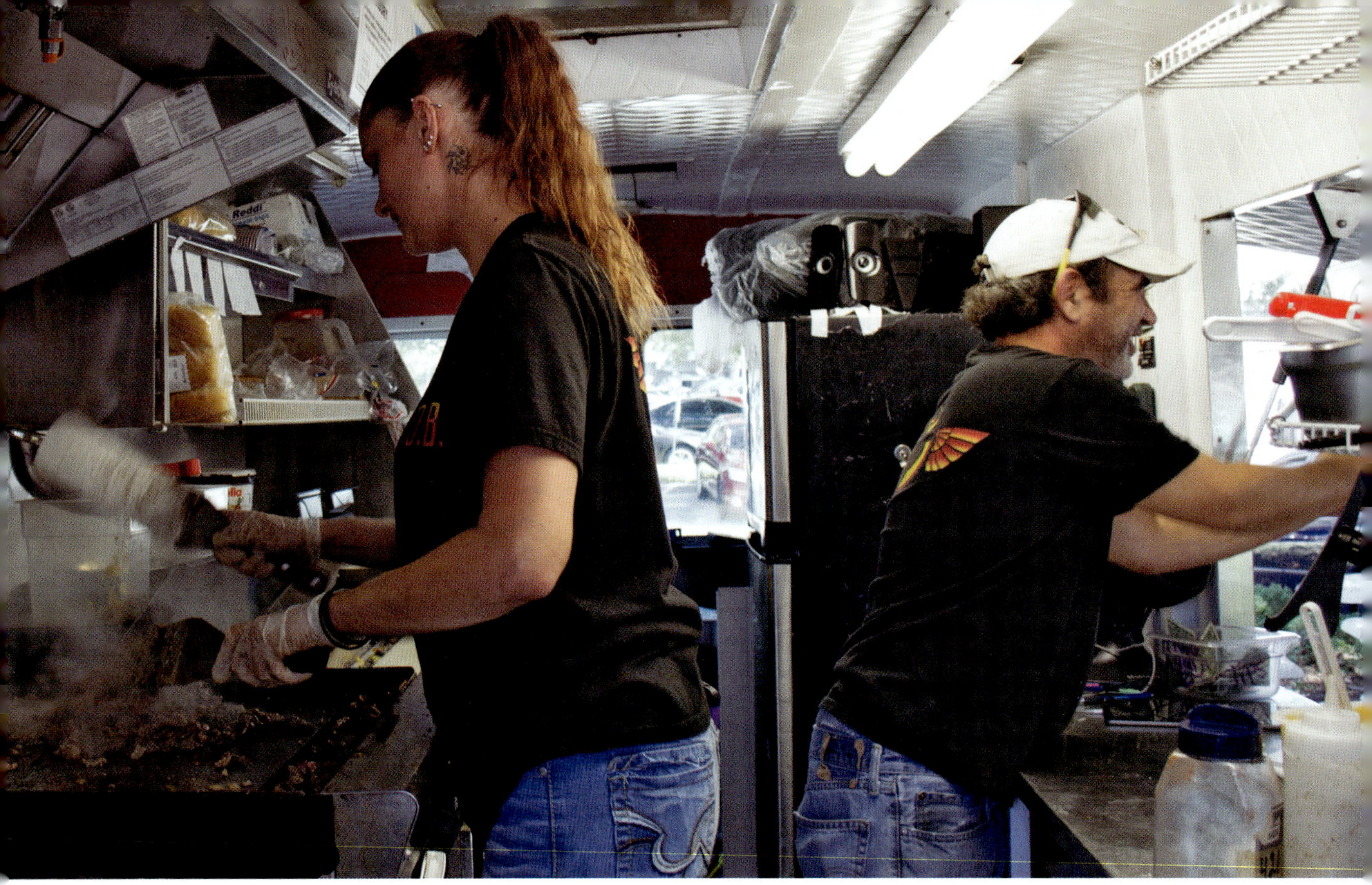

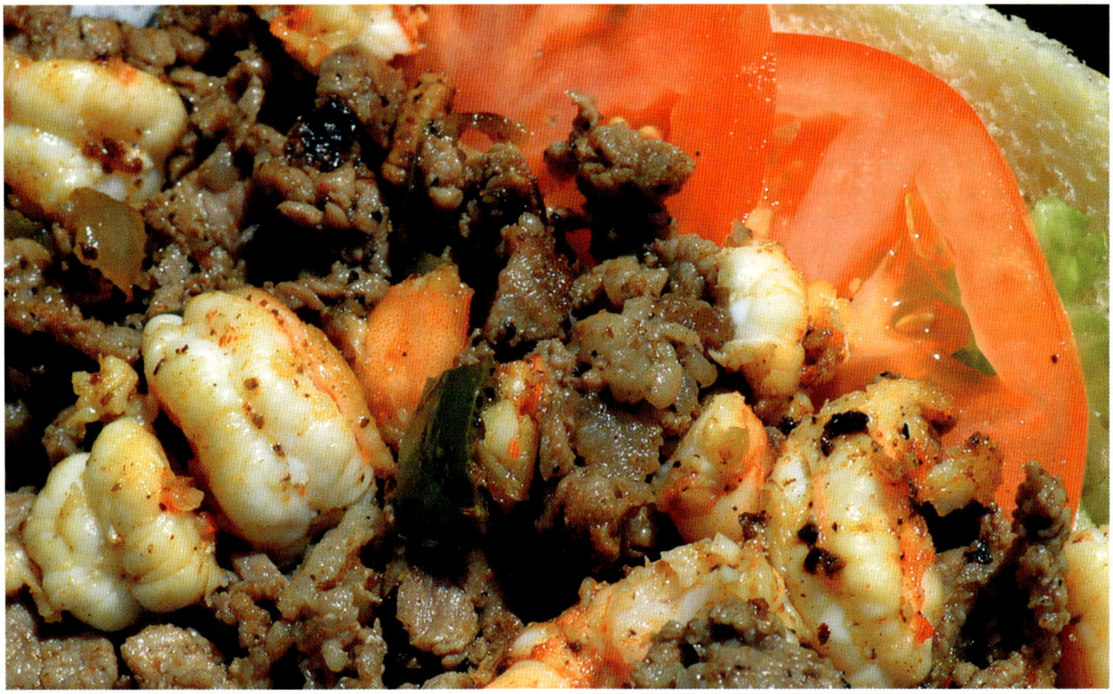

Above: Danyelle and Randy work the lunch rush.

Left: The Mayport SOB.

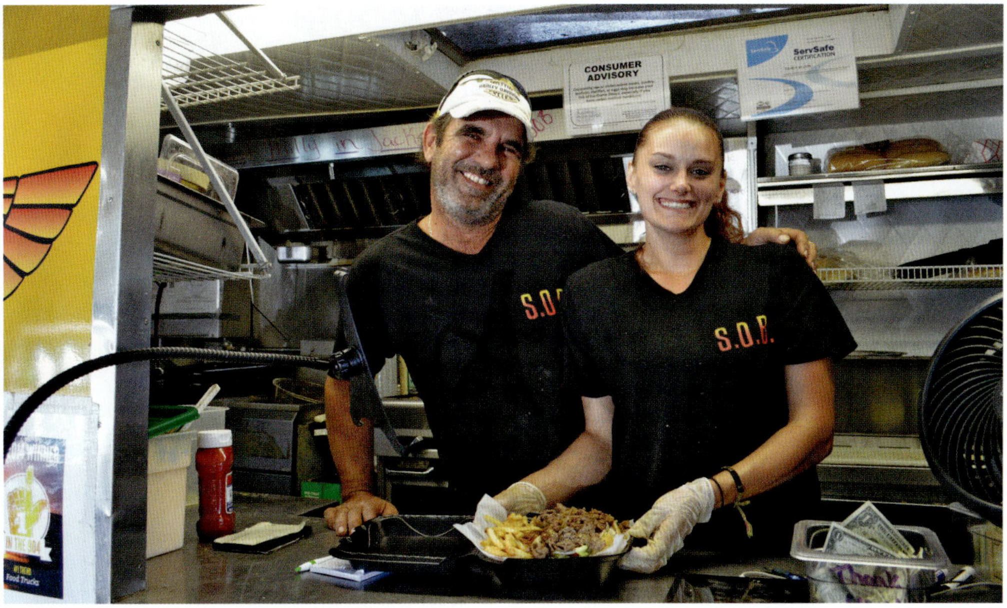

Randy Leibl and Danyelle Smialkowsky, owners of Son of a Butcher.

Shrimp Po'Boy and Shrimp Tacos, Randy weighed his options and polled his customer base—did his customers want fresh Mayport shrimp or a larger portion of frozen shrimp? Fortunately, 60 percent agreed fresh, local ingredients were the way to go. I stand with the 60-percenters.

Another awesome choice on their rotating menu is the Rich SOB—hand-cut filet mignon sliders, grilled to order and topped with mini crab cakes.

This is in stark contrast to, you guessed it, the Poor SOB—butcher-quality grilled beef bologna with American cheese and mustard on grilled fresh white bread.

Randy loves how laid-back, fun and real people are in Jacksonville. He and Danyelle have seen a great reception for their food in just a few short months. He hopes that as the local food truck industry grows and improves, the people will compel the city to embrace and support it more fully.

You can find the bright yellow SOB truck online at www.jaxsonofabutcher.com or look it up on Facebook at jaxsonofabutcher and on Twitter (drop the *r*) @jaxsonofabutche.

SOUTH IN YOUR MOUTH

Donny Trauthwein and Rachel Baldwin-Trauthwein

Armed with the best ingredients and an unrelenting love for food, Donny Trauthwein and Rachel Baldwin-Trauthwein have set up camp—Fish Camp, that is.

South in Your Mouth is one of those lucky few mobile food businesses that has a permanent lunch spot. Browns' Creek Fish Camp on Heckhser Drive is Rachel's family's business and her and Donny's home base. Rachel is vice-president of operations for the full bait and tackle shop and surrounding property, a hub for the local fishing community. They are open Monday through Friday at Browns' Creek, and they hit the road on weekends for events, catering gigs, festivals and such.

They started designing their trailer in July 2013, working with M&R Specialty Trailers to bring it to fruition. The bright yellow rig with its provocative slogan and playful graphics is easily visible from the road. Parking is plentiful, and there are a few picnic tables for customers to enjoy their lunch on the premises. They are just a short drive from the Port of Jacksonville, the Marine Corps base, BAE Systems and Jacksonville Electric Authority. That, along with word of mouth among regulars, has earned them a solid customer base in a relatively short time.

Even though his mostly blue-collar male customers don't spend a lot of time on Facebook, Donny tells me they will check his page to see what's on special for lunch. There are at least one hundred "regulars" who Donny and his crew know on a first name basis. Many of their customers call their orders in so they are ready and waiting when they get there. Donny and the team do most of their business in the first thirty to forty-five minutes each day, so if you want a more leisurely lunch experience, wait until the crowds die down a bit; however, you might miss some of the daily specials. When they are out, they are out! On the other hand, you might get to sit and enjoy lunch with Donny himself.

Donny mans the smoker and "drives" the food business while Rachel manages the bookings and helps out at bigger events. Their dream is to create a restaurant with a family playground behind the existing store at the Fish Camp. Meanwhile, their food enjoys a growing fan base as it spreads their brand recognition far and wide.

Their very first event was a doozy: They had just gotten the trailer and were invited to do Bike Week 2014 in Daytona Beach. They were parked at the White Eagle, a Daytona Beach bar. They were the only concession trailer in a sea of food vendors in tents. After observing hordes of hungry customers making their selections from the large photos of food being served at

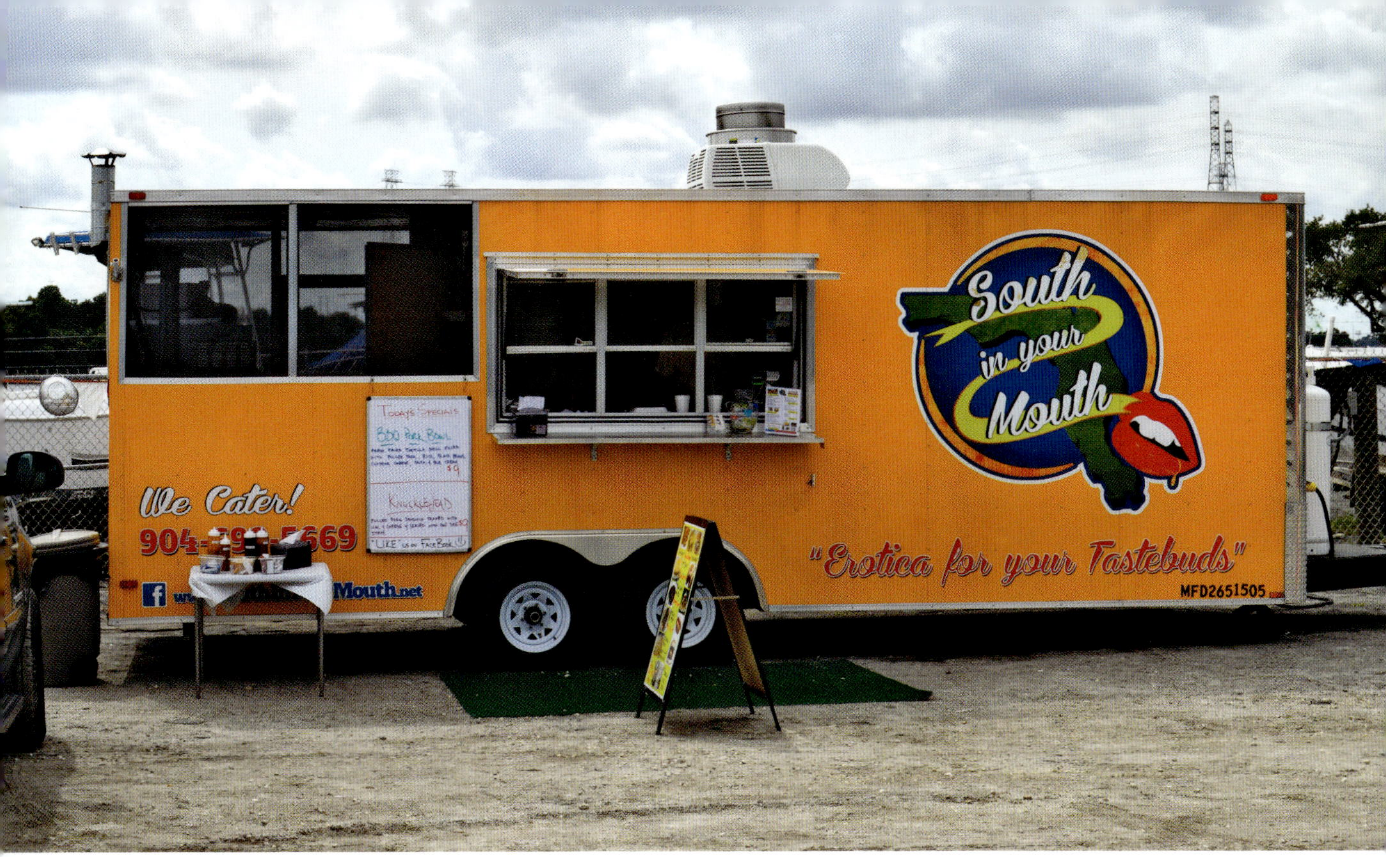

South in Your Mouth.

each tent, Rachel quickly replaced her chalkboard-style menu with a signboard featuring color photos of their items, a technique they have used ever since. They got the hang of serving the diverse Bike Week crowd during the ten-day stint.

After Bike Week, they came back to Jacksonville and held their grand opening at the Browns' Creek Fish Camp at the end of March 2014. At first, they did made-to-order breakfasts in addition to their lunch service. They were almost too successful at that and decided to stick with lunch, where they could focus on their mouth-watering barbecue pork and beef. Donny credits his father with teaching him everything he knows about barbecue, and while it's an important component of their menu, they don't want to be known as just a barbecue truck.

They had their biggest sales day ever at the Jacksonville Boat Show. Donny says big events are fun but take extra time away from their three children, so they weigh their options carefully. They were in Food Truck Alley at Everbank Field for the Jaguars versus the Steelers, and they returned to Daytona Beach for Biketoberfest in October. They served a majority of the diners at the annual Kingfish Tournament last year and have been present at most every fishing-related event in town. Visitors to St. Augustine Distillery Company's Sugar Cane Harvest lined up at the big yellow trailer to get a little South in their mouths.

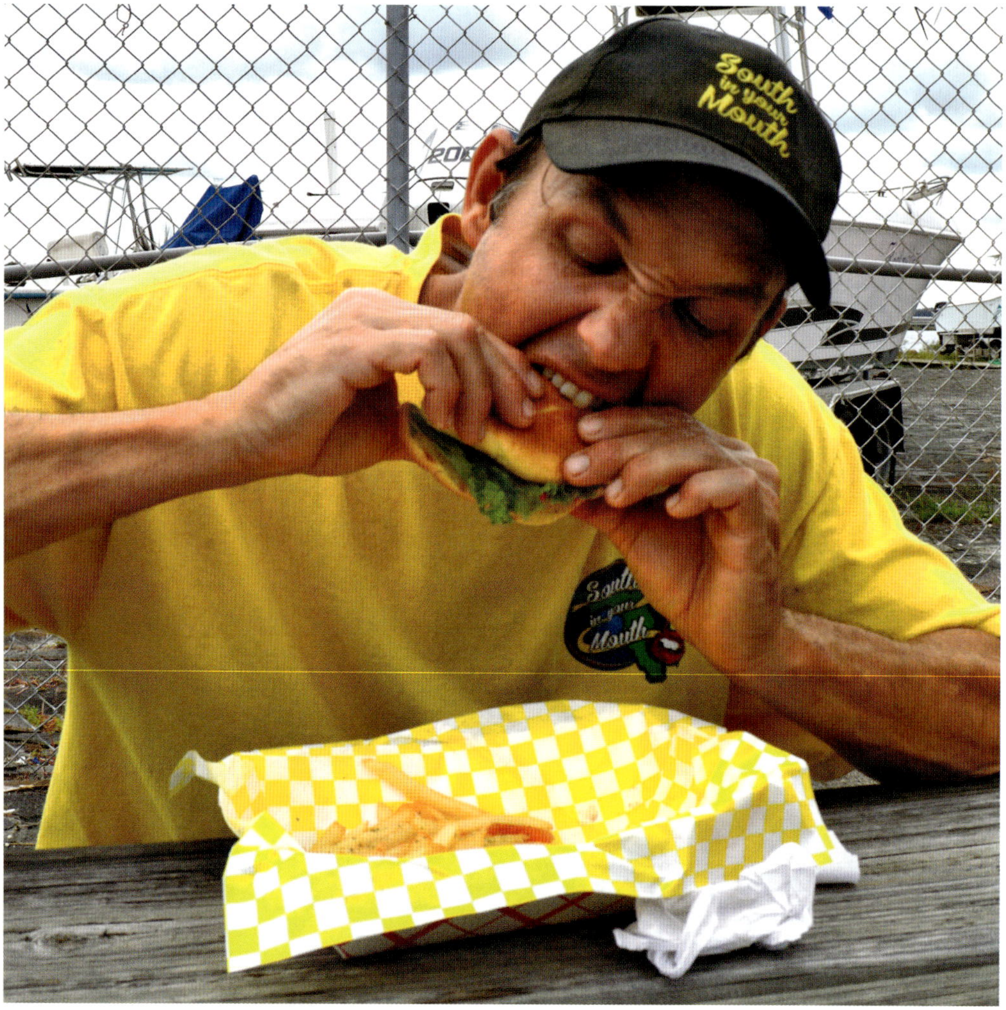

Donny Trauthwein, co-owner of South in Your Mouth.

Pulled pork is on the menu every day. Donny used to ride motorcycles, and with South in Your Mouth's debut at Bike Week came the Harley Davidson–themed names for a trio of pulled pork sandwiches: the Panhead (the original succulent pulled pork sandwich), Knucklehead (the same, topped with creamy mac and cheese) and Springhead (piled high with Carolina slaw). I ordered the Springhead my first time out. Donny told me they were looking for a name that went with the "motorhead" theme but got across that this one had green veggies on it too. Thus the "spring" came to be in Springhead. Any of these three sandwiches would be a mouthful, but this one was so huge it became lunch *and* dinner.

Burgers are a half pound of fresh Angus beef that is hand pattied and cooked to order on the grill. It takes eight minutes to cook them through, but it is worth every minute for the juiciest, most flavorful burger. I'm getting this next time I go.

Wednesday is "Ribs Day." Fresh St. Louis ribs are smoked for hours, and they are super big and meaty. Donny and Rachel make their own rubs and spice mixes for this and all their meats.

On Thursdays, they do smoked brisket: tender beef brisket, smoked for over sixteen hours. Get there early, or better yet, phone your order in. They open at 11:00 a.m., and they

The Springhead.

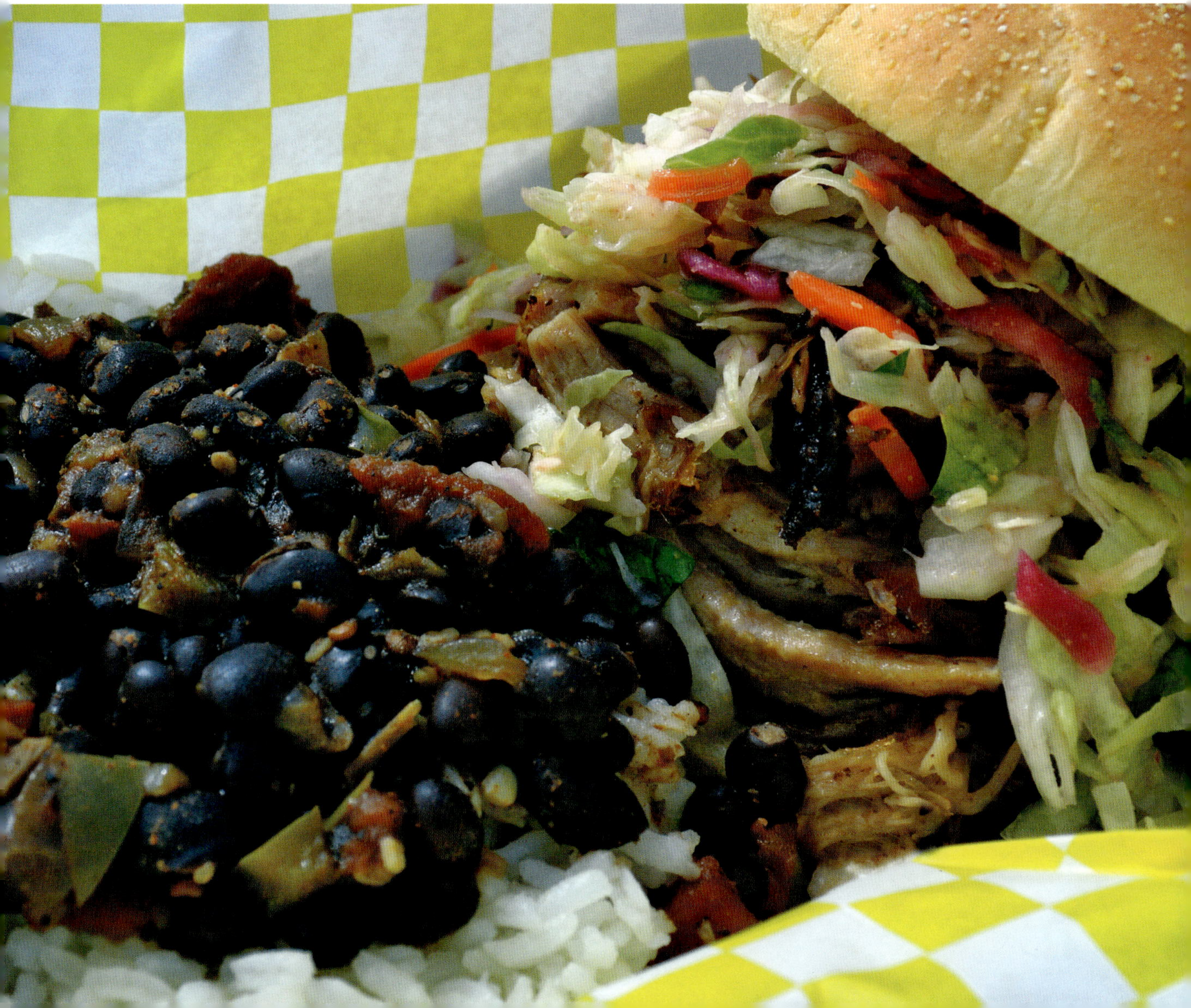

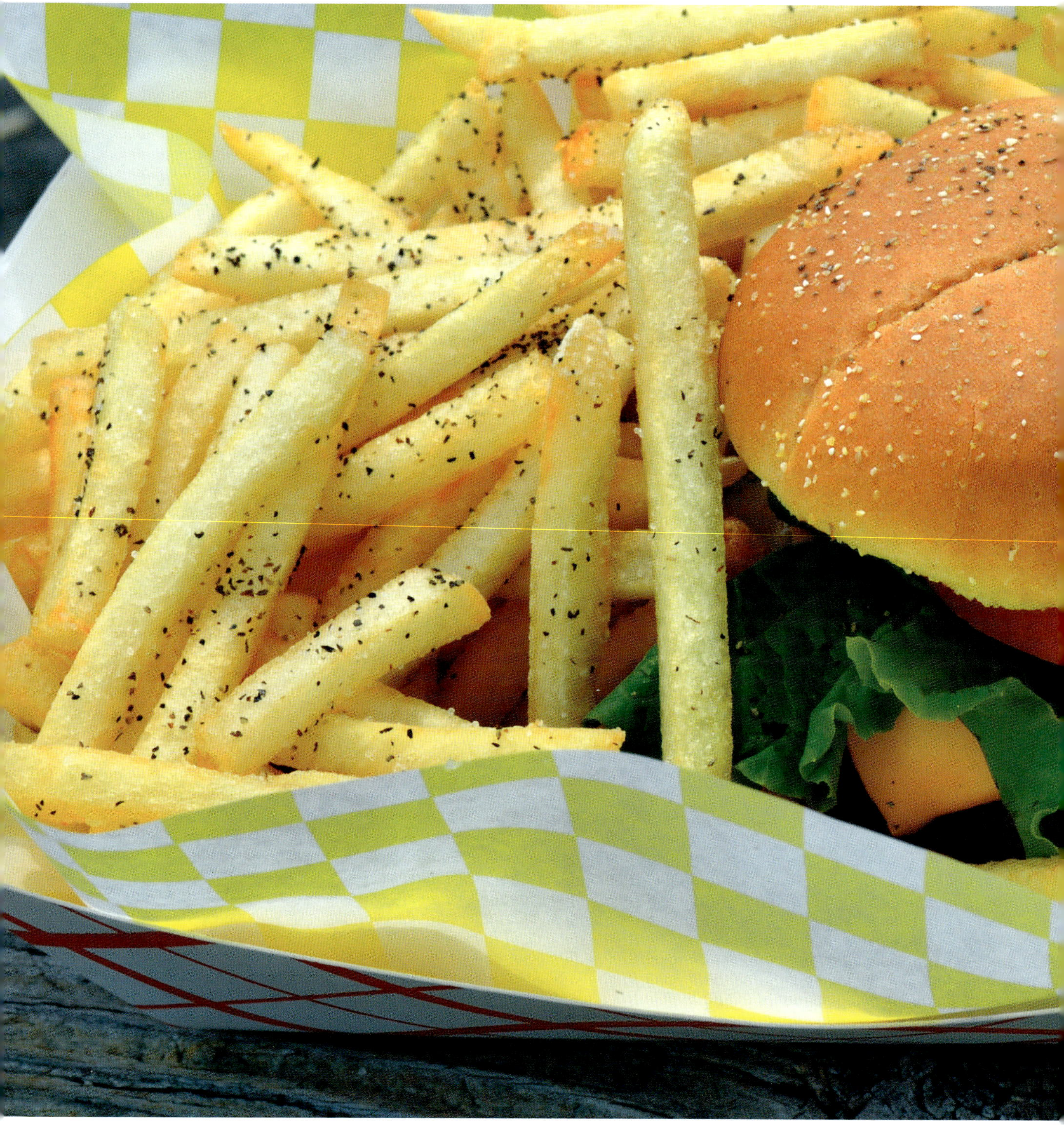

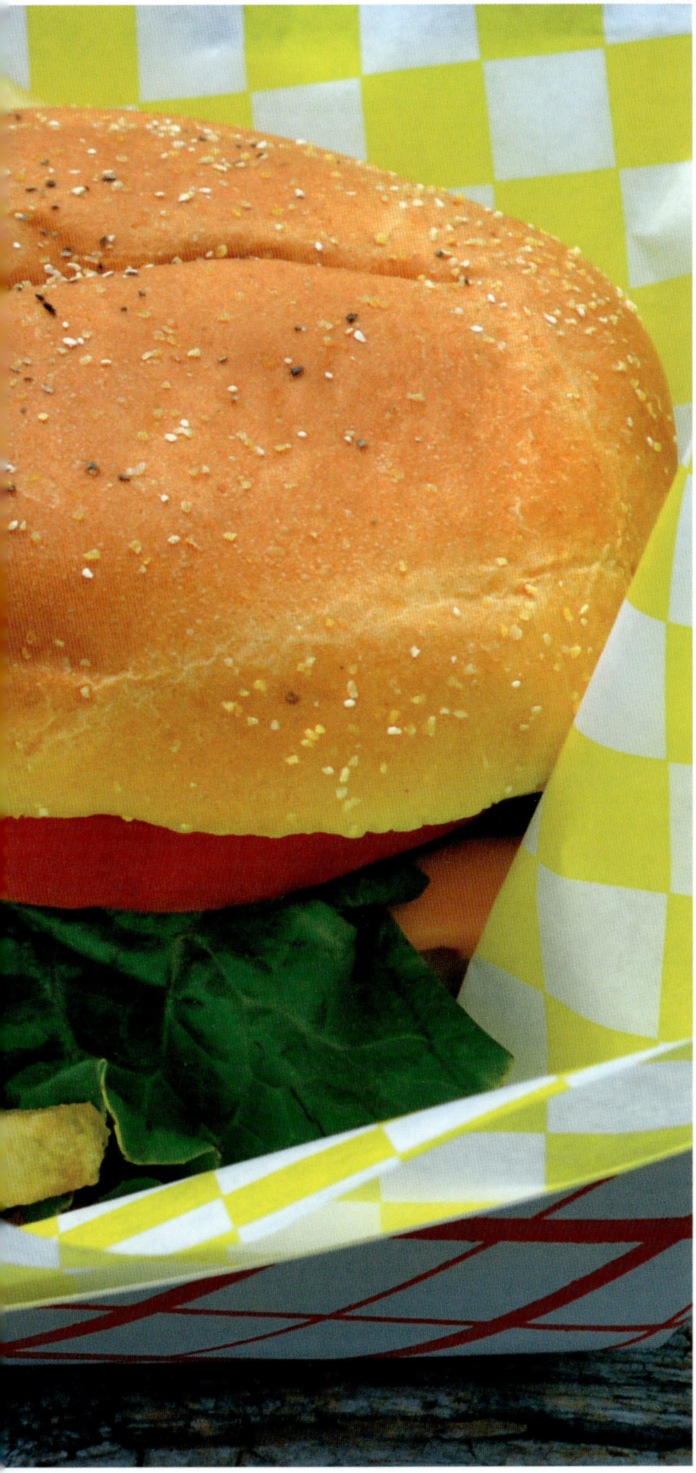

will sell out of thirty pounds of brisket by 12:30 p.m.

They serve specials with your choice of crispy French fries, black beans and rice, mac and cheese or Carolina slaw. I tried their black beans and rice, and I get why they are the most complimented side dish on the list. Sometimes you just want a healthier choice than the fries and mac, and South in Your Mouth's black beans and rice deliver—in the most flavorful way possible.

The massive Pork Bowl is another great choice, featuring black beans and rice in a fried tortilla shell, along with a generous heap of pulled pork, cheese, cilantro, sour cream and salsa.

Sausage and Home-Fried Potatoes with green peppers and onions is so popular it sells out in fifteen minutes every time it is offered.

My new obsession is the Beef Brisket Philly: juicy, tender smoked brisket, melty provolone cheese and onions folded into a fresh bun—yes, please!

Donny was born in Hamilton, Ohio, a suburb of Cincinnati. His Cincy-style family recipe is the basis for his Dixieline Chili. It is served one, two, three, four or five ways, and if you have never gone to the "full five," you are missing out, my friends. I lived in Cincy years ago, and it was this dish that first drew me to South in Your Mouth. I was skeptical that Donny

Burger and fries from South in Your Mouth.

SOUTH IN YOUR MOUTH'S DIXIELINE CHILI

Recipe from Donny Trauthwein

1 quart cold water
2 pounds ground beef
10 ounces tomato paste
2 large onions, finely diced
¼ cup chili powder
1 teaspoon cayenne pepper
1 teaspoon ground cumin
1 teaspoon cinnamon
¼ teaspoon ground cloves
1½ teaspoons salt
1 tablespoon Worcestershire sauce
4 cloves fresh garlic
1 whole bay leaf (optional)
1 tablespoon apple cider vinegar (optional)
1 tablespoon unsweetened cocoa (optional)
1 15-ounce can red kidney beans (optional)

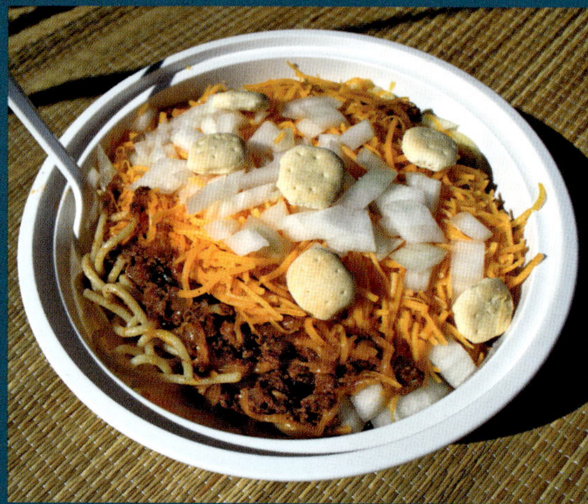

South in Your Mouth's Dixieline Chili.

In a large (3-quart) pot, combine water, ground beef, tomato paste and onion. Crumble all contents of the pot together with your hands until ground beef is all separated. (I usually wear gloves for this process; there is an interesting glaze on your fingers if not.) Heat mixture over medium heat.

Add dry spices, Worcestershire sauce and fresh garlic, as well as any optional ingredients (except the beans), and then reduce heat to medium-low. Stir chili frequently until it begins to simmer, reduce heat to low and cook for 3 hours. After 2 hours on low, cook red kidney beans, if using, in 2 cups of chili until heated through.

could pull off a genuine Cincinnati-style chili, but I was pleasantly surprised when I finally got to taste it. It's even better than I remembered. I was thrilled when Donny offered to share his "super-secret" recipe with us here. All I can say is if you can't get to South in Your Mouth and you have always wondered what the fuss is about Cincinnati chili, try this one.

Come to Browns' Creek Fish Camp for the full-on South in Your Mouth experience and visit Donny and Rachel online to check out the rest of their menu or to contact them for catering and events. You'll find them on Facebook and on their website at www.southinyourmouth.net. On Twitter, follow @southmouthjax.

SUPER FOOD

Richie Haugk and Dale Stoudt

Call the Super Food Truck to fight your hunger super-villain!

The colorful, cartoon-clad Super Food Truck can regularly be found patrolling the streets of Riverside, Southside and downtown Jacksonville looking for hungry patrons in need of saving. Well, OK, that's an exaggeration. What I mean to say is if Dale and Richie are not serving lunch at McKesson in Southpoint or in the parking lot at EverBank Plaza in Riverside or at the city lot at Main and Forsyth Streets downtown, look for them in downtown Jacksonville at their new brick-and-mortar location.

The Super Food Truck was custom fabricated by M&R Specialty Trailers in Macclenny, and the whimsical graphics were created by Atlantic Imaging in Atlantic Beach. Color-coordinated chairs invite diners to sit and wait for their orders or scarf down their fresh, hot lunch in the

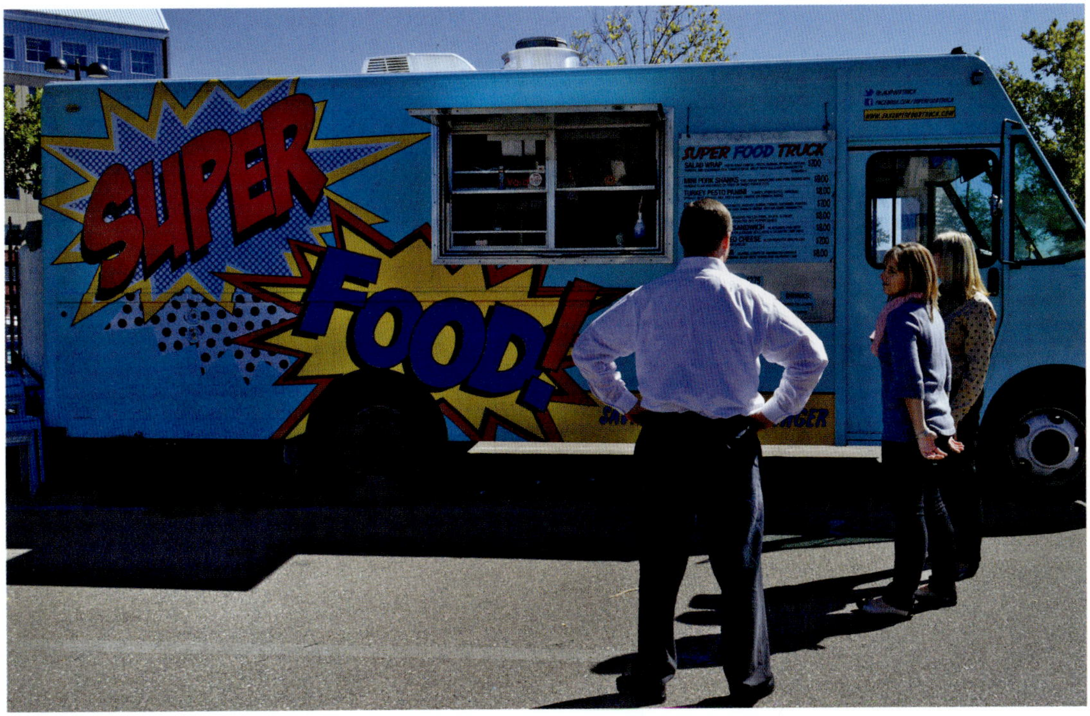

Super Food at EverBank Plaza.

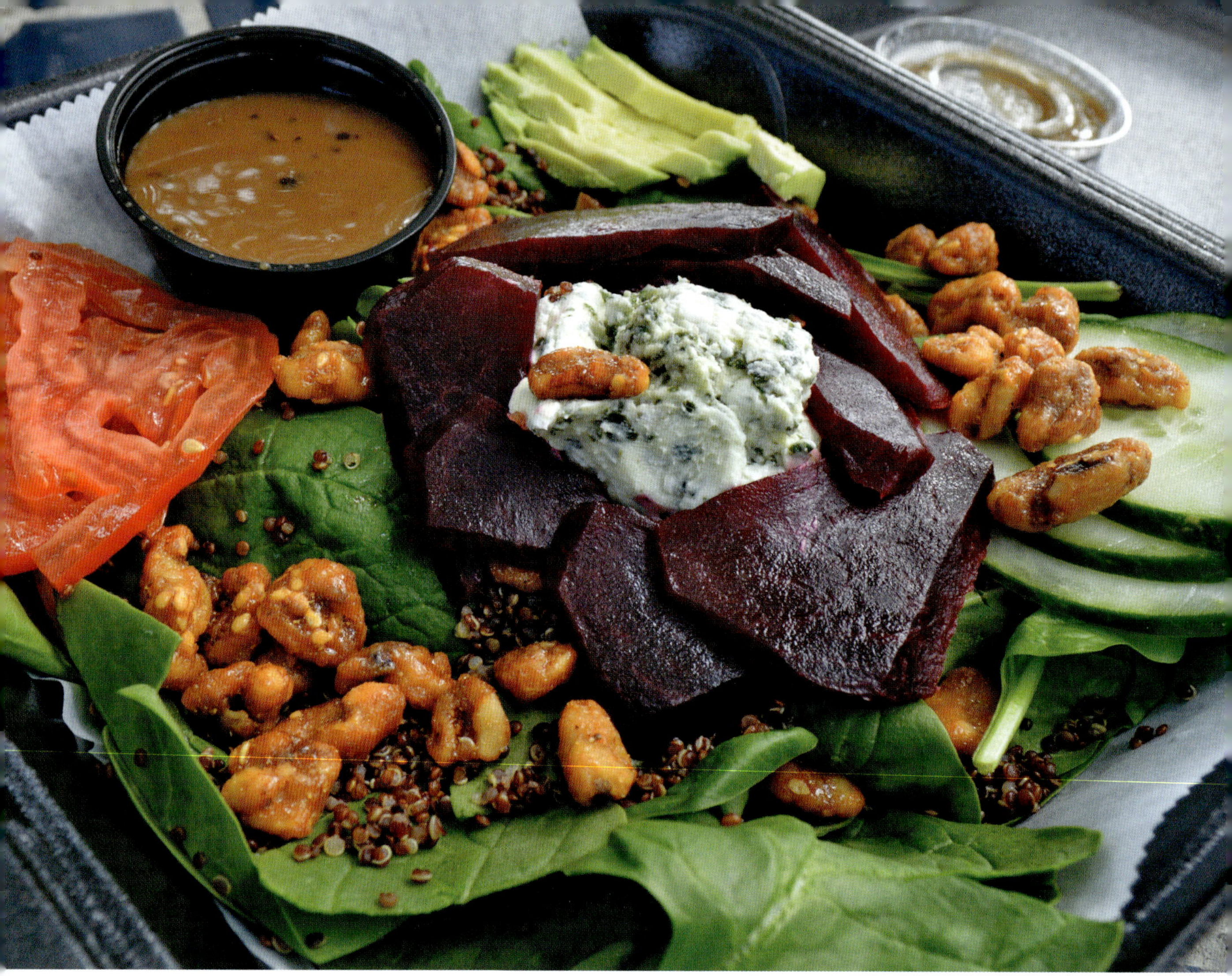

Super Food's Beet Salad.

great outdoors, before heading back to the beige world of cubicle row.

Chef and co-owner Richie Haugk is a twenty-year veteran of the restaurant industry. He came out of some of the best fine-dining kitchens at the beach, as a sous chef at Marker 32 and chef de partie at the Ponte Vedra Inn and Club.

Super Food's cuisine is based on fresh, wholesome "super foods," the nutrient-dense, good-for-you stuff, but Ritchie and Dale make it look and taste way better than most of our moms did while we were growing up. Take the beet salad I got from them the last time I visited. They were parked at McKesson, in an office complex parking lot that hosts a rotating variety of food trucks throughout the week. The salad was a beautifully arranged plate of roasted beets, avocado, quinoa, tomato, cucumber, toasted walnuts and herbed chevre over a bed of fresh spinach greens, with a fresh balsamic vinaigrette dressing. The portion was mammoth!

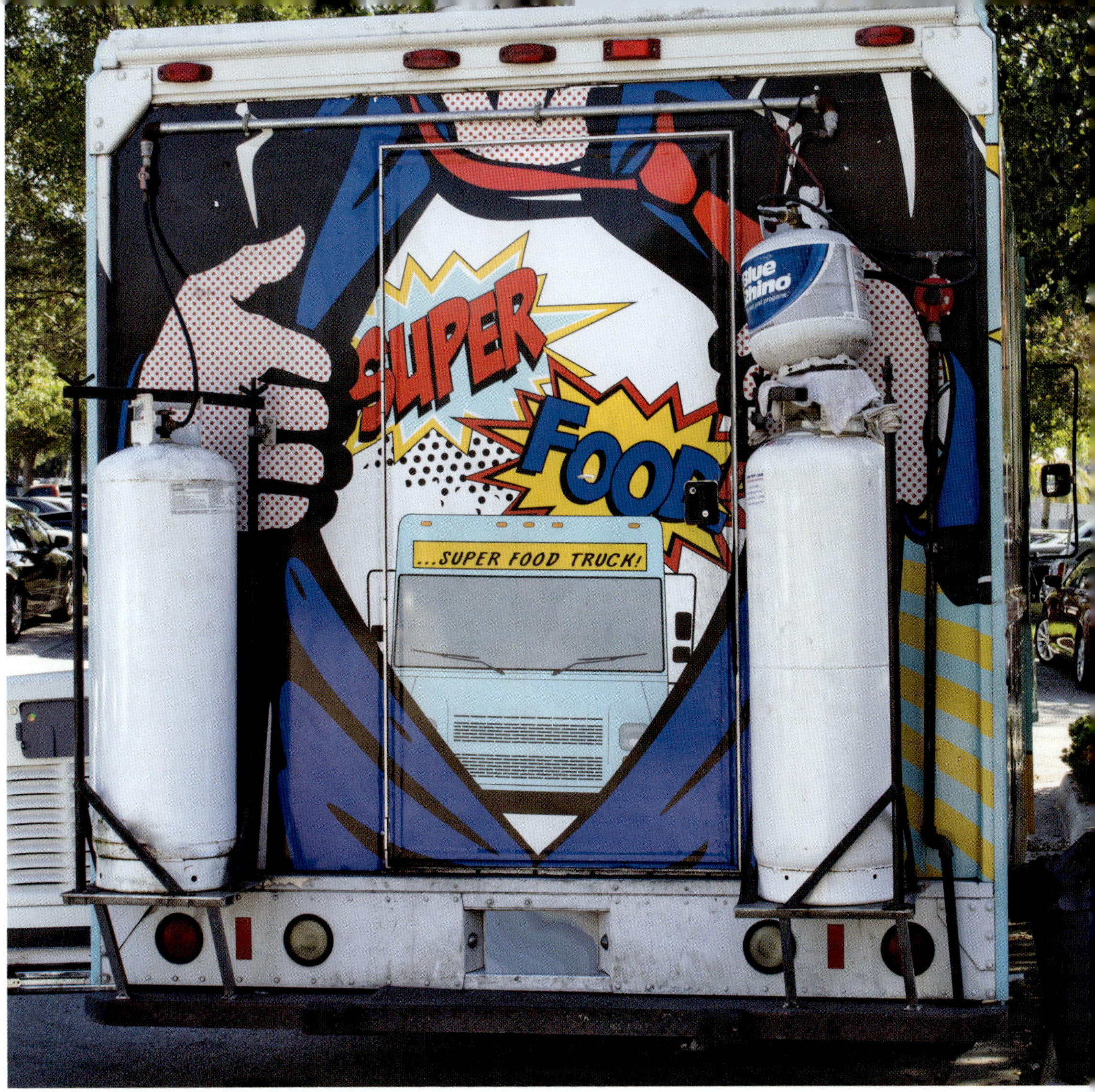

Super Food.

Super Food is a crowd favorite at events big and small all across the First Coast. The truck will do corporate functions, private parties and luncheons. It even catered a wedding, food-truck style!

Super Food has done the Players Championship and the Clean Water Festival in Ponte Vedra, a wedding reception at St. Augustine Beach, Ferry Fest in Mayport, Jaguars Tailgating at EverBank Field, the Natural Life Festival at Metro Park, ArtWalk, the Auto Show, Community First Saturdays, Jaxsons Night Market and One Spark in downtown Jacksonville, just to name a few. It's fun to travel behind the truck in traffic, too!

A hugely satisfying chicken bánh mì sandwich was the first thing I tried at Super Food, one sunny afternoon at Everbank Plaza. I love grabbing lunch there, because of the plentiful parking and great views of the St. Johns River. But I digress. About that bánh mì, seared chunks of marinated chicken

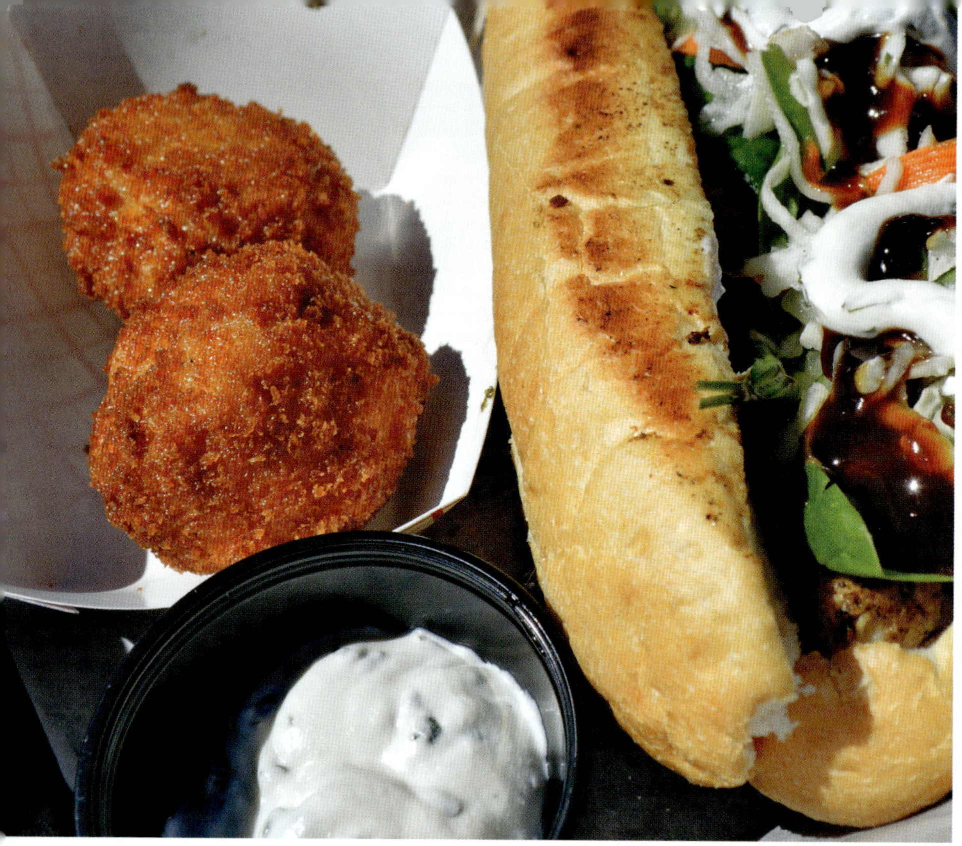

Left: Mac 'n' Cheese Balls with Chicken Bánh Mì from Super Food.

Below: Super Food's Sweet Potato Tots.

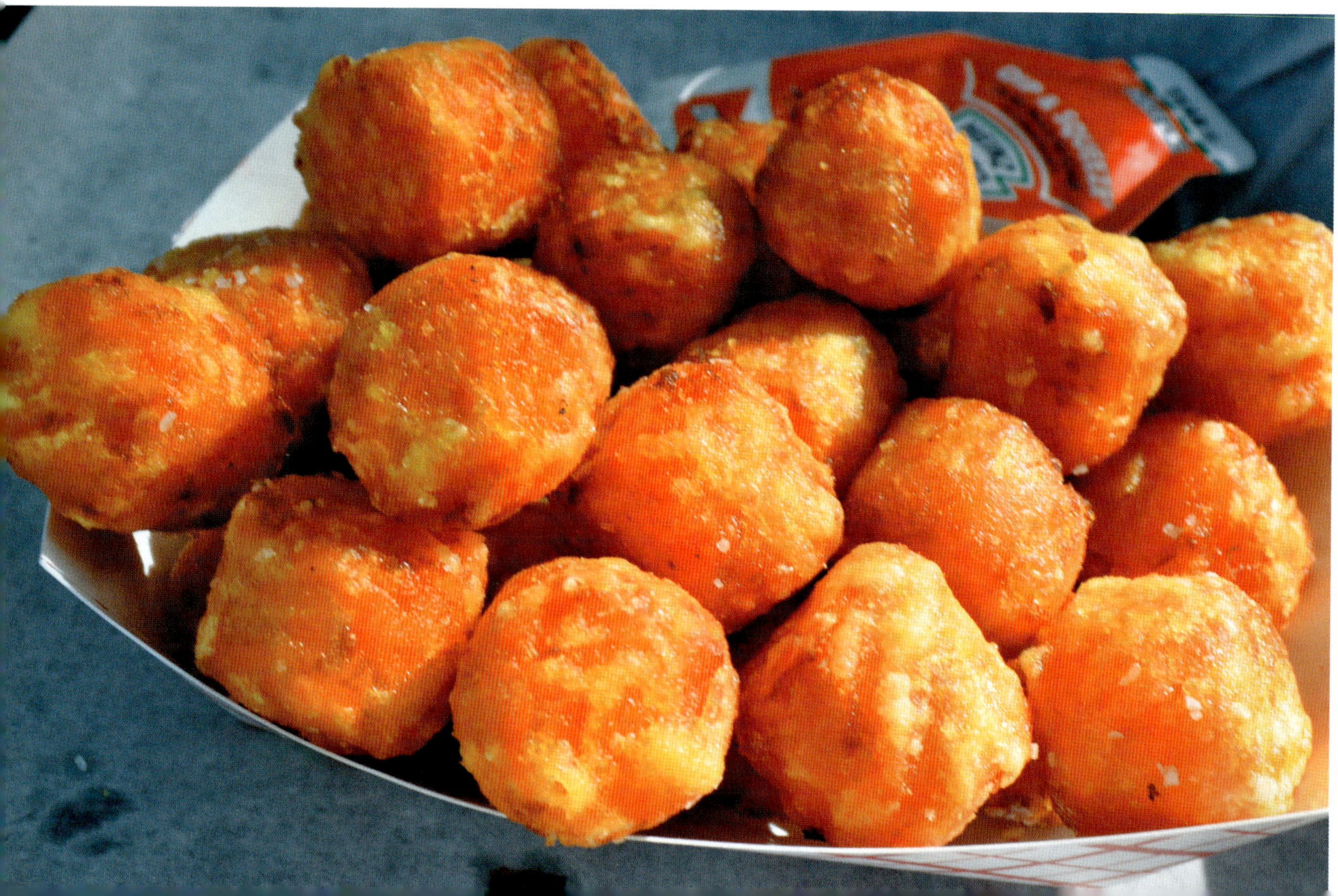

fill a toasty French baguette, along with a quick-pickled slaw of carrots, cucumber and daikon radish. They even tuck some fresh spinach in there (because it's super food, of course), and then the whole thing is festooned with lavish amounts of hoisin and cilantro-lime aioli. I'm pretty sure I nearly fainted when Dale handed this down to me from the truck window.

As delicious as it was, the sandwich was eclipsed by the seemingly mild-mannered and subtly addictive Mac and Cheese Balls I ordered on the side. Two gigantic orzo pasta balls, stuffed with cotija and mascarpone cheeses and roasted peppers, are rolled in seasoned panko breadcrumbs, chilled and then fried. I guess it's the combination of textures here that make these such a memorable dish.

The "crime-fighters" daily menu rotates with the seasons and availability of fresh ingredients. A Turkey Pesto Panini on flattened French bread gets a flavor boost from prosciutto, avocado, spinach, tomato and herbed chevre.

Mini Pork Shanks are savory fall favorites. Two hoisin barbecued mini pork shanks are presented with cabbage slaw and your choice of fries

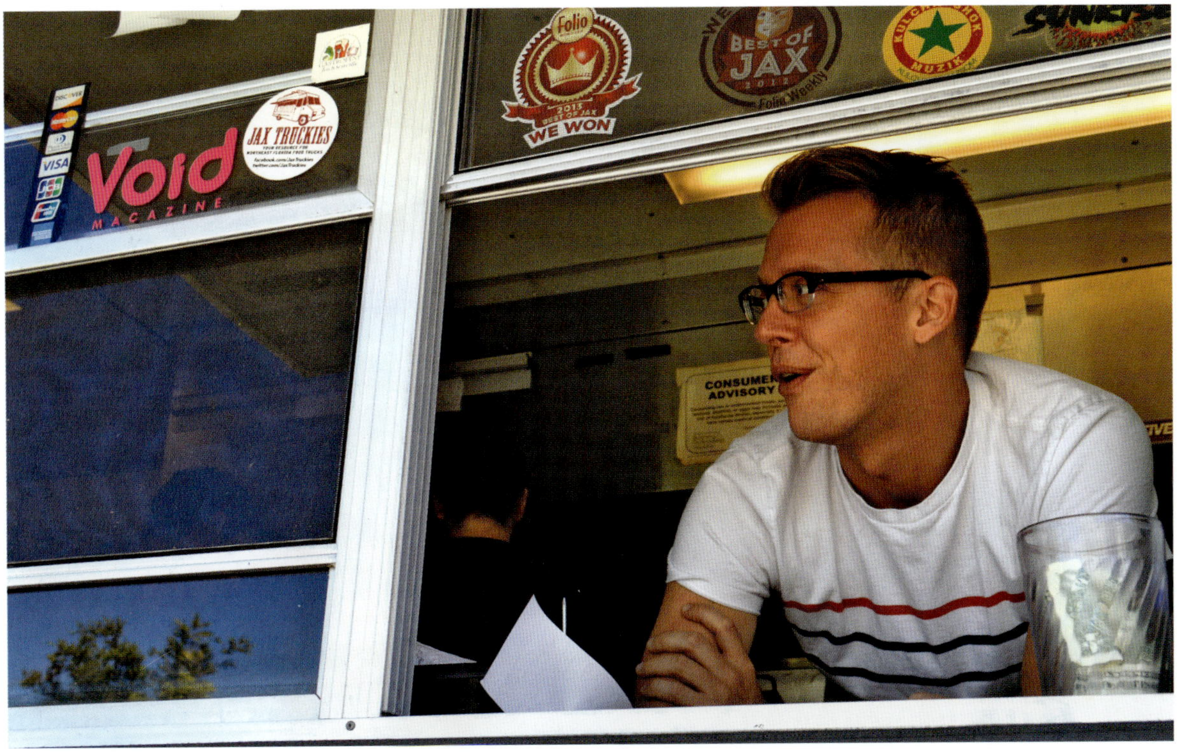

Dale Stoudt, co-owner of Super Food.

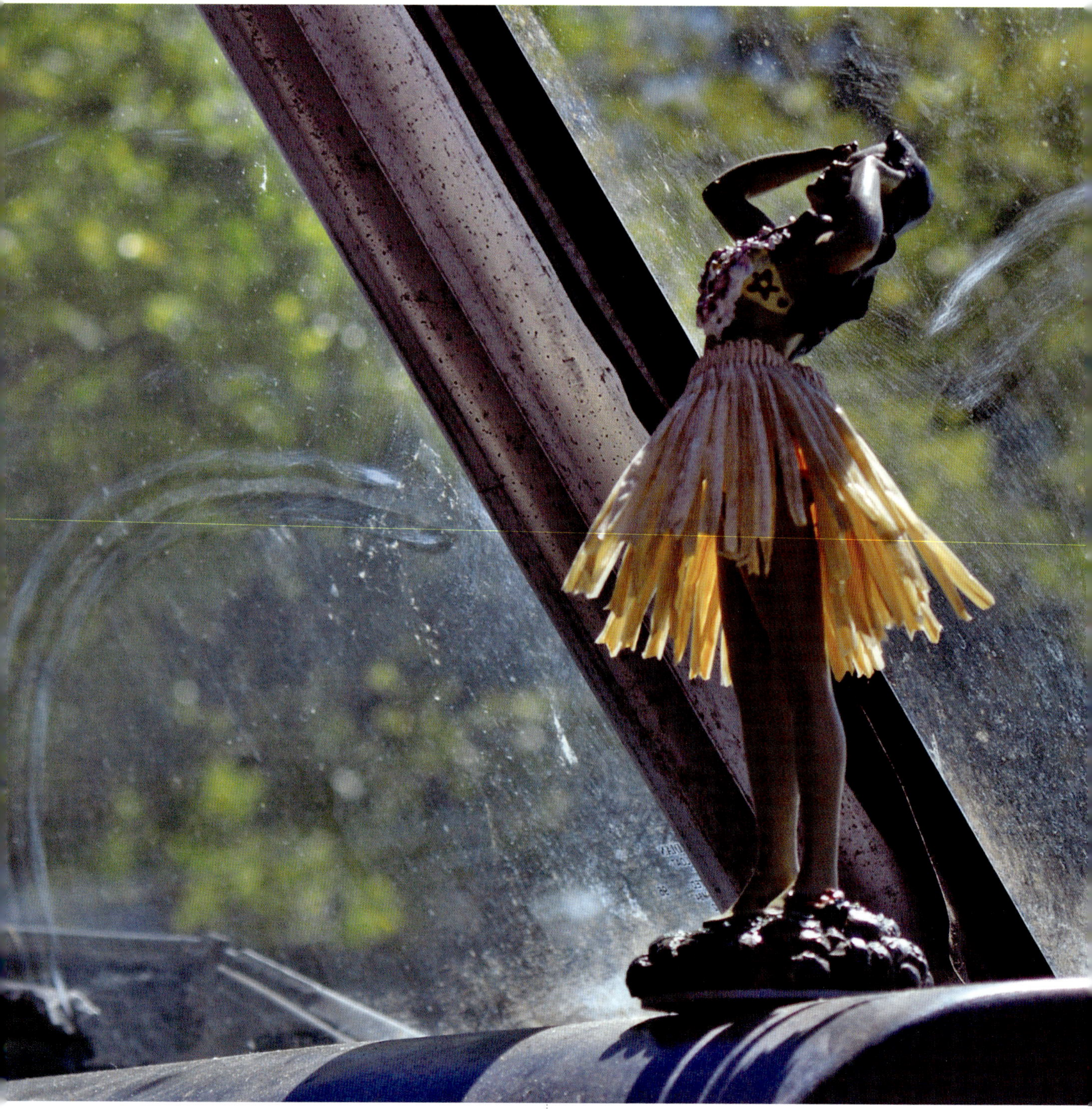

On the dash, Super Food.

or sweet potato tots. If I may, go for the tots, dudes and dudettes.

Dale was instrumental in helping to shape the city's food truck legislation. He represented truck owners during forums on the subject after Councilman Reggie Brown proposed a bill saying stricter controls were needed. As a result of the open dialogue, Councilman Brown formed a committee of local stakeholders and revised the bill.

What's next on the crime-fighting agenda for this super duo? It's a truck, it's a restaurant…it's Super Food and Brew! Dale and Ritchie are planning to open a restaurant in the 11 East Building at Main and Forsyth Streets downtown. They figured the build-out on the former Starbucks location would take four to six months. Once they open a brick-and-mortar restaurant, they will stop offering daily lunch service from the truck, but they will still do catering and special events.

Follow Super Food Truck on Facebook and Twitter (@Jaxfoodtruck) to see where they are each day.

TADO STREET

Tay Nguyen and Jennifer Vu

Let's cruise down to Tado Street for some Vietnamese street food. Oh, you want Mexican? No hay problema!

Tado Street introduced its Vietnamese and Mexican favorites to Jacksonville's hungry street food fans beginning in 2012 in front of Rock Solid Automotive on Beach Boulevard.

The truck rocked the dinner shift and continued serving in that location several nights a week, from 7:00 p.m. to midnight. Encouraging community-style dining, Tay and Jennifer put out tables and chairs that were filled within minutes of their opening. The location was great for their demographic, and their faithful customers sought them out for their nightly specials of authentic Vietnamese and Mexican dishes. The menu for the night would center on a few staples and a nightly special, and they would often sell out. Things seemed to be going great; they made it two months, and then they suspended service and were out of the picture for two years.

Tado Street draws a crowd.

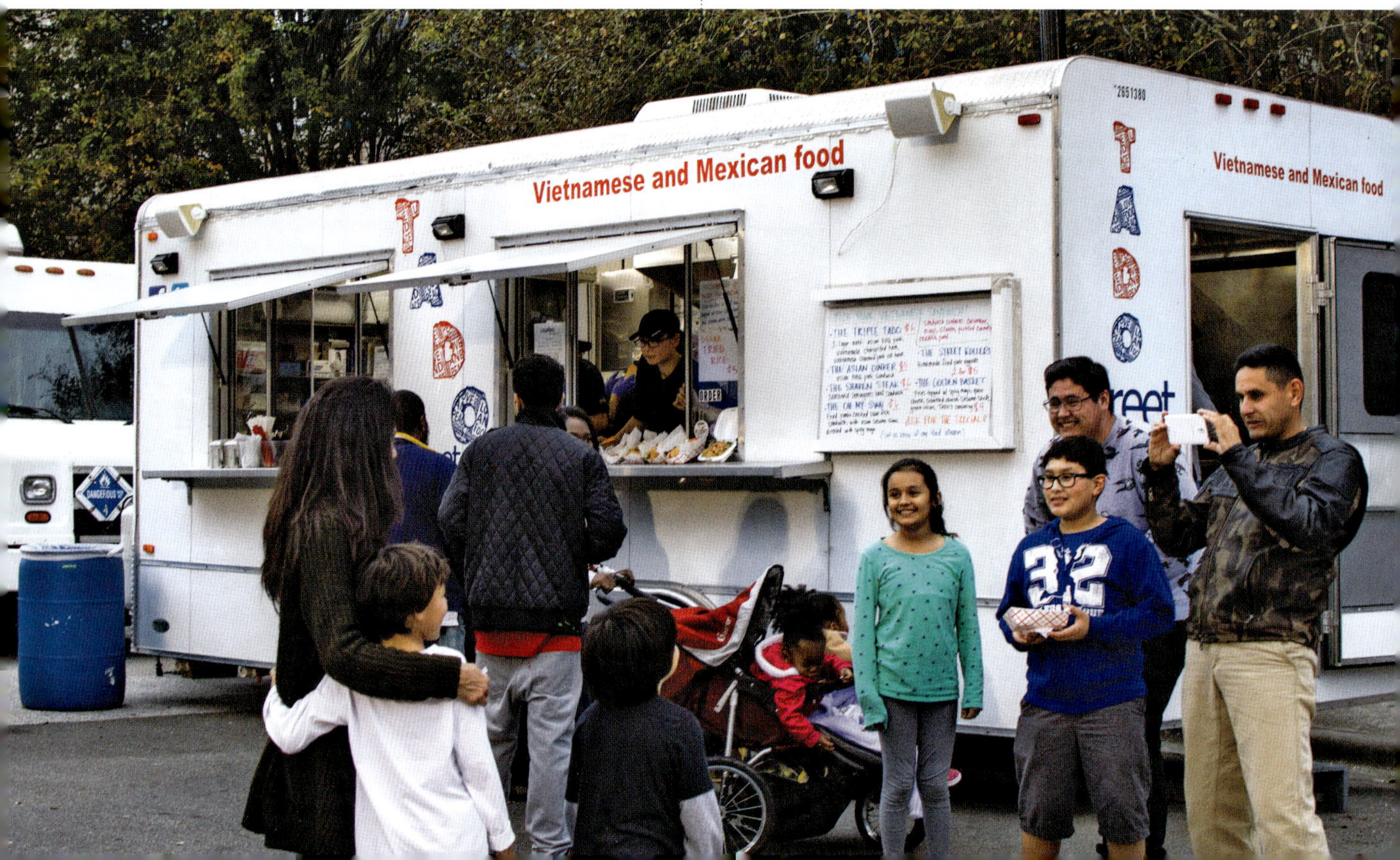

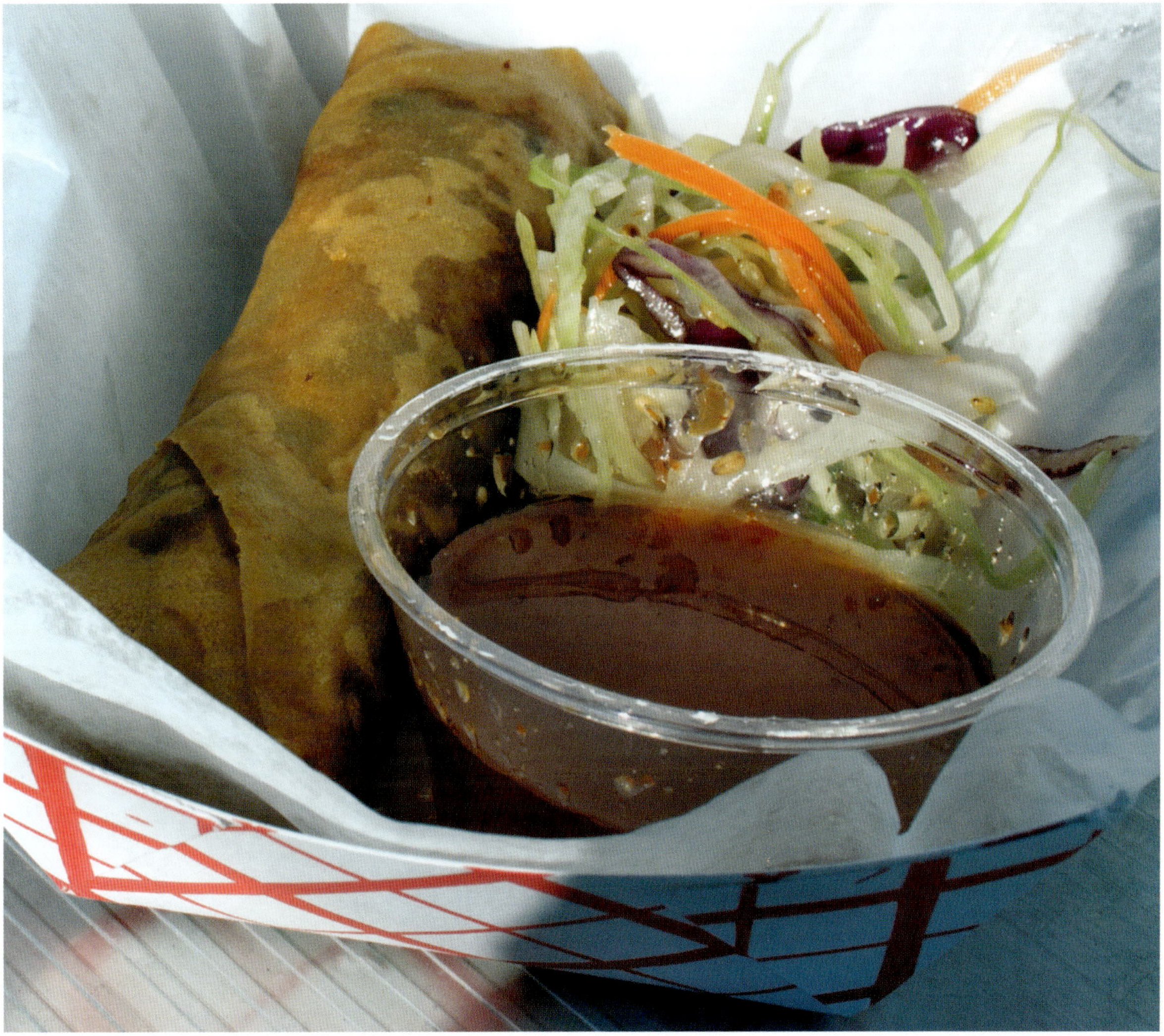

Pork Spring Roll from Tado Street.

I missed out on the lengua, chilaquiles and tortas they sold back then, so now I need to make up for lost time.

Similarly, Vietnamese bun bo hue (spicy beef noodle soup) made appearances in 2012, along with the more tame beef pho, and sweet-toothed customers loved che dau tran (black-eyed peas in coconut milk) and che ba mau (three-color dessert) with yellow mung bean paste, red azuki beans and green tapioca noodles layered on top of one another to create a colorful mosaic in a cup. Topped with sweet coconut milk and crushed ice, the real fun is fishing out all the chunky "bits" as you drink it. I hope we see these brought back.

The menu may have changed, but Tado Street offers the same experience.

The crew is super friendly and happy to explain dishes to curious diners. Crew members put sample dishes out on their order counter so you can see what your money is going to get you. Not that there's much to worry about—their prices are great. They offer iced Thai tea and Vietnamese coffee, so the caffeine component is there, too.

I caught up with Tay Nguyen and Jennifer Vu at the big white Tado Street truck in Neptune Beach, where they had set up at Sliders' Octoberfest breast cancer awareness

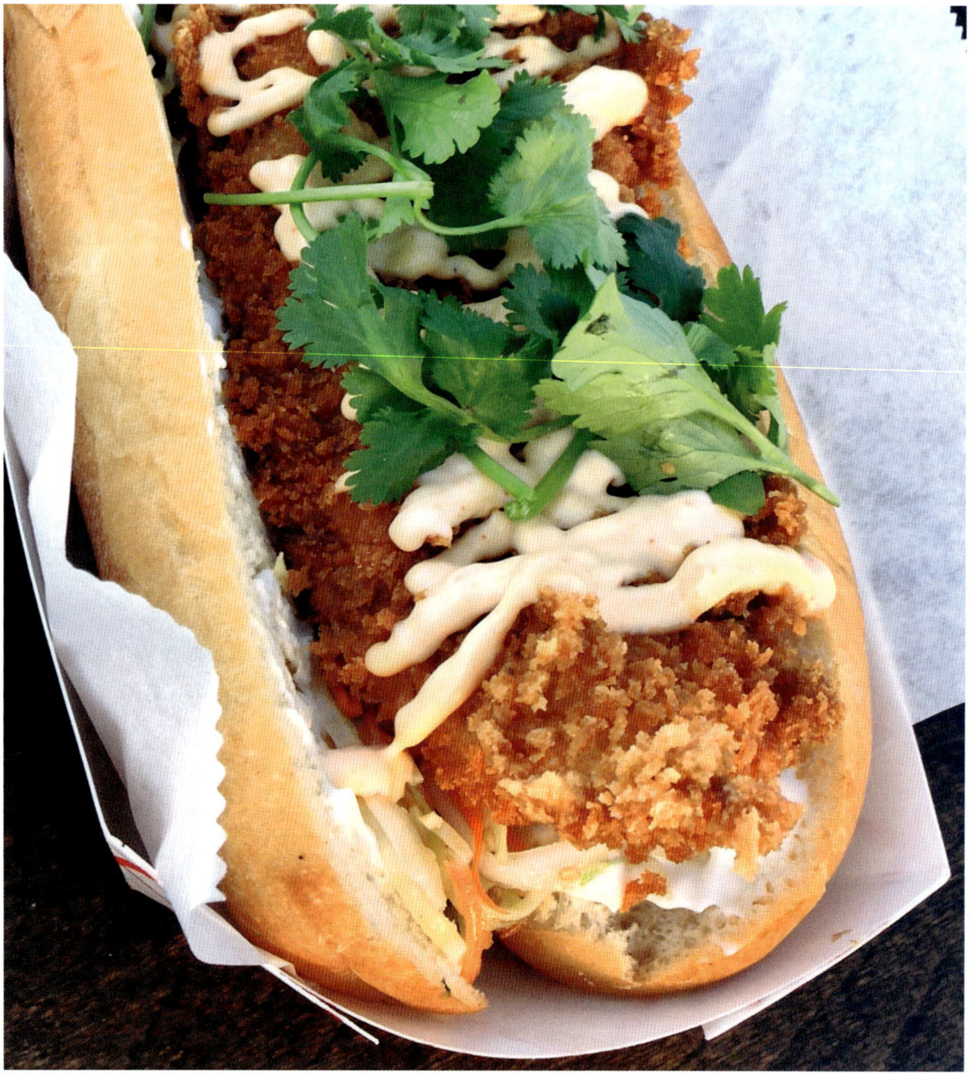

The Oh-My-Swai Bánh Mì from Tado Street.

fundraiser for the Donna Fund. I really appreciated seeing them out there since I knew it was an extra expense and time involved for them to get a special permit from the city to vend there for that one day, and there were two other trucks. Theirs had some of the longest lines throughout the afternoon, though, and it wasn't because the food was cooked to order and took a while. The large crew is very efficient on that truck and turns orders pretty quickly.

My friends ordered the Oh-My-Swai bánh mì and it was a huge hit—literally huge. A heavy panko coating lent a satisfying crunch, and the sandwich was devoured in minutes. I got a nibble of it and made a note to order it when I brought my mom out to the truck—she always gets a fish sandwich if there is one on the menu.

Another simple but tasty option, the Golden Basket is just plain fusion comfort food. First off, it has a cool name, right? Big, hot, golden crinkle

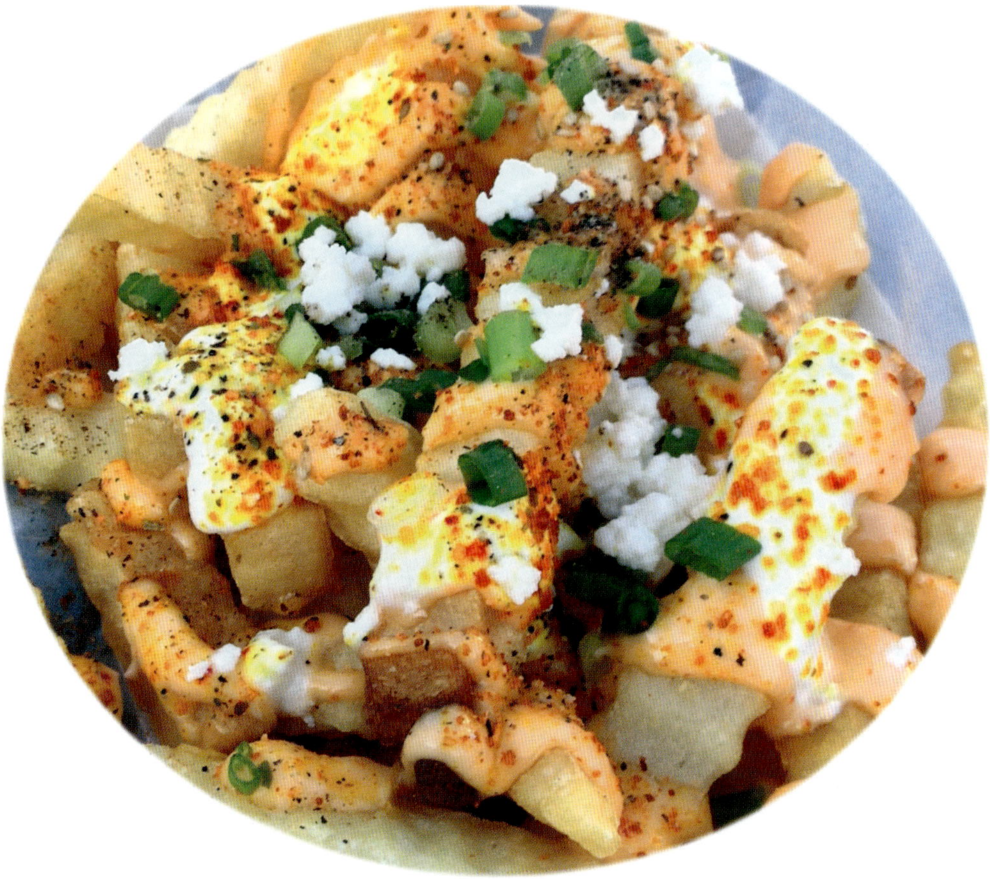

The Golden Basket (seasoned fries) from Tado Street.

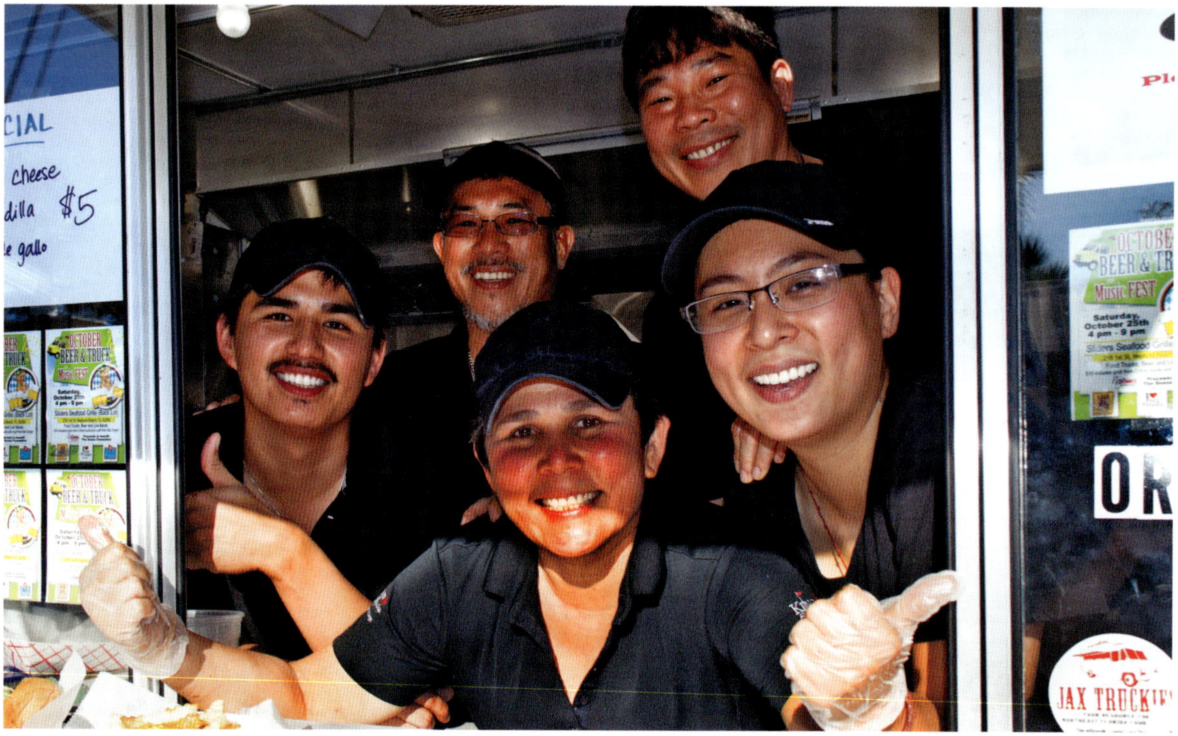

Tado Street's friendly crew.

fries come out of the fryer and into a paper basket. They are seasoned, doused with spicy mayo, scallions, sesame seeds and crumbly cheese. I was invited to nosh on these but showed remarkable restraint and tasted just a couple of them. I made a mental note, though: next time, you are *mine*! I got a spring roll that was full of pork, pleasantly crisp and greasy. It was accompanied by an Asian sesame slaw, cilantro and spicy mayo. It did not disappoint, but I couldn't help but think how great it would be with more of those fries.

At the Jax Truckies Food Truck Block Party at the Jacksonville Landing, I got a small portion of Tado Street's pho with rare steak, and it was pretty great, actually. I pulled a typical me move, though, mixing a little bit of the accompanying hoisin and Sriracha into the broth to begin with (that's just how I roll, deal with it), and there was an uproar on the truck! I was good-naturedly chided for not tasting it first to see how the broth was without add-ins. I realize now that would have been the polite thing to do. But I eat pho quite often, and I almost always end up adding both sauces; so, I figured in the interest of time…I'll know better next time. What I saw was people who are passionate about the dishes they hand out the window, and that is enough to keep me coming back time and again.

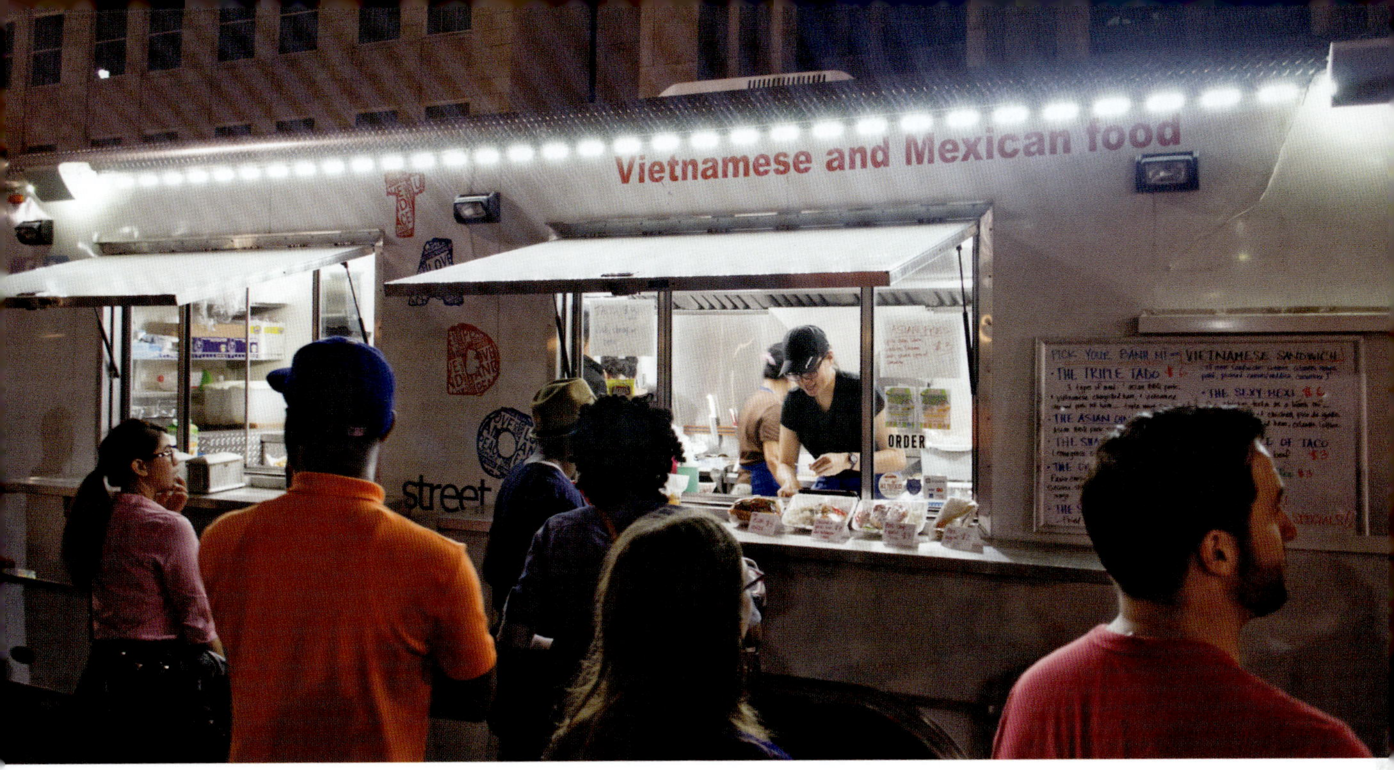

Tado Street at Jaxsons Night Market

The fall of 2014 saw Tado Street out in the evenings at Aardwolf Brewery and downtown at Jaxsons Night Market and doing lunch service at Fanatics, among other spots. Then, in early 2015, they suffered a temporary setback that had them sidelined as I was finishing this story. I hope they are going to be back soon; we've only just met, and I think we could be good friends!

Look for the big white Tado Street truck on Facebook at www.facebook.com/tadostreet and on Instagram and Twitter @Tadostreet.

TASTE BUDS EXPRESS

Billy Ross and Terrence Webb

Taste Buds Express rolled out for the first time for the River City Pride 2012. The truck, operated by Billy Ross and Terrence Webb, offers a huge variety of menu items each day. Houston-style Tex-Mex is what self-taught chef Billy Ross grew up eating, and since October 2012, he has been bringing it to Jacksonville's taste buds on the Taste Buds Express.

It's not all Tex-Mex, all the time, though. Southern home-style and American seasonal items make regular appearances. I got the Pastrami Dip sandwich once, and it was so good I forgot to take its picture before devouring it. If you follow #nourishthebeast on Instagram, you know that hardly ever happens. In June 2013, their fan-fusion-tastic Chicken Schwarma Flauta won the Best Sandwich category at the Jax Truckies Food Truck Championship at Burrito Gallery. Of course, I had to sample one for you. Grilled chicken, onion and peppers get a stacking of French fries, are wrapped tight and then deep fried or grilled toasty. The

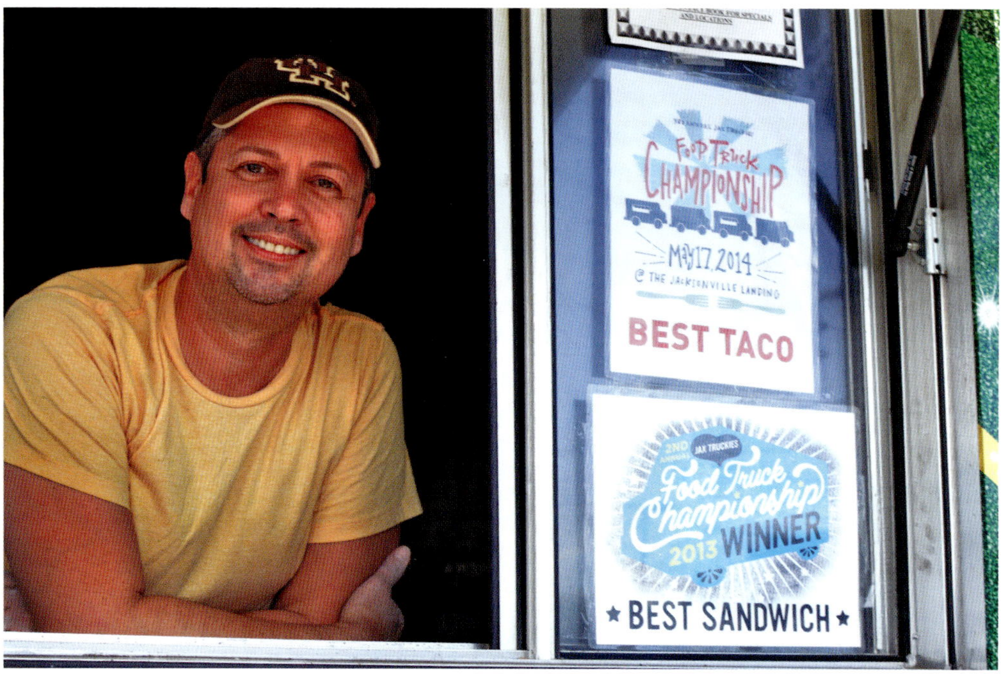

Billy Ross mans the kitchen at Taste Buds Express.

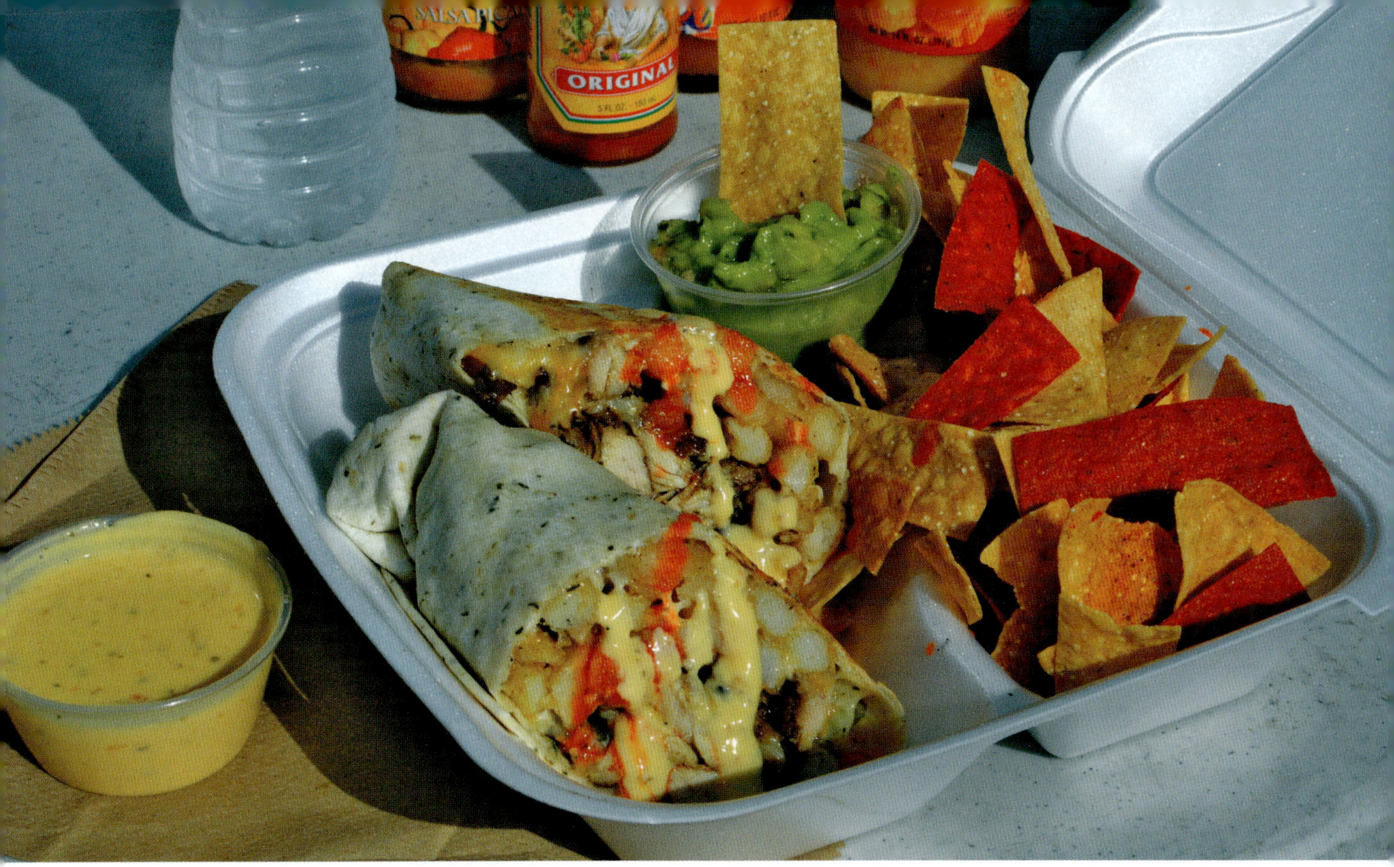

The award-winning Chicken Schwarma Flauta from Taste Buds Express.

sandwich is served with fresh corn chips and Taste Buds' house-made guacamole and queso. It's a belly buster, so plan to share it or stash half of it away for your dinner.

Tacos Al Carbon are a mouth-watering selection, with your choice of steak, hickory smoked pork or grilled chicken, topped with fried jalapeños, wonton crisps, cheese, pico de gallo and cilantro in a soft flour tortilla. There's a Carne Guisada Taco for all you fellow brisket lovers out there, or you can get your carne on (braised beef brisket and gravy) over Taste Buds' veggie rice and served with warm tortillas.

Billy's Favorite Taco is the crowd favorite—again with your choice of protein, plus bacon, blue cheese, sautéed mushrooms, bell pepper, pico de gallo, wonton crisps, jalapeño crisps, cilantro and cheese. This bad boy took Best Taco honors in the Jax Truckies 2014 Food Truck Championship.

Beyond the taco, Billy created a Southwest version of poutine that gets heavy with a heap of their tender pulled pork. Hand-rolled southwestern egg rolls feature their spicy rice mixed with vegetables, rolled and deep fried. Did I mention these are spicy? There, I said it again. They are served with their top secret Green Sauce, which helps quench the heat just enough to make you want to take another bite, and another, and another. Wraps, burritos, flautas and quesadillas have all made

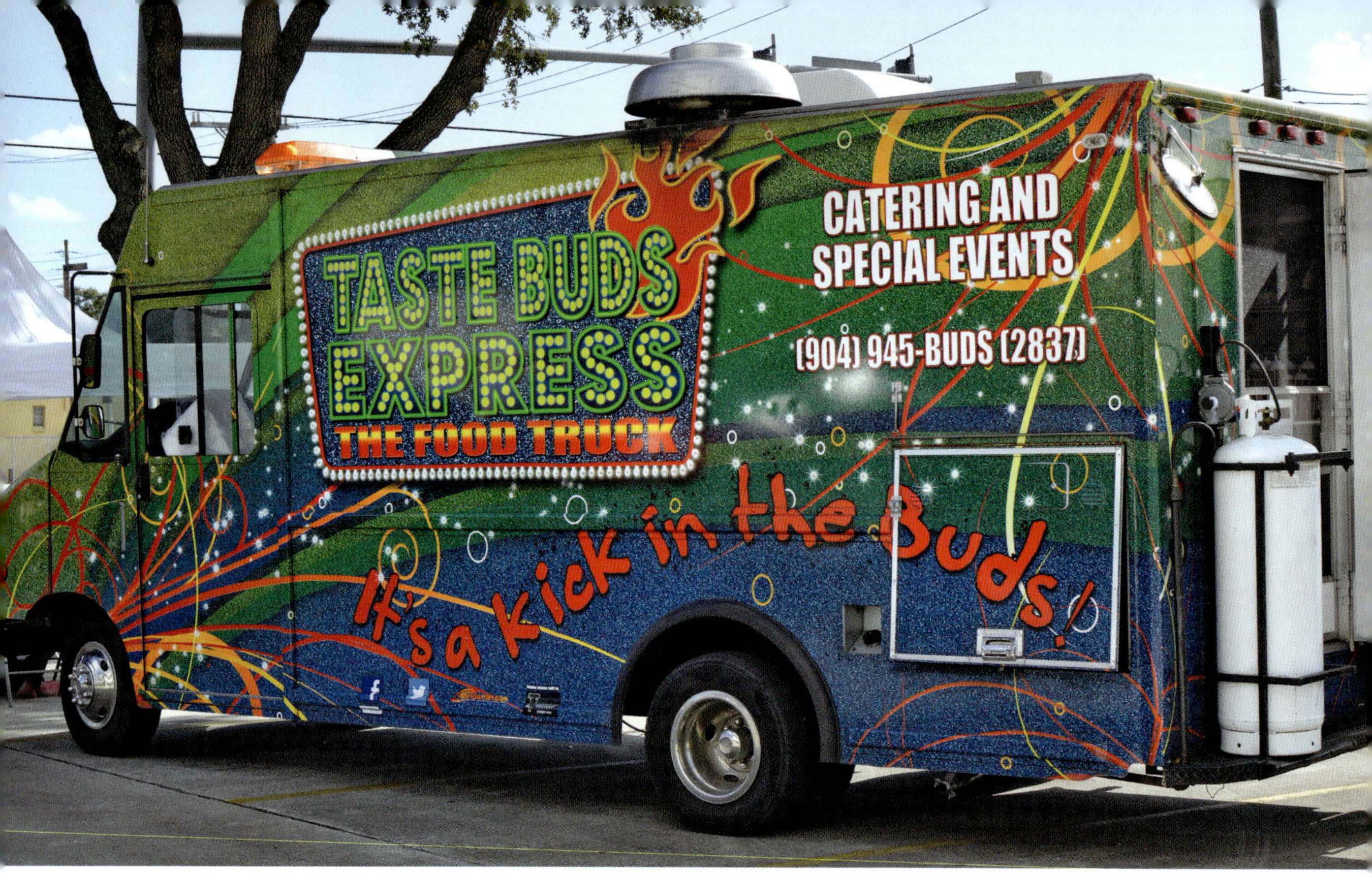

Taste Buds Express looks like a party on wheels.

appearances, either on the extensive regular menu or as specials.

The truck can be found downtown at the Main and Forsyth Street lot, Interline Brands, AvMed and Jax Federal Credit Union on Park Street. Billy and Terrence had a great thing going at the Metro Entertainment Complex in Riverside, and they have been seen at festivals and fundraisers throughout the First Coast. In 2014, they were recognized as Jacksonville's Best Food Truck at the LGBT Community Awards banquet at the Karpeles Manuscript Library Museum.

Check in with award-winning Taste Buds Express when you're planning your next event. You'll find the truck on Facebook. It's a kick in the buds!

UP IN SMOKE BBQ

Tom and Jennifer Wilbers

With generations of barbecue experience, true southern hospitality and out-of-this-world barbecue, Tom and Jennifer Wilbers own and operate Up in Smoke BBQ. Fueled by their passion for food and meeting new people, they run two bright red food trailers, the largest of which has been a frequent sight at Hemming Park downtown.

Talk about tradition—some of their homemade southern barbecue uses Tom's grandmother's sauce recipes from almost eighty years ago. Up in Smoke began selling its "que du jour" from a pop-up tent at RAM on Saturdays.

I visited Tom and Jennifer at Hemming Park last summer and was excited to get to try their beef brisket. It sells out most days, and I scored the last order on the truck that day! Super pink from the smoke, it also had those burnt ends I love. I got baked beans and

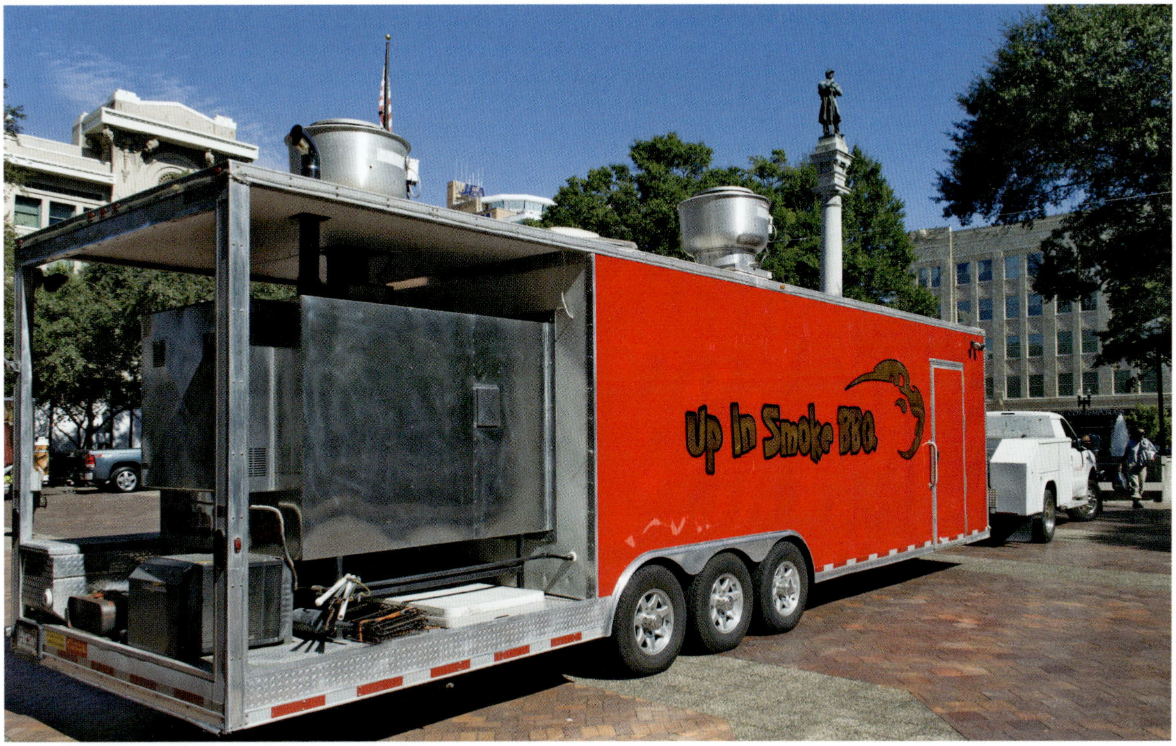

Up in Smoke at Hemming Park.

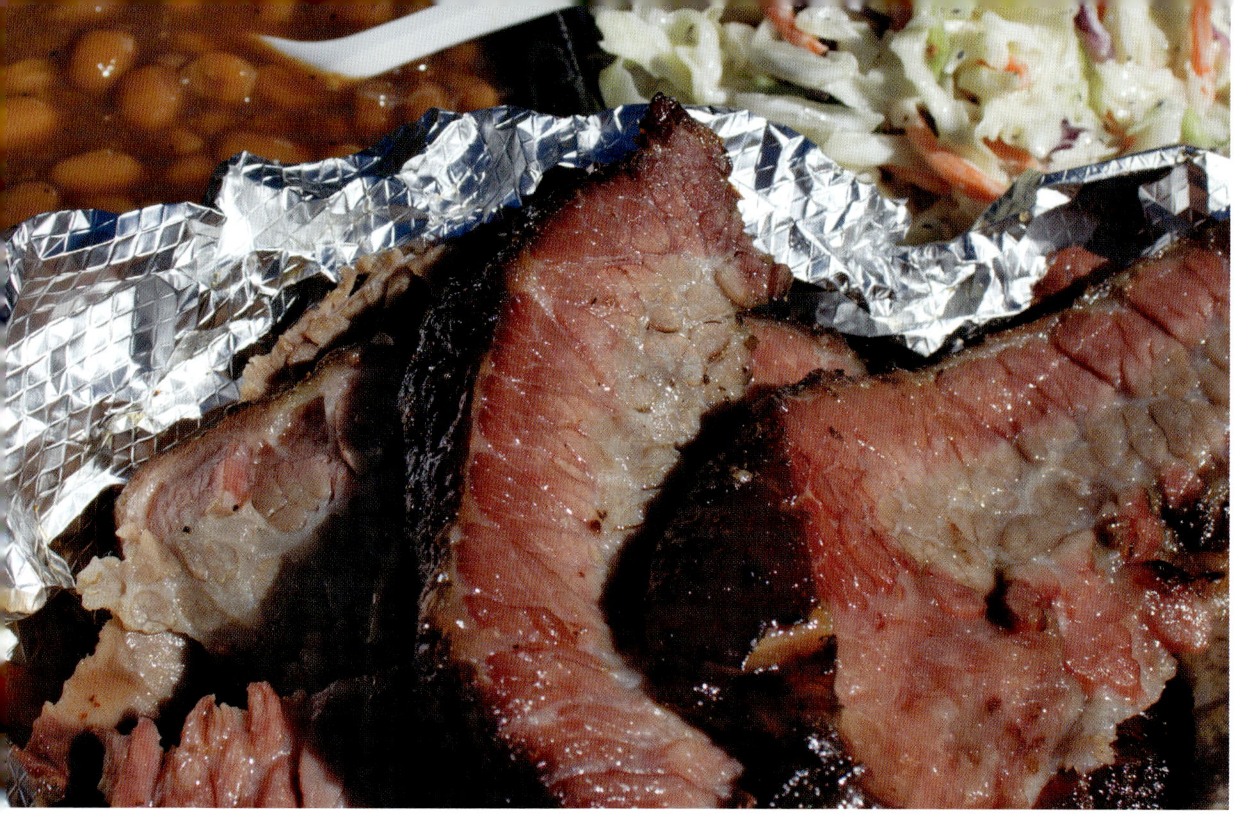

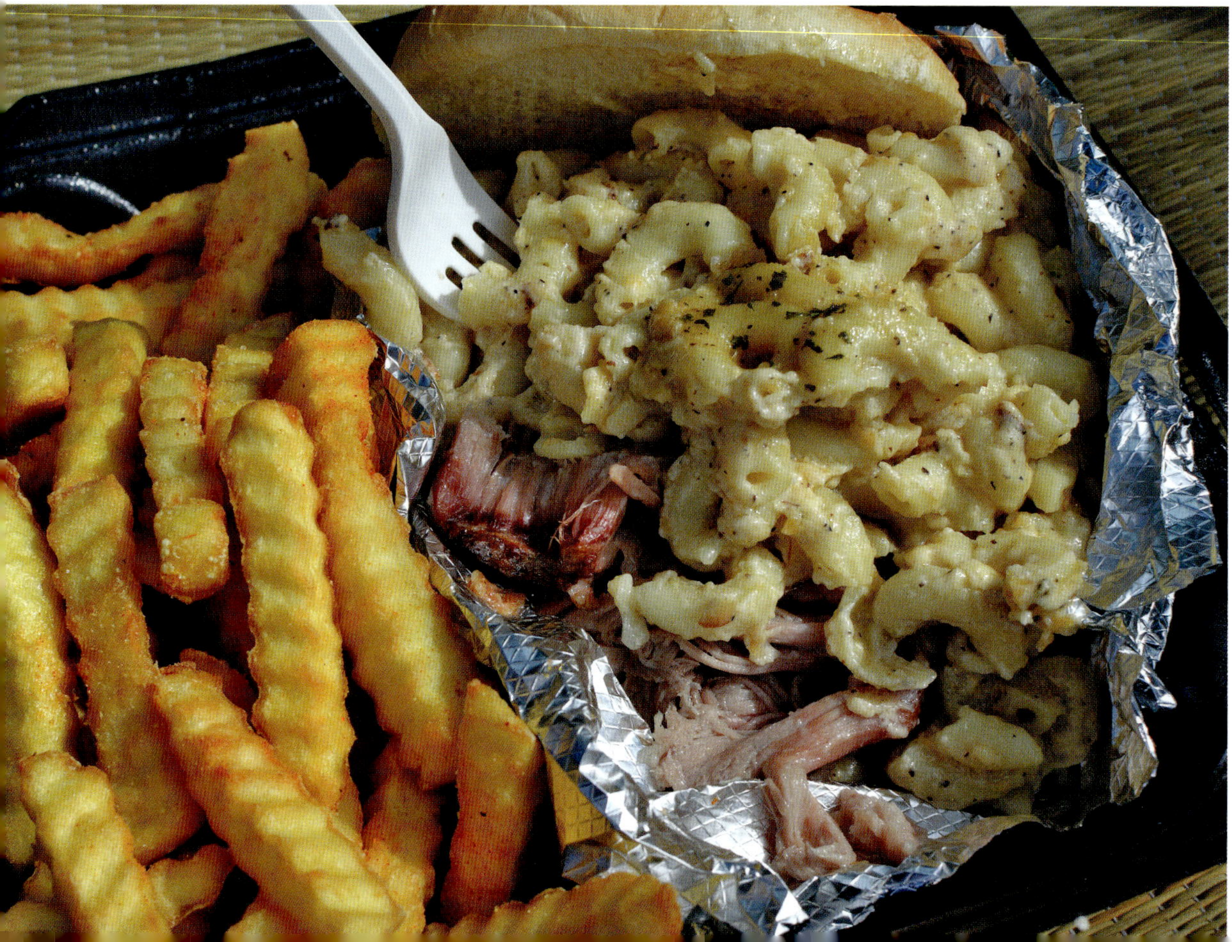

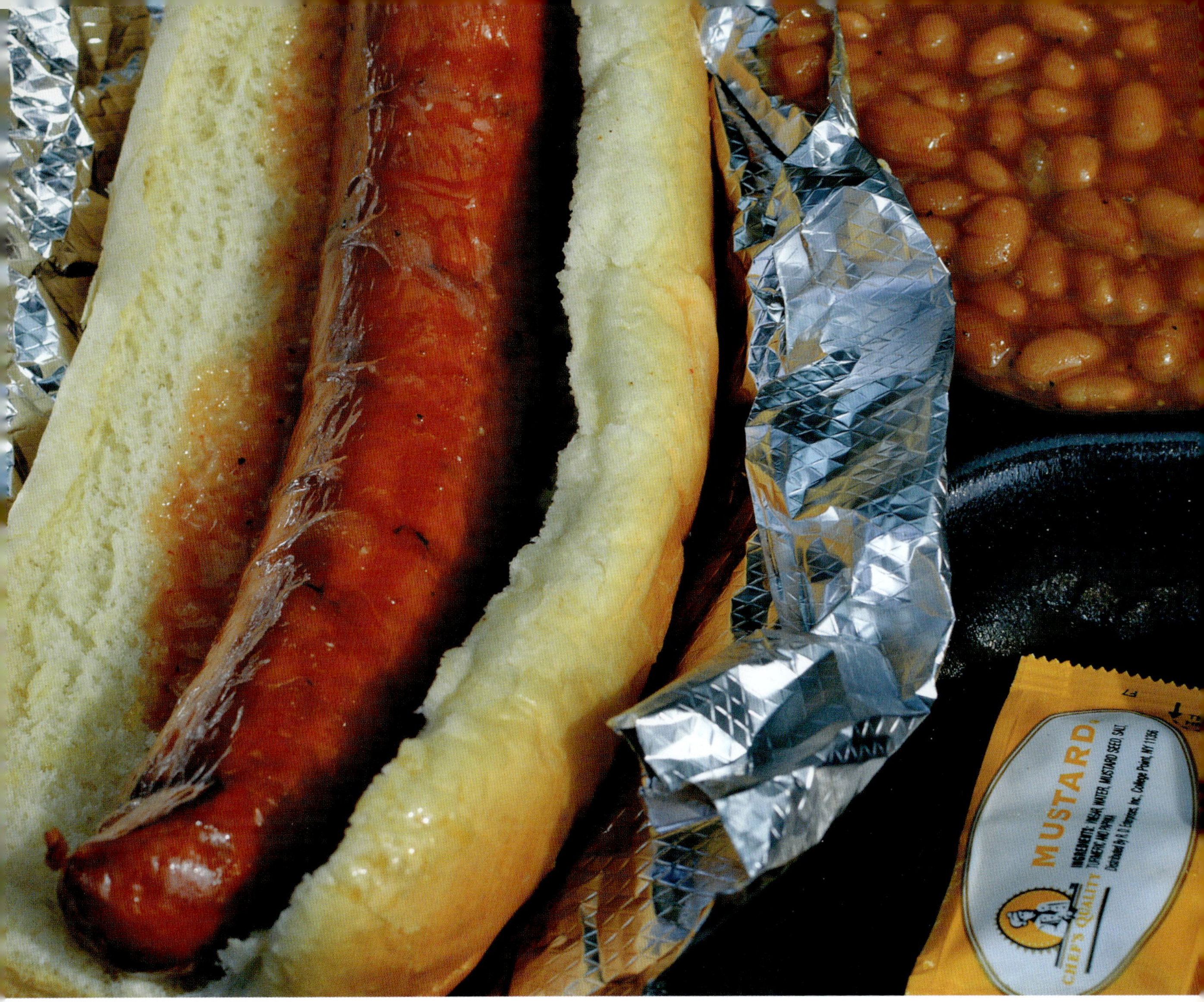

Smoked Sausage from Up in Smoke.

Opposite, top: Up in Smoke's Beef Brisket.

Opposite, bottom: Behold, the Muncheech, from Up in Smoke.

coleslaw for my sides, and both were the perfect accompaniment to the fatty, tender beef. If you like brisket, get in line at the big red trailer.

They have fed the hungry crowds at EverBank Field, the tailgating venue during the Jaguars game, and they love to do events and festivals across the First Coast. The first time I met them was at the Players Championship at TPC Sawgrass in Ponte Vedra in 2014. They had made a special item for the event—a pulled pork slider topped with a generous portion of their pimento cheese. It was the best thing I ate all day, and I am pretty sure I at least tasted everything in the place.

I found them set up at Capital Plaza at Deerwood one afternoon, and I asked Tom what their most popular item is. He told me by far that would be the Muncheech, a mega-huge sandwich piled high with their succulent pulled smoked pork butt topped with a huge scoop of their creamy mac and cheese. Wow. You go, Jacksonville! The big red Q mobile and the Muncheech are making waves everywhere they go! They sold out at Jacksonville's first One Spark Festival a few years ago and then came back with even more the next year. They took the Top Sales award at Food Truck Wars in St. Augustine in October 2014, and that was a huge event by any standards.

Personally, my favorite thing I've tasted at their trailer is the smoked sausage sandwich. It's a huge, juicy sweet pork sausage with the perfect snap. The flavors are well balanced, and those baked beans are the best thing to go with it. Why complicate it? I add mustard, maybe some onions, and I'm good to go. It's what I'm getting next time I go, and I recommend, if you haven't yet, that you try it, too!

Up in Smoke BBQ does a lot of work with events, and it is set up to do anything from the largest events to intimate, backyard barbecue parties.

Tom and Jen, along with Alex Montanez from Gourmet Aviator, are also managing members of Jacksonville Food Trucks. Tom can be found most days doing custom fabrication on trucks at the JFT Warehouse on Powers Avenue. He and Jen both enjoy working with other JFT truck operators, and I've heard from more than a few of them just how much that has meant to them personally and to their businesses.

Find Tom, Jen and Up in Smoke online at www.foodtruckjax.com

BIG TASTES FROM SMALL PACKAGES

A sweet trend took shape in the Jacksonville Food Truck scene in 2014 when two restored Scotty campers began popping up at Jax Truckies events, the breweries and various downtown venues. Jacksonville was charmed.

Bold City Pops

Rhonda Ryan and Suzanah Raffield of Bold City Pops sell delicious gourmet ice pops from an adorable restored 1969 Serro Scotty camper. Their pops are crafted by hand in small batches with all-natural ingredients.

What I love about Bold City Pops is the "farm to freezer" business model it has built. I love that Rhonda is telling me about her and Suzanah's trip to Harrietts Bluff Farm to pick berries while I'm eating their blueberry-buttermilk pop. Picking their own fruits and making individual connections with the producers of their fresh ingredients, they carry all of these stories with them when they serve their pops.

Bold City pops up all around town and does corporate and tenant events, parties and weddings. Recently Rhonda and Suzanah at Hemming Park, the Jax Food Truck Food Court and Academy Sports. Suzanah's dad helped the two build an even smaller version of it pulled by a bicycle—they call it the Bold City Pop-Cycle! Their custom concoctions are always innovative and made with the freshest, best-quality local ingredients available. Look for Bold City Pops on Facebook and follow @boldcitypops on Twitter and Instagram .

Vagabond Coffee

Will Morgan is the owner-operator of Vagabond Coffee. Theology student turned barista, he started his handcrafted coffee business out of a vintage '68 Scotty HiLander camper. As low-tech as it looks, the camper is equipped with a bangin' pre-infusion espresso machine for cranking out serious caffeinated brews. A friend from Bold Bean Coffee Roasters gave him a coffee crash course, and Will was on a roll.

Within a year of launching his truckie-style coffee business, his passion for the bean, his standout style and great coffee helped him win Jacksonville's first Food Fun(d) crowd-funding event in 2014. It also earned him the attention of a downtown developer who invited him to open a brick-and-mortar store on the ground level of the Barnett building downtown. Not one for laurel-resting, Will orchestrated a Poppin' Holiday Pop-up Market in Hemming Park to encourage holiday shoppers to spend locally and support small—sometimes really, really small—businesses. Tweet to Will @vagabondcoffe.

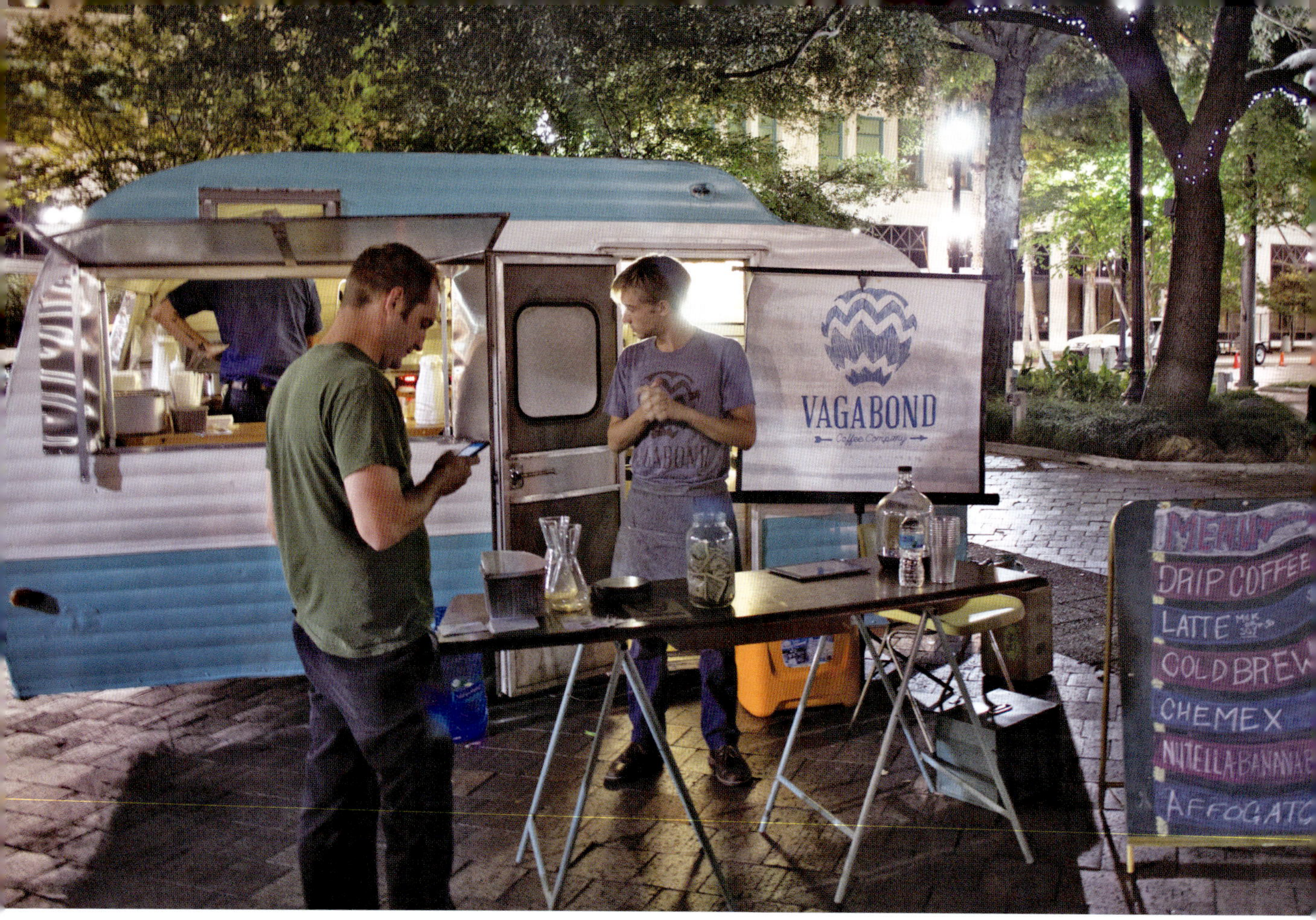

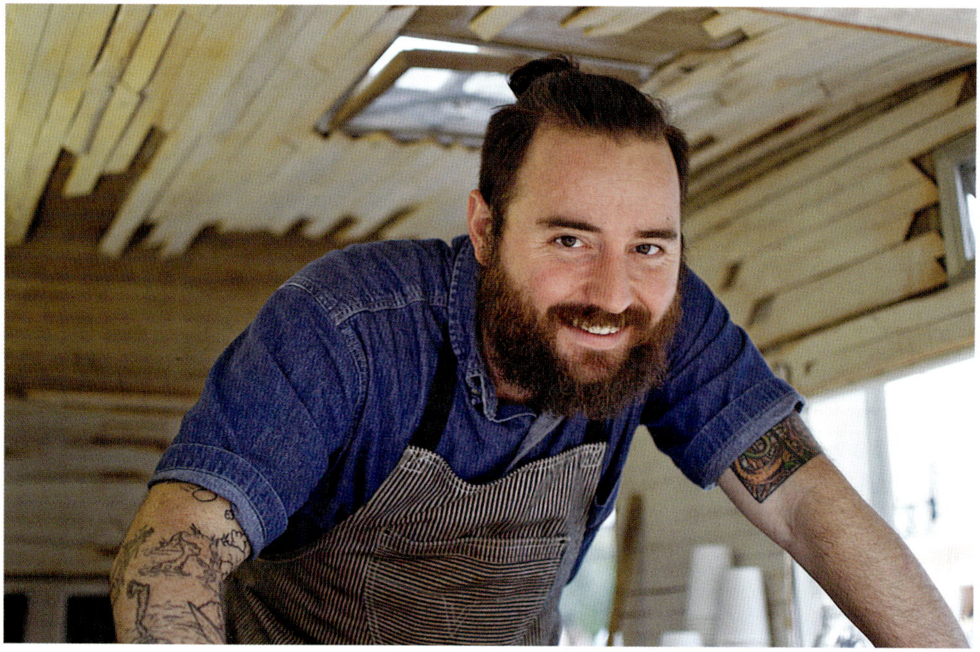

Above: Vagabond Coffee.

Left: Will Morgan, owner-operator of Vagabond Coffee.

RESTAURANTS ROLL ALONG WITH FOOD TRUCKS

The South is nothing if not hospitable, and many restaurant owners are embracing the food truck scene here. Blue Bamboo's chef Dennis Chan indulged his fantasy of owning a food truck by creating a suite of "virtual food truck" menu items—two per week—throughout the summer of 2014. In October, he reprised the dishes with a special dinner event. At Neptune Beach, where new regulations had only just been put in place to allow trucks to operate at events, Sliders Seafood owners Valerie and David Pickett hosted a group of food trucks in the courtyard behind their restaurant, for a fundraiser to benefit breast cancer awareness nonprofit the Donna Foundation in October 2014.

Just as many truck operators were grabbing for the brass ring of restaurant ownership, restaurants were adding "Truckie" to their list of accomplishments. Some restaurants have branded their catering trucks and trailers in food truck style. Most justify the expense as a must for catering operations and participation

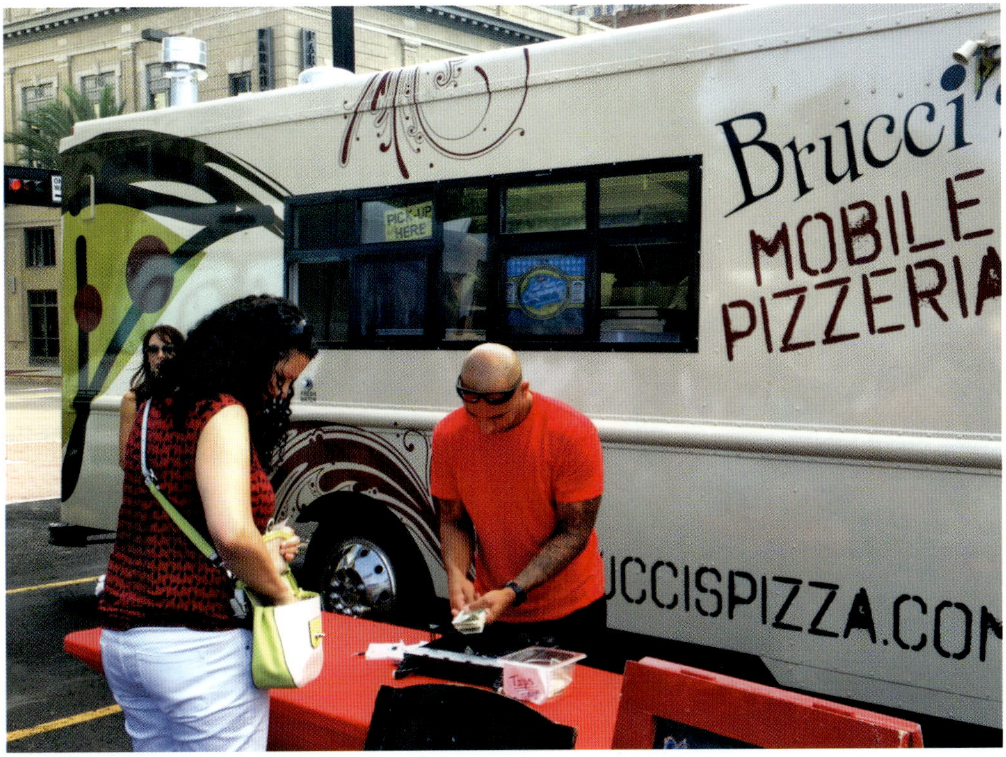

Brucci's Pizzeria on wheels at the 2013 Food Truck Championship.

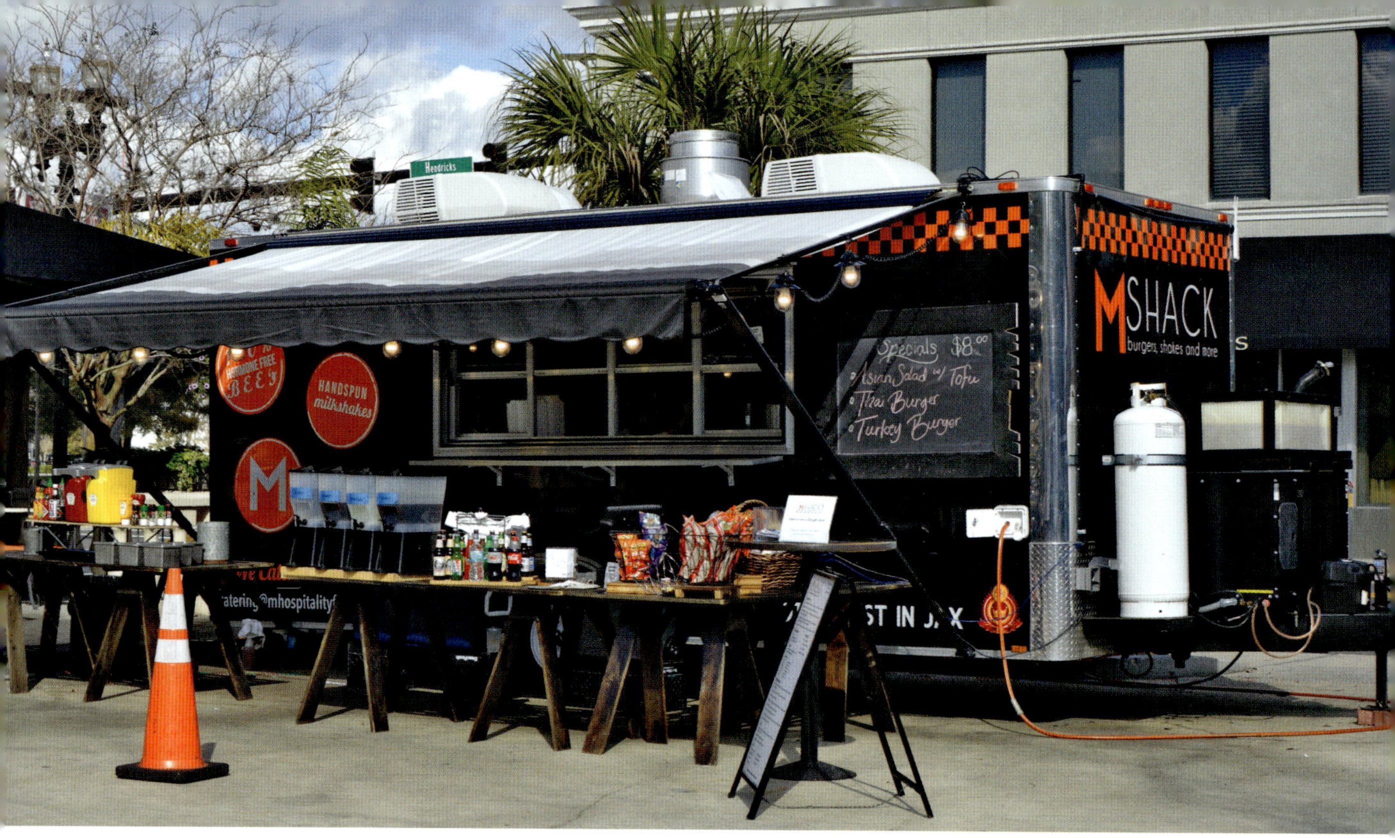

M Shack operates in front of its namesake restaurant, across the street from Matthews in San Marco.

in large events, but increasingly, these mobile kitchens are being pressed into daily service as sales outlets and ambassadors of their brands.

Bono's Bar-B-Q operates a large food truck called Bono's Bar-B-Q Express. It launched in May 2014 just in time for TPC Sawgrass. M&R Specialty Trailers extended the frame of the truck to fit the Southern Pride cooker. They have a ten-foot awning to keep diners and condiment shelves out of the elements and a full wrap with a fun brick wall graphic. A big screen monitor displays the menu. As far as we can tell, it is only being used for large events and catering.

Brucci's Pizza has been sending out its big beige Mobile Pizzeria Food Truck to events and festivals since March 2012.

One of the earliest food trucks in Jacksonville was actually a converted 1999 International bus. **Bus'in Your Chops** mobile kitchen was owned and operated by brothers Drew Cavins of Mossfire Grill and Curt Cavins of O'Brothers and served fare from each of the Riverside restaurants. Disenchanted by the resistance from the city and not finding a steady customer base to support the operation, they were in circulation for just a few short months before calling it quits.

M Shack had a catering trailer it decided to put to daily use as a food truck location. It started serving out of its commissary parking lot in San Marco in 2014 and had the trailer wrapped with the fun M Shack branding in November. The restaurant used it to build excitement and a customer base for its third brick-and-mortar location in Five Points Village, serving once weekly from the parking lot there while the retail space was being developed.

I stopped at the truck when it was at their San Marco location recently to grab a Cross-Fit Burger: two grilled patties, lettuce, tomato, avocado, grilled mushrooms, peppers, onions, bacon, fried egg and no bun. I guess I missed the point since I ordered fries on the side. This was another one of those orders I wasn't prepared for. It was a thing of beauty, but it was also a beast. The San Marco spot also has covered patio seating and adjacent parking. Find M Shack online at www.mshackburgers.com.

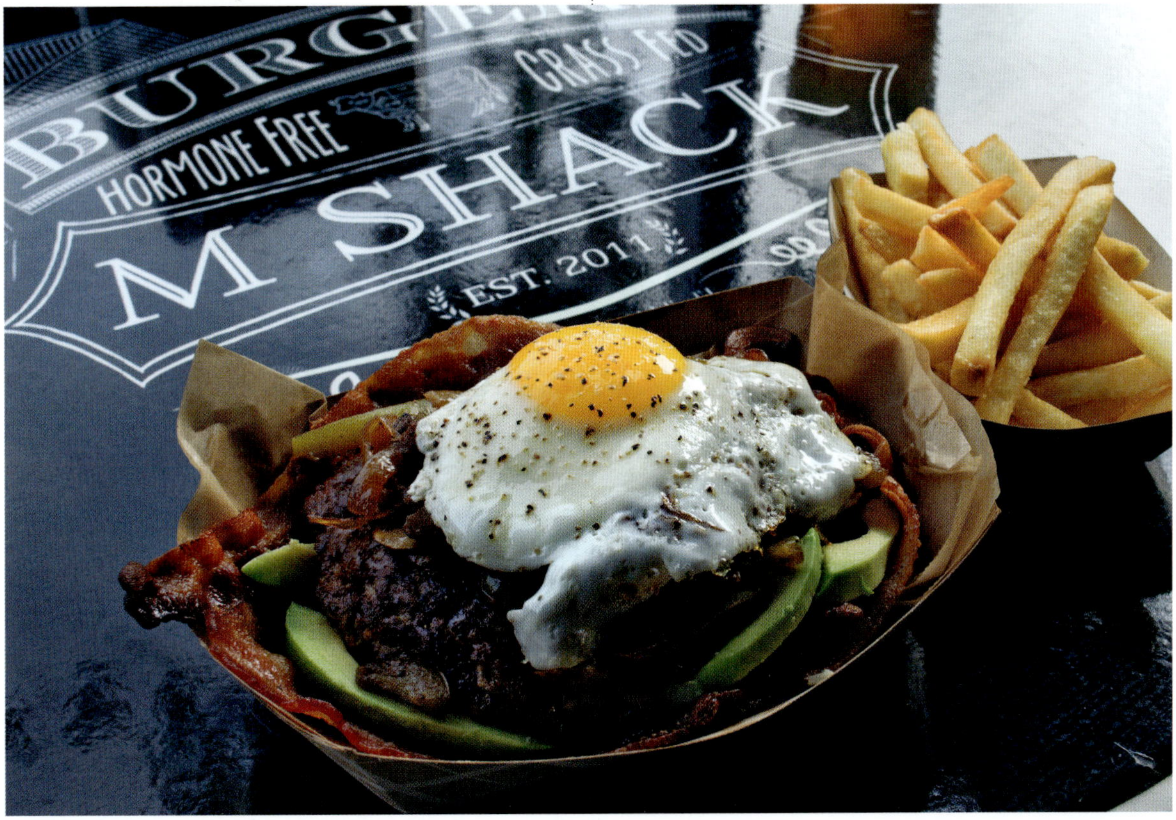

The Cross Fit Burger from M Shack.

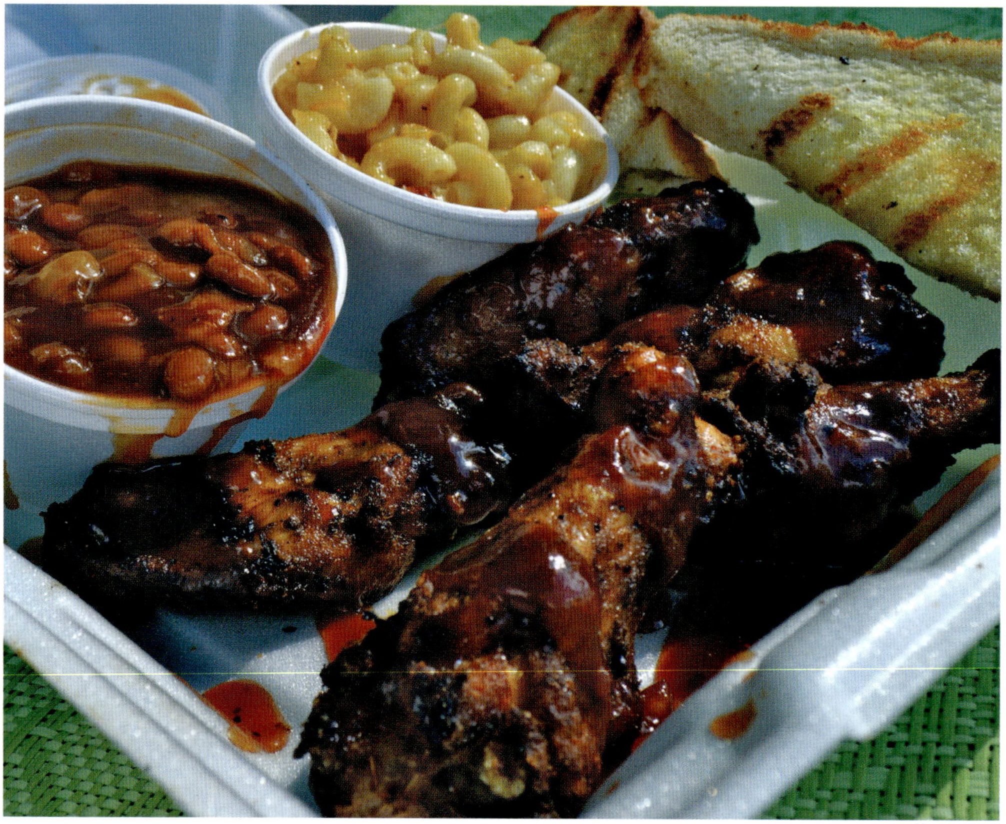

Monroe's On the Go Chicken Wings.

Opposite, top: Monroe's On the Go.

Opposite, bottom: Sweet Pete's Candy at Jaxsons Night Market.

Monroe's BBQ launched its **Monroe's on the Go** food trailer in February 2011, selling most of the restaurant and catering business's popular smoked meats and sides. Owner Keith Waller had the custom-built mobile kitchen constructed ten years before, but he was only using it once a year to cater the annual NHRA Gatornationals in Gainesville.

Monroe's started setting up for lunch rotations at EverBank Plaza in Riverside and Capital Plaza in Deerwood and did gigs at Intuition Ale Works, where I first encountered the truck. The restaurant is one of my favorite local barbecue places. (I know, I'm not supposed to have favorites, but there it is.)

The MOTG trailer was hugely successful from the first outing and shows no signs of slowing down even today. In August 2012, the restaurant hired Jeff Avera, who—along with his dad, John—had just sold his bright red **John's Grab-n-Go** food trailer that he had operated at nightclubs and roadsides around the city since March

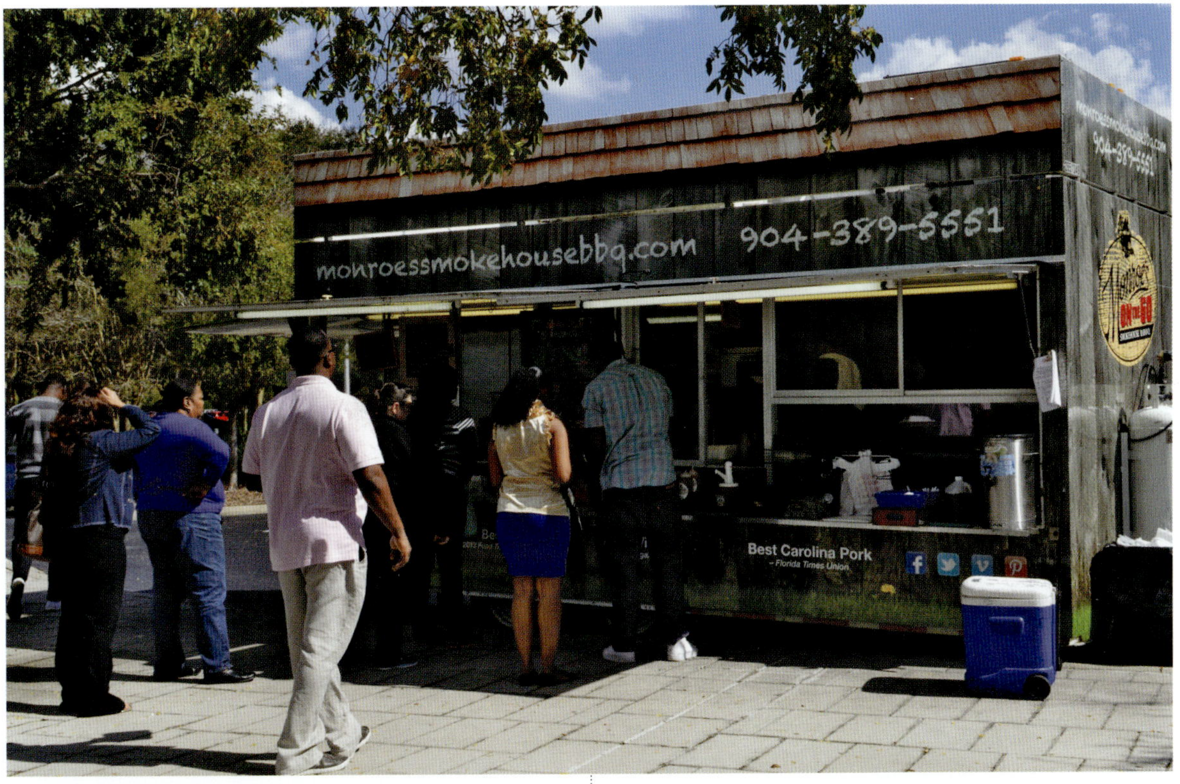
monroessmokehousebbq.com
904-389-5551
Best Carolina Pork
– Florida Times Union

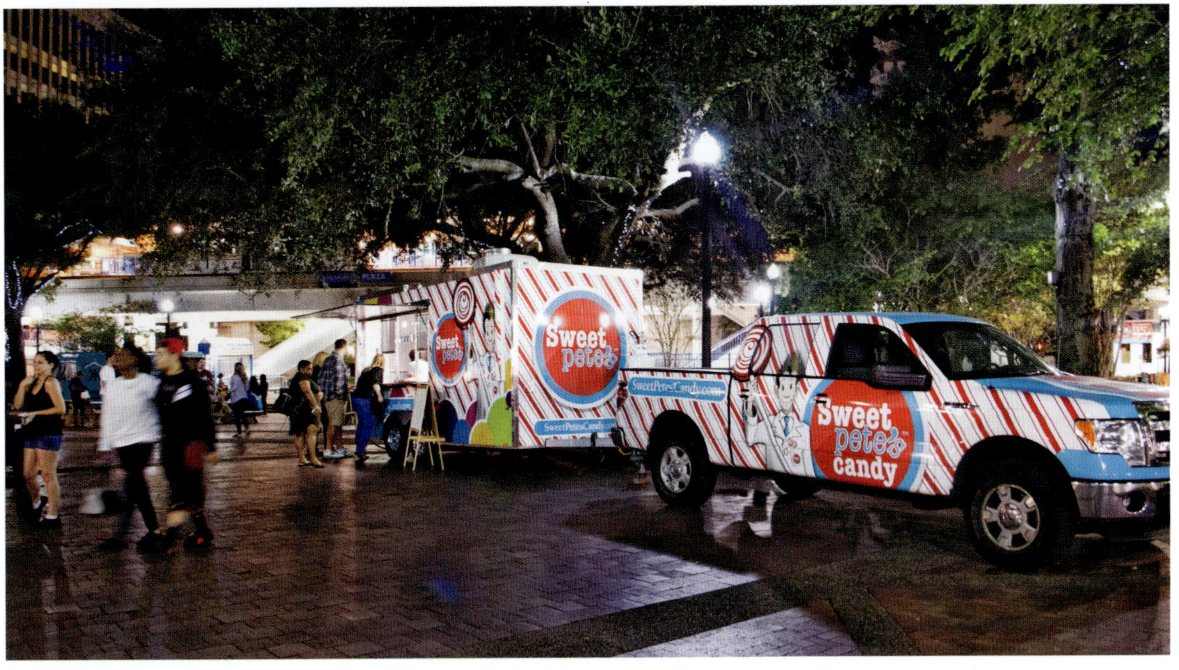
Sweet pete's
SweetPetesCandy.com
Sweet pete's candy

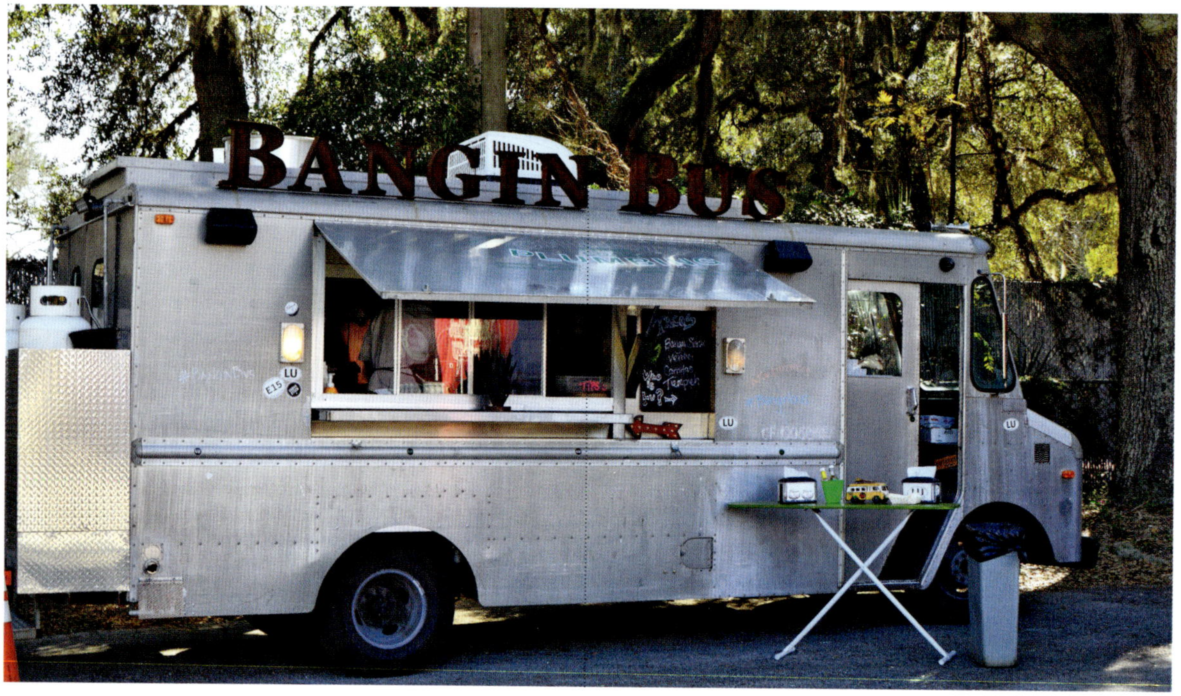

TacoLu's Bangin Bus is back. The Jacksonville Beach restaurant's mobile outpost is becoming a regular sight at community events.

Opposite, top: TacoLu's Bangin' Shrimp and Verde Chicken Tacos.

Opposite, bottom: A replica of the original Bangin' Bus, a TacoLu legend.

2011. Jeff still works at MOTG, and he shared his story with me the last time I visited. He's one of the youngest of the old-school food truckies I've met, and he really knows how to work a crowd. In 2013, Monroe's on the Go took the prize for Best Taco in the Second Annual Jax Truckies Food Truck Championship. The trailer recently got a new wrap that resembles a distressed-wood smokehouse.

Freshly spun cotton candy is just one of the sugary delights being handed out of the windows of **Sweet Pete's Candy** trailer. Candy cane striped and pulled by a matching wrapped truck, it is a sight to behold. I got a kick out of watching Peter "Sweet Pete" Behringer roll fluffy cotton candy onto a stick and present it to customers at Jaxsons Night Market in Hemming Park, cater-corner to Sweet Pete's new home in the former Seminole Club building on Hogan Street. Sweet Pete's went mobile when Marcus Lemonis of CNBC's hit show *The Profit* struck a deal with the Behringers to expand their business. Find their new site online at www.sweetpetescandy.com and follow them on Twitter @sweetpetes.

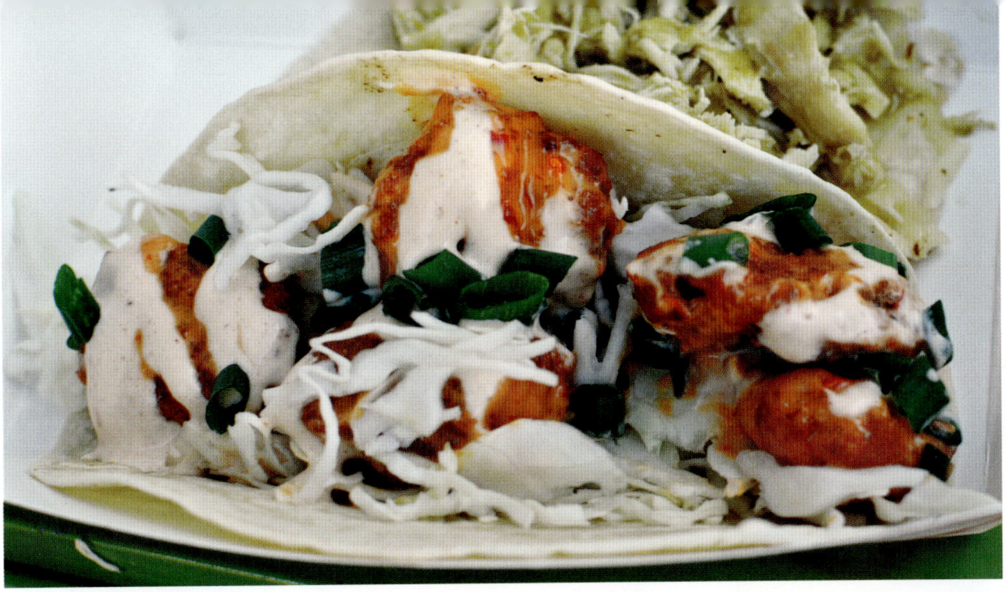

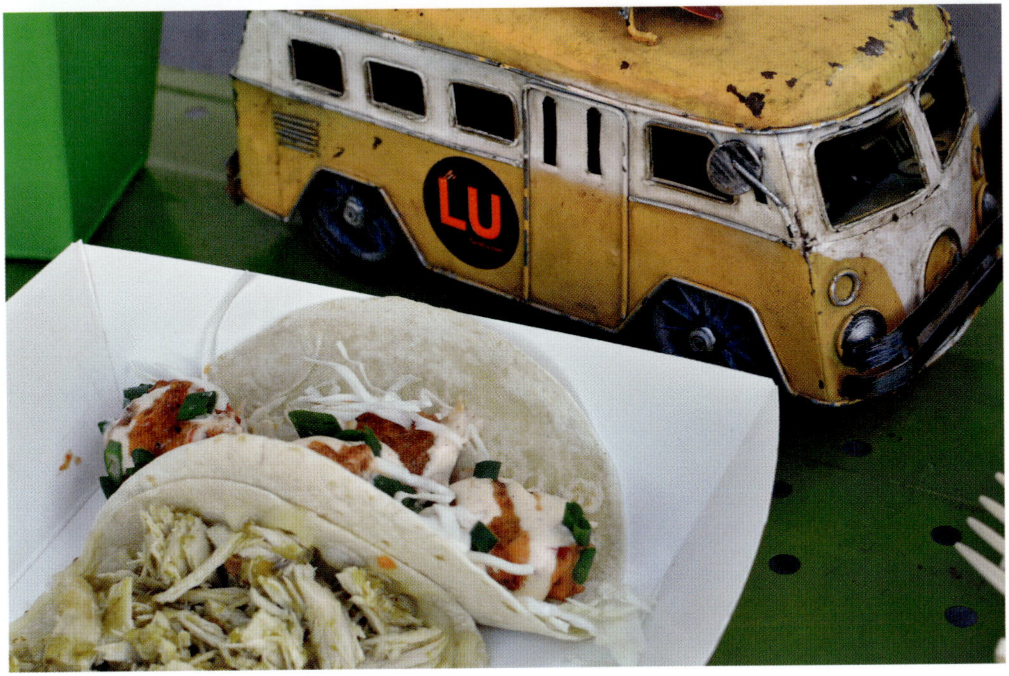

Who doesn't love the Lu? After a rough early start, the **TacoLu** Bangin' Bus hit the road in the summer of 2014, making its public debut at Jaxsons Night Market. Deb, Don and the Lu crew set up at events, usually with a pop-up replica of their "nearly famous" mural set up nearby for selfie-snapping fans. TacoLu is online at www.tacolu.com.

These catering and event arms of conventional restaurants have been participating in the food truck movement locally and have helped to blur the line between brick-and-mortar and mobile food. It's all good, y'all!

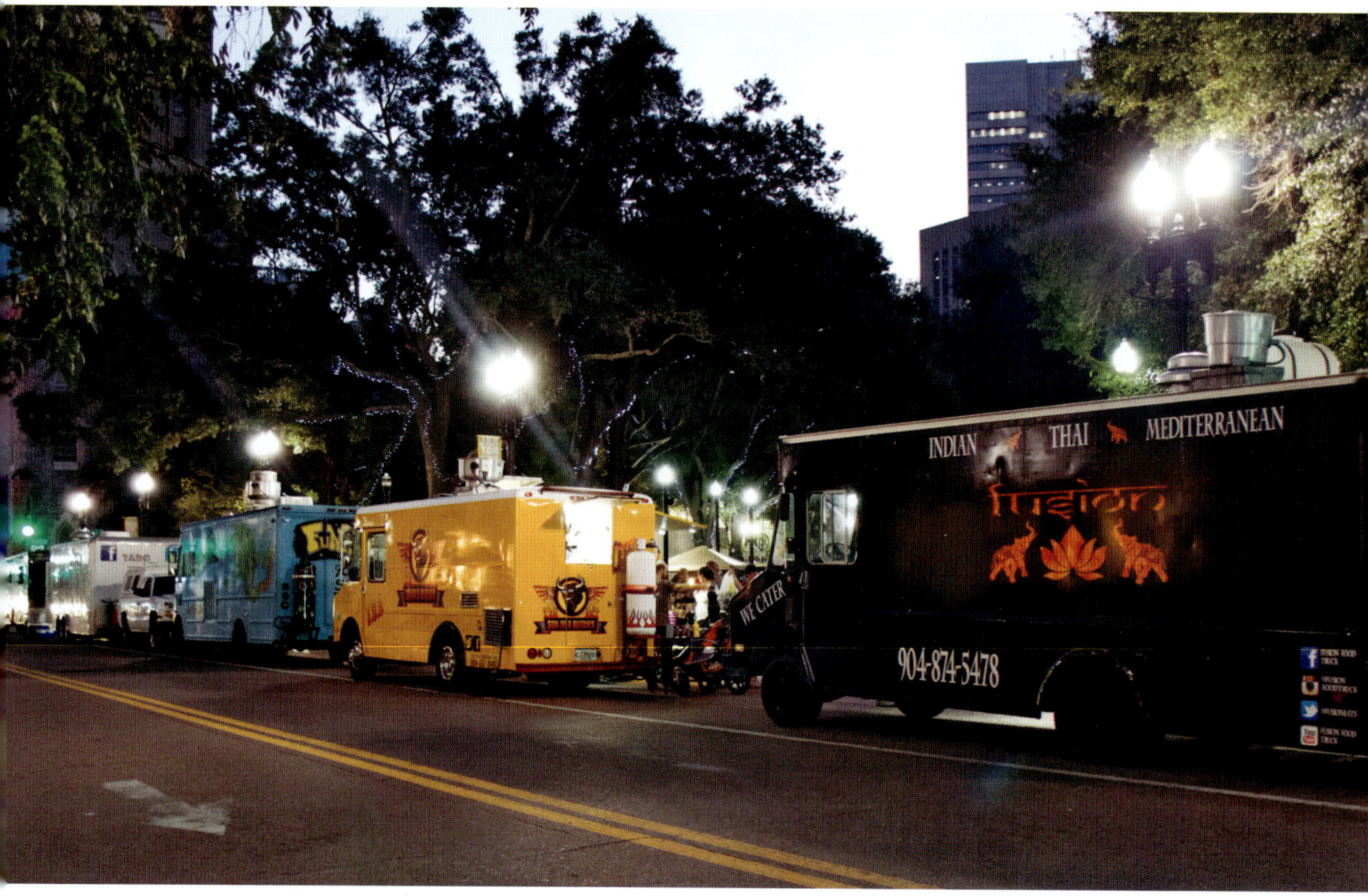

Trucks line North Laura Street during Jaxsons Night Market.

THE ROAD AHEAD

Advice for Prospective Food Truck Owners

During the course of writing this book, I asked many of the truck operators if they had any advice for would-be truck operators. As you might imagine, there were many recurring themes.

First and foremost, this is hard physical labor we're talking about. Just about every last truck operator I spoke to said he or she knew it would be tough, but just how tough was the most surprising. It was the number one thing the truckies I spoke to wanted to impress on newbies and wannabes—shopping, prepping, packing, loading, hauling, unloading, cooking, cleaning, packing back up and then starting all over again. One truckie told me it's like going on a camping trip every day, twice a day.

In no particular order, here are some nuggets of wisdom gleaned from Jacksonville's food truck veterans, with a few of my own tossed in for good measure. I share them for anyone who is interested in hitting the road.

- The food truck business isn't really the way TV and movies portray it. You're going to have to work, hard, for everything you get, 24/7/365.
- Know the rules; follow the rules. Be familiar with the numerous setup and operating requirements your business will need to meet and pass city/state inspections. Check with the Florida Department of Business & Professional Regulations (DBPR).
- Share the road. Make friends with your fellow truckies. They're competition, but they are also family. Ask for help if you need it and give help when asked. If you're just getting started, find a mentor who has been there.
- Focus on one thing and do it right…and don't make that one thing barbecue or tacos (substitute whatever

is prevalent in your area). Take into consideration your expertise, your target market, your budget and what your competitors are already serving so you can differentiate your menu from theirs.

- Don't base your brand on what's trendy today. Your menu should stand the test of time.
- Keep your business name simple and, if possible, include the food item in the name. Think the Happy Grilled Cheese or Driftwood BBQ.
- Your truck is a twenty-foot billboard. Hire a designer who gets that. Don't get in his/her way.
- Your website and social media outlets are extensions of your brand. Give them as much thought and attention as you would your menu or any other aspect of your business. Be consistent and always let people know where you're going to be next.
- Know your crowd. You'll find diners are more adventurous at some events than others. At a standard lunch service, most people are looking for something a little more accessible and familiar. At large events, make sure you have some smaller, "taster" portioned items for those people who want to sample several trucks. Price them accordingly and make sure visitors know they are special for that event.
- People love the trucks, and they want to be part of something when they patronize your business. Wow them. Make sure each and every customer or visitor to your truck knows how happy you are to see him or her. Every. Time.
- Have fun out there!

A LIST OF FIRST COAST FOOD TRUCKS

Trucks come and go, just like any small businesses. Here is a list of trucks that were currently active when this book went to print. For current information on food trucks, visit JaxTruckies.org or JacksonvilleFoodTrucks.com. For interviews and reviews of local food trucks, visit eatdrinkjax.com.

Truck Name	Contact(s)	Website
3 Moms Ice Cream	Jeff Olson	www.3momsicecream.com
5Loaves 2Fish	Toben Stubee	www.5loaves2fishtruck.com
A La Anna	Thomas Biagioli	www.alaanna.com
Baby's Badass Burgers	M. Earl Pulliam II	www.babysbadassburgers.com
Backstreets Catering	Ulka Shriver	www.backstreetscatering.net
Backyard Pops	Ashlee McCormick	www.backyardpops.com
Big Island Bowls	Brendan Schneck	www.bigislandbowls.com
The Blind Rabbit	Jeff Stanford	www.theblindrabbitwhiskeybar.com
The Blu Claw	Toni Davis	www.bluclaw.com
Blue Pacific Grill & Taco Bar	Izzy Tahil	www.facebook.com/BluePacificTacos
Blue Wave Coffee	Don Henrichsen	www.bluewavecoffee.com
Bold City Pops	Suzanah & Rhonda	www.boldcitypops.com
Bono's Bar-B-Que Express	Chance Gerisch	www.BonosExpress.com
Cats Meow Culinary Express	Fawn Turner	www.thecatsmeowculinaryexpress.com
Celeb's Corner Kitchen	Niki Brunson	www.celebscornerkitchen.com
Chew Chew	Blake Burnett	www.chewchewfoodtruck.com
Chunky Tomato	Debra Ford	www.facebook.com/pages/Chunky-Tomat
Corner Taco	Chris Dickerson	www.cornertaco.com
Cravingz Mobile Kitchen	Johnny	www.facebook.com/pages/Cravingz-Mobile-Kitchen
Dagwoods	Ron Perry	www.facebook.com/DagwoodsFoodTruck
Danilo's Famous Lumpia	Darryl Sayas	www.facebook.com/danilosfamouslumpia
Delish Kebabs	Sandro Oliveira	www.facebook.com/delishkebabs
Dirty Birds Wings on the Fly	Eric Peterson	www.dirtybirdswingsonthefly.com

Truck Name	Owner(s)	Website
Driftwood BBQ	Patrick and Amy O'Grady	www.driftwoodbbq.com
Front Porch Kettle Corn	David Harrison	www.facebook.com/frontporchkettlecorn
Funkadelic	Jerry and Amanda Asker	www.facebook.com/funkadelicfoodtruck
Fusion	Chef Ashley Amin	www.fusioneats.com
Gourmet Aviator	Alex Montanez	www.GourmetAviator.com
Guanabana Artisan Ice Pops	Oliver and Julieta Mosqueda	www.guanabanaicepops.com
The Happy Grilled Cheese	Anthony Hashem	www.thehappygrilledcheese.com
Jalepeño Truck	Kerri Dennis	www.jalapenotruck.com/
Kona Ice–Jax	J. Feheley and G. Greco	www.kona-ice.com
Latin Soul Grille	Gary Lahion	www.facebook.com/pages/Latin-Soul-Grille
Le Petit Cherie Cupcakery	Lisa Wheeler	www.facebook.com/pages/Le-Petite-Cheri-Cupcakery
Lewey's Crab House	Torrey Lewey	www.leweycrabhouse.com
The Little Family Crêpes	Lucie Little	www.facebook.com/TheLittleFamilyCrepesLlc
The Loving Cup	Matt Lennon	www.thelovingcup.net
LuLi's Cupcakes	Janeen Damiano	www.luliscupcakes.com
Mama's Food	Natalia Lorincz	twitter.com/Mamas_Food101
Mister Softee of Jax	Millie Albano	www.mistersofteejax.com
Monroe's on the Go	Keith Waller	www.monroessmokehousebbq.com
Mother Truckin Pizza	Kellie Rice	www.mothertruckinpizza.com
Muzzi's Madhouse	John Scaramuzzi	www.muzzismadhouse.com
Nonie's Place	Debbie Matthew	www.noniesfoodcart.com
On the Fly Sandwiches & Stuff	Andrew Ferenc	www.ontheflyjax.com
PDQ	Kelli Marts	www.eatpdq.com
The Pink Cupcake	Kelly Haser Pickens	www.cupcakefriday.webs.com
Rat Race Phillies	Franchesca Albano	www.ratracephillies.com
Repicci's Italian Ice	Dan Clifton	www.italianice.com
River City Smoke	Nick Griffith	www.facebook.com/rivercitysmoke

Truck Name	Owner(s)	Website
Rolz Food	Michael Tumlin	www.rolzfood.com
Say Cheese	Chriss Brown	www.facebook.com/SayCheeseJax
Simply Sweetie's	A. and D. Rivers	www.facebook.com/ simplysweetiesentertainment
Smoke It Up BBQ	Kelham Stephenson	www.smokeitupbbqkitchen.com
Son of a Butcher	Randy Leibl	www.jaxsonofabutcher.com
SOS Diner	Jesse Dowling	www.facebook.com/pages/SOS-Diner
South in Your Mouth	Donny Trauthwein and Rachel Baldwin-Trauthwein	www.southinyourmouth.net
Super Food Truck	Dale Stoudt and Richie Haughk	www.jaxsuperfoodtruck.com
Sweet Pete's Candy	Allison Behringer	www.sweetpetescandy.com
Taco Lu Bangin' Bus	Deb Nicol	http://www.tacolu.com/
Tado Street	Tay Nguyen	www.facebook.com/tadostreet
Taste Buds Express	Terrance Webb and Bill Ross	www.tastebudsexpress.com
Taste of the Islands	Rich Thomas	www.facebook.com/ TasteOfTheIslandsMobileCafeLlc
Taste of Ukraine	Rich and Vita	www.facebook.com/ TasteTheUkraineky
Transcend 2000 Snowballs	Derek Davis	www.facebook.com/pages/ Transcend2000-Sno-balls
Vagabond Coffee	Will Morgan	www.vagabondcoffee.com
VonZippers Mexican Grill	Eric Walter	vonzippersmexicangrill.com
What's the Catch	Glenn Connelly	www.jaxcatch.com
Wiki Wiki Hawaiian Shave Ice	Dianne Darabi	www.wiki-ice.com
Wrap It Up	Nikol Zrihen and Kobe Fedida	www.facebook.com/wrapitupinjax

INDEX

I

J

K

L

M

N

O

W

Y

ABOUT THE AUTHOR

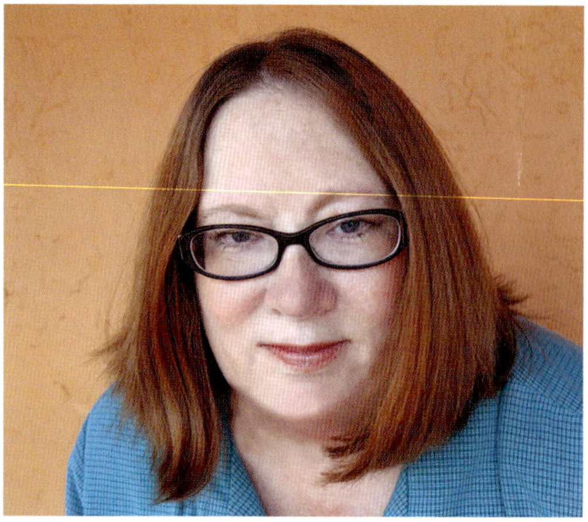

Nancy White writes about food and culture in her blog, NourishTheBeast.com. She writes the weekly Dining Notes column and critical restaurant reviews for the *Florida Times-Union* and is a regular contributor to Jacksonville's *Arbus* magazine on the topic of local restaurants and food-related events. A self-described food truck enthusiast, she serves as an advisor and social media contributor to Jax Truckies, Jacksonville's first and most respected food truck community. A resident of the First Coast since 1998, Nancy works behind the scenes to help local food trucks and food-related businesses find a collective voice and ensure their continued success in the region. Follow her drool-inducing photography on Instagram, @nourish_the_beast and @jaxtruckies.